'Michael's vision and courage were key c⟨...⟩
Church in South Africa to challenge and to⟨...⟩
divisive systems in the world, namely apartheid.'

S. Doug Birdsall, Honorary Co-chair,
Lausanne Committee for World Evangelization

'This is truly a "must-read" book! Full of detailed, moving accounts of
personal stories – including miracles and gripping accounts of faith in
action, courage in situations of high tension and danger, and reconciliation.

This biography of a man whose faith led him to make a unique contribution to the promotion of peace and equality in South Africa is profoundly
inspirational – and a glorious Christian witness for the rest of Africa and,
indeed, of the world.'

Baroness Caroline Cox

'When it comes to all things African, Michael Cassidy is a Christian
statesman who walks his talk. He has invested decades of prayer, preaching
and tireless advocacy on behalf of Christ's kingdom on the most ancient
of continents. *Footprints in the African Sand* is Michael's remarkable and
highly personal story of how Africa touched his heart . . . and he, in turn,
reached deep into the heart of Africa. If you enjoy captivating stories
about missionary zeal, this is a must-read.'

Joni Eareckson Tada, Joni and Friends International Disability Center

'Michael Cassidy has lived a life of Christian nobility. Numberless people
are in the embrace of Christ's love because of his faithful efforts.'

Gordon MacDonald, Chancellor, Denver Seminary

'Michael Cassidy is an apostolic figure who, like his friend Festo Kivengere,
towers over the scene in Africa's rapid evangelization. His vision of mission
is holistic, holding together the need to proclaim God's reconciling love
in Jesus Christ and to bring about reconciliation among mutually hostile
groups of people. In particular, this attitude was honed in apartheid
South Africa, where Michael played a significant part in providing the
gospel underpinning for the downfall of that nasty ideology which was
sometimes justified by dubious appeals to the Bible.

His involvement in the justice issues surrounding the racial situation in
his country and elsewhere does not prevent him from being assiduous in
bringing people to personal faith in Christ, both in one-to-one evangelism
and through mass rallies that draw thousands. In fact, the two sides of the
gospel are shown, in this book, to interpenetrate and inform each other.

The book shows that redemption can be personal as well as social and that there can be godly resistance to evil which does not fall into the trap of emulating the ways of the oppressors. Michael has been able, in his own life, to overcome the divisions of race, denominations and theological emphasis with simplicity and integrity. I have learnt much from his example. I know that others will too.'

Bishop Michael Nazir-Ali

'Perhaps no other mission agency has had the impact AE has had in the cities of Africa.'

John Ortberg, author, speaker and pastor

'This story is the life's work of not only a friend but a true brother in Christ. Michael Cassidy has been an inspiration and shines forth with the love of Christ. His mission has been to preach the word of God and he has seen lives transformed at all levels of society, especially in his own country of South Africa.

This book, delivered with such grace, will encourage and challenge all ages to understand the unifying power of the gospel.'

Lady Susie Sainsbury

'God has given Michael Cassidy the ability to make significant contributions to the body of Christ and to society as a whole. With others, Michael has gathered the Church together for times of reflection on its witness and mission. He has tirelessly helped others to make evangelism essential to the mission of the Church. He has stood for biblical truth, and has written widely on important issues touching the foundations of faith, apologetics, social ethics and growing with God. Michael has also given national and international leadership in defining the biblical view of marriage and promoting it as a fundamental building block in society.'

John Tooke, Director, Michael Cassidy and Friends Legacy Foundation

'I've learned that prayer involves listening as much as talking, aligning us with what God wants done in the world more than what we want God to do for us. Michael Cassidy's life models that principle.'

Philip Yancey, author and journalist

Michael Cassidy, a South African brought up in Lesotho and educated at Michaelhouse and Cambridge, founded the work of African Enterprise in 1961 while still a student at Fuller Theological Seminary in the USA. Its aim was to preach the Christian message in the cities and among the leadership of Africa. This work has been prosecuted very successfully by ten teams planted around the continent. Apart from preaching the Christian message in cities, universities and schools, Cassidy and African Enterprise have been involved in many practical projects of compassionate care, social concern and reconciliation. In the latter regard Cassidy played a major role behind the scenes in the 1994 South African election which enabled the Inkatha Freedom Party to come into the election at the very last minute, thereby averting civil war in Natal. He is the author of many books, one of which, *A Witness for Ever* (Hodder & Stoughton, 1995), tells the story of the 1994 elections. He has an honorary doctorate from Azusa Pacific University. He is also the honorary co-chairman, succeeding Dr John Stott, of the Lausanne Movement for World Evangelization. He is married to Carol with three children and eight grandchildren, and lives in Pietermaritzburg, KwaZulu-Natal.

Also by Michael Cassidy:

Bursting the Wineskins

A Witness for Ever

The Church Jesus Prayed For

So, You Want to Get Married?

Thinking Things Through

The Politics of Love

The Passing Summer

Chasing the Wind

What on Earth Are You Thinking for Heaven's Sake?

Christianity for the Open-Minded

Where Are You Taking the World Anyway?

Prisoners of Hope

The Relationship Tangle

Together in One Place

A Passion for Preaching

Making an Impact

FOOTPRINTS IN THE AFRICAN SAND

My life and times

Michael Cassidy

First published in Great Britain in 2019

Society for Promoting Christian Knowledge
36 Causton Street
London SW1P 4ST
www.spck.org.uk

British Library Cataloguing-in-Publication Data
A catalogue record for this book is available from the British Library

ISBN 978–0–281–08101–1
eBook ISBN 978–0–281–08102–8

1 3 5 7 9 10 8 6 4 2

Typeset by Falcon Oast Graphic Art Ltd
First printed in Great Britain by Ashford Colour Press
Subsequently digitally reprinted in Great Britain

eBook by Falcon Oast Graphic Art Ltd

Produced on paper from sustainable forests

For CAROL
– supremely –
as well as my family, children and grandchildren,
plus friends and colleagues in African Enterprise
and other works of the Lord,
especially younger leaders everywhere, both risen and rising

THANK YOU

Megan
Brenda
Carolyn
David
Gavin
Tony and the folks at SPCK

Contents

Contents

Foreword

————— ◆ —————

'The Candle and the Bird' is one of the most powerful essays written by my favourite essayist, F. W. Boreham.[1] With his brilliant sweep of God's work in history, Boreham traces how revivals spread from continent to continent. He observes that, when the brilliant flame of God's movement in the hearts of people appears to be dying out in one place, a fresh spark ignites a God-breathed revival elsewhere.

Boreham distinguishes between extinguishing a candle and chasing away a bird: when you extinguish a candle, the light goes out; when you chase away a bird, it sings its song from another bough. Hence his title, 'The Candle and the Bird' – a beautiful metaphor.

So, he concludes, 'Let no person become unduly depressed because, here or there, the good work seems to flag. If, with us, the sun seems to be setting, you may depend upon it that other people, far away, are gratefully greeting the dawn.'

Perhaps Boreham's words are a fitting reminder whenever we pick up a memoir recounting incredible memories of years gone by. And yet, how moving to know an author in his 'sunset years' whom God continues to use to touch countless lives. Such is Michael Cassidy's story. From his opening pages to his concluding ones, one theme overarches *Footprints in the African Sand*: God is the gracious Grand Weaver of our lives, working through us far more than we can ever hope or imagine. At times and in places when the candle of God's blessing appeared to flicker, the tireless efforts of Michael Cassidy saw the bird singing its song on another branch.

Blessed with a rich memory and a treasure trove of family letters, Michael Cassidy has woven together a fascinating account of his life in his beloved Africa. Michael is a man gifted with remarkable vision, compassion and wisdom. As a young adult, he helped to launch African Enterprise to further the cause of Christ by serving the needs of Africans across a vast landscape. I remember in my undergraduate days, hearing of that vision and impact. Later, when 'the darkness and despair about apartheid' weighed upon him, he shares how God allowed African Enterprise to be 'a ministry of hope' (p. 337). Michael was a key instrument in bringing an end to apartheid, modelling Christ's charity and love even in hostile settings.

His extraordinary impact was born out of his commitment to Christ and a firm belief in the transforming power of the gospel. He writes, 'Throughout my life and work subsequently, I think what has delighted me most has been to try to live *sub specie aeternitatis* (under the aspect of eternity), as the medieval theologians used to urge. So, on the cover of my diary I have a quote from Martin Luther which I love: "There are only Two Days in my Diary. Today and That Day"' (p. 442). That should be the motto for all of us.

Michael Cassidy's many years of faithfulness and fruitfulness are testament to what God accomplishes through one life lived for his eternal purposes. It is a great privilege for me to offer the Foreword to his remarkable story. I am grateful for our many years of friendship and his steadfast commitment to our Lord. I will never forget the meetings we shared together in the nation he so loved. His name is a household word in many a home that has known of his impact at a difficult time in the history of a continent. As you read his memoirs, his name and his impact will be the same in your home. It would be his desire that in hearing his story, you will love even more the Saviour whom he upholds – especially in troubled times such as ours. You will be richly rewarded by the pages before you.

Ravi Zacharias, author and speaker

Preface

My testimony is of a weak vessel that the Lord decided to use in a very complicated context to make a difference in it through the power of his Spirit. I have lived through a convulsive and revolutionary period of contemporary history, especially African history, and over the years it has been my privilege to meet and know some exceedingly interesting people.

But of course the most fascinating Person I've ever met and got to know is Jesus Christ. Yes, for sure, meeting and knowing him since October 1955 has been the single most exhilarating and inspirational experience of my life. And for my life and work, the most dominant and pivotal. So my story in the main has him as its major point of intersection, thread and motivation, and my steps have been given and guided by him. Most of them, anyway.

And telling about *that* is something I do truly want to do. I have been his 'passing guest', as the psalmist calls himself (Psalm 39.12), these more than threescore and 22 years on Planet Earth, and he has hosted me, frail sinner that I am, more graciously and patiently than my wildest deservings. To testify to that experience, that inner soul journey and that adventure of mind and spirit, and to affirm his Amazing Grace and matchless faithfulness does indeed excite me as much as it makes me tremble that I could ever do justice to all I have seen him do and bring forth. But I am open to trying. So yes, I do want to bring testimony – while I yet have time.

I knew I wouldn't finish this endeavour without the considerable help of Carol, family, friends and colleagues, not least my dear departed mum and dad who wrote to me faithfully from the time I left home in 1946 to go to boarding school, all the way through high school, university and seminary, and who kept all those letters in orderly form so that these records, among others, could be drawn on now for this project. Thank you, dear ones, as well as so many others who are part of the warp and woof of life as I've known it, and without whom all would have been futile and fruitless.

Of course in telling a tale like this anyone would realize that there are hundreds of people and scores of places and incidences which, for space and time reasons, could not find their way into this text, deserving as they might have been. I am sad about this, but of course it was inevitable (*please see p. 443*). For those of you who are interested you can visit the Michael Cassidy and Friends online archive where many of these stories have found a home: <https://michaelcassidyandfriends.org/>.

I began writing this book on 30 January 2011 while I was alone on retreat with the Lord at Hyrax Cabin on the Kariega River on Doug and Edie Galpin's farm in the Eastern Cape. For me Doug and Edie represent so many of the Lord's salt-of-the-earth people who have enriched my life along the way and enabled many gospel exploits to come forth. This remote forest riverine hideaway, only accessible by river or four-wheel drive, is one of Planet Earth's most magical spots for me, and one I have enjoyed annually for years for my major annual solitude retreat. Birds, bees, butterflies and crickets, with the music of Kariega's lapping waters six metres away, were the background orchestra of delight, sharing with me those moments of decision to start telling you about my 'footprints in the African sand'.

Hilton, Pietermaritzburg
South Africa

1

A walk on the beach

───────•◦•───────

Ex Africa semper aliquid novi. (Out of Africa always something new.)
(Pliny the Elder)

There was a warm glow on both sea and sand that early Liberian morning when I went down to the beach to talk to my Lord.

The midsummer heat and humidity of the West African state were oppressive, but down at the beach where the waves washed in it was cooler, and both outer and inner man felt relief. Like the heavens and mountains, the ocean always announces Something Bigger. Man is not so mighty after all and certainly not 'the measure of all things'.

The beach, that July 1961 morning, looked pristine. As if no mortal had ever set foot upon it. Beyond the sand, the dense tropical bush seemed just as it had been for centuries. I was to be the lone intruder on it all. And that was fine by me. Because all I wanted was some solitude and quiet to reflect and pray.

I was 24 years old, South African born and bred, and possessed of a crazy but persistent longing to take the news of Jesus Christ to every city in Africa. The whole of Africa.

This wasn't just some fly-by-night notion but had crept up on me and been encouraged by many others. Our nation was needy. In so many countries, not least my own beloved South Africa, the brokenness was heart-wrenchingly evident. Who could see it and not long for a solution?

By the time I was walking on that Liberian beach, I was not alone in my endeavour and the fledgling organization African Enterprise (AE) was already under way. Our hearts were at peace and our minds settled, but we were signing up for a big job. What on earth would the evangelization of Africa through word and deed in partnership with the Church look like long-term?

That was what was preoccupying me on that beautiful Liberian beach.

The waves, with their to and fro and coming and going, seemed to beckon me forwards. And the beach in the early light seemed to call to me as if from God himself: 'Come walk with me.'

The Lord, my Lord, felt very near. All I wanted to do was tell him he was mine and I was his – by purchase, by conquest and by self-surrender.

But more than that, I wanted to claim our partnership in this gospel endeavour.

I drew an enormous outline of Africa in the sand and wrote: 'Claimed for Jesus Christ'.

I then asked the Lord for 50 years of ministry in Africa, 'a year for every state presently on the African continent'.

Then, to clarify things further, I started to walk.

'Lord Jesus, I am going to walk fifty paces and put fifty footprints in the sand. And I want each one to represent one year of ministry on the African continent. That's what I'm asking you for.'

With deliberate steps I made my 50 footprints in the African sand, and made my earnest ask to the Lord of heaven and earth and sea and sky. Then, above the prints and parallel to them, I wrote again in huge letters: 'Claimed for Jesus'.

My lone footprints were etched for an eternal moment on that deserted sand and I was satisfied. I was already sure of the Lord's call on my life. Now I had made my own firm commitment to it and to the Lord, and I felt my prayer had been heard. We were in this together!

So how did it all begin?

Footprints in the African sand

Part 1

FORMATIVE YEARS

2

Roots

*Where you will sit when you are old shows
where you stood in your youth.*
(Yoruba proverb)

My mum and dad, in my naturally unbiased opinion, were the best of the best and, through them, I was the blessed of the blessed.

To them under God I owe the gift of life and the matchless privilege of being deeply loved, rascal though I was!

I had a wonderfully happy home and idyllic childhood in Maseru in old colonial Basutoland, which is now Lesotho. Dad, after being moved there by his Johannesburg company, was the senior mechanical and electrical engineer in charge of power, electric light and water. Mum for me was in charge of everything else.

My parents – Dee and Charles Cassidy, Chaka's Rock, Natal, North Coast, 1950

Charles's parents – Catherine and Stewart Cassidy

Dad came of Irish stock, of 'the very ancient Celtic family of Ma Cassidi or O'Cassidy',[1] from the village of Ballycassidy.

In our tribe there was an archdeacon, a doctor, a parish minister, a colonel and a musketry instructor, no doubt alongside their fair share of rogues and scallywags.

Anyway, my dad's father, married to Catherine Startin in 1892, became a sailor and rose to become captain of a Union-Castle ocean liner and was regularly rounding the Cape of Good Hope before the opening of the twentieth century.

He died at sea, and his men placed a plaque in his memory in the Seaman's Mission chapel in Cape Town. It is still there with its inscription: 'Charles Stewart Cassidy. He was ever the Christian gentleman.' I saw it long ago and photographed it with pride.

Mum's lineage went back to the House of Craufurd, and included the renowned Scottish patriot, Sir William Wallace, who was popularized in the modern film *Braveheart*. So if you detect a touch of militancy in me now and then, or a tiny trace of aggression, blame it on my predecessors! The family, ever proliferating, and based mainly in Ayrshire, in due time had a castle all of their own. It was 'ever so grand' according to my sister Olave who has been to see it.

My mother's mum, Ada Mary Craufurd, born in 1863, and nicknamed

Molly, decided to follow her adventurous younger sister, Helen, out to South Africa where Helen had just married an engineer working on the proposed new railway line from Cape to Cairo.

Molly did her homework and finally tracked Helen and her husband Gordon Buchan down in the Northern Cape in a remote British garrison town called Mafeking, just as the Second Anglo-Boer War broke out between the British and the Afrikaners (Boers).

The Siege of Mafeking captured the imagination of the world. And General Robert Baden-Powell, later to found the Boy Scout movement, with his British garrison resisted the Boer assault.

Helen and Gordon introduced Molly to General Baden-Powell, who put her in charge of the children's hospital as she had some basic nursing skills. I remember as a child being so proud of my granny. She put together a makeshift hospital where she nursed the wounded, both Boer and British. My mother, equally proudly, told me that for this and other acts of courage she was awarded the Royal Red Cross, the women's equivalent of the Victoria Cross, for highest bravery. Later in the war when Baden-Powell had taken up command of the British troops in the Free State town of Bloemfontein, he asked Molly if she would come and nurse the Boer women and children following the scorched-earth policy of the British by which they burned down hundreds of Boer farmsteads and took the women and children captive.

Also in the Free State was a certain English cavalryman, Captain Edward Reading, who was gearing up for a battle against a strong Boer force. Although the British carried the day, Edward was wounded and moved to a hospital in Bloemfontein where he was capably looked after by nurse Molly Craufurd. They fell in love and the rest is history.

After Edward, or Ted as he was known, and Molly married, Ted joined the British South African civil service. They both had profound regrets over the Boer War and saw it as an unnecessary and tragic consequence of Britain's empire-building. Their view was that this had achieved little and turned the Boers into implacable enemies of Britain.

I well recall Ted and Molly impressing on me that the Anglo-Boer War was a tragic mistake and that military and political greed brought only bitterness and the desire for vengeance.

After the horrors of the war Grandpa, or 'Dah' as I called him, and Granny Reading were posted to the Free State town of Parys where Dah took up his first magistracy. Mum and her twin sister were born in 1906, Mary Tyrell and Mary Craufurd, who were nicknamed Tweedledum and Tweedledee. Mum was known as Dee all her life. They were inseparable

Dee's parents – Molly and Ted (Edward) Reading

best friends so my mother was inconsolable when Dum died of pneumonia in 1910 at the age of five. I don't believe Mum ever recovered fully from this heartbreaking loss.

But life had to go on. In 1910 Dah was transferred to Heilbron, another Free State town and not that far from Parys, again as the senior magistrate. There he established a friendship with Deneys Reitz, the legendary Boer general. Out of this friendship the two former combatants taught each other much about reconciliation and forgiveness.

In fact, in my office I have a framed letter from Deneys Reitz to my grandfather in which he writes:

> The fact that I was able to speak of 'battles long ago' without bitterness as early as I did was largely thanks to you. When first I came to Heilbron I still nursed a good many narrow prejudices and I might easily have followed a far more rigid pathway than I did but for your having been my friend.
>
> I am thankful to know that the road you and I have trod is now being justified by racial concord such as this country has never known and to you personally I owe an eternal debt of gratitude which this letter is a feeble attempt to express.[2]

This letter followed Reitz's self-imposed exile to Madagascar where he had struggled for a couple of years with his bitterness over the British. Dah seemingly played a significant role in persuading him to return to South Africa.

Dah was then made Chief Inspecting Magistrate and Inspector of Prisons for South Africa. This kept him and his little family constantly on the move all over the country in what my mother as a child felt was 'a wretched existence'.

After initial education from a private governess, Mum went to boarding school at Roedean, Johannesburg, which gave her some stability, and she did well with her schoolwork, and even opened the bowling for the school cricket team! She was head girl for her last two years and also developed her extraordinary gift for the piano. In her final school concert she played Beethoven's 'Appassionata', one of the more demanding sonatas, from memory. This opened the way for her to go to the Royal College of Music in London, after which she returned to Roedean (in Johannesburg: the sister school of the one in Brighton, England) as a graduate to teach piano.

But in 1929 misfortune struck the family with the stock-market crash. My grandfather lost everything. In despair he took to drink and became almost suicidal until the intervention of some Christian Scientists who brought my grandfather back to normal life, and even into their own faith tradition. I believe my grandparents, by this rather unorthodox route, later on came to real faith in Christ. Which is very much how I remember them.

In Johannesburg, at a tennis party, Mum was soon to meet my dad, a young electrical engineer from Scotland, Charles Stewart Cassidy.

Charles had been raised in Glasgow by his single mum, Catherine, a devout Christian who apparently mixed with people from the highest, such as Prime Minister William Gladstone, to the lowest, for example prisoners just released from prison whom she took in, and former prostitutes whom she had rescued and who came to her home. Dad had decided, after doing Engineering at Glasgow University and finding himself jobless due to the stock-market crash, to move to Africa.

After working on mines in different parts of Africa, he eventually responded successfully to an advertisement for an engineering company in Johannesburg, only too happy to escape the world of mining.

My parents fell in love and their engagement was blissful, as many letters reveal.

Dad was 31 and Mum 29 when they married in 1934 and then settled into a simple home in Johannesburg. Whether together or apart, as quite often required by Dad's work, they explored each other's thoughts and worlds. In early 1936 Dad wrote:

> I loved your letter today all about mint sauce [I suppose Mum was growing mint in their garden], and the Bible . . . But life is a curious mixture of these sorts of ingredients, so there is nothing strange really in writing about both in the same letter.[3]

Charles and Michael, Johannesburg, 1937

Mum continued her piano teaching at Roedean until pregnancy required her to stop.

I arrived pretty well on schedule on 24 September 1936, even rating a mention in the birth columns of the London *Times*.

I was given three names – Charles, from my father and paternal grandfather; Michael, after Dad's brother; and Ardagh, the omnipresent Irish name in the family tree.

I'm not sure why I took the second name for daily use, and not Charles. Possibly so that when my mother called for male assistance from one or other of the two men in her life, the appropriate one would show up for duty.

Or maybe it was because in Ireland, from where Dad's ancestors came, every Tom, Dick and Harry is called Michael!

The South Africa into which I arrived was one of upheaval. The Representation of Natives Act had just been passed. Black people in the Cape were no longer eligible to be on the Common Roll, but were placed instead on a separate roll and denied the right to run for public office. Black people throughout South Africa were thereafter to be represented in government by four white senators. Talk about a recipe for future trouble.

In addition, in the same year, a number of land acts were passed, meaning that the black population, accounting for about 61 per cent of the general population, was forced to live on only 13 per cent of the total land in South Africa. So the ratio was extraordinarily unjust. As a result, many blacks were forced to seek work in salaried employment away from their families and culture, in white residential areas or on large white farms, or in white industrial urban centres.

The South African government was presiding over something that would explode in their faces.

Nearer to home, my mother's experience as a young mum was nothing if not trying, as she reported in a letter to her parents: 'Michael has screamed nearly all day, kicking violently and clenching his fists and going red in the face.' Finally, in desperation, she called the doctor:

Luckily Michael was screaming when the doctor grabbed him, shook him, and slung him under one arm so that his head hung down one side and his feet the other, as she strode up and down the room airily and said he just wanted handling properly. Michael, little devil, stopped howling at once and hung upside down with a seraphic expression on his face. She then said there was nothing the matter with him but temper, and asked for the weighing machine, dumped him down with his bare arms and legs waving in the air (not a sigh of protest from Master Michael) and said he weighed 7 lbs 15 oz – a gain of 8 ozs since we left the home six days before – which apparently is quite excessive. So she waved a hand, as if to say I told you so, and said 'He's getting too much food, you see', she having exhorted me to get him to take at least 4–5 ozs at each feed, only two days before. She always rather takes the wind out of one's sails . . .

By Jove, it is all far more complicated than I ever bargained for![14]

3

Shadows of war

———◆◆◆———

We are fighting to save the whole world from the pestilence of
Nazi tyranny and in defence of all that is most sacred to man.[1]
(Winston Churchill, House of Commons, 3 September 1939)

My very first memory and the first sound to register consciously in my
ears was a clanging gate.

And the very first words I remember were these: 'Well, it's come.'

The date was Sunday, 3 September 1939, and the place Maseru,
Basutoland, where my father had been posted by his Johannesburg-based
engineering company to run the power, electric light and water for the
territory.

Mum, Dad and I, three weeks shy of my third birthday, were standing
in the open, dusty space outside the Maseru Hotel. St John's Anglican
Church was on our left. I was too young even to have begun to terrorize its
Sunday school classes, as I later did, but I remember it being there.

Michael, aged around three in the garden at home, Maseru, Basutoland, 1939

The hotel gate behind us clanged shut as the strong spring automatically banged it back into place. The gate was dark green. I remember that too.

A man, very tall, with a straight and erect back, but grim-faced, walked straight towards us. My little soul sensed something serious.

As the stranger walked past, without even turning his head towards us, he uttered the memorable words: 'Well, it's come.' His eyes were fixed forwards, maybe already staring into the world's and his own uncertain future.

At 11.15 a.m. that Sunday morning in the House of Commons Neville Chamberlain had announced: 'Britain is at war with Germany.' A final ultimatum, sent to Hitler at 9.00 a.m., had expired at 11.00 a.m.

By five o'clock that afternoon, France had followed the British lead. Italy, Japan, China, the Soviet Union and the United States also became major participating countries in what was to be a six-year war. The Second World War became the deadliest conflict in human history, with the first ever use of nuclear weapons.

The mysterious, grim-faced stranger joined the war effort at once.

He was dead a few months later, according to my parents.

Unfolding events in Europe

My family, of course, like all the world, and certainly all in the British Commonwealth, had been watching with apprehension the events unfolding in Europe in the years leading up to 1939, particularly the rise of the Nazi Party in Germany under Adolf Hitler with its aggressive foreign policy.

My paternal grandmother, 'Granny in England' as we called her, had been very anxious and wrote to my dad in October 1938 about everyone being 'under this awful dread of war. The suspense from hour to hour we shall never forget. I shall not at any rate.'

With the horrors of the First World War still in her memory she spoke of people, especially mothers with children, packing up from Dover, where she lived, a place in line for a German assault, and going to Devon and Cornwall to be further away from potential German raids. 'Trenches are being dug in readiness, just to make us feel a little more secure. Gas masks are also being handed out.' She commented that the wonderful thing, however, was 'all the prayer', and how all would 'love to see a miracle'.

Dad's brother, my 'Uncle Mike in America', in due time signed up for military service when the USA entered the war. Having been transferred

Michael with his father (Charles), 1938

from Johannesburg to Basutoland, my own dad, however, now had His Majesty's Government to take into account. In fact the Basutoland government had said he was the *only* person in the whole territory who could *not* go to the battle front. He was needed to keep all essential services running.

As a child I used to worry about whether my dad was 'important', because he wasn't in the colonial 'Administrative Service' which seemed to be top of the pops.

I could not have understood when I was little that my dad, who wanted desperately to enlist in the British Army, was considered 'too important' to be allowed to leave Basutoland. Even though I was told this, I never really believed it. It was to leave a wound in my funny little soul.

On 10 May 1940, the day Holland was occupied by the Nazis, Mum wrote to her parents:

> I've been trying to make myself realise these happenings and last night I did dimly imagine them and felt panic coming over me, so after all it seems better to go on without realisation. It is going to do no one any good becoming nervous and jittery. But I do feel we ought to be doing more – at least I ought to be.
>
> I wonder what news you have of the home people. From Charles' mother we have only post-cards and hurried notes with no news at all except that

14

she is saddened by the loss of one of her brothers – a good deal older than her. But she must be working [in the war effort] from morning till night, so she never seems to have a minute to write. Of course all knew this assault must come in the spring, and I suppose the fierceness of the attack must have been expected.[2]

Dad remained mortified that he couldn't go off to war, in spite of several fresh applications. While Mum felt an inevitable relief, she also coveted for him

the marvellous experience, and chance of expanding . . . if only there was not this ghastly possibility of anything happening to him . . . of course I realise what I would be feeling tonight if the answer had been different [to his latest application], and he were going.[3]

But in the meantime, not only was there a handful of a little boy to raise but February 1940 saw a baby sister arrive, Olave Mary Craufurd Cassidy. I decided I liked my little sister a lot. In fact we became like two peas in a pod.

A little later Mum reported:

Michael is more adoring of Olave than ever. It is difficult in some ways, as she gets too much attention and noise. He rushes in saying, 'where's my sweet Olave – I just want to kiss her.' Then he makes her laugh and gets her to grip onto one of his fingers and he just pores over her. She knows him and laughs directly she sees him, and just follows him with her eyes.[4]

Michael with his mother (Dee) and sister Olave, 1941

First prayers

Spiritual nurture and training of their children 'in the way they should go' (see Proverbs 22.6) naturally assumed an important place in our parents' efforts on our behalf.

Because my memory obviously cannot serve me well for this period of my life, my prolific letter-writing mum must remain my primary source of information for this time. It effectively makes her a co-author!

Thus Mum tells of me at age five 'entering a religious phase. Charles is reading him *Peep of Day*, every day.'[5] This was a famous mid-nineteenth-century children's devotional book by Favell Lee Mortimer, seemingly a classic which sold literally hundreds of thousands of copies.

When I was first reminded of Dad reading this to me, I was intrigued. My dad was a regular Anglican communicant, every Sunday without fail, but he was a shy person, private and retiring in terms of verbalizing his faith. I *do* remember him, when I was about seven, one night at my grandparents' home, coming into my bedroom after my lights were out, and saying: 'My boy, I think you should pray every night.' That made a deep impact on me and I began a little nightly litany: 'God bless Mummy and Daddy, Olave and Judy [my second sister, when she arrived], Punch [my horse], Dingo [my dog], Jackie [my cat] and Uncle Roger [my godfather].' Poor Uncle Roger! Bringing up the rear after all the family and the animals! Anyway, in my adult years, I always saw that experience as decisive, as the moment when God became more than a word.

Intrigued about this daily bedtime reading of *Peep of Day*, for which I have no memory, I recently secured a republished version of it. Its preface says:

> From very early on in her child's life, a godly mother will try to teach her child about our Creator and the Lord Jesus Christ, who came to be the Redeemer.
>
> This little work aims to convey systematic instruction to the child as soon as the child's mind is capable of receiving it. Children can understand religious truths at a very early age. The child easily perceives that there must be a God, and acknowledges His power to be great; the only objections he raises to any doctrine are such, in general, as have never been solved by man while the child finds no difficulty in believing that God's understanding is infinitely superior to his own.[6]

To discover late in life that Dad was avidly reading to me as early as four years of age nightly, from something quite theological, was quite a revelation. How or where Dad got hold of this book, I will never know. Maybe his own mother had read it to him.

After reporting on the nightly dose of *Peep of Day*, Mum writes:

> So Michael now says 'Good morning God' rather ostentatiously when he wakes. And if I make no comment he says, 'I just said Good Morning to God.'
>
> But he has his doubtings and comes straight to the point with 'Well then, who made God?'[7]

But my agnosticism did not prevail. In any event, whatever Dad did on the reading front, Mum seemingly supervised the prayer side. She reports on this with obviously endless chuckles:

> When Michael was saying his prayers the other night, he said, 'Often when you say prayers, you have to say "Chart in Heaven", don't you?' So now he insists on saying The Lord's Prayer which I've tried to explain to him, as they say it at school, and he had no idea what it meant. His prayers are really killing, and chiefly about the weather! So when I suggested he should thank God for a comfortable home and clothes and food, he said, 'Thank you for our house and thank you for laying our floors.' Incidentally when I said that 'Thy Kingdom come' meant that we want Him to come and be King on earth, he said, 'You better be careful if you say that, or He'll come, you know!'

Michael and John Leckie, Maseru, 1943

17

But he seems quite happy about his ideas of God and heaven and the hereafter, as presented to him by his friend John Leckie, so I am relieved. As he was worried about all those things at one time, I didn't talk about being angels with wings and all that – but John has quite convinced him that he'll be an angel and able to fly, and he is thrilled.[8]

John Leckie was one of two good friends of mine in my young childhood, the other being Jeremy Pollock. John's dad was big in the Agricultural Department, and Jeremy's dad was away at the war. We three adored each other and played with delirious happiness most of the time – apart from occasional inevitable collisions!

After writing about my belief in angels, Mum reports:

His prayers are getting a bit too amusing. I have to cut them short and say, 'I think that will be enough now.' He was thanking God for Ruth Kennan's pigeons the other night and broke off to say, 'You know Ruth Kennan's rabbits . . . well they're dead!' And so on![9]

But it was not all plain sailing:

Michael refused to say his prayers tonight, and Charles remonstrated with him. Later Michael grumbled to me that he was too tired to say his prayers. And in any case he never heard God talking and never heard His voice. All very difficult for me at any rate.[10]

However, things have a way of looking up. And Mum was able to write in February 1942 when I was six:

Michael wants to say his prayers every night now, since going to school. He was never very keen before and I didn't want to force him. He always makes up his own prayers. Last night he said, 'Thank you, Lord, for the rain. Don't let it come too hard, but it *is* lovely. Everything is lovely and I love everything so much.' And he often prays for the Parys River, 'Please look after Granny and Dah and the river at Parys. I love it so much.'[11]

First smokes!

The following month Mum was writing:

John [Leckie] is allowed matches and Michael has been a perfect pest this week asking for matches or sneaking off with a box and eventually trying to smoke. I found him hiding a cigarette behind his back, so made him smoke it to the end. He hated it, but grinned defiantly in between each puff, and stuck to it to the end. I hoped it would make him sick, but he didn't turn a hair! So my friend Denys advises me to get a strong Turkish cigarette and when he asks to smoke again, to give him one of those! And he has asked since, rather to my surprise, so I must have this cig in readiness. In the evening when he was going to bed after the cig I told him he could have two the next day. So he said, 'No thank you very much, mummy. I don't think I'll have another cigarette until I am quite used to smoking. You see, that was my first cigarette, so I don't like it very much.'[12]

Several years later, the addiction having grown by then, our gardener, Jacob, found me smoking in the stable. Mum decided to sit me down the next afternoon and made me smoke a whole packet of 50. I grinned and bore it with radiant courage and resolution. Mum's only sense of triumph came when she said next day she wanted me to smoke another packet of 50, and I politely declined.

This silly indulgence, incidentally, continued all my schooldays, mainly on stolen cigarettes. But at conversion my good Lord wisely intervened and told me to stop! Thus when people offered me a cigarette as a young adult, I could truthfully say: 'No, thank you. I gave up smoking when I left school.'

English bombs

The war came very close to home when my father's mother had her house in Canterbury – to where she had fled when St Margaret's Bay was imperilled – bombed and obliterated while she was out at a prayer meeting of all things. When she went back, she found her flat in ruins.

Her cable to us read: 'Mercifully uninjured, safe, well, but homeless.' My mother was particularly upset about the loss of treasured photos: 'One imagines everything like that has probably been blasted and burned.'[13]

Although she was told not to go upstairs, my grandmother went and poked about, thankfully finding all sorts of things among the bricks and mortar which had more or less escaped: knitting wool, and some clothes and a few treasures. The Duke of Kent apparently came round in response to the bombing and spoke to her, asking if there was anything he could do for her. My mother said that Granny thought it might have been her white hair which had drawn his attention! Friends of hers lost everything they possessed. She told of one couple who were sharing a mackintosh and had on a garment or two they'd managed to snatch.

'Granny says she wonders why she has been spared so miraculously, when so many young lives are being wasted,'[14] my mother commented in her letter to her parents relating the incident.

One of my own memories of that time is sitting on a hillside not far from our home watching all the Basuto troops, day after day, marching off in battalions down to the Maseru station to leave for the war.

I used to sit there a long time, pondering.

After a visit from my godfather Roger Haldane, who was going back to England for the war, Mum commented:

> Michael is such a mixture – so difficult to get at and reason with, and yet deeply affected by things which do not usually worry children.
>
> Last night he was very subdued and said he felt like crying during the day because Uncle Roger had gone. Then he hesitated, and I said, 'What were you going to say?' He wouldn't tell me at first. Then he said, 'You see he might never come back. When people go to the war, they may get killed, and we may never see him again.'
>
> He was upset in the same way when this last contingent of troops went off a few days ago, marching down to the station to drums and a bugle just as day was breaking. It struck him as terribly sad that they were going to war.
>
> In the half-light this bugle did sound rather poignant, I must say.[15]

For me as a little boy growing into self-awareness, the war rested deep in my subconscious so that for decades of my adult life, maybe into my sixties, I had regular dreams of being in a war situation with planes overhead and bombs being dropped on us as we dived for cover with bullets flying, my gun always seemingly unable to fire properly because it had no bullets.

4

When I was a child

————◄••►————

*Our childhood memories are often fragments, brief moments
or encounters, which together form the scrapbook of our
life. They are all we have left to understand the story
we have come to tell ourselves about who we are.*[1]

(*Edith Eger*)

By God's grace and provision, I was blessed with not one but two wonderful sisters, Olave, and then Judy, who arrived in 1944. I loved them way back then and still love them to bits now.

My sisters

Mum wrote to her parents when Olave was two and a half:

> Tonight Michael and Olave and I were singing nursery rhymes but in the end he and she were shouting their songs and breaking off into peals of laughter. They are just beginning to be companionable together. When he is not teasing her, they enjoy each other's company.
>
> He is quite upset if I interfere. Olave won't settle till Michael comes to bed and then she's content. She's also a bit jealous. She says to Michael: '*MY* mummy', and he says 'Yours *AND* mine!'[2]

The teasing thing occasionally got out of hand; for example, as Mum reports, 'tonight he rubbed his bread and butter over Olave's face.'[3]

Then came Judy. I was apparently very proud when a friend's mother said Judy was the nicest baby in Maseru. And she was certainly as cute as a button. 'Michael is always poring over Judy and saying, "I do love her." And if she is yelling it really upsets him, and he pats her and sings to her and then says, "You know, she liked that song."'[4]

It seems that Judy picked up on God's power at a young age. On one car journey Olave was going through the Lord's Prayer, asking me 'What comes next?', then repeating it after me with Judy echoing whenever she

Judy as a baby

could get in a phrase. When Olave said, 'For thine is the kingdom, the power and the glory', Judy echoed, 'For thine is the kingdom and the power station . . .!', thinking of the Maseru power station which occupied Dad on a daily basis. 'Just over there,' she said and waved in the general direction. When one day we passed the immense River Klip power station on the way to Johannesburg and my father pointed out that it too was a power station, she said quietly, 'Two power stations'.

Judy was always her own person, forming her own ideas, living happily in her own little world, almost like Frank Sinatra singing, 'I did it my way.' Whatever Olave and I did, Judy always ended up doing it better, whether in academics, sport or whatever! Initially hopeless on a horse, Judy later rose in her time to be the best jumper in Basutoland.

Horses

My love of horseback riding all started with a generous gift from our next-door neighbour, Ken Nolan. He was a prominent Basutoland trader, grandfather of my mate Jeremy Pollock and father of Johnnie Nolan, who is even now a faithful supporter of African Enterprise.

'Michael,' he said to me one day, 'you don't yet have a horse, and I would like to give you one of mine. He's an old fella, nearly twenty, and will probably die in a year or so. But he is yours if you want him. His name is Ponooga!'

I could hardly contain my excitement. And thus began a friendship

Olave, Michael and Judy, Maseru, 1947

which surprisingly lasted four or five years. My dad also had a new horse, Punch, and we rode together virtually every day in the early mornings when Dad used to go down to the town's reservoirs by the River Caledon to check the water levels.

Joining us with wild exuberance on these rides was my dog Dingo. He was a pedigree Rhodesian Ridgeback (as they were then known), given to me as a Christmas present by my friend Pat Duncan as I turned seven. I

Siblings on the beach, Chaka's Rock, Natal, 1952

23

Judy and Dee with Punch and Ponooga, Maseru, 1954

had called him after the famous story by Rudyard Kipling of a dog by that name. The celebrated Pat Duncan, son of the former governor general of South Africa in the prime ministerships of Albert Hertzog and Jan Smuts, lived opposite us. As I write later, he became my childhood hero.

The image of the horses, Dad and me and Dingo, at full stretch in the early morning glow, remains indelibly printed on my mind even now. Halcyon days indeed!

When it came to horses, white Maseru divided into two communities – those who played polo and those who took part in gymkhanas. We were in the latter group. Thanks to Ponooga and later Punch, and then weekly riding-school lessons given by Ralph Tennant and his family, I won Basutoland's Best Rider Under Twelve cup, and later the cup for the territory's Best Rider Under Sixteen.

To this day I can remember the names of assorted horses belonging to different families, maybe in competitions with me, all around Maseru.

When old Ponooga finally had to be put down, and I found him in the stable with a bullet through his head after the vet had gone, I wept tears enough to flood the River Caledon.

Mercifully I had few tumbles while riding, but after one very perilous fall at high speed I lost my nerve for a while. Mum said I had 'no reason at

Michael on Punch

all' to baulk at riding. But the hidden reason, well concealed by me, was that I was running scared.

> We have had such a tussle to get Michael to ride these holidays. It is a sort of stupid business developing into a 'red rag' for no real reason at all. He just turns obstinate at the mention of riding. However on Tuesday we had a set to and I said he *had* to go to riding school. He went off looking black as thunder and kicking out at everything including the horse, and came back singing 'Annie Laurie' at the top of his voice, and shouting out that he had jumped Mrs Tennant's horse three times. I refrained from comment![5]

However, at the next annual gymkhana, I refused to compete. Mum then adopted the ruse of forbidding me on any account to ride. That did the trick. I would defy her, and ride.

In the jumping competition, John Leckie went ahead of me, was thrown at the final jump, and landed up unconscious and carried from the field. That didn't help my nerves. Anyway, too late to back out in public, I did a clear round. And won the Jumping Cup!

My nerve was back. Never again to be lost.

In one 1945 letter to my dad, I ended: 'Give my love to the horses, Dingo, Jackie [the cat!], and Olave and Judy!'[6] In that order!

Birds nesting

I soon developed another passion, Pat Duncan having wildly enthused me about birds. In reality, everything Pat did was wildly done – he was surely one of the world's ultimate enthusiasts. Collecting birds' eggs was a big thing for me. It brooked no compromise. It was worth risking any danger for. It suspended all morals.

I didn't bat an eyelid at taking all the eggs from a nest, even though both British and ornithological etiquette required one to leave at least one or two. A nearby neighbour, Mr Gordon, kept turkeys. I therefore quite often took a shortcut through his yard on the way to school, stole a few turkey's eggs, and then quickly dotted and spotted them with a few colours from my paintbox. At school I would take a few boys aside, one at a time, present these with much acclaim to my wide-eyed friend as coming from a rare eagle or vulture, and then swap the egg for the best and rarest egg in my friend's collection! I even once broke into the school after dark, opened a museum showcase of rare eggs presented by the parents of a young man who had gone off to the war, and stole two or three to add to my now burgeoning top-of-the-range collection of eggs.

Oh, no wonder the Bible says: 'The heart of man [and even of boys] is deceitful above all things and desperately wicked' (see Jeremiah 17.9).

The dangers related to securing eggs were all worth running. If the nest was at the top of a tall poplar tree, I would climb it till it bent itself almost double to yield its treasures. Rock pigeons' nests on the cliffs of

Michael with Dingo

26

mountains? No problem. I would risk life and limb on a rock face to bring the joy of the prize to me, and grief to the pigeon. Once I put my hand in a snake hole. The snake left like a bolt of lightning, kindly deciding not to bite this boyish intruder.

Pretty faces

My passions as a boy were not all about animals and birds. Seemingly my first love affair was when I was five. I fell for Little Bo Peep at a local school concert, telling my mother what a lovely face she had and please to invite her to play. 'Michael always notices people's faces, whether it's a "nice" face or not. But I hope he's not always going to be so susceptible . . .!'[7]

Anyway, in case Little Bo Peep thought she was going to have it all her own way, Mum reported fresh developments on the romantic front a few months later:

> He has now fallen for another 'lovely face'. I took him to Mary Whitworth's dancing class yesterday. Some of the big girls from his school were dancing and he has talked of nothing else since. He murmurs one girl's name over and over, 'Avis . . . Avis . . . Avis . . .' and keeps on saying 'I can't think of anything but Avis' face, mummy. Do you think she knows me? I feel I want to be with her all the time.'
>
> Charles has just told me Michael said to him this morning that Avis has a face like Jesus![8]

Mum, an accomplished pianist, was always being asked to play the piano for this function or that, including dancing, in which I participated. She went on to say:

> Michael talks about [Avis] incessantly. It is quite an extraordinary thing I think at his age, and I wish he'd hurry up and get over it. But I don't think it is any good squashing him about it, though I have said impatiently once or twice that I was sick of Avis! And that she's no different to other people.[9]
>
> Perhaps he'll have a surfeit of dancing and get bored with it, and then Avis will lose her allure. But it looks as if there'll always be another.[10]

Cubs

With Mum's godfather being Lord Baden-Powell, founder of the Boy Scouts movement, and Lady Baden-Powell being Olave's godmother and founder of the Girl Guide movement, I was bound to get into Cubs and

Scouts. I was a washout at both, to the great disappointment later of Lady Baden-Powell.

Mrs Bell was our Cub mistress, a large and formidable lady, who scared most fellow Cubs to death. Seemingly not me.

One day Jeremy Pollock showed me a huge two-by-three-metre German swastika flag his father had secured as British troops crossed the Rhine and began the final conquest of Germany. With Mrs Bell in view, my mind began to race. Our Cub troop met in a little room within the Basutoland Council Chamber where all court cases and formal government proceedings were carried out. Outside it, ever so grandly, flew the proud Union Jack on a tall pole. The latter flag I managed to lower, and the former flag I managed to hoist. I then vanished into the Cub room to bury myself in distinguished Cub duties to conceal my guilt and impress Mrs Bell.

I waited.

Finally, and a little late and flustered, Mrs Bell arrived. There billowing out before her, in full bloom and in all its giant glory, was the swastika. I don't think she concluded in her fury and apoplexy that Rommel's Panzer divisions had done a lightning strike out of North Africa to capture Basutoland, that colonial jewel in the king's crown. Powerfully entering the room chest-first, the only way she knew how, she realized at once with compelling logic that among her loyal and devoted little Cub pack lurked a traitor of serious wickedness who needed rooting out.

You know what? I don't remember the outcome. Maybe I got it all blamed on Jeremy Pollock! Serves him right for snitching that flag without his father knowing about it!

Sunday school

My mischievousness was no less uppermost in that most sacred of places, Sunday school! Which as an institution also gave my parents something to think about.

Mum wrote: 'I've been annoyed with one or two things Michael has been passing on from his Sunday School teaching, and I now don't really want him to go.'[11]

She reports a visit from the local vicar trying to get us all to attend more of his communion services:

> I told him I did not like the idea of the Communion service for children.
> So we had a discussion for two hours. He is not a bad old chap, tolerant of
> other religions which is rare, saying he has doubts himself, and has many
> differences of opinion with the church but finds for himself personally that

the Church of England seems the most complete. But everyone has to find what appeals to them.

After the communion service, which she made a point of attending with me, she writes:

> I must say I hate all this 'Lord have mercy', and 'sin', and the 'Tempter' etc. Religion especially for children should be a happy thing with one's head high. But I am a bad one to judge, as the whole subject to me is one of discomfiture and irksomeness due to laziness probably. I hate joining up with other people in church. It depresses me *beyond words*, but it becomes a more complicated question when one has children, I can see![12]

I am afraid to say that Mrs Trapp, the vicar's wife and our Sunday school teacher, regularly consigned me to the Disgrace Pew, namely the right-hand empty side of the church, the children all sitting on the left. But the fact that everyone had to close their eyes for prayers provided me with a God-given opportunity to return to my seat! This was very trying for Mrs Trapp. One crime which sent me to the Disgrace Pew was looping a girl's plaits over the back of her seat and tying them with a rubber band, so that when she stood up she almost dislocated her neck, to my enormous delight.

Maseru Preparatory School (MPS)

My local school was Maseru Preparatory School, or MPS as it was known, which received the children of all the Basutoland government servants, plus a few others. But there were no black children, as was the colonial way. They had their own schools, good ones as it happened, but separate. Oh dear!

In early reports Miss English declared me 'a bright and cheerful little pupil' – and 'promising'. But she was over-optimistic about my arithmetic: she pronounced it 'weak' but believed that 'with patience and care he will master this subject'. Flat wrong. I never did!

As to my handwriting, still lamentable, Miss English reported that 'the entire staff has gone to much trouble to help Michael improve his writing. He *must* make more effort himself now.'

Well, Miss English, I'm still making an effort at 82, though I think you'd still say now: 'Michael's writing keeps deteriorating!'

I did get top marks every term for Recitation – I suppose of poetry, which seemingly I enjoyed, particularly the sound of the words. Miss English told my mother that I was 'artistic and alert with a very acute ear'.

Mum commented to her parents about my love of words when, at our night-time prayers, I recited part of a psalm: 'Though I take the wings of the morning and dwell in the uttermost parts of the sea, even there shall Thy hand lead me and Thy right hand shall guide me.'[13] Psalm 139 is still my favourite psalm; those verses (9 and 10) were always Dad's favourite in the whole Bible. Perhaps he had helped me memorize them.

Mum adds: 'Michael talks glibly of Hannibal and Carthage and Alexander the Great and Bucephalus and so on. I feel quite ignorant.' By the way, Mum, Bucephalus was Alexander the Great's horse. Important to get people's horses right, you know.

Quite often I would take Miss English a bunch of flowers picked while taking a shortcut through her own garden on the way to school. Behind my angelic smile lurked wicked satisfaction that I could thus take her in!

Not that she didn't try to exert some control: she once washed out my mouth with soap in front of the whole school for swearing, and also made a school rule that no one was allowed with me when I had my bicycle, so dangerous was I in regularly taking two or three extra passengers on my crossbar or back carrier, to the horror of the parents of the said passengers.

Once I decided the school needed the spectacle of a major explosion. I therefore went across the road to a neighbour and told her in a flat lie that Mum needed some matches and a bottle of methylated spirits. This paraphernalia I took to school, announcing to all my friends that if they came round the side at morning break, they would see a major explosion. My local fans gathered. But little Margaret Brown, to my eternal rage, ran to Miss English and 'sneaked' on me. Even now I can see Miss English's frantic eyes as she raced round the corner to seize me and interrupt my venture, just before I put a lit match into the bottle of meths. Well, thank you, Margaret Brown, wherever you are. You probably saved me from losing my sight due to exploding glass. Ever thereafter, into the folklore of colonial Basutoland, came the embellished tale of 'the boy who tried to burn the school down'.

The end of the war

The omnipresent news of the war led me avidly to start a scrapbook which I have to this day. It has pictures of all the key players, then one picture of the Archbishop of Canterbury, Dr Geoffrey Fisher. Perhaps I really saw him as holding the key to the outcome of the war!

Anyway, VE Day came at last – Victory in Europe, 8 May 1945. I was in Parys at my grandparents' place with Mum, and I wrote to Dad telling

Michael's war scrapbooks

of us 'tearing all over town in Dah's car', enjoying all the celebratory fire-works, though one sight which scared me was a drunk woman rolling around on the roadside next to a drain. Mum used it as yet another op-portunity to impress on me the 'perils and horror' of alcohol! That was a hobby-horse of hers!

Then again my scrapbook reveals a magnificent two-page picture spread of George VI superimposed upon a Union Jack, with his words:

> Throughout this bitter and terrible conflict, I have never doubted that the response of my colonial peoples to all calls made upon them would be swift, wholehearted and complete. It is a wonderful thing for me to reflect that the promises of loyalty and support which so many of you sent to me in the darkest days of our history have been redeemed many times over.[14]

Maseru always had a good eye for any opportunity to party and we all enjoyed the 'Victory Balls'. Mum also writes of my solo performance as a Cub in a ceremony at the Cenotaph:

> Michael was the only Cub in uniform so he paraded on his own! Not to be done out of an official occasion! He was in a new shirt and trousers, and

very smart. There had been such a rush to get him all ironed up and ready in time too![15]

Off to boarding school

I think I finally became too much for MPS, for Miss English and for Basutoland. The stage was set for me to be sent away to boarding school in Johannesburg.

Parktown School (PTS), where one of the two heads, Douglas McJannet, a great pianist and musician, was known to my parents, was the considered choice.

So in January 1946, aged nine, I was put on the train to Johannesburg.

5

Boarding school

---

*Education without values, as useful as it is, seems
rather to make man a more clever devil.*[1]

(C. S. Lewis)

My retrospective judgement is that I was too young, at nine, to go off to
boarding school.

But at the time I was full of excitement at the prospect, which reassured
Mum: 'In a way it makes it easier to part with him. It would be awful to
feel he was unhappy. I really doubt he will be homesick. I hope not.'[2]

One attractive feature of leaving home was that while going around
Maseru saying goodbye to people I could expect a few monetary gifts. I
must have hinted at this as much as possible because I managed to collect
21 shillings in farewell tips! 'I got my bicycle lamp,' I announced trium-
phantly to my parents![3]

My parents drove me from Maseru to Marseilles just over the border
in the Free State and there I caught the big mainline train from Durban
through to Bloemfontein where we had to change trains and catch
another one overnight up to Johannesburg.

There were probably tears, visible or suppressed, and next day (29
January 1946) Dad wrote:

My Dear Michael,

We all felt very sad seeing you puffing off in the train yesterday and I
expect you had a little bit of a sinking feeling in your tummy too. Never
mind, though, we all feel the same when we have to go away from home,
especially for the first time on our own. Actually, I think it is a bit worse
for the people left behind, as they have to go home to find it rather dull and
lonely and not much fun – rather like having a nice bike with the chain
broken so that you can't go for rides on it. Mummy is feeling very like that
and we are all missing you very much.

I have a lot of work to do now so I won't write any more just now. We
are all looking forward to having a letter from you soon. I am sure you will

love school once you get settled in. If you feel a little lost at first don't worry. You have heard the story of Jonah who was swallowed by the whale. Well, somebody once said 'When you are feeling down in the mouth (that means depressed) remember Jonah, he came out alright.'

Best of luck, old chap, and much love from,

Dad[4]

For my part I did my best to let my parents know I was all right, certainly on my many journeys on that train: 'You will be glad to know I am not doing anything hare-razing (*sic*), like leaning out of the place where the carriages join, or standing on the heater and leaning out of the window',[5] clearly contrasting that particular journey with my normally 'hare-razing' way of behaving!

Parktown School was, like most boarding school experiences, a set of mixed blessings.

On the bright side, I did well in schoolwork and usually got the form subject prizes for Latin, French and Afrikaans. I loved sport, which was well taught at the school, and before long I was in the first teams for both cricket and soccer. I also began to take an interest in boxing.

In football (or 'soccer' as we called it) I became quite a legend around Johannesburg schools for fearlessly diving full length on even rough gravel fields to save otherwise certain goals.

Michael acting a bad cricket shot, PTS, Johannesburg, 1948

Michael, a good goalkeeper for PTS First 11, Johannesburg, 1949

In cricket I was a good wicket-keeper, and I have told my great cricketing son-in-law, Gary Kirsten, that I believe I should be in the Guinness Book of World Records for once stumping I think at least seven or maybe all ten batsmen in a match we were playing – admittedly against a much weaker opposing team. Jeremy Pollock was the magical spin bowler enabling this!

I loved my music lessons, especially with Douglas McJannet, my music master. I recollect sitting sometimes, in the evening, on the dining-hall steps leading up to the second floor and listening to McJannet playing the Chopin Ballades, which Mum also played on our little Bechstein Grand at home. To this day those Ballades are part of my internal musical DNA.

And I had my good friends from Maseru, Jeremy Pollock and John Leckie. Hence an early letter home around the time of John's birthday:

Dear Mummy and Daddy,

Please will you send me about five shillings to buy John a birthday present. Send it quick as you can because his birthday is on Wednesday and I have not got him anything yet. Why I want to get something fairly expensive is because he has told me what he is giving me for mine, and it is something jolly expensive. If you send me the money I know what I will get for him. I am in the sick room with a slight temperature. Send the money as quick as possible. This is only a note to ask for the money. That is why it is not very long.

Love Michael xx[6]

Jeremy Pollock and Michael in boxing combat, PTS, 1949

In fundraising circles that's called 'staying on the money and sticking to the message'!

Seemingly I also enjoyed art, and reported home on 24 September 1946, my tenth birthday: 'I have painted some pictures which you must look at from far away. They aren't very good. You must look at the pictures from a distance.'[7]

I can hear my folks chuckling. The best view of the pictures was probably from just out of eyesight.

Classroom mischief

There was plenty of mischief in the classroom.

Chain-smoking and hot-tempered 'Bulldog' Richmond was in charge of Geography. He loved putting elaborate maps on the blackboard. But I was more attentive to his cigarettes; his chosen brand was a yellow-boxed Cape to Cairo, if I remember rightly, which he smoked during class!

One day, while Bulldog busied himself with a fancy map of Europe, I lifted his burning cigarette from his desk where he'd left it and signalled to the class the procedure I was proposing. Then I took a huge puff, kept it un-exhaled in my mouth, and passed the cigarette to the boy next to me; he followed the same procedure, no exhaling, and thus round the whole class. As Bulldog turned from his work of art on the blackboard, I gave the signal and the whole class exhaled, enveloping Bulldog in a cloud of smoke – at which, apoplectic, he exploded in ballistic rage, seized his box of 50 cigarettes and tore it into shreds in front of the hysterical class, scattering tobacco all over the floor!

As to Hippo Armstrong, who took us for History and Shakespeare, we had to read aloud around the class chapter after tedious chapter of kings and queens and battles and executions. When it came to my turn, at the end of each page, I would turn three or four pages at once and carry on blithely as if the normal text was following. My friends knew this trick, and followed along with me while the half-asleep Hippo was constantly amazed that we could cover the whole of sixteenth-century English history in just a few minutes!

In consequence I know almost nothing of English history, though I have heard of Henry VIII.

Shakespeare was also a fun class as we read the Great Bard's plays, one after the other, all of us thankful that, somewhere between Hamlet's soliloquies, Romeo's love stuff and Richard III yelling 'A horse, a horse, my kingdom for a horse', one could find mischievous potential in juicy references to something sexy or suggestive. Each such reference produced a sea of hands asking Hippo the meaning of the thing, as if we didn't already know the answers!

This finally induced Hippo, somehow deceived into imagining we were all in blissful ignorance of these things, to have Mr Lawlor, the headmaster, give us a sex talk. Lawlor complied in equal embarrassment with a 'birds and bees' explanation of things which, as ever, short-changed the birds and the bees but was star entertainment to us wicked little blighters.

Cruelties and caning

School photos from 1946 to 1949 reveal a change in my demeanour as time went on. First I was a smiling, happy little fellow, but later I became an angry rebel with the face of a thundercloud.

Perceived injustices from some masters initiated war as far as I was concerned, a war against authority which I didn't call off until much later in my school career. Then there was the prevailing culture in boarding schools of the time, involving serious bullying. There was a 'law of the jungle' among the pupils where you either led the pack to crucify someone else, or had the pack turn on you with equally ferocious, even avenging, force. Really you had little choice but to set your jaw and aim to survive.

There were also some terrifying initiation practices. When I reached the senior dormitory, for example, I was required to run the gauntlet through the dormitory as each boy lashed me on a bare back with either a belt or a wet knotted tie. The thing of course was never to cry.

The particularly cruel practice called 'rorfing' involved punching, kicking, and pulling the victim's hair till tears and fury finally extracted some mercy from the gang. During the day the word would go round that someone had been picked out to be 'rorfed' that evening. It was like the secret police were coming to get you. The attack would usually come before supper, the victim being pulled out onto the veranda where 20 or 30 boys would kick and bash him to the ground and unleash the shattering assault. It was a horrendous business. I have never forgotten the day when I realized I was to be the victim.

Caning and corporal punishment were part of the school regimen, though punishment preference was given to writing out hundreds of Latin verb 'principal parts', in consequence of which I know my Latin principal parts exceedingly well.

I found something amusing in one caning I received. Twenty or so boys had been taken on a long walk on a rainy afternoon. Midway through the walk, on a pleasant hillside, the master in charge said we could have 'free time' to cut out for 30 minutes on our own. We had to report back on time. Or else.

In the event, we got back about 15 minutes late. So a stick was found. As I reported to my parents:

> I at once volunteered to go first, and get the ordeal over . . . As I bent over he hit me quite hard, only one cut, but it broke the stick clean in half. It was so funny. Anyway the others got off their stick, because there was no stick.[8]

It was a desperate time in a number of ways, although I was probably getting my just deserts. The school authorities must have known of the bullying and were culpable in not putting a stop to at least the more brutal or brazen aspects of it. In school assemblies, regularly occasions for little pep-talks, this kind of behaviour should have been forcefully addressed, as contradicting a cultural code supposedly embraced by the school.

But ne'er to my recollection was any such message ever conveyed. The law of the jungle, and of *Tom Brown's Schooldays*, was left to run its course on the assumption that it would finally make men of us and teach us to manage life, even if some would end up doing so as among the walking wounded.

Perhaps all this instilled some aggression in me, because my interest in boxing developed into a passion. Joe Louis, world heavyweight champion, was my great hero, followed by Johnnie Ralph, the South African heavyweight champ. If there was a big fight overseas, such as Freddie Mills versus Bruce Woodcock for the heavyweight title of Britain, I would borrow a radio, set an alarm, and listen to it during the night with the radio under my blankets.

I once asked Mum and Dad if they wouldn't 'adopt Joe Louis', but seemingly the proposal never got off the ground.

Diaries

In what is the first diary I seem to have kept (1947) I recorded daily routines religiously. Never missed a day, or a detail. I could even record on 3 October 1947, the rare entry, 'Did nothing'. The page for 10 December 1949 has the highly intellectual statement, 'Fooled around'!

A typical entry might be this, on my eleventh birthday:

Woke up. Opened my parcel from home. Came down to prep. Shooting. English, Maths. Played hot-rice at 11 o'clock. Latin, Shakespeare. No sweets. Got two letters and *Fight Magazine*. Played cricket. Carried on with game from previous day. Played [first 11] wickie [wicket-keeper] for first time this term till half time. Supper. Had my birthday cake. Gave some to Fry and John. English Reading, and lights out at half past eight.[9]

The 'hot-rice' referred to here was a game played in the schoolyard where a tennis ball was thrown with full force at a batsman's body, the aim being, while he defended himself with a cricket bat, to hit him somewhere on his anatomy. Anywhere. If successful, the batsman was out, and the ball thrower in. Most of us had colourful circular bruises on chest, backside or legs where we had been hit!

We were allowed to buy sweets once a week – if we had the money. Otherwise it was 'no sweets', recorded numerous times!

'Shooting' refers to the school requirement to learn to use a .22 rifle. As I had one of these at home for holiday use, I became quite adept and could score regular bullseyes.

Another entry tells me I 'got a stripe in Reading for eating cake'. A stripe was a written punishment, and once one had accumulated a stipulated number of these, one was duly beaten with three strokes by the headmaster!

These diaries and their non-emotional, disciplined, matter-of-fact entries intrigue me. I'm not sure why I did all this record-keeping. Or how I got into it. Except that my maternal grandfather Reading was a disciplined diarist, and he gave me a diary for 1948, and my paternal grandmother, Dad's mum, gave me one for 1949. Perhaps they knew I had started on my own in 1947, and they were just encouraging this modestly eccentric childhood interest.

Thus did diary-keeping enter my DNA, and I have remained an inveterate chronicler, perhaps at heart a frustrated historian, ever since.

While the prep-school diaries record nothing of interest spiritually, at least I noted that the school had daily assembly and prayers, and Scripture classes were diligently, even if not memorably, taught. We were taken to church every Sunday, attending a little Anglican church down below the hilltop school in the suburb of Orange Grove, very close to where Mum and Dad had lived when I was an infant.

Holidays

Of course there were holidays to change the pace of things. Dingo would go mad on my return and race crazily around the garden for 10 or 15 minutes at a time!

I loved being back with Dad on our daily early morning rides, plus every evening Mum would read aloud from the classics. PTS always set us what they called 'a holiday task'. This was a classic book we were required to read during the holiday period, and then on return to school we were tested on it. If we passed the little exam satisfactorily we were awarded a 'Holiday Task Half Holiday', when we were released from school to play on the 'koppie', a forested wonderland for kids of many acres. We were given a cake and a fizzy drink to add to the jubilation.

I had also been encouraged to take an interest in plants and again the inevitable scrapbook was produced. And, yes, it is still in my possession. Goodness, what a hoarder I have been!

A wistful Mum wrote to her parents:

> Michael's holidays are going so horribly quickly. I have not made use of them myself this time, and regret the little I see of him. He is of course very keen on football and on playing with the other boys. He has regimented all he can gather together and they all go together to the school field every afternoon. I gather he captains them, and rules them like a lord. Yet he is very matey with them too, and seems to have a respect for smaller children. 'He's a nice little chap, you know', is his usual remark about the small guy![10]

She added:

> Somehow he and I seem suddenly to have reached a complete understanding of each other. At one time I used to think it would be the reverse. But now I think we are so alike in so many ways and feel and think alike, and react to things the same way, so that these holidays have been just glorious. He has been out as usual a tremendous lot with his friends and yet always seemed glad to get home, and would come in at once, eager to tell of some excitement or interesting happening. And he seemed to want Charles and me to be with him, and would say, 'Oh you must come, can't you come? I don't want to go without you.' Such a change from some time back when he seemed so impatient of home restrictions.[11]

Prep-school wrap-up

One memory of my last months at prep-school is that Mum and Dad came up for an end-of-year school play – *Puss in Boots*, I think – and I was fourth cat, or fifth citizen, or whatever. But they came in our new, ever so modern Studebaker car, which had a fancy new elongated shape, a colourful dashboard that lit up and electric indicators. I felt heaven had arrived, plus some reputational rescue, as I had always been ashamed seeing my Jo'burg friends' parents' ever so fancy and gadgety cars.

Now – my parents had one too! I could hold my head up high. We had arrived. We were moving up in the social stakes. No one could look down on me now.

I blush to record any species of embarrassment or shame over anything to do with my precious, devoted parents, let alone their car. But there you are. The world of a child is stitched together with many imponderable emotional threads.

Curiously enough, my diaries through these years never recorded any such feelings – nor indeed any unhappiness. So maybe after all, it was all much more normal and manageable than some of my later retrospective perspectives might suggest.

My diary for my last day at prep-school records matter-of-factly: 'Played around. Swam illegally. [Oh dear, a criminal up to the last.] Dad fetched John and me at 3.00 pm. Left Johannesburg. Travelled down to Parys. Had supper. Went on to Maseru during the night.'[12]

Next day's entry has me immediately into holiday things without skipping a beat: 'Went for a short ride. Went down town. Got my breeches. Went to the library. Joined it myself. Read. Went for a ride. Went to concert.'[13]

The Nationalist victory and the demise of PTS

It was the policy of apartheid after the Nationalist victory in 1948 that eventually sounded the death knell for the school.

We, as pupils, had been politically modestly conditioned and were told that this 'apartheid idea' was very bad. So strongly did Lawlor and McJannet, the two heads, abominate the new policy that they immediately declined the government educational subsidy which was the crucial and indispensable financial lifeline for the survival of a small (75 pupils) private school such as PTS. The school staggered on for another decade. And then closed.

McJannet made his own eccentric statement by buying a pipe whose large bowl was carved as the head of Dr Malan, the new prime minister.

'It seems to please both sides,' he noted with a twinkle. Malan's supporters saw him literally 'puffing' their leader, while Malan's opponents saw him setting fire daily to the new prime minister, and roasting him good and proper!

Things were certainly changing in South Africa, and even before I moved on from prep-school I was learning fast about politics.

One of my mentors was the redoubtable Pat Duncan, my neighbour and firm friend.

6

Patrick Duncan – childhood hero

Michael follows Pat around like a dog . . . I think he gets too wild
with Pat and over-excited. He's been with him all afternoon.[1]
(Dee Cassidy)

Pat Duncan, a rising political thinker and anti-apartheid activist, and
now a British 'Colonial Servant' living in Maseru and next door to us,
was 'the perfect adult for a small boy',[2] as his biographer Jonty Driver
put it, while commenting on his friendship with young Michael Cassidy:

> Duncan knew something about everything a small boy might be interested
> in – birds, butterflies, wild animals, stones, fossils, stars – and when he did
> not know he would go to great trouble to find out. Everything done with
> him was an adventure.[3]

And we certainly had adventures!

On one occasion, when I was riding one of Pat's ponies, the animal ran
away with me and I remember Pat tearing up next to me at full gallop.
With glee and delight, rather than alarm and fear, he seized the reins
of my bridle and helped me bring the pony under control. 'Wasn't that
exciting?' exulted Pat.

He also urged me to climb very high trees with him and, once I was
poised dangerously at the top, he would call my nerve-racked mother to
come out and see. In fact she was always terrified of our shared adventures,
most particularly when Pat bought a huge bow and arrow. He would fire
an arrow several hundred metres into the sky directly above us and then,
with my horrified mother looking on as the arrow began to descend, he
would pull me to this side or that and ensure in the end that we avoided
the arrow going straight through one of our skulls and bringing one or
other of us to a sticky end!

One of Pat's legs was stiff in consequence of untreated osteomyelitis,
his mother denying him medical treatment for it because of her Christian
Science convictions. So Pat walked, rode, climbed trees, ran . . . all with a

Michael's seventh birthday: Granny and Grandpa Reading,
Michael and Charles Cassidy, plus Pat Duncan and Olave

stiff leg. I accordingly marvelled and for a year or so walked with a stiff leg myself. My mother of course thought it was all absurd.

I also remember one day when I was cycling I heard a car hooting behind me. I moved to the edge of the road. The car hooted again and came closer. Unnerved I went right down a bank, and to my astonishment the car followed me down, almost turning over. Of course it had to be Pat. The car had gone where no car could go and then it got stuck, to Pat's hysterical delight. And mine! Not sure how we got it out.

Then there was the afternoon when Pat invited me on an errand to Hobhouse, a Free State town a couple of hours' drive from Maseru.

On the way back in the late afternoon his car, an old Hudson which he called Henry, began to make the most extraordinary engine noises, along with nerve-racking stutterings and loss of power.

Pat's solution was to talk to Henry vigorously and pat the dashboard affectionately like a father urging along a recalcitrant child, and at the same time depressing the accelerator flat! This in consequence of his zero knowledge of mechanics.

'Now, Henry, you can't let us down. You just must keep going. Imagine us getting stuck out here for the night with no garages. You can do it. I know you can. No, no, don't stutter. You keep going, Henry.'

Then he would beam at me. 'Michael, this is fun. We're going to get home. You watch. Henry is listening to me . . . Now, Henry, I don't like that noise. It's getting louder. You must stop clanging like that. It's an awful sound. Don't give up.'

More lusty pats on the dashboard.

I sat and watched, riveted. A collapsing car listening to the voice of its driver!

And so we trundled along those dusty, corrugated Free State roads, every second an adventure of fun and marvel for a child, and finally limped into Maseru and to our house with Henry the Hudson almost on his last legs.

'I knew you could do it, Henry,' said Pat, giving the exhausted vehicle a final couple of pats of approval.

Another time, after Pat had bought Riverside Farm just over the Caledon River border, he asked me if I would come for the weekend and help him plant poplar trees along the willow-treed banks of the river.

Never did I work so hard for two days planting those hundreds of young poplar saplings with Pat. But what made it fun were the regular breaks to tear apart huge brown loaves of fresh bread and smother them in peanut butter, all washed down with hot tea from a huge thermos flask!

If you go today to Riverside Lodge and look down on the veritable forest of gigantic poplars lining the Caledon River for hundreds of metres, just think of a small boy digging and planting for hours and having fun with his childhood hero!

Any capacity I now have to seek out fun is due in no small part to Pat.

Pat and Maseru

Colonial white Maseru was an interesting place – full of very interesting people, ranging from two very lugubrious civil servant brothers we nicknamed Calamity and Catastrophe Damant, through to the more so-called jolly 'Colonial Servants'. These latter were people of substance, by and large Oxbridge, and very well educated. They were of course Church of England, and everyone went to church. The front pew on the left was reserved for the 'Resident Commissioner' (of a rank like that of a governor) and his family. No one, on pain of severe socially raised eyebrows, would dare to sit in 'the RC's pew'.

People's homes and marriages were stable and sound, and in all my childhood I never knew of a divorce anywhere. I understood very early that marriage was for keeps.

Commitments to the welfare of the Basuto and Basutoland were deep and real. No government servants got rich, and salaries were modest, the only perk being that every five or six years people could go 'home' on long leave to Britain by Union-Castle ocean liner. But no one was on the make.

Developing legal and administrative systems, building schools, advancing education, teaching crop rotation, arresting soil erosion, promoting contour furrowing, providing responsible policing, running good postal services . . . all were tasks passionately embraced by Maseru's little clan of civil servants.

It was, or so it has always seemed to me, the sunny side of the much-maligned 'colonialism'. But the long arm of Britain's control was everywhere evident. My dad once had to put up an electric power line to a new school on the edge of town, and got permission for this project signed by Anthony Eden, later to be Colonial Secretary, Foreign Secretary and finally Prime Minister of England! And administrators who did well were honoured in the King or Queen's end-of-year honours with an OBE (Order of the British Empire) or MBE (Member of the British Empire). At the end of the day before he mopped up in Basutoland, even my dad was awarded an MBE. Resident Commissioners who excelled were generally knighted.

There was even a time in my teens, while considering the colonial service as a career, when I rather fancied Her Majesty's sword resting on my shoulder, and hearing the words 'Arise, Sir Michael!'

It was into this world that the young Patrick Duncan stepped in February 1941 to serve in His Majesty's Diplomatic Service as Assistant District Officer for five years, before becoming Private Secretary to the High Commissioner, Sir Evelyn Baring, in Cape Town. After his stint in Cape Town he returned to Lesotho and became Judicial Commissioner in 1951.

Though born in South Africa and educated at Winchester and Oxford, Patrick's ancestry was Scottish and German. He was the eldest son of a South African cabinet minister, also a Patrick Duncan, who, as earlier mentioned, later became Governor General of South Africa. 'On the day of his birth, one of his father's colleagues sent a telegram welcoming the birth of "a future Prime Minister."'[4] In fact for a while Pat came to believe he might become 'the first Prime Minister of a non-racial South Africa'.[5]

Sir Patrick, Senior, hailed from Fortrie, a remote Aberdeenshire village in Scotland. Himself a brilliant classical scholar from Balliol, Oxford, he came to South Africa to join the civil service in the Department of Inland Revenue as Secretary to its chairman, Alfred Milner, another Balliol classicist. Milner then promoted him to be Colonial Secretary at the head of Milner's 'one-man-show' government in the former Transvaal.

It was said that Milner and his 'kindergarten', a cluster of Oxford-educated rookie administrators, including the famous architect Herbert Baker, whose buildings add architectural distinction all around South Africa, laid the basis of the South African state.[6]

Patrick Duncan Senior had married Alice Dold, a gracious lady of German extraction from Kokstad, a town in KwaZulu-Natal. 'From that day onwards,' wrote Alice, 'for the rest of our married life I enjoyed a happiness with Patrick which I think was as great as that of the happiest married couple, and was welcomed by his friends in a most whole-hearted manner.'[7]

In this process of forming the United Party, Patrick Duncan Senior had played a central role, not least in persuading a reluctant Smuts to work with Hertzog to address major issues, especially the economic crisis of the early 1930s, when Hertzog gave him one of the most important cabinet posts as Minister of Mines. Patrick Duncan now took out South African citizenship.

Duncan Senior's great desire and unsparing efforts were focused on erasing the old animosities of Boer and Briton, which was his own version of a United South Africa.

The issue of black participation in a United South Africa was not yet seriously in view. It would be the cause that his son, Patrick Junior, would in due time take up.

By 1936, Duncan Senior was becoming wearied with the battle in Parliament to achieve a South Africa with Boer and British unity. Hertzog perhaps discerned this and, recognizing his statesmanlike qualities, asked

Lady Duncan (Pat's mother)

him to become Governor General of South Africa, and urged the British to confer a knighthood on him.

Duncan finally and reluctantly agreed to the knighthood and told his son, Pat, 'I wear it like an ill-fitting garment.'[8]

By this time of course the political clouds were again darkening in Europe. And if Britain went to war with Germany, would South Africa enter on Britain's side, or remain, as per Prime Minister Hertzog's commitment, 'benevolently neutral'? But Smuts favoured South Africa's entry on Britain's side, and carried the day by 13 votes.

Hertzog was appalled and asked his governor general to dissolve Parliament and call for a general election to take place on the issue of entering the war on Britain's side.

Sir Patrick declined Hertzog his request. This momentous and lonely decision put South Africa once again at war with Germany. Hertzog resigned to rejoin Malan and his Nationalists, and Smuts became Prime Minister.

Smuts was later to tell Lady Duncan that her husband's 'decisiveness had saved the Southern Hemisphere by denying the Germans a base in South West Africa'.[9] John Duncan, Pat's brother, now deceased, told me that Smuts' exact words to his mother were: 'It was an act of Providence that Hertzog made your husband Governor General.'

The war directly affected the Duncan family. Andrew, the second son, who had been decorated with the Distinguished Flying Cross (DFC), went missing in North Africa (later confirmed killed), while John, always a very close friend of our family, was interned in Algeria after the loss of his ship in the Mediterranean.

Duncan Senior died at Government House in Pretoria on 19 July 1943 and was given a state funeral, while his ashes were interred in the stone pillar with the name of the Duncan Dock on the reclaimed foreshore of Cape Town. They are known as 'the Duncan Docks' to this day. At Duncan's funeral, Smuts said: 'we all trusted him.'[10]

Lady Duncan, no longer First Lady of South Africa, left Government House and moved to Maseru to be near Pat. For the Cassidy family generally, and for me specifically, it was a happy conspiracy of circumstances.

Religious convictions

Pat eventually married and had four children of his own, but when he was still a bachelor he sought company and loved coming in and out of our home – and Mum and Dad loved receiving him.

Thus some 1943 letters can record:

> On Saturday Pat Duncan came to lunch and stayed to tea. The Sunday
> before he'd asked Michael to have lunch with him. He's rather refreshing,
> full of great debates and emphatic ideas – thinks everything is going to be
> marvellous after the war, if soil erosion can be stopped![11]

> Pat was in here again to supper tonight and has now gone on to church
> with Charles.[12]

I find myself curious that Pat would be going to church with Dad – who
never missed either Holy Communion or Evensong. Pat really struggled
with Christian faith. Mum describes debating with him on the subject: 'Pat
is very anti-Christianity – says it is outmoded and finished. To him it is
synonymous with Roman Catholicism which he hates with a bitter hatred.'

Interestingly enough, Pat never tried to influence me towards his
notions of the Church and Christianity. Later, we would discuss as adults
what true Christian faith was all about. Back then it was all disillusionment, which may, in-between all his exuberance of life, have contributed
to his regular fits of depression.

Thus Mum reported how one Sunday evening he came over and

> fooled around with Michael and seemed very cheerful. Charles went off
> to church, but Pat stayed on for a while in apparent good spirits. But just
> as he was leaving he blurted out, 'Do you ever get depressed? I am so de-
> pressed; I don't know what to do with myself.' And when we got outside
> it was raining and lightning and dark and he said, 'what a dreadful night,
> isn't it simply terrible.' And he looked just too miserable for words.[13]

As a child I never saw that side of him.

Biographer Jonty Driver comments on Pat's religious views in these
terms: 'He was attracted to a peculiarly Anglican version of Christianity,
though it never took deep spiritual hold of him . . . He had no real grasp
of theology.'[14]

Royal visit and Nationalist victory

In 1947, when King George VI and Queen Elizabeth together with their
two daughters, the princesses Elizabeth and Margaret, made a memorable
visit to South Africa, Basutoland was on their itinerary and I was given a
special holiday dispensation from school to enjoy it. I remember the new
stop-sign at one of Maseru's intersections and the freshly tarred roads – all
for the royal entourage.

Pat Duncan, royal visit, 1947

I also remember Pat Duncan in his snow-white uniform, white plumed helmet and regimental sword, ready for the Pitso, the Sesotho name for a mass gathering. Seventy thousand people gathered that day – and I almost wrecked it for my parents by slipping out of their sight and vanishing!

Their minds went into high gear. Michael could only be heading for the royal car and Princess Margaret (with whom I had fallen in love), and the rest of the royals. They frantically squeezed through the pressing throngs, and finally got to where the vehicle was gently trying to ease its way through the crowds. There they saw me with my nose pressed against the car window, about ten inches from the startled king, either swearing undying allegiance to His Britannic Majesty, or else perhaps asking for his daughter's hand in marriage!

Meanwhile, in South Africa, D. F. Malan's Nationalist bandwagon was gathering speed, intensity and political strength.

And his 'separate development' notion was gaining in appeal to many sectors of the white South African electorate, especially Afrikaners. The National Party intended to divide South Africa on a large scale along racial lines: black, white, 'coloured' and Indian, and to pass further legislation which would affirm the already divided society.

Smuts, whose eyes were on the wider world, the developing United Nations and the British Commonwealth, did not realize the political tide was turning against him.

When the National Party defeated Smuts' United Party and came to power in 1948, ushering in the long dark years of apartheid, Pat took me

Royal visit, Basutoland Pitso, 1947

for a walk on a hillside at his Riverside Farm and told me this was 'a catastrophe and calamity for South Africa'.

'Michael,' he passionately declared, 'this is a tragedy. We are going as a nation down the wrong path. The price we pay will be terrible.'

This was an utterance I never forgot. My childhood hero was stating a conviction and a political truth which etched itself indelibly into my young mind and soul. I embraced Pat's conviction, and believed it for ever.

While Pat knew he had to oppose apartheid with every fibre of his being, he also told me it had to be done 'non-violently'.

Thus he proceeded to tell me about Mahatma Gandhi and his friendship with Manilal Gandhi, Mahatma's brother. For Pat, Gandhi was a saint, and his philosophy of *satyagraha* (the use of soul force and non-violent resistance) was Christianity in action.

This was partly why any such positive views as he may have had of Christianity were focused on its political possibilities; hence his support even of the notion of a Christian Democratic Party. Twenty years later, when I founded African Enterprise, Pat expressed great approval because of what he saw of its political potential.

While Pat never challenged Christianity in front of me, and probably helped me to believe that Christianity had political potential, nevertheless he did try to instil his Gandhism in me, young though I was, so that the ways of non-violence became part of my DNA.

Family friendship

Mum felt sorry for Lady Duncan when she first moved to Maseru to 'that dark and bitterly cold house with a gloomy garden', as she described it to her parents. The two saw each other regularly and I was always proud of her saying that 'the Cassidys' little sitting-room was the loveliest room in Maseru'.

She also had an eye to my own education in etiquette. Mum records one example:

> One evening, she asked me to go for a walk with her and Michael came too. But at every gate she drew back and said: 'No, I am anxious Michael shall learn to open gates [for ladies]. Now, Michael come along.' It really is not her place to bring up Michael, though I am very glad he has the chance of having 'chivalry' awakened in him.[15]

I'll never forget her coming into our home as the war ended with her son, John, just released from the Navy. I was dazzled by his snow-white naval uniform! Not long afterwards he married Pamela Reid, whom his mother called a 'Fairy Princess'. And John and Pam remained dear family friends. They both became powerful Christian witnesses after their conversions later in life.

Pat also brought other interesting people into our lives, along with much intellectual stimulus. A case in point was Elizabeth Feiling, daughter of Sir Keith Feiling, the famous Oxford historian, who had at one time been an advisor to Churchill. She and Pat were quite close and my folks always enjoyed being party to their conversations, quite often in our home. Mum wrote:

> When Elizabeth and Pat get going together, I feel so illiterate and such a fool altogether. One does become a vegetable when one just sews and knits and never reads. Charles holds his own quite well because what he reads sticks, and he can discuss most things, and it is obvious that Pat enjoys his long talks with him.[16]

Mum short-changes herself here, as she read widely and was an extraordinary conversationalist herself.

By 1952 Pat had resigned from the colonial service and gave himself fully to passive resistance against apartheid. He started and edited a fortnightly newspaper called *Contact*, which had a considerable impact on people of all races and backgrounds with its strong stance on various issues. He often found himself arrested or serving banning orders, which were an attempt to curtail his political activities around the country.

In 1955 he became a co-founder of the Liberal Party of South Africa and became an active agent for change within the party, and in 1963 he resigned to become the first white member of the Black Nationalist movement, the Pan Africanist Congress (PAC).

Patrick Duncan – childhood hero

Pat Duncan speaking at a Liberal Party meeting, Nyanga, Cape Town, 1959

He eventually became the party's representative in North Africa and later went on to work with a relief organization called Comité Chrétien de Service en Algérie. It was while in Algeria that Pat contracted a blood disease called aplastic anaemia. He died in London in 1967.

Jonty Driver, Pat's biographer, later recorded an episode which much encouraged me after all my years of prayer for Pat. He had been very unwell, almost delirious from his blood problems, while out on a safari in the Algerian desert. He seemingly called in desperation on 'Jehovah', after which he was flooded with a tremendous feeling of well-being and strength so that he could finish his safari in a fit state. Pat described this as 'one of the most remarkable things I have ever experienced'.[17] I really believe this was an answer to prayer. And more especially so because he was rereading *The Pilgrim's Progress* when he died. Seconds before he died he had what may have been a vision of heaven, and his last words were, 'It's just like an El Greco painting.'[18]

7

Michaelhouse

A man's tone, moral and spiritual, as well as intellectual,
is largely determined for life by his school.[1]
(James Cameron Todd)

I began my last chapter talking about Pat Duncan as my childhood hero. And I have got a bit ahead of myself. So I now need to double back to January 1950 when a new adventure opened up for me. This happened as my parents sent me off to Michaelhouse, a private school for boys at Balgowan in Natal.

They chose Michaelhouse over rival school Hilton College because the headmaster or, as our school heads are called, the rector, Fred Snell, was warmer and friendlier on that particular day than the head they met at Hilton.

My folk were very ambitious for me and wanted me to have a private school education, although it would reduce them to a life of financial

Michael leaves for Michaelhouse for the first time, 1950

54

struggle, scrimping and scratching to make ends meet through the next four or five years.

I was aware of their sacrifice and proud that Mum had made all my school clothes, including blazer and grey flannels, rather than having bought them at posh shops in Bloemfontein, Johannesburg or Pietermaritzburg. I was proud too in a funny way only to have ten shillings pocket money a term, when other boys had five or ten pounds. And I accepted that while other boys had their parents visit them regularly, mine could hardly ever afford to drive the 400 or so kilometres (about 250 miles) down from Basutoland. Maybe once or twice in five years.

However, I had a few lessons to learn about how to manage with little money. On the midwinter train back to Basutoland, I tried not only to do without a bed so seven shillings could be saved, but to avoid having my ticket clicked by the conductor so I might use it again on another journey. When my dad heard of these well-intended efforts, he gave me the roughest scolding I ever got in my life. I was later very proud of my father for this. It vividly demonstrated what integrity was all about – honesty in detail. I was also introduced to the notion of 'false economy' by my angry parents when I got pneumonia as a result of freezing all night on the train without a bed.

Early days

So, in late January 1950 with a few Basutoland friends travelling with me on the Bloemfontein to Durban train, we had to stop and disembark at Balgowan station at 4.30 a.m. We then walked together up to the school in the dark.

My first letter home opens with the words: 'I am having a wonderful time here.' But the reality was a regime that rocked my system.

We rose at 6.00 a.m. for cold showers, a rusk and a cup of coffee, then roll call at 6.30 a.m. – and then into our first period at 6.35 a.m. Then breakfast. Then daily chapel. Then classes all morning. Then a half-hour rest after lunch. Then compulsory sport. Then seventh period at 5.20 p.m. Supper at 6.00 p.m. Prep time in our classrooms from 7.00 p.m. to 9.00 p.m. Lights out at 9.30 p.m.

Meals, to be honest, left me always hungry. In fact, registering that I lived mainly on institutional food from age 9 to age 26 (when I left seminary), my retrospective judgement is that I would have developed better physically on a diet more approximating to home cooking! There was other growing up to do. 'We have no one who looks after us,' I wrote home. 'Our clothes and laundry are all our own responsibility.'[2]

Daily sport came naturally. Cricket started fine, but I wasn't seeing the ball well. Unbeknown to me I had failing eyesight. I wasn't making high runs, and before the end of the year was banished to what they called 'House Leagues', the 'rabble' of sporting non-starters. Once in house leagues, unless you scored several fifties or centuries in a row, you were relegated for ever. Having gone to Michaelhouse with a reputation as a potential cricket star, I was devastated at this development. And I always felt bitter towards the cricket master, known to be a man of favourites, who made no effort to discover the reasons for my poor performance. It was step one in my loss of self-confidence. And it intensified my reaction to authority.

Although I'd played only football (soccer) at prep school, I nevertheless seemed to start out well as a rugby fly-half beginner who could convert a ball between the posts with accuracy from almost any angle. But rugby requires physical bulk and strength, and because I didn't really grow physically till I was almost 17, I found myself again failing to fulfil initial promise. This was step two in my loss of self-confidence.

But then there was squash, hockey, and of course boxing, which I embraced wholeheartedly and did well until I lost a fight against a friend who later played rugby lock for Oxford! I decided then that people were now hitting a bit too hard for my liking, and being a rather devout coward, I thereafter refrained from entering boxing tournaments.

I took to squash like a duck to water, playing for the school first team and later for my college at Cambridge. Once, while in Maseru, I made the quarter-finals of the Free State provincial squash championships.

Hockey was rather frowned on by the rugby thugs, but I ended up captaining the second 11, never quite making it to the firsts. I was moving towards being Mr Average. Nothing to write home about, even if I did so!

I made friends quite easily my first year. My old buddy Jeremy Pollock, from Maseru, was in another house so we mainly caught up on Sundays when it was usual for the boys to be taken out for the day.

Confirmation

On the spiritual front, most boys in their second year (C Block, as we were called) found themselves on a sort of conveyer belt which trundled them along towards confirmation. I was all right with this and found myself in a fine confirmation class taught by our headmaster, Fred Snell.

My family were greatly supportive of my being confirmed and all wrote with their encouragement for the Big Day.

My dad wrote:

This is just to wish you every blessing for your Confirmation next Sunday. It is an important step in your career and will I am sure stand you in good stead in the years to come. Mummy and I are so sorry that we can't come down to school for it, but you may depend we shall be thinking of you especially on that day. As you grow older and, even now, you may hear uncharitable things about the Church and the way of life it teaches. But Christianity is a very beautiful religion in its essential simplicity and there is no doubt that it is only its teachings which can bring relief to a much tired world. And the condition of this world is, of course, due to what people think, and what ideal they attempt to live up to. So stick to its essentials all through your life and you will find more real happiness than by following other and seemingly more attractive causes.[3]

Mum's letter said:

We shall be thinking of you on Sunday and how I wish we could be there! I hope that you find that it really means something to you and that your religion will be a great help to you always. One needs it, I am sure, if one is going to be a really fine being. People who have it show it in their lives and conduct and have something which is lacking in those that haven't a faith. So I just hope you have that gift of faith, which isn't given to everybody. It is a wonderful thing to have, obviously.[4]

My granny in Parys, with her hands paralysed from arthritis, had to dictate a few lines, and wrote movingly:

Darling Michael, this is to tell you that I shall be thinking of you on Sunday. I pray that God will bless you and guide you all through your life. Listen always for the voice of His Spirit, and hear no other call. Fondest love, dear, from Granny.[5]

Padre Lean, my rector in St John's, Maseru, penned these lines both to me and another Maseru friend, Paul Chapman:

There is just one thing that I would like to say. Make up your minds before your Confirmation that you really intend to be faithful members of the church, and to attend its services at home as well as at school.[6]

These were dear and meaningful communications to me. And retrospectively I deeply thank God for them.

The Big Confirmation Day finally came. I felt it was a serious moment and resolved two things. First I would put one shilling in the collection, and not my usual 'tickey' (three pence!). Second, I wouldn't smother my hair with styling wax, as other confirmees in Pascoe, my school house, were doing, in order to discomfort the Bishop as he laid hands on the head of each candidate, only to find them sinking into slimy slugs of hair cream!

Bantu studies

The Junior Debating Society addressed some of the serious topics of the day. One motion with awful wording was 'In the opinion of this house the native should be educated and finally become a citizen.' The motion on the first count was won 23 to 14 and I was for it. But in the final count we lost 16 to 25. 'I think some idiots must have voted twice,' I wrote to my parents.[7]

The Bantu Education Act of 1953 enforced racially separate educational facilities. It was a terrible thing, among the worst of apartheid's segregationist laws. While schools were the places primarily affected, universities also tragically became 'tribal', and homogeneously one group.

Church mission schools were deeply hit and all but three in the country chose to close down, this partly determined by the loss of government subsidies. In 1959, by the Extension of University Education Act, distinguished universities such as Fort Hare were taken over and degraded to being part of the Bantu Education System.

Hendrik Verwoerd, Minister of so-called Native Affairs at the time, even came up with his notorious utterance: 'There is no place for the Bantu in the European community above the level of certain forms of labour . . . What is the use of teaching the Bantu child mathematics when it cannot use it in practice?'[8]

The fact that this kind of motion could be debated at all and even lost, in a school like Michaelhouse in the 1950s, shows just how far we were, for the most part, from grasping the shameful political realities of South Africa, even then.

Personal shame

My physical development, aged about 15, was modestly average. I weighed 108 lb (49 kg), and was five foot, six-and-three-quarter inches tall (1.7 m).

That was sort of all right. But there was one problem. I was about the same size two years later. I just did not grow at the time. My self-esteem was now being affected by my own body.

This opened up for me a far worse situation than I had to put up with at prep school. Teasing and snide remarks and cruel jokes at my expense, even after lights-out at night, became routine as I entered my third year.

And I could do nothing about it. Like an African teased for being black. I couldn't suddenly produce big muscular arms, which remained a complex for me for ever. I couldn't in the showers, nightmarishly required twice daily, suddenly sport huge genitalia and Amazon forest pubics to match the Crown Jewels sported all around me! I was naked, outside and inside. And ashamed.

Worst of all in my developing isolation, I suddenly found special friends distancing themselves from me, including one of my closest new buddies. I couldn't then, or even now, blame him. Social and peer-group pressures are real.

Of course I learned certain coping mechanisms. My developing faith was real. I even stuck with kneeling by my bed at night to say prayers, while the odd slipper was heaved my way, amid scornful giggles. Mercifully there were friends in other houses. And in the school holidays there were my mum and dad. Mum found me a little book on 'How to Gain Weight'! But if school food is bad, a little book about good food is hardly a solution.

On the sexual side I began in due course to register the hanky-panky that goes on in boys' schools in this regard. But when other boys bragged of sexual conquests during the holidays or on the school trains, I basically despised them, my mother having made it as clear as the sun on a cloudless day at noon that sex was for marriage. That conviction I embraced unequivocally as a cardinal tenet of belief for life.

Pranks

But not everything in my life was grim. I was as keen as the next boy to be in the vicinity of girls on the few occasions when school life permitted it.

Thus when the annual school dance came round for 'A Blockers' (seniors), I decided I needed to get in by hook or by crook, even though I was only in B Block, which meant I wasn't among those allowed to the dance.

I reported home as follows:

> The dance was quite an occasion and packs of girls came up from all over the place. Robert Lewis was the only B Block chap supposed to be going (as a barman, i.e. handing out *cokes* etc) as he had booked it long beforehand. However Russel Collins and I wangled it with Hugh McNiel (the chief electrician) that we should go as electricians and work the lights and floodlights etc![9]

Now, there's a 'how'd you do'! Though Dad was an electrical engineer, I knew nothing about electricity other than how to get a shock! But now I was an electrician, no less, for the school dance. My dad must have howled himself into near cardiac arrest at the thought!

I bided my time. Finally the band leader called for 'a Paul Jones' – an arrangement where girls and boys revolve in two huge circles going in opposite directions. When the music stops, you dance with the girl opposite you. I edged into the boys' circle.

How did I work it? I don't know. But when the music stopped I was opposite Bridget Forsyth-Thompson, my childhood flame from Basutoland. So I danced with her! Bliss had arrived!

When I was asked by a master what I was doing as a B Block pupil at the dance, I replied 'Electrician', which raised a roar of laughter but passed muster.[10]

My ongoing piano lessons with the legendary John Hodgson, teacher and lifetime friend, introduced me to the great compositions of Beethoven, Brahms, Liszt, Mozart and Rachmaninoff, enriching my schooldays.

I wrote home, telling of the School Prize-Giving Day in 1952 when I certainly did not win any prizes but took comfort from the remarks made by guest speaker Geoffrey Clayton, Archbishop of Cape Town: 'You boys who are prize-winners today have the gift of concealing your ignorance. But you who have not won any prizes, you have the gift of concealing your knowledge.'[11] That surely applied to me!

My sixteenth birthday came shortly after this and my dad wrote with his loving wisdom:

> I don't usually admire new born babes, but I remember thinking you were a very presentable specimen – perhaps because you were our first! Anyway, I think you aren't too bad at your present age and I feel sure you will grow to be a man we shall be proud of. Only don't do it too quickly, for that will mean I shall be old and I don't feel like being that just yet! Life is opening out before you and I hope, more than I can say, that it will be a happy, interesting and fruitful one, not only for yourself but those around you. Do the best you can at whatever you are doing, and don't worry if others do better.[12]

As to my behaviour, I was still quite a rebel, a naughty guy, 'bit of a crim' (criminal), as some boys put it. I would, for example, run absurd expellable risks at the school stationery shop, leaping with remarkable agility over the counter, while the attendant's back was turned, to steal a rubber or pencil, effectively of virtually no monetary value. Shoplifting was a special skill, and once in Pietermaritzburg with a Basutoland friend, Alan Bowmaker, I got the shop lady to hunt something down at the far end of the shop while I stole a cake and vanished out the door. For me it was just a clever prank.

But then came a life-shaping remark in my school career. Alan said to me: 'Michael, if you go on like this, you'll steal a motor car next.'

I thought to myself: Hey, you know what? That's right. And I decided there and then never to steal again. And I never have.

Holiday fun

As always, my holidays were active and full of fun.

I remember going down the Caledon River in tubes, even when it was dangerously flooding. Then there was tractor driving for Pat Duncan. As I said previously, Pat had left government service in 1952 and bought a farm just over the Caledon River border from where he ran a bookshop, did his politics and a little gentlemanly farming. I had always wanted to be a tractor driver, among my many ambitions, so I relished ploughing fields, constructing and grading farm roads, making contour furrows, and doing errands like fetching bricks from Maseru to build a pump house on the farm.

I became reckless. On one such errand to the Maseru brick factory with a big trailer hitched to the back of the tractor and a young African farm-hand helping me, I embarked on a rather typical Michael prank. At the top of the hill coming out of Maseru and heading down a long flat stretch, then round a corner to the border post, I put the tractor into neutral, the young Mosutho lad in alarm clutching the tractor's mudguard next to me.

The tractor, with a ton or two of bricks behind it, picked up speed to about 90 kilometres per hour (55 mph). Some little ol' Maseru colonial servant almost succumbed to cardiac arrest as he suddenly had a tractor and trailer and a hysterically laughing teenager thunder past him like a racing driver in the Monte Carlo Grand Prix. My young African friend concluded that his last day had come as we hurtled down at breakneck speed to the border post. There, mercifully, the tractor's brakes held and we came to a spectacular standstill before the gobsmacked police officer manning the border gate.

Final year at high school

In my final year at Michaelhouse, I wrote home reporting that:

All the chaps at school call this place 'a hole', and say 'what a frightful hole' this is! It was therefore very funny in house prayers when Mr Ibbotson, while lecturing us said, 'We are all part of a whole.' Everybody just roared. Mr Hammond, our House Tutor, who likes a good few drinks now and then, sometimes reads at House Prayers. Thus on Friday when he said, 'renew our spirits' there were some rather suppressed giggles![13]

Chapel did mean quite a lot to me, and I went to voluntary communion every week. But I refused point-blank to say one of the prayers in the Communion Preparation Manual: 'O God, take me, make me, and use me, to your honour and glory.' This struck me as an absurdly extravagant self-offering and I refused to say it. If God got hold of me like that, he would resolve to make me miserable and send me to a monastery. And I surely knew, even then, I was not the monastic type!

I still saw school authorities as 'agin' me, though that was probably just part of my own paranoia in interpreting assorted disciplines that came my way in response to my naughtiness.

At about this time, Langdon Ibbotson, my house tutor (and acting housemaster while Jim Chutter was out and about with his politicking for the Torch Commando, a local anti-apartheid pressure group), decided that maybe there was something good in young Cassidy, and he gave me a responsibility – to be in charge of Pascoe's senior day room. I had to see it was well supplied with magazines and daily newspapers and that it was generally kept looking nice.

It was a tiny thing but a turning point. Someone, at last, was believing in me. I responded wholeheartedly, and called off there and then my war against authority. And I looked after the little recreation day room as if I had the keys to Buckingham Palace, procuring good newspapers and magazines for it, as well as quite a handy radio.

The shy Langdon Ibbotson was thus a key player in my school career. Later we became firm, lifelong friends.

Another key player was the great Ken Pennington, who brought his famous mathematics skills and his genius for encouragement to bear for a term or two upon my lamentable maths. Without him I would have failed maths, failed my 'matric' (school-leaving exams), never got into Cambridge, and who knows where I would have landed? On such small hinges can the big doors of life turn.

Decades later Ken's son, Rex, at one point a distinguished rector of Michaelhouse, would become a very dear and true friend, along with his wife, Sarah.

There was general agreement that I would benefit from a year of post-matric, which set me up for a leadership role. In anticipation, in October 1953 I was made a house prefect, to the scorn of some of my

A Block mates. I was able to muster the courage to conceal my mixed emotions and wrote home positively on 25 October 1953:

> You will be very pleased to hear that I am writing this in the prefect's room. I was made a prefect on Wednesday together with Arthur Reynolds. It is almost certain I will be Head of House next year – but don't go saying that to everyone in case I'm not. I have two skivvies (Cullen and Curry) who clean my shoes every day, brush my blazer, take my books to classrooms, fetch my wash, buy my haberdashery and do book-room for me. As prefects' duties in the house I have to see that the chaps fill in the games chart and the Sunday free bounds book and as school duties ring the chapel bell and serve in the tuck shop.[14]

When I was made Head of House and awarded my school prefect's badge at the final assembly of the school year, some of my detractors came to congratulate me, one of them in apologetic tears. That was quite healing.

It was a huge relief to get matric, a nightmarish exam, out of the way. For most of my adult life, my recurring nightmare was that maths matric was only days away, and I didn't know what the heck was going on!

Happy days

My post-matric year was psychologically restorative. I loved trying to 'clean up' Pascoe from some of the stuff that had prevailed in the last few years; for example, I banished bullying and teasing and made it a capital crime. I stopped any ragging of boys who seemed to be so-called 'religious'. I even re-initiated an after-prep prayer meeting in the Crypt Chapel which I had started in my matric year to the scornful ridicule and indignation of my contemporaries. This sometimes had 30 or 40 boys attending. My actions made our chaplain, the Revd Bill Burnett, later Archbishop of Cape Town, put it to me that I 'might be a candidate for the ministry'. This I briefly entertained while exploring other options such as doing photography for *National Geographic*, working for Shell Oil, or entering the legal profession, even the colonial service.

When Mum heard that somewhere, perhaps even remotely, in the mix was the idea of Christian ministry, she exploded: 'I would rather be dead than see you in the church!' I guess that slowed me down a bit!

Even so, the ministry notion had never been dead and my dad, concerned, had picked this up with my former headmaster, Fred Snell, who had by this time moved to then Rhodesia (Zimbabwe) to found Peterhouse School.

Fred had then written me an extraordinary letter which reached me as I entered my post-matric year and which deserves setting forth in full:

Peterhouse, Marandellas
January 21st 1954

My dear Michael,

I have been thinking of you since I got your father's letter telling me that you were wanting to go into the ministry. He asked me to write to you before the end of the holidays. What I think about it all in general is this:

1. The call of God – 'vocation' – is a very real thing and it is generally mediated to us through the thoughts that come into our minds, through the apparently chance meetings that happen to us, through the things we hear or read or see – in short, through any or all of the circumstances of our lives. Such 'vocation' is not of course confined to a call to the ministry. But if that be the 'vocation' in question it is a particularly serious matter because of the high responsibility involved.

2. If the call is of God, to refuse it is certainly the road to frustration and unhappiness.

3. But the devil is a cunning devil and not above concocting the symptoms of 'vocation' for his own ends. If you prefer to substitute for 'the devil', 'the depths of our subconscious pride and the rest' – the practical effect is little altered.

4. In a matter of such importance therefore as a vocation to the ministry it is not wise to act precipitately unless circumstances are such as to compel immediate committal. How then is one to be sure whether a 'call' is of God or otherwise? This is of course the crux of the matter. Generally I believe by living with it – holding it as it were in the presence of God as best one can, till it either fades or settles into firm conviction. Sometimes also I believe that the sense of call may do neither of these – the doubts remaining. In such a case, and when 'the call' is one which, as in your problem, involves real sacrifice, it probably means that it is authentic and that He is testing one by refusing the comfort of firm conviction and forcing one to walk 'by faith and not by sight'. By holding it in the Presence I do not mean continual praying about it consciously – though there must be conscious prayer about it from time to time – I mean never shutting God out of the debate. Sooner or later either the 'call' will fade away or the thing will be brought to crisis by the necessity for some decision which must be either acceptance or refusal. If then the 'call' is still nagging in the conscience I believe it is pretty certainly God's call.

5. But all through this long, and often painful process the first essential is that one should be continually disciplining oneself to the submission

of one's own will to His will – striving to desire before everything that one may do His will. The primary conscious object of prayer should thus always be this submission – which is itself His gift. I wonder if I have been able to get that clear to you. I hope so. I am convinced it is the root of the matter.

6. As far as the present is concerned, and on what information I have which is very possibly incomplete, I believe you should continue with the course previously mapped out, finish Michaelhouse, go to university and get a degree in Science or what you will, all knowledge and truth is His, and if you eventually go into the Church He will know how to use it through you. The final crisis of decision may well be delayed till the degree is behind you and you then have to decide whether then to go to a theological college or not. But if and when your duty to God is clear to you it must be followed at all costs even if necessary that very high cost of going against the wishes of the parents to whom you owe, and I am sure pay, your love and duty and gratitude. Also if a particular course of action is in accordance with His will, material difficulties will sort themselves out – though not perhaps in the particular way you would choose or desire.

Bless you. Yours ever, F.R.S.[15]

How deeply blessed I was, and privileged, to be the recipient of such schoolmasterly care, and counsel and wisdom!

I was finding a deep spirit of care for the boys in my house. This first alerted me to the fact that I was a people person, and had some pastoral instincts in me.

My studies allowed much more free time to read classics, do some basic German, start on philosophy, try my hand at painting and improve my piano playing. I even did a piano piece in a school concert! Terrifying ordeal.

As Head of House I was also in charge of discipline, which I carried out conscientiously.

Cambridge possibility

When it came to thinking about university, Mum and Dad had set their minds over-ambitiously on Oxford or Cambridge, and were steering me away from South African universities for political reasons.

In August 1954 I wrote home: 'I think Oxford and Cambridge, including living during vacs etc, come to about £400–£500 per annum! So it looks as though there's no hope there. I am finding out about the entrance to London University.'[16]

*Speech Day, 1954, final year at Michaelhouse: Mr Brookes (Latin master)
and Mrs Brookes, Michael and J. B. Chutter (housemaster)*

At this point I suddenly decided it was string-pulling time and went to see the rector (headmaster), Clem Morgan, an Oxford man, to ask if he could help me get into Oxford. Morgan reflected a moment and then said: 'You know, I think your housemaster, Jim Chutter, might have more strings to pull at Cambridge.'

So off I went dutifully to the great Jim. He was a distinguished graduate of St Catharine's College, Cambridge, known as 'Caths'.

'Cambridge? Jolly good idea, old boy,' he exulted, and promised to write to his old college. He wanted to do something for his house captain, having concluded that while I was 'of average ability' I was a pretty good all-rounder.

In the rector's testimonial, I was apparently 'not outstanding intellectually' but had 'a good fund of common sense . . . he has a real gift of responsibility and also a certain natural charm'.[17]

Well, whoever heard of getting into Cambridge on average ability, a non-outstanding intellect, some common sense and a little charm? But Jim found a way, sending my father a form with the words 'Please kindly also on the form fill in Michael's nationality. He doesn't seem to know what he is!'[18]

And that was that. Normal entrance exams, which academically I would never have managed, were waived. Miracle of miracles.

I was into Cambridge University. One of 120 out of 2,000 applicants trying to get into Caths. By some judicious string-pulling. And the grace of God!

Or was I? The fact is another miracle was needed. A financial one. Mum and Dad simply did not have the necessary resources.

Then they heard the Basutoland government was going to 'give' them a government house. This they had coveted for years, instead of the tiny little privately owned home, now ever more difficult for us all to squeeze into. Bless them, they decided to sell this little home and got £1,000 for it. But Cambridge required £300 per year, plus £400 expense money for the balance of the year (six months) when students were not on campus. So £700 ideally was needed for the third year.

Did my parents pray? I don't know. Probably. Anyway, a miracle was indeed shaping up. My dear maternal grandfather, Edward (Dah) Reading, had missed out himself on university, having gone into the Royal Canadian Cavalry straight after school. This university education gap made him passionate about the idea of his only grandson one day getting to university.

Now the other bit of the story. In the 1920s or 1930s, my grandfather had invested a substantial slug of his savings and earnings in shares on a gold mine which went bust. He lost his shirt on it. Effectively he went bankrupt. Out of that trauma he turned to drink for a while, almost to suicide. And the shares, still in his possession, remained valueless. However, several decades later, just when I needed money to go to Cambridge, uranium was found in the defunct mine. Its shares shot up overnight in value. My mum, who had inherited the shares, promptly sold them.

The sum which came in?

Exactly £700!

I could go to Cambridge! I would study Law.

So thank you, dear Dah, for hoping and maybe praying – because he had become a person of prayer – that I would get to university! And then posthumously making it possible.

And thank you, God.

In my last term at Michaelhouse I was made a senior prefect. The journey, nearly complete, had taken me from bliss in my first two years, to bitter pain, loneliness and desolation in my next two, to fulfilment and happiness and some modest achievement in my last.

I had gained much from Michaelhouse for which I could never be adequately thankful. But I also received into my being a mortal emotional wound of inferiority or inadequacy.

On balance Michaelhouse was a wonderful time of growing and equipping. Nor could I have dreamed that one day I would send my son Martin to Michaelhouse and even Pascoe House for five happy years.

Michael home for the holidays, while teaching at PTS; Riverside picnic, August 1955

8

Cambridge and conversion

———•◦•———

*We are really delighted you are going to Cambridge . . . It is
one of the biggest things that will ever happen to you.*[1]
(Pat and Cynthia Duncan to Michael)

The months before going up to Cambridge were very happy ones. I was now a man. I could smoke openly if I wished. Down a beer-shandy when I wanted to, even with my parents looking on. I could wear a sports jacket and fancy tie, even a suit, and no longer a school blazer.

What's more I had a job as a schoolmaster at Parktown School in Johannesburg, where I had been as a child. I taught, if you can believe it, Latin, French and Divinity, and took the boys for cricket, soccer, hockey and boxing. Also on staff was Nina Wynne, a marvellous teacher of the really little ones, and we became great friends. In fact in 1961, during my tour of Africa, she asked me to be her chauffeur to drive her to the church on her wedding day when she married Charles Baber. Juliet, their first child, became my goddaughter and we are close to this day.

'It all comes very naturally,' I told my parents. In fact I loved everything about that job.

I have kept one of the notes given to me by some boys when I left:

> No more Latin, no more French,
> no more sitting on a hard old bench.
> If the teacher interferes,
> knock him down and box his ears.
> And if that doesn't serve him right,
> blow him up with dynamite![2]

Setting sail

I sailed from Cape Town on the *Stirling Castle* amid great excitement:

There were masses of people at the docks – waving streamers, and lots of shouting. Cape Town looked superb, and it must surely be one of the most beautiful and dramatic ports in the world. The sea was an incredible blue and there were wisps of cloud floating across Table Mountain and all the time the crying of gulls. The thrill as we started moving was terrific – first two tugs pulled us away from the dock edge and once clear the engines started up and I immediately felt a shudder. Then we were off – through the gap in the wharf and out into Table Bay. The first time I walked I nearly fell down and for the first two or three minutes I walked very gingerly getting the feel of the roll which was quite considerable due to the Cape Rollers.[3]

The day before I left home, my dad had taken me on one side: 'My boy, I just want to warn you that once people get on board ship, they go quite dotty!'

Indeed, when the ship put in at Las Palmas in the Canary Islands and many of the young lads went ashore for a few hours, my little protected universe was shaken to its foundations by what I gathered they got up to.

Not surprisingly, I didn't escape one of those legendary, flibbertigibbet shipboard romances. I was confident enough, and danced with the girl a lot. But that was about it!

Once off the boat train from Southampton, I was met in London by my old Michaelhouse piano teacher, John Hodgson, who was in the UK

Setting sail for England and Cambridge at last (Table Mountain,
Cape Town, in the background), September 1955

on leave. My letter home recorded: 'After a shambolic hour or so trying to get my luggage, we caught a taxi straight across London to Euston. John pointed out the Houses of Parliament, St Paul's, the Thames of course, the Festival Hall – all very hurried.'[4]

After a magical few days with John Hodgson in Preston, even listening on radio to the *Last Night of the Proms*, to another few days with family friends in Kent, and then a brief visit to my dad's old 'aunts' in Painswick, I linked up in London with my dear godfather, Roger Haldane, one of the world's consummate gentlemen, who drove me up to Cambridge.

St Catharine's College

There are, I imagine, few people who can arrive in Cambridge and not find themselves catching their breath at the awesome loveliness of the place, arguably the most beautiful university town in the world. Oxford students would of course deny this, but the truth remains all the same!

I was put in digs at 45 Newnham Road, with Alasdair Macaulay, ex-Michaelhouse, brother of my friend Ranald and a law student, having already read a Bachelor of Arts in Law at Natal University. The third occupant was Michael McGowan, an Anglican ordinand, whose calm existence was severely shaken by these two rambunctious and rowdy

Cambridge

South Africans, one of whom (Alasdair) played jazz records half the day, while I played classics on a record player or on the hired piano.

Mrs Askham, our landlady, a severe woman who ran a sweet shop with her husband on the ground floor beneath us, was appalled when my hired piano was squeezed perilously up the stairs.

I vividly recollect walking down King's Parade with Alasdair Macaulay on our first evening in Cambridge. We were both awed by the place. The bells of Great St Mary's were booming out into the cool night air and for all I can remember I might even have thought of God in those moments. We wandered on through dimly lit streets and shadowy cloisters, trying very hard to affect the sophistication of third-year men. But no one with eyes to see would have been taken in, for we were wearing, as required after 6.00 p.m., our academic gowns, which were bright and new, while the gowns of third-year students bore little or no resemblance to the article that leaves the manufacturers.

During our first few days, like all freshmen, Alasdair and I were inundated with every possible letter and pamphlet, the majority of which informed us that we could not truly claim to have been in the University of Cambridge unless we had belonged to the society they were promoting. I cautiously refrained from committing myself anywhere. Alasdair, more impetuous, kicked off by joining the Heretics Club, a strange organization whose speakers spend their time expounding, for example,

Michael and Alasdair Macaulay in the sitting room of 45 Newnham Road, 1955

the innumerable benefits to be derived from joining a nudist colony! The other club he threatened to join was the Buddhist Association. And that after a church-school education!

One society, however, did its propaganda by personal visitation. Thus one evening there was a timid knock on the door of our sitting room. We opened it to admit a pleasant undergraduate with a gentle, retiring manner. He was fumbling a lot of cards. Had we heard of the CICCU, he asked nervously. We hadn't. He looked relieved. His name was Christopher Wilson, he said, and he was from the Cambridge Inter-Collegiate Christian Union – CICCU for short.

To this Alasdair replied with an impatient little laugh, 'You can forget about me – I'm an agnostic.' If there was any religion which interested him, he said, it was Buddhism. Christopher met this opposition by visiting us almost every evening during the next three weeks. Alasdair countered by joining the Buddhist Association. The daily discussions which now followed on the subject of religion normally degenerated into vigorous argument, with Alasdair holding a lone position against the frontal assaults not only of Christopher and Michael McGowan, but also of myself, as eager and determined a defender of Christianity as anyone. Indeed the Christian religion meant enough to me to make me plead with Alasdair to give it a try.

In the first few days, like every other freshman, I went to a number of

Michael McGowan and Alasdair Macaulay

freshers' 'squashes' – the idea being to squash as many people as possible into the meetings, usually in a very confined space! These were run by various clubs and societies in an attempt to win the support and the membership of as many freshmen as could be persuaded. Among the squashes I attended was that of the CICCU.

The men in it struck me as exceptionally friendly and genuinely interested in me and my welfare. They invited me regularly to coffee in their rooms, and helped me in the inevitable business of where to buy books, where to go for lectures, and how to find this tutor or that professor. They put me in contact with the secretaries of various clubs, and the captains of various sports. In fact they generally looked after me, as they endeavoured to do for the other freshmen, particularly those from overseas, who found the necessary adjustments to Cambridge life a more radical business than their British counterparts.

Moreover, in talking of their faith they seemed so enthusiastic. Christianity clearly meant more to them than it did to anyone I had met before. One day I approached Robert Footner, a keen CICCU man, and asked him if I could join. To my amazement he discouraged me from doing so and said he thought I should wait a while and give it 'a little more thought'. Apparently my request caused some amusement among the CICCU men in the college as there was the vaguest suspicion that I might not yet be a truly committed Christian.

Robert Footner, who led Michael to Christ and mentored him

On my first Sunday I was taken to the CICCU Freshers' Sermon. The sermon struck me as splendid and when the preacher asked at the end of the service that all those who had 'accepted Christ' should go forward to the front of the meeting and collect a booklet from him and shake his hand, I went up. I recall liking the idea of personally meeting such an impressive man. 'Have you accepted Christ?' he asked me. 'Oh yes, long ago,' I replied unhesitatingly as I took the booklet from his hand.

I learned later from Mike McGowan how he had been praying earnestly for me and how ecstatic he had been when I went forward. But his bubble of joy was rudely popped next day when I told him that I had only gone up for the booklet! Unbeknown to me, the CICCU members re-intensified their prayer for me.

One evening Christopher asked me what I thought had happened on the cross. 'Jesus died for my sins there,' I replied without hesitation. 'Yes, that's right,' he said. Even so, he was not convinced I understood the cross and I recall for my part being mystified by his saying the whole business really depended on how one regarded the cross. Anyway, about one thing there could be no mistake: intellectually I could say that I knew Jesus had died for my sins. I had been taught that all my life.

While things were moving towards a climax for me spiritually, I had to face another big issue – namely whether I should change my subject from Law to Languages. I had suddenly felt I had signed up for the wrong degree. I didn't really want to do Law. (As Carol always said to me later: 'You'd have made a hopeless and lousy lawyer. You'd be letting everyone off.' Maybe!)

Out of the blue in my first days at Cambridge I met a student who said he was doing a degree in Modern and Medieval Languages.

'What's that?' I asked.

'It's basically a degree majoring in French and Latin. In fact modern and medieval French. Classical and medieval Latin. Plus Provençal – the medieval language used in Provence, in the South of France.'

I was smitten by the idea. As I explored it, I saw that the course would qualify me much better than law for a career in teaching. The schoolmaster's life struck me as constructive in the true sense and eternal in effect, shaping the lives and personalities of young people who in their turn would shape others' lives and personalities. I wanted my epitaph to be written not on a block of stone but on the hearts of people. It seemed such a positive life. Unlike a doctor's work, schoolmastering was not rescue work. Unlike the ministry of the Church, as it seemed to me, it was unrestricted.

Change of course

So I approached my tutor, Dr Gooderson, about a change of course. I immediately found myself swept along by the tide of circumstances. My tutor sent me at once to the Modern Languages supervisor, who thrust a piece of French prose into my hand and told me to translate it and return it to him in two days' time. As I walked out into the dark college quadrangle, I realized that this was the most important bit of work I was ever likely to do. On it depended my course at Cambridge, on my course at Cambridge might well depend my whole future career, and on my career could depend my life's happiness.

I was sufficiently awed by the whole business to commit the matter to God. I felt that if the prose satisfied the French supervisor it would represent the 'green light' from God to change my subject. Two days later after reading the prose, the supervisor commented: 'You'll just make it. You won't do well, but you should scrape a third.' My supervisor, you see, was an optimist.

My Latin tutor, Mr Lacey, gave his consent, for some reason which is still to me a mystery, to my taking Latin without even requiring so much as a recital of *mensa* from me. I might just have been able to do this, but had he asked me to translate a Latin prose I would most certainly have ended up reading Law. My Latin was far worse than my French.

So, I changed my course to study for the Modern and Medieval Languages degree – or 'Tripos' as the exams are known in Cambridge. O happy day! As it was, the extent to which I had fooled both these men and myself was to become evident only too soon!

Soon we were into lectures, tutorials and assignments. I was alarmed by the standard and the academic pressure. We all felt it.

Mr Lacey, my Latin tutor, sent me off for special coaching to a retired Cambridge don, 80 or 90 in the shade, affectionately known around Cambridge as 'Malaria Jones' because he had written a learned tome whose thesis was that the Roman Empire fell as the result of an outbreak of malaria in an Umbrian swamp in central Italy. After a few sessions with Malaria Jones, he handed me back a Latin prose translation marked with more of his red ink than my black ink, and said in a tremulous, quavering voice, accompanied by giant twittering eyebrows: 'Young man, when I think of you and the Tripos, I get so *frightened* for you.' I cycled back to Caths ready myself to jump off one of the spires of King's College Chapel. I was in academic despair.

On a lighter note, in a Classical History lecture, the lecturer referred to Polybius, the great Greek historian (204–122 BC), whom I to my now immortalized shame had never heard of, and I wrote down 'Bolivius' in my notes. This caught the eye of Bob Beramian, our Caths captain of squash sitting next to me, who promptly exploded into paroxysms of uncontrollable laughter which lasted for the next three years. Crowning me Cambridge's leading ignoramus, he called me 'Bolivius' ever thereafter. 'Bolivius,' he would say, bending double with laughter, 'we are playing St John's this week. You'd better win!' With my place having been well and eternally secured at the bottom of the academic heap in Cambridge, my only redemption with Bob was that I pretty consistently won all my squash matches for the college. 'Bravo, Bolivius! You're a champ!'

Conversion

One Saturday evening about three weeks after I arrived in Cambridge, Robert Footner asked me if I would like to go to Sunday communion with him the following morning. He said he knew of a very nice church. I replied that I'd be delighted to join him.

Next morning, leaving the famous Round Church, a Norman masterpiece, we had half an hour to kill before breakfast which was at nine o'clock. The date was 23 October 1955.

Robert suggested we go up to his room and kill time there. We killed it all right – and by the time I left Robert's room I had made the most important of all life's decisions. I had decided to commit my life unreservedly to Jesus Christ. I had decided, in Studdert Kennedy's words, to 'bet my life' that Jesus was the Son of God. It happened like this.

Robert asked what I had thought of the service. I said I had enjoyed it as much as any communion I'd ever been to, that is, not much. But I was careful to add that Rome was not built in a day and I expected that in due time communion would come to mean something to me.

Taking the initiative rather suddenly he asked, 'Michael, have you found Christ? Do you know him?' I imagine I looked as confused as I felt but I managed to blurt out, 'Er, yes, I suppose I have,' not really knowing in the foggiest what he meant, but believing that as a regular churchgoer I presumably had 'found' Christ, and knew him. In reality the notion of 'knowing Christ' was just so much gibberish as far as I was concerned. In fact the expression 'knowing Christ' was anathema to me. Though I don't remember how I replied to this question, I am sure my answer must have been unintelligible.

I know I was very put out and immediately branded my questioner a religious fanatic whose acquaintance I proposed to drop at my earliest convenience. Robert told me later that he went on to explain the whole gospel to me, speaking of sin, the Saviour, Calvary, the need to commit oneself unreservedly to Christ, the difference between 'knowing' him and 'knowing about' him, and so on. I recall very little of this and certainly nothing about the cross, which I did not really come to understand in any sense until about 18 months later.

They say it is the final straw that breaks the camel's back, and it was certainly the final questions that broke mine.

'Have you ever asked him into your life as your Saviour, Master and Friend? Have you surrendered *yourself* to him?'

By this time I was not just put out. I was angry. I deeply resented this invasion of my privacy and felt such insolence to be damnable. Who on earth had the right to speak to me like this? But despite this rush of rebellion I found myself thinking – and thinking hard. Certainly I had, I thought, done most things in the religious life – I had been baptized, confirmed, been a regular communicant for years, even served at the Communion Table; I had taken the collection at services and read the lesson; I read my Bible every night, had said my prayers daily since I was seven – but as for giving or surrendering *myself*, I wasn't sure I had done that. Maybe that was the all-important thing. Maybe that might account for the deadness of my faith. I admitted to Robert that I didn't think I had given or surrendered myself to Christ.

'Would you like to ask Christ into your life now – here?' Robert asked. 'We can just kneel down here. Don't be embarrassed.'

Once again I was hit by a surge of rebellious feelings. Praying in somebody's bedroom! What plain, unadulterated nonsense! Dammit – I couldn't call my life my own. I couldn't even take this sacred step by myself. I had to take it on the dirty floor of a student bedsitter in a scruffy hostel. Hell, no! I'd just tell him I'd rather not. But all the time he was looking at me – probably realizing the struggle that was going on inside me. And it was just this spirit of love and understanding that prevented me from telling him I wouldn't. I felt vanquished – and was. The ramparts of my rebellion came down.

'Do you know that verse of Scripture in Revelation 3.20?' he went on. '"Behold I stand at the door and knock: if any man hears my voice and opens the door I will come in to him, and will sup with him and he with me." You see, that is a promise – when you've done your share it is then over to the Lord to do his. You can be sure he will.'

We knelt down and after Robert had said a short prayer I mouthed to Christ a few confused words to the effect that I wanted him in my life as a Ruler and Friend. I opened the door of my heart to him. I asked in sincerity; that I know. But my faith was blind and hesitant and I had little real understanding of what I was doing – and had no idea whatever about what would follow.

As we rose from our knees Robert looked ecstatic – and expressed his feelings saying, 'Now, you really *have* asked Christ into your life. Isn't that grand!' I wasn't sure that it was.

After breakfast I began to grasp the significance of what I had done. I began to see that I had taken a very big step indeed – a step, I felt, that would prove or disprove the reality of Christ, depending on the effect produced in me. Robert had said Christ would change my life for the better if I accepted him. Well, I had accepted him and would now put him to the test. I would challenge God to prove himself by changing my life. Exerting every iota of faith I possessed, I claimed the verse in Revelation and held on to the promise for all I was worth. I had opened the door of my heart and life. He must now come in.

Three hours later I knew he had.

No words are adequate to describe what happened. But gradually during that Sunday morning I became aware of a Presence. It was uncanny – almost frightening. Somehow he was with me, in me, beside me. I left my room. He came with me. This was something new. Robert had talked about 'knowing him'. That was about the nearest I could come to expressing what had happened. I had come to 'know him'. He had introduced himself to me personally. I did feel a new person. Those weren't just words. They expressed what I felt – new, remade, reborn. And with this came a new joy and peace, hitherto unexperienced. I quickly recalled my words to Alasdair a few weeks previously. I had said I had never been happier. But now I was experiencing a happiness that certainly transcended the feeling I had spoken about to Alasdair. This was something deep, and not a momentary frothiness.

That evening I went to church in Holy Trinity and for the first time in my life understood the Blessing, which was part of the liturgy: 'The Peace of God which passeth all understanding . . .' Previously these had been just words. Now they were proven experience and I rejoiced in them. After church I rushed round to an old school friend of mine in Jesus College and told him of my new experience. He did not pour cold water on my story, which surprised me. But not so Alasdair. He was thoroughly sceptical, and understandably so. Here was the person who had been vigorously proselytizing for Christianity coming to him now with a story that he had only become a real Christian himself that very day. Who wouldn't be sceptical – or if not sceptical then mystified beyond measure?

Afterwards

I was making friends quickly, chiefly South Africans, with our common concern about South Africa drawing us together. I soon became close to two of these, David Millard and Michael Nuttall.

David and I had met on my first day. He was a very fine sportsman who went on to secure a Blue for Cambridge against Oxford in both cricket and rugby. He was also a man of strong Christian conviction who happened to be studying theology. ('What's that?' I remember asking myself!) Shortly after our first meeting he said, 'You and I seem to run on the same wavelength,' and with a cheery chuckle he mounted his bicycle and disappeared into the night.

Michael was someone I immediately felt to be a kindred soul. He had had a brilliant academic career at Natal and Rhodes universities and was very patient with me and my fumbling, mediocre mind. His maturity and balance were just what I needed to keep me modestly level-headed. And his faith was very real.

The first thrill of conversion was over and the first germs of doubt were squeezing their way in. I had been told to make prayer and Bible study a regular habit and had failed to take this seriously. Life was going on much as usual and my academic work was proving more and more oppressive. My initial zeal for that frightful practice of 'buttonholing' people to talk about Christ was wearing off. I had caused much offence and harm, incidentally, by this habit and I shudder when I recall the numerous occasions on which I collared some poor unsuspecting undergraduate and submitted him to the ordeal of having the state of his soul examined. I offer retrospective sympathy to those who suffered at my hands in this way.

However, two weeks after my conversion I found myself so far slipped away from my initial certainty that I went to a CICCU friend and asked him to furnish me with ten proofs as to the existence of God. He looked suspiciously at me and then told me simply that I had been lazy. Without giving me so much as one proof of God's existence he sent me packing, with the exhortation to devote more time to prayer and Bible study. I saw Robert Footner the same day and told him too of my awful doubts. He tried to clarify things without much success.

As an afterthought Robert mentioned Romans 10.17: 'Faith comes by hearing and hearing by the word of God.'

'What was that?' I asked eagerly. 'Say it again.'

I pondered the words, felt they had the very solution to my needs, and went back to my digs, sure that if I was to increase my faith I must devote more time and care to the study of God's word. Next morning I did not read my Bible in bed or say my prayers beneath the warmth of the blankets. I got out of bed, and spent 20 minutes on my knees. And as I developed this habit of the daily 'quiet time', so my doubts were dispelled and my college friends once more had cause to be on guard.

St Paul had put it so clearly: 'Anyone who belongs to Christ has become a new person. The old life is gone; a new life has begun!' (2 Corinthians 5.17 NLT).

Then I read of Temple Gairdner, an Anglican missionary to Cairo, writing soon after his own conversion: 'That sense of newness is simply delicious. It makes new the Bible, and friends and all mankind, and love and spiritual things, and Sunday, and church, and God Himself. So I've found.'[5]

Billy Graham

A few weeks after regaining my spiritual feet I heard that an American evangelist, Billy Graham, was coming to Cambridge to lead a mission lasting for a week. The name rang a bell. Just. But now the university and seemingly all England were in an uproar. A famous fundamentalist (whatever that was) was coming into an academic environment. The columns of the London *Times* sizzled with heated correspondence. Mainly between clerics. The leaders of the Church of England seemed to be at each other's throats. For the first time in my life I realized that not all Christians in the Church of Jesus Christ see things the same way. The problem was, said the letters to *The Times*, that Billy Graham took the Bible literally. And you can't do that in these modern days. Yes, you can, said many. I was very perplexed.

There had been numerous threats on the part of certain students to kidnap the evangelist, but there must have been a miscarriage in the plans of the kidnappers because he arrived safely and on time! The evening before the mission opened, Dr Graham addressed the CICCU and delivered a powerful message on the need for greater consecration. During the concluding prayer some fireworks were thrown into the meeting through the window of the Union Debating Chamber, and I recall being highly amused at the not inconsiderable antics performed by the unfortunate worthies among whom the thunder-crackers landed. The explosions over, Dr Graham finished his prayer and the meeting dispersed.

The following six evenings I heard the evangelist preach, and these addresses did more than anything to inspire me to deepen my faith by deepening my knowledge of the Scriptures and lengthening my times of prayer.

About the third night there was great rejoicing in 45 Newnham Road (my digs) as Alasdair returned from the meeting and announced that he had been convinced of the truth of Christianity and had decided to commit his life to Christ. My boundless joy at this was shared by Mike McGowan and particularly by Chris Wilson whose regular visits for weeks had at last borne fruit.

I also learned from my South African friend Mike Nuttall that he had decided to remain behind after one of the meetings, feeling that, although committed, he had never publicly nailed his colours to the mast. He decided to go forward to meet the evangelist, the arranged way of signifying that a decision for Christ had been made. Michael was a great inspiration to me at this time, and not a day passed without our meeting for discussion and prayer. The synthesis of his simple faith and enormous intellect never ceased to amaze me, and I counted myself fortunate to have found such a friend.

After the Graham mission my faith was more childlike and my spiritual vision clearer than at any other time. I felt Christ's presence at work and at play and found that even while cycling I could rejoice in the fact that he was there to talk to.

A stolen bicycle

One Thursday I left the Modern Languages library to discover that my bicycle had been stolen.

Telling the police was an option that I rightly or wrongly considered out of the question, when I had an all-powerful and all-seeing heavenly Father to turn to. So I prayed for the return of my bicycle. I spent the rest of Thursday being late for my various appointments and lectures and getting fed up. On Friday morning I decided not only to continue praying for the return of the stolen vehicle, but to pray for its return by 7.00 p.m. that evening. At lunch I told Robert Footner what I was doing.

'You can't do that,' he said in a horrified voice. 'You can't ask God for things like that. You just can't, you know.'

I didn't see why not and said so.

A stolen bicycle: St Catharine's College in the snow

All afternoon I held on in faith that I really would find my bicycle that evening if only I did not waver in faith. At about 5.45 p.m. I set out in a 'Cambridge Drizzle' for another Latin tutorial with my famous Dr Malaria Jones. I arrived late, and he was not pleased. Afterwards I walked back to college thoroughly depressed and roundly cursing the day I had ever changed my subject from Law to Languages. I found myself late for supper, which infuriated me further. So I had to wait for the next sitting. I decided to go and call on Pam Geldard, a South African I had met a few weeks before and who lived very near our college. Suddenly I registered that evening was here – but not my bicycle. Again I claimed in faith that my request would be heard. With these thoughts in my mind I walked back some 20 minutes later. While doing so, I looked to my left down a dark alleyway. Suddenly the moon glinted on something propped up against a wall. A bicycle. I walked up to it and looked again. The old-fashioned sloping crossbar was recognizable anywhere.

It was *my* bicycle. One among 8,000 bicycles in the town! I almost fell on it, like a child seizing a new Christmas present – so great was my joy, and then with a twinkle in my eye I looked heavenwards and said: 'Thank you, Lord. Thank you so much.' Back at college, just before 7.00 p.m., I saw Robbie Footner. 'Oh, by the way,' I said as casually as possible, 'my bike's back.' His jaw dropped in amazement, and then snapped back into place! All we could both do was dissolve into helpless laughter.

Study weariness

The Old Testament book of Ecclesiastes says: 'Much study is a weariness of the flesh' (12.12). That is really an understatement. It is difficult to describe the burden that I found my course to be. If my French essays earned any grade at all, I was pleased. But usually I had to be content with something very low, or minus minus. The effort required to turn out even abysmal essays was considerable and probably amounted to three or four times the number of working hours my fellows needed.

On many occasions I was almost reduced to tears by my maddening inability to string together a number of French words in anything like tolerable French grammar. But as this burden of work became greater, so *pari passu* my reliance upon Christ deepened, for I felt more and more that I would never come anywhere near the grade in my work unless I had his supporting hand. So nearly every essay I tackled was preceded by prayer that I should have the ability to produce something even approximating what my supervisor wanted. Besides, I felt my work was a sphere in which I ought to do my best for the sake of him to whom I belonged.

Much more hopeful was the fact that Jesus Christ was becoming a part of my life in a manner I could scarcely comprehend.

9

Theological perplexities and politics

———◆———

Perplexity is the beginning of knowledge.[1]
(Kahlil Gibran)

In my letters home I told my parents everything about everything. And they were pretty concerned about all the religious stuff!

Dad wrote to me some advice about guidance:

> The fact that you feel guided to take up the courses you are now doing will be a source of great strength to you in carrying them through, for as Drake said, 'It's not the beginning of any great endeavour but the continuing of the same until it has been thoroughly finished which yields the true glory.' However, as we are all very human it is sometimes worthwhile considering how much our inspirations are influenced by our own desires at the time. In this I can only speak for myself, although I have observed the same tendencies in others. As a seeker after truth you will realise that all across the ages people have done very fine as well as very bad things as a result of feeling guided, although in the case of the bad, they must have deceived themselves as to the source of their inspiration. Please don't think that in underlining the rather obvious I want to undermine your faith in your future or in God but only to try and disentangle the curious and remarkable mechanism of the mind from self-deception.[2]

My mother wrote the very next day, eager to be supportive yet anxious that I not become too self-preoccupied or let dreams of success run away with me:

> We feel so glad to know how convinced you are that you are doing the right thing. That must be half the battle towards achievement. And what you are feeling now must surely be a sort of shield and buckler with which to face life and its pitfalls. You will meet so many clever people of different and varying convictions and hear so many opinions, theories and philosophies that you might well be shaken and bewildered – so that with your coming to a definite conclusion, and you having had as you say a profound experience of what faith can do, you should be better able to come through

unscathed. It must be quite a tough world to face at Cambridge – as Pat Duncan says life there can make or mar you. But at least you have the chance of seeing and hearing everyone else's standards and ideas, and of deciding finally on your own.

As you know I've never had your gift of faith. I have always been a Doubting Thomas, but I have envied those that had it and have applauded the vital spark in them which is lacking in people like myself. Granny and Dah had it, Granny in England (Dad too), and they all stood out as shining examples when troubles came, the testing times which I guess have to come to all of us. I had faith in their faith, and have it in yours and Dad's.

I had of course told my folk about hearing Billy Graham in a packed Great St Mary's, and how 'the most adamant sceptics and agnostics had found Christ and given their lives to Him'.[3] Later I was to meet him in person, and wanted to defend him to my parents:

When Billy Graham came here many students went along with the specific purpose of seeing whether he spoke emotionally, for here as anywhere else people do not like having their emotions played upon. I only heard one or two out of the vast numbers that heard him, criticise him on the ground of being emotional. A lot of people criticise him and become antagonistic to him because they realise that he has something – something that is only going to make terrific demands on them, and which they do not want to accept. He has terrific sincerity, yes, but that is not enough to bring people to an awareness of Christ. The thing that he has, as someone said to me, is quite obviously the power and blessing of God.[4]

Sunday school teaching

Michael Nuttall and I were now teaching Sunday school in the little Anglican church in Grantchester, made famous by reference to it in one of Rupert Brooke's poems. As it happened, this turned out to be one of the activities I enjoyed most during my student days. The vicar there, Pat Hewat by name, received us most warmly when we offered ourselves to help in the Sunday school.

But of course the idea that I might be teaching my new-found faith to Sunday school children filled my mother with alarm:

As far as you yourself are concerned, Mitie [one of Mum's pet names for me], we must leave it to you. It is too difficult to judge at this distance. We just rather hope though that you are being an ordinary, cheerful and normal young man, enjoying life thoroughly and with a zest, not entirely springing from religious fervour, but just because you are young and keen

Revd Pat Hewat, Vicar of Grantchester

and surrounded by wonderful opportunities to enjoy life. And we rather hope you are not making it all too obvious, and are not in ordinary life being the evangelist or ramming it down other people's throats!![5]

Of course this is exactly what I was beginning to do, so this maternal caution was in order.

She went on: 'Somehow it seems to me that something deep down inside is usually unobtrusive, if it is strong and worthwhile. It is the same with any venture. If paraded and flaunted, it often ceases to be a virtue.'[6]

'As to children's missions,' Mum thundered, 'I want most strongly to protest.' She explained:

Mitie, it is not natural, normal or healthy for a child to be thinking about the Lord or coming to Christ. A child's outlook is simple, uncomplicated, just accepting things as they seem matter of fact and ordinary. They accept their parents as their security, their unfailing source of everything they need. Their Sunday School and what they learn of Jesus is just another aspect of the parent relationship. They don't want to have to think of things unseen or abstract and least of all of any hereafter. Once the idea of there being an end to life occurs to them, fear enters, but it is dispelled by the reassurance of having parents. With their parents they are not fanciful, pushy or flattered by any interest taken in them and their affairs. It is accepted as a matter of course.

87

But when anyone who is not their parent comes along, showing a particular personal interest in them the effect is immediately unhealthy and detrimental.

If you want to help children, contribute to feeding and clothing schemes or Dr Barnado's Homes!

She concluded:

I have great respect for Dad's ideas. He was saying that to come to faith through the trials and tribulations of this life, and to arrive at and build up deep conviction as a result, seems to him a more solid foundation than to start too much in the heights and then perhaps to fall and face disillusionment and reaction. I have no doubt your faith will stand the test of time, and will prove itself. But in the meantime it is as yet untested, and you are not yet exactly qualified to 'go out and preach.' It is wonderful that you can feel as you do, darling, but let it stand the test of time before you proclaim it too much to all and sundry.

What a difficult letter to write, I suppose it may carry no weight whatsoever. At any rate, I hope it does influence you or rather convince you a bit. I do feel so strongly about it. Let the poor children enjoy the sea and sun and beach and the thrill of just being alive without having to worry about their souls. They are far more naturally akin to God than adults.[7]

Well, here was food for thought. For sure. Dad wrote again too in more restrained terms:

Life is very perplexing and complex, so I think you will understand if we appear a bit dampening at times. This is not intended to put a brake on the natural enthusiasm of chaps your age whether for religion or politics, but only to point out the possible snags of over-simplification. Like Mum, I don't take too much to the idea of being 'saved' in one go, as I think one has to go on battling all the time to lead a reasonably decent life.[8]

My parents were so loving in their honesty. I did take seriously what they said and resolved to seek advice from respected Christians about theological approaches and evangelism so I would be better equipped to make a careful judgement for myself.

A week or so later I wrote to reassure my parents:

Your words have been far from vain and I really am going to get my views on all this absolutely taped before I leave Cambridge. I can see your points of view perfectly and fully understand how you feel and why you feel it. I have great respect for your opinions, but do feel that there are other sides to the picture which I must find out about, so that I can speak authoritatively about the whole thing.[9]

Theological perplexities

The two theological issues which were causing debate within our friend-ship circle at the time were the authority or otherwise of the Bible, and the different standpoints on Church and society of the so-called Evangelicals and the so-called Anglo-Catholics. Those issues wax and wane to this day, of course.

The problem of biblical inspiration and its related question of author-ity was new to us, and one we had to live with and think through for ourselves. There could be no abdication of responsibility here. We were confronted with one of the most important theological questions in the Christian faith, and evading it would be as unsatisfactory intellectually as it would be detrimental spiritually.

The question was whether the Bible was the word of God and the final authority in all matters of faith and morals. The Evangelical answer was an unequivocal yes. Other sectors of the Church were equivocal, certainly those of liberal outlook. That was the confusing bit to my young mind.

As I wrestled with this, particularly as it related to salvation, which was preoccupying us at the time, I came to see that the claim of Jesus was key when he said, 'I am the way, and the truth, and the life; no one comes to the Father, but by me' (John 14.6). I saw no suggestion of any alternative way. Jesus was *the* way, not *a* way. And if we reject the validity of his claim to exclusiveness as I saw it, we reject him. The truth of his statements and the fact of his divinity stand or fall together. And would not passengers on an ocean liner think little of the captain who encouraged his helmsman to be tolerant and follow any route haphazardly into the harbour? A captain with any sense would urge that the map, the chart, the guidebook and the compass all be followed closely.

I became convinced that tolerance here of any except the charted route would lead to catastrophe.

Thus it was that a book came into my hands called *Fundamentalism and the Church of God* by a man called Gabriel Hebert. He held to it that final authority for life and faith lies in the official teaching of the insti-tutional Church. This is what J. I. Packer describes as the 'traditionalist view', namely: 'What the Church says, God says.'[10] So, Hebert said, we find the mind of God in the Church's historic tradition. And we accept that we receive the word of God via the fallible words of human writers. Was this just the historic creeds? Or did this include the theological writings of the Church's best scholars? And what if these things clash with what the Bible seems to say? In some of our minds we saw this formula ('what the Church says, God says') as a major risk, especially in places where the Church's teachings seemed manifestly contradictory to Scripture.

Soon thereafter a reply appeared by a rising young theologian called James Packer. *'Fundamentalism' and the Word of God* was his title. He affirmed the Bible as fully inspired, reliable and the final authority in all matters of faith and morals. He rejected the label 'fundamentalist' and preferred the label 'evangelical', and this is the label used more commonly today and expressing the oldest traditional creeds and faith statements of the Church. Packer rejected the 'fundamentalist' label because it had become associated with rigidity and negativism and to an evangelicalism that was less than its best.

What brought clarity to my mind and thinking on the authority of the Church was the fact that when the Church began formally to define the limits of the New Testament canon, it only *recognized* the authenticity and authority of those books which already had apostolic authorship or authorization. The task under the guidance of the Holy Spirit was one of discerning which books were apostolically authored or authorized. The Church *recognized* the authority but *did not confer it.* It would be rather like claims made for a painting as a genuine Rembrandt when it would take the discerning eyes of the art connoisseur to recognize the painting as either a genuine Rembrandt or a fake. I found all this persuasive enough. Thus for me, as an enquiring undergraduate and a young Christian, I came to believe that the Church's authority was under Scripture, not over it. The Church only recognized an authority and authenticity already there in the biblical text, but did not confer this. Martin Luther saw this as he challenged the erroneous teaching of the Church, and he brought forth his cry of *'sola scriptura'* (Scripture only) as the only authority for faith and morals. John Wesley affirmed the same as he faced the Church in late eighteenth-century England. For them the teaching authority of the Church had to submit to the teaching authority of Scripture.

Divisions among friends

The whole situation was aggravated for me when friends began to lean towards Anglo-Catholicism, a movement which put forward an Anglican threefold formula, a sort of three-legged stool, as the locus of authority, namely Scripture, tradition and reason, rather than simply the Bible. So where would Scripture stand if tradition or reason seemed to contradict it? Obviously this would affect how we understood the sacraments (e.g. is the bread/wafer just a memorial or is it transformed in some way?), the efficacy of baptism (are people made regenerate through it or just brought into the visible Church?), new birth, salvation, the uniqueness of Christ, other religions, and so on. All of these teachings, which produced a sort of middle way on everything, hung on where spiritual authority lay: in the Bible, or in the three-legged-stool formula? So it was a pretty key issue.

Presumably this kind of discussion was to be expected in a university, which if nothing else sought to stimulate thought and encourage students to rethink ideas and beliefs. But it was difficult when it affected friendships.

How to hold this truth in love was a lesson we had not learned, nor had we grasped the fact that, among the three great virtues of faith, hope and love, love is the greatest (1 Corinthians 13.13). We were unlovingly intolerant of what we considered to be false doctrine. But it is not for intolerance of what we saw as error that apology need be made, but for the spirit in which we demonstrated that intolerance. In an age when tolerance is considered almost the virtue to end all virtues, there is surely a great need for Christians to restate their convictions, but lovingly, that there is no other way of salvation except through Christ and the biblical faith. The apostles certainly had this conviction, as I saw it, so that Peter could say: 'Neither is there salvation in any other: for there is no other name under heaven given among men whereby we must be saved' (see Acts 4.12). And had not Paul added, as I reflected on it all, 'Though we, or an angel from heaven, preach any other gospel unto you than that which we have preached unto you, let him be accursed' (Galatians 1.8 KJV)?

The Bible and apartheid

Soon I was to confront a different challenge on the subject of the Bible. And it related to my beloved homeland, South Africa.

Father Trevor Huddleston, an Anglican monk and leader of the Community of the Resurrection in England, came to Cambridge just after the publication of his book *Naught for Your Comfort* – on South Africa. His visit caused a sensation. I soon devoured the volume. There I learned how some sections of the Church in South Africa, most notably the Dutch Reformed Church (DRC), actually sought to justify apartheid from the Bible. That was a shock. Because here was I, a new and big enthusiast for the Bible, now being told that the Dutch Reformed Church in South Africa used the Bible to justify the dreadful discriminatory system which even as a child and schoolboy I had come to hate. Why, even Jim Chutter, of chapel comedy fame at Michaelhouse School, was strongly convinced that the Bible condemned apartheid. Another South African churchman who had visited our school had said the same thing, namely the famous Alan Paton, whose classic book *Cry, the Beloved Country* was a fearsome indictment of the whole apartheid system.

But Huddleston's revelation to me was a bolt of lightning. Clearly we could not hold the Bible in one hand and the policy of apartheid in the other.

Going public

I was therefore ready, even though still struggling with the Scripture issue, to join with Michael Nuttall, Alasdair Macaulay, Arthur Jenkins (a South African PhD History student) and John Reeves (son of Ambrose Reeves, the Bishop of Johannesburg) in forming what we called the Margaret Thlotleng Society, as a kind of South African political pressure group. Margaret Thlotleng had been a great African saint in Sophiatown in Johannesburg, much admired by Trevor Huddleston for her daily attendance at Mass.

Thus did I find myself, along with Alasdair Macaulay, co-signing with Michael Nuttall a letter to the editor of the London *Times* which Mike had basically drawn up, with Alasdair and me making a few suggestions for alterations in the final draft copy.

Our letter, which produced quite a stir around the UK, and even in South Africa when it was reprinted in a number of papers, read as follows:

> Sir, It is very striking, and very heartening to us as a group of young South Africans studying at Cambridge, to see the affairs of our country being so seriously thought about here. It seems almost presumptuous to contribute to the discussion in your columns, and yet there is a point we would very much urge.
>
> It is this. Nothing is more rooted, it seems to us, in the average white South African mind than the capacity for self-deception. It is sometimes deliberate enough to amount to sheer, blatant dishonesty. We deceive ourselves into believing that apartheid will work even though we know, deep down, that to work it will require large land grants to the African, and that the European farmer upon whose vote we depend will not give up his land. We deceive ourselves that the removal of the Coloured people from the common electoral roll is a vital step on the apartheid ladder and that the Statute of Westminster has made constitutional entrenchments void, when we know, deep down, that in this belief we have debased the moral currency. We deceive ourselves that separate worship among the races is

Michael with Alasdair Macaulay (left) and Michael Nuttall (right), Cambridge, 1956

necessary for geographical and linguistic reasons, when we know, deep down, that it is really that we do not want to sit in the same pew and drink from the same cup. The cancer of dishonest self-deception is one of our greatest diseases, and we sincerely believe this to be no exaggeration or distortion of the facts.

Now, the worst possible thing for white South Africans is to have this evil either spread or placated by the sympathetic remonstrances of well-intentioned Englishmen. The great temptation to the white South African (ourselves included) is to exploit the complexity of his problems, and to hide behind facts which conveniently obscure the issues at stake. Mr Strydom is reported in one of the papers to have answered Father Huddleston with the significant refutation that the Nationalist Government has spent more per capita for the African population in South Africa than any other Government in Africa. This is wonderful news, and we are proud of it; but, ever so subtly, it evades the basic issue. A spiritual and a moral challenge is answered by a material rationalization. It is like Great Britain saying, in support of her defence programme, 'We have spent more per annum on atomic weapons than any other country in the world,' when the real criterion for judgment should be how 'much effort she had expended in the cause' of international disarmament.

The western areas removal scheme can rightly claim to have provided better housing for a section of Johannesburg's African population (and we rejoice in this fact), but this is no answer to the invasion of freehold rights in Sophiatown. The Bantu Education Act can rightly claim to have brought more African children into school, but this does not invalidate the ultimate purpose of the Act, which is to teach the African that he is different and inferior and ought to be separate. If there were 36 million Africans in Great Britain (if we may adopt Lord Brand's hypothesis) it is likely that white Englishmen would desire a colour bar as much as white South Africans, but the *tu quoque* argument, so appealing to the apostle of self-deception, does not exonerate or excuse the white South African in any way. It merely shows that the Englishman is likely to be as evil as he! Yet such a hypothetical comparison is accepted by the average white South African as a real exoneration, and with a sigh of relief he relaxes once more into the 'immensity' of his problem.

We love our country. There is a great work to do there. We would urge, in humility, that well-meaning sympathy be not confused with honest thinking about fundamentals. It is tragic that the conscience should be stilled when it ought to be stirred.

Yours faithfully,
Michael Nuttall
Alasdair Macaulay
Michael Cassidy[11]

The fact that Mike Nuttall had done the letter will lead you to deduce the sort of mind he has – lucid, fertile and clear. After the letter was published we received about 20 personal letters, all without exception brimming over with congratulations and good wishes. Among the letters were several invitations to stay with people from odd corners of England and to call for a meal or drinks if ever we were in such-and-such a part of the country. One old lady, who had family ties in South Africa, told us that she had been praying daily for many years that God would raise up South African students and young people to face the situation in South Africa with a brave front. Similar prayers were going up in churches and homes all over England.

Mum and Dad's reactions sought to be encouraging, but were filled with anxiety and some racist double-think about what would happen if the 'colour bar' really came fully down.

Pat Duncan was delighted beyond measure. Here was his young mentee at last flying his own colours:

How right you are to stress the urgency of the whole situation! If white South Africa goes on behaving in this way for another 30 years, then a generation of black South Africans will have arisen to whom it will have been irrefutably proved that black and white cannot live together in this country. There is only one way, and that is for whites to help in the elimination of the Colour Bar, realising that the future is the chancy one of being a minority with a bad record in a non-white majority.[12]

Of course, there were other things to think about in Cambridge other than theology and politics – namely getting through Part I of the Tripos in Modern and Medieval Languages.

10

An academic mountain to climb

*The best way to treat obstacles is use them as stepping stones . . . Laugh
at them, tread on them, and let them lead you to something better.*[1]
(Enid Blyton)

Apart from our college and university Bible studies each week on
Wednesdays and Saturdays respectively, including a weekly one-hour discipling time with Robbie Footner, plus my squash and hockey, there was
time for little else but revision. I never went out to dinner (couldn't afford
it anyway), or to a movie, or play, but did fit in a very occasional concert, even going down to London a few times with my old Michaelhouse
friend, John Wace, to Beethoven or Brahms concerts at the Festival Hall.
I never dated at all in my entire three years, other than a blind date at
the May Ball just before graduation. I am not sure who was more blind,
she or I.

Christian friends were both alarmed and startled when I announced
that I was 'praying for a second-class honours' because, I claimed, Revd
Dick Lucas had said in a CICCU Bible study you could ask God for anything, and God was obliged to answer because his glory was at stake if he
did not.[2] I was strongly, but to no avail, cautioned about this posture. My
friends held their breath.

They were thankful, however, when they could drag me away occasionally from my desk for something recreational, like a brief punt on the
River Cam.

'I had my first outing on the river last week and my first fall in,' I reported in a letter home.

> The punt pole caught on a tree, and of course rather than leave the pole
> and stay on the boat, I jumped for the branch and to the hysterical delight
> of Mike Snell, Mike Nuttall and John Wace, hung there for a few seconds
> before the branch broke and I splashed into the river. The sight apparently
> was unique – just a pair of spectacles visible above the water! Such is the
> extraordinary eccentricity of Cambridge University that there is a club

Exams: Michael studying in his bedroom at Cambridge

called the Dampers Club for which one becomes eligible on genuinely fall-ing into the river fully clad. The club has a tie and an annual dinner![3]

A final act of desperation was to go to Paris for my April vacation before the exams in May (1956) to immerse myself in the French language.

Paris

I found a cheap air ticket which would get me to the French capital for £10, but the day I was to leave, in my 'quiet time', my eyes lighted on a verse which changed all that. Jesus said: 'You compass sea and land to make a single proselyte' (Matthew 23.15). That was that! The Lord was guiding me to go by sea so that I could win someone to Christ! So cancel the air ticket. Go to Dover.

On the train I tried to witness to an old lady. But she turned out to be Russian. 'Not speakie da English!' Abort number 1.

Going over by Channel boat to Boulogne, I was all the time trying to hunt down my potential proselyte. One person on the ship looked lonely and isolated amid the stormy crossing. I tentatively approached him. As I got close to him, he leaned over the side of the ship and vomited violently. End of witness session number 2!

The train ride from Boulogne to Paris was equally uneventful in evangelistic terms.

Outside the station in Paris, a taxi saw little lost ol' me, having no clue where I was going. Or what I was doing. 'Cité Universitaire,' he yelled. Maybe this was God guiding me again!

'*Oui, certainement*,' I called back.

'*Allons*.' (Let's go.)

Talk about Abraham 'going out, not knowing where he was to go' (see Hebrews 11.8). That was I!

Paris

Arriving at the 'university' in the south of Paris, I enquired after a room! The clerk at the desk looked at me as if I were a nutcase. Arriving out of the blue at a university and asking for a room! I sat down dejected. I took out my Bible to look again at Matthew 23.15 by which I had been supposedly 'guided' to change from air travel to 'sea and land' instead. Oh, no! Oh dear! Oh me! Oh my! I hadn't looked at the context: 'Woe to you, scribes and Pharisees, hypocrites! for you traverse sea and land to make a single proselyte, and when he becomes a proselyte, you make him twice as much a child of hell as yourselves.'

While heaven was no doubt filled with giggles, I was filled with alarm and despondency. Clearly I had a few things to learn about how God guides from Scripture!

At this point, the door to the student reception area opened and in walked a bearded hippy sort of student. I must have looked forlorn and pitiful because he came right up to me and asked in English if I was all right.

'Well, not quite. I'm from England and I'd hoped to find somewhere to stay – but they say they have nothing.'

'Well, my name's Terren, by the way. You could come and stay on the floor in my room. But only after 10.00 p.m., because I'm having an orgy until then.'

'Oh,' I gulped. Then, mustering courage, I replied, 'Thank you, Terren. That would be wonderful.'

About three hours later, the orgy over, I was summoned into a darkened room, lit by a purple light, and with incense sticks burning all over the place. A floor never looked better. Nor the proffered blanket. I lay down, exhausted, and slept the sleep of angels. No doubt with heaven still chuckling!

Next day Terren told me he was 'a professional student' who just got one scholarship or bursary after another to keep him indefinitely entrenched in student life. His attitude was so casual that he had once checked in to sign the register at five to ten for a nine o'clock lecture. The lecturer had exploded.

'Sir, you should have been here at nine o'clock.'

'Why, what happened?' Terren had innocently asked – as he told me – to the apoplexy of his lecturer!

Of course Terren inevitably asked me about myself. And I gave him my testimony about Christ.

You know what? He didn't reject me but said he would hear me again. I resolved to visit at a later date.

I tracked down some accommodation in a garret room on the fourth floor of an apartment building on Avenue Victor Hugo, very near the Arc de Triomphe. The room was about four metres by three. A Madame Miltat was the lessor and I the grateful lessee as the room was dirt cheap – it had to be with the so-called ablution set-up being worse than medieval.

There I got stuck into my French and Latin, day after day. I lived on bits of baguette, yoghurt and cheese.

On Easter Sunday I went to a church which met in a small cinema near the Arc de Triomphe, the pastor being the famous Dr Donald Caskie who had an amazing story of helping fleeing French soldiers escape the clutches of the Nazi occupants of France. His book, *The Tartan Pimpernel*, was a bestseller for years.

But now here was the thing. I had run out of money, apart from 20 French francs (approximately two shillings) in my pocket. Two shillings was my normal weekly tithe. Now what was I to do as the collection bag approached me down the rows in front of me?

Soon after my conversion, I had been taught to tithe one tenth of my weekly pocket money as an act of spiritual obedience, and had been shown the astonishing promise in Malachi 3.10: 'Bring the full tithes into the storehouse . . . and thereby put me to the test, says the LORD of hosts, [and see] if I will not open the windows of heaven for you and pour down for you an overflowing blessing.'

But could I still give my tithe, when broke, and without money or food for the next two weeks? Could I trust God?

As the collection bag made its relentless way towards me, my crisis of faith intensified. It was a life-determining moment. Would I – could I – believe the word of God and receive its promises as authoritative, inspired and trustworthy?

'Put me to the test,' says the Lord. 'Bring the tithe. Then watch me. See what I'll do. Watch me open the windows of heaven.' 'Prove me now,' says the King James Version. '[I will] pour you out a blessing, that there shall not be room enough to receive it' (Malachi 3.10 KJV).

Could I act on God's word?

The bag arrived.

Yes! I could. And should. And would. And did. Into the bag went my last 20 francs.

I had no money for food. And two weeks still to go in Paris.

At the end of the service as I was leaving, Dr Caskie rather casually said to me, 'Michael, would you like to come over to my apartment and have *quelque chose à manger* [something to eat]?' My heart leapt.

'Oh, I'd love to, Dr Caskie. Thank you.' He could never have guessed my relief.

Lunch over, I bade the good doctor farewell, and with some trepidation headed down the four flights of stairs to the street. What now?

As I got to the exit, a distant voice from high up the stair-well called down: 'Michael!'

'Yes?' I shouted back.

'Come back up here, will you?'

When I was back at the door of his apartment, Caskie said to me: 'As you were going downstairs, I kept hearing a voice within me saying "Give that boy some food." So come with me.'

Once in the pantry Caskie filled to the brim a huge cardboard box with groceries and everything under the sun.

I staggered back to my little garret at the top of Madame Miltat's staircase, put my cargo down, fell on my knees and wept. What had been given me, I calculated, was several hundred times what I had put in the collection a few hours beforehand.

I told the Lord I would never doubt his faithfulness in finances and I would never stop tithing. And I never have. Malachi 3.10 is a proven, tried and tested passage of Scripture. It is true. Like the rest of Scripture.

Also, shortly after that, a £10 money order, sent three weeks previously by my parents, arrived. Mum said, 'I woke wide awake in the middle of the night and knew I just had to send you some money.'

Terren, my hippy friend

On Saturday 14 April, four days before I was due to sail for England, I suddenly realized I had not been back to visit my hippy student friend, Terren, at the Cité Universitaire. My excuse was that I had been too busy, but now time was running out, so I resolved to go that very afternoon. I spent some time in prayer to God that I should find Terren, the professional student, in his room when I called.

After lunch I set off on my long journey through the tangled tunnels of the Metro to the Cité Universitaire. I found Terren at home and I entered his sanctuary in fear and trepidation, not knowing for a moment how I would broach the subject of spiritual things with a person who I was sure would remain resistant to my message.

But soon I saw that my fear was far surpassed by his need, and after a while the prayed-for opportunity to speak of Christ arose quite naturally. Lying on his bed and staring intently at the ceiling, my friend began speaking in a quiet and serious voice. 'The last few days have been unbear-able,' he said. 'My nights have been filled with such frightful nightmares that now I literally dare not go to sleep. The very thought of sleep terrifies me. So I spent the whole of last night just roaming the streets, tormented by fear of every person I saw and every shadow that moved. I wondered whether it wouldn't be better to end it all . . . I suppose it's my conscience,' he added with a nervous little laugh.

'Not your conscience,' I insisted, 'but God's voice. Surely you don't think you can go on living like this without incurring God's wrath for flouting even the most elementary of his moral laws.'

I then recounted more of my own conversion experience and told of all Christ could do in a life. What I said did not, to my surprise, meet with antagonistic reaction. Instead there followed a few moments of sad si-lence during which a look of pathetic remorse came into my friend's eyes. He then made a disclosure which at once staggered me, and convinced me more than ever that my meeting with him was in truth totally God-planned, as I amusingly 'compassed land and sea to make one proselyte'!

'You know,' he whispered, 'I had a conversion experience, like the one you describe, when I was eighteen, and Christ meant as much to me then as you say he means to you now.'

So the man I was speaking to had not only heard the gospel before but had actually embraced it and accepted Christ as Saviour. My meeting him made sense more than ever. Demonstrating unspeakable compassion and love, Christ was seeking out a 'lost sheep' and trying to bind its wounds and restore its health.

My friend explained how he had slipped a little after his conversion, and when he had failed to recover himself a spiritual landslide had set in. 'I feel too ashamed now ever to return to Christ.' He went on, 'I have sinned far too grievously against him.'

I was trying to explain that Christ's mercy knew no bounds, when the door of the room opened slowly and in stepped his roommate – back from a trip to England. Not to be daunted I continued, and the newcomer joined in the conversation, maintaining, with little apparent desire to be convinced to the contrary, that once sin had gripped a person he or she could never be released from its insidious shackles. I retold the gospel but found that Terren evinced no desire to recommit his life to Christ and test the Lord's claims to save to the uttermost. Unlike Moses he was prepared to enjoy the pleasures of sin for a season, even if it cost him his eternal life.

I was utterly frustrated by the fact that nothing I now said made either of these young men move from the position each had taken up – the one maintaining he could not return because of his shame, the other insisting that repentance was impossible and sin worthwhile. Neither had anything to lose but his chains, yet both clutched at their slavery. Neither really wanted to reject Christ, yet both did so. Firmly and insanely they held out against every principle of common sense, thereby demonstrating that their wills were held captive by some force outside themselves. And for the first time I came to realize with deep conviction that 'we wrestle not against flesh and blood, but against principalities, against powers, against the rulers of the darkness of this world, against spiritual wickedness in high places' (Ephesians 6.12).

Disappointed and discouraged, I retraced my tracks across the French capital. The afternoon appeared to have proved fruitless.

Anyway, who knows? Maybe one day in heaven a bearded hippy will come up to me and say: 'Well, Michael, here I am. In your immature ignorance you did indeed compass land and sea to make one proselyte. And guess what? You made one. Here I am! I finally got back to the Lord. Thank you. Let's rejoice together.'

Yes, my belief is that the 'Hound of Heaven' would have chased after him and finally embraced him.

My Parisian adventure was over, and the money Mum and Dad had sent me was enough to get me back across the Channel to England.

Exams

The day my first-year exams ended I was overcome by deep gloom. I had not properly finished a single paper and, humanly speaking, my chances appeared hopeless. I felt too sick at heart to pray and so instead retired to my room and lost myself and my worries at the piano.

I had been playing some time when there was a knock at my door. It was John Wace, deeply depressed as well. Recovering myself, I endeavoured to comfort him and assure him that God would not fail us, as we had trusted in him. I urged John to hold on in faith to the Lord's faithfulness and love. Results would take several weeks to come out and I resolved to be as carefree as possible in the meantime.

As the days passed I began to recover my former spirits and hope. Exams were over, Christ was alive and May was here. How truly sang the old ballad:

> There are twelve months in all the year,
> As I hear many men say,
> But the merriest month of all the year
> Is the merry month of May.[4]

And May is merrier in Cambridge than in most places, even if the merriment is often born of one's yielding to every innate inclination to idleness. Time not spent lazily on a sofa with a good book and one's feet up is spent lazily in a punt with a good book and one's feet up; that is, until some tiresome individual insists that one take a hand at the controls.

This punting is a distasteful task. The fact is that not only does one get very irritated with a machine that does not appear to respond to even the elementary laws of navigation, but one usually ends up providing comic relief for the inevitable crowd of tourists and 'landlubbers' who are a painful feature of King's Backs in spring. By this I mean that one usually ends up either perched precariously on the end of a punt-pole while the punt drifts pathetically downstream, or else half-drowned in the slime that is a marked feature of the bottom of the River Cam. At least the American tourist then has something to write home about.

Eventually results day arrived and, leaping on to my bicycle, I hurried round to the Senate House. Feverishly I scanned the noticeboards. At last I saw it. 'Tripos Pt. I Modern and Medieval Languages.' In confident faith I looked immediately at the list of second-class honours passes. The 2:1s (second-class honours, upper division). My name not there. And then 2:2s (second class, lower division). My name not there. It must be the wrong board. I checked. No, this was right. I looked in the list of third classes. Several times up and down ran my incredulous eyes. My name was not there either. Frantic, I looked at the list of 'ordinary' BA passes

Merry month of May: River Cam

– those people who had not made the honours grade but had qualified for an inferior pass that contributed to an ordinary BA degree, which was lower in standard and kudos than the honours degree. My name was nowhere to be found.

I was stricken in my tracks. There must be a mistake. It could not be true with God on my side, after all my prayer, all my work, all my confidence in him. It couldn't be true after I had demonstrated my faith and told others he would not fail me. God might not grant me a second-class result, but it was unthinkable that he should not grant me even a third or an ordinary pass. No, it must all be a test of my faith. He must have planned a printer's error to see if I would give up hope.

Yet at the back of my mind I knew the Cambridge University Press was not in the habit of making printing errors. The impossible had happened. I had totally and completely failed my exams, and my days at Cambridge were over.

My first thought was escape – from people, noise, high spirits, laughter and above all sympathy. There was nothing I despised more than pity. Besides, I did not want to grovel and crawl around before my failure like a whipped dog. Nor did I want other people to crawl around either, with their well-meaning but ineffectual words of comfort. The situation after all could not be changed by words, only developed by action. As far as possible one needed to put up a bold, brave front.

The place to which I chose to escape was the college chapel. I knelt down and opened a Bible. My eyes fell on Proverbs 3.5 (KJV): 'Trust in the LORD with all thine heart; and lean not unto thine own understanding.'

They were the words I needed. They provided *an* answer at least – that God had done something I could not understand at the present – and in this I placed my wavering faith.

I did not want to face even my best friends, let alone all the others. I have never been blessed with great natural courage, so this situation was far from easy to face, especially as I was not of the temperament that could laugh off a serious blow with a joke and a 'couldn't care less' attitude. The trouble was that I cared desperately, particularly because of the shame that would fall on my family at my having to leave the university. My friends knew how I cared, and that was the trouble.

That afternoon Dr Edgar Brookes, the prominent South African historian, writer and parliamentarian, was to address a few of us in our rooms on South African affairs.

I remain sure that my attending that tea and political discussion was the bravest thing I have ever done. What would I say to Dr Brookes by way of greeting? I know. I would say, 'You've got a good day to be in Cambridge, sir.' With this in mind I pushed open the door of our sitting room and stepped in. Immediately there was a silence. They all knew I had seen the results. I stepped forward to Dr Brookes. A meaningful look in his eyes, he held out his hand and said, 'I'm so sorry about the exam.' All eyes were on me and I felt as if I had been knifed. I went deep scarlet and blurted out, 'You've got a good day to be in Cambridge, sir,' and then bolted for the back of the room and a seat. Nothing said at the meeting registered on me at all.

When I finally went to bed all the feelings I had suppressed burst loose. I didn't care if the college authorities chucked me out. One day, I swore, they would be proud to have had me as a college member even for one year. I would show them. I would achieve something despite this false start. I would shake my fist and laugh at the tricks of Fate. But I wouldn't curse the college administrators. I would just show the devils they had chucked out the wrong man.

After I had worked all the aggression out of my system, I lay limp and exhausted.

'Failure! Failure! Failure!' I shouted bitterly into the emptiness of my room, and then fell sound asleep.

Encouragement

To every thing there is a season, and a time to every purpose under the heaven . . . a time to break down, and a time to build up.
(Ecclesiastes 3.1, 3 KJV)

Thanks to the encouragement of friends, the sure words of Scripture, like those above, and above all the Lord's wonderful closeness to me at that time of trial, I became assured that my exam failure had a definite purpose. I held on to the word of God, which promises that 'All things work together for good to them that love God' (Romans 8.28 KJV), and states as axiomatic that 'The ways of the LORD are right' (Hosea 14.9). In addition I looked back on his past faithfulness to me and, knowing that he is unchanging, I was assured of his future faithfulness. And even at this time, when I could not understand the full purpose of his working, I could see that the humiliation had done me good. 'The pride of your heart has deceived you,' God says in the book of the prophet Obadiah. He then affirms: 'Though you soar like the eagle and make your nest among the stars, from there I will bring you down' (Obadiah 1.3–4 NIV).

The day after the posting of the results I called on my tutor, having prepared myself for the news that I would have to leave the university. But boundless was my surprise and joy when he made no mention whatever of my leaving and only insisted that I come up to the university for the long vacation to put in some extra work. 'The exam you have just done,' he said comfortingly, 'would be of final year standard at any other university in the Commonwealth or the United States.' But I wasn't out there. I was here. And I had to survive here.

He then explained that although French Honours Part I was normally done by most students in their first year, the option to do it in two years was also academically legal. But it would be a fearful sweat, as I also had on my plate Latin Part I, which was normally a two-year course. Now I would be trying to do almost three years' work in one! It would be daunting. But I accepted the challenge.

Rejoicing now in the knowledge that at least I was still *in statu pupillari*, I went down from the university and proceeded to a students' conference at High Leigh in Hoddesdon. This was a time of deep spiritual strengthening and a time used by God to begin his work of building me up anew after he had broken me down.

I saw this teaching in many parts of Scripture, and took heart. 'He has torn us to pieces but he will heal us; he has injured us but he will bind up our wounds,' writes the prophet Hosea in chapter 6, verse 1 (NIV). 'My son, do not despise the LORD's discipline,' says Solomon, 'and do not resent his rebuke, because the LORD disciplines those he loves, as a father the son he delights in' (Proverbs 3.11–12 NIV). And in quoting this Scripture the writer to the Hebrews adds in comment:

> Endure hardship as discipline; God is treating you as his children. For what children are not disciplined by their father? If you are not disciplined – and everyone undergoes discipline – then you are not legitimate, not true sons and daughters at all. (Hebrews 12.7–8 NIV)

One thing I resolved: no, I would not collapse. I would take a fresh grip on life. My limping feet would recover strength. And, God helping me, I would not collapse.

On getting back to Cambridge for the opening of a new term and my second academic year, I learned to my relief and delight that on a re-mark of papers I had been given an 'ordinary BA pass'. *Deo gloria!*

But not honours. The first important consideration for me thereafter was whether I was going to follow on my ordinary degree pass by taking for the remaining two years the easier ordinary BA degree course, or whether I was going to embark on what was humanly speaking a very bold, precarious gamble – trying for the honours degree. If I did the former I would have an easy time and have no difficulty whatever in surviving the remaining two years. If I attempted the latter I would be taxed to my extremities and might well come down again in the exams at the end of my second year.

If the latter unhappy contingency arose, there would be no alternative for me but to leave the university. One Tripos failure was bad enough. Two would make my case hopeless. The first alternative offered a safe and comfortable ride through to a mediocre achievement. The second, while fraught with risk and difficulty, would, if successful, lead to a higher academic qualification for teaching and a much more satisfactory achievement. I knew fairly well what I was up against. It would be a gruelling, almost impossible assignment, I could see that.

But the easy way out did not seem the Christian way out.

Moreover I saw the decision in the final analysis as Christ's. And prayer on the matter only entrenched me further in my conviction that I should attempt the honours course and leave the issue in God's faithful hands. 'Commit your way to the Lord; trust also in him; and he shall bring it to pass' (see Psalm 37.5).

Thus my second year of studies at Cambridge was as difficult and challenging to my faith as I might have predicted. I wasn't trumpeting any more that God's glory was at stake if he didn't get me through! My prayers were now more silent, secret and considered. Bravado had given way to a deeper and more desperate surrender.

Brush with the law

I was scarcely into the foothills of my academic Mount Everest in my second year when I had my first brush with the law!

I duly reported home:

> I am probably going to be summoned to court this week . . . I was cycling at high speed on my way to a squash match and while approaching a road junction the policeman on duty put up his hand to stop the traffic on 'my' road. I applied all my brakes to no effect and cruised past him with a wave which made him livid! I misheard his direction to me to stop, but clearly heard his second which was a veritable roar! He then came up to me in the most belligerent fashion waving a nasty little charge book in my face. He then said he was going to test my brakes. Putting on both front and back

breaks as hard as possible he then proceeded to wheel the bicycle happily along, the wheels going round quite normally while I fairly chortled with mirth. He then said, 'Where's your bell?' 'Bell? Bell? Oh, bell?' said I scrutinising the bike carefully, 'I'm not sure.' So he had me on three charges. 1. Not stopping at his signal. 2. Not having brakes. 3. No bell. Actually I had taken my bike into a shop that afternoon to have the brakes seen to, but they had said they were overloaded with work and couldn't do it. Anyway there we are. This I imagine is the first of many criminal charges, the rest of which no doubt will come in due course from the South African Government![5]

Shortly thereafter I had my day in court and sent my parents an update:

I was heard third. On 'Charles Cassidy' being announced I stepped smartly out into the 'accused's box' and stood there while the magistrate read the charge. My friend, the copper, then stepped into the witness box and proceeded to give evidence against me. In thick cockney. He said he had been on duty at Market Street and when he put up his hand to stop the traffic 'oi nowticed that the defendant had sum difficulty in stoppin.' At this stage, to the disapproval of the judge, I burst out laughing! Anyway the long and the short of it is that I was fined £1. A pleasant surprise. One man being charged with speeding did not appear but sent a letter and open cheque for £2 saying 'that if there was anything left over it should be given to charity!' The magistrate promptly fined him £5 saying he was sorry about the charity![6]

Exam inspiration

As I headed towards the Tripos exams of French and Latin Part I, plus Provençal, I realized I needed to declare a state of emergency. I found myself still unable to translate more than one or two exam portions of Latin poetry or prose in the three-hour allotted time frame. And the exams, which were closing in, required getting through six. It was terrifying. What on earth could I do?

An inspiration came to me. I would ask Tom Barlow, a dear Christian friend and fellow South African, to lend me his big reel-to-reel tape recorder. Then I would take the famous Loeb translations of all writings classical, and would slowly read great chunks of English translation from the Latin on to the tape. This I did.

Then I got the Latin texts, and with the tape recorder running, I would 'read' the *Latin* text for hour after hour after excruciating hour with the English translation running. Ah! I see how *that* Latin word or phrase turns out to mean *that* in English. As I came to a word I'd never seen, I would stop the tape, look up the word, add it to my vocabulary list, and then press on. Day after laborious day, and week after terrifying week, I simply 'read Latin' while listening to the English translation.

And, oh, how I prayed!

The exams finally arrived. In a mix of faith and terror I entered the exam room for Latin Prose, and then Latin Poetry.

And you know what? *Mirabile dictu*, marvellous to relate, I got through. I passed. Third class admittedly. But an honours degree nevertheless. Not an ordinary BA! I had made it. Both in French and Latin, plus Medieval French, Medieval Latin, and even Provençal. There had been no room for failure. Had I not made it, I would have been out of Cambridge. A class-act academic failure. Forever living with 'if onlys' or 'what might have beens'. But the Lord, bless his holy name, had seen me through.

Gloria in excelsis!

The future?

A third year at Cambridge beckoned, but in the meantime I had been wondering about the future and what work I might do.

During the tough academic struggles, I had clung to some words of Martin Luther which had been quoted at that same conference that had so encouraged me after my first year: 'May I never cease to believe that God has a great work for me to do.'

Were I to aspire to such a future – and I did – what might that 'great work' look like?

11

A 'great work'

May I never cease to believe that God has a great work for me to do.[1]
(Martin Luther)

'The longer I am at Cambridge, the more I realise the tremendous revolution, intellectually and spiritually, that it has brought about within me,' I wrote to my parents in my second year.

I went on to reveal the new thought that was growing in my mind. 'The desire to do a theological course grows day by day and I hope the Lord will make this possible.'

Still with the idea of teaching in my mind, I had realized I would like to teach Scripture, or Divinity as some call it, as well as my academic subjects.

There was in fact an excellent Anglican theological college in Cambridge, Ridley College, and I decided to enquire about a scholarship. I had no money for such a new study venture.

'We'll only consider you,' the college authorities said, 'if you can guarantee us you will go into the ordained Anglican ministry.'

I didn't feel free to give such a guarantee, but I continued to gain experience in teaching during my long summer vacations from Cambridge.

My first summer teaching post was at a prep school called Kingsmead in Hoylake, Cheshire, where I taught classes in French and Latin. I enjoyed it all so much that I wrote home to tell my parents: 'I think the last four weeks at Kingsmead will mark one of the big stages in my teaching career, for I have seen now what I want to aim for and I am going to go for it with all my might and main.'[2]

The second teaching job the following summer was, amazingly enough, in America.

And it was in America that a clear new direction emerged for the future.

The New World

It all came about because of a legacy left to me by my grandmother.

Mum wrote and said that Granny in Parys had left me £100 in her will. To me the sum seemed astronomical. And it was the provision I had been seeking, because I had been invited by Uncle Mike (Dad's brother) and Aunt Gertrude to visit them in New York for the summer. I had seen a little advert, almost buried on one of those cluttered college noticeboards, for a 'student charter flight to New York. £87 return!'

I would do it, I decided. With Granny's £100. And I would even have £13 pocket money for the three months of the vac!

Our initial problem was that there was so much wrong with our odd-looking charter aeroplane and its engines that it took three days of starts and repairs, and false starts and more engine repairs, and more false starts, and more repairs, until we finally cluttered and bumped down a Heathrow runway headed for Reykjavík in Iceland and then New York.

In an upper-class English accent, one student announced loudly for the 80 to 100 of us on board that he was 'jolly glad' he was 'by the emergency exit', so he could 'jump first'!

Uncle Mike, a gynaecologist, and Aunt Gertrude, also a doctor, met me in New York and took me to their lovely home in the wooded suburb of New Rochelle. No kindness was too much for them. They showed me the 'Big Apple', the Empire State Building, the Hudson River, the Statue of Liberty, the spectacular local planetarium, the grand local yacht club and the tennis club (where I got extra lessons), plus their magnificent five-acre plot nearby, wooded, lush, blessed with a small lake, believe it or not, and

Summer in the USA: Aunt Gertrude

112

New York

thick bush which they wanted me to clear for $10 a day. Pocket money! Suddenly I was rich.

It was also through my aunt and uncle, who knew about my aspirations to teach, that I was given the chance to work in the summer school of Choate, one of the greatest private schools in the USA.

My summer-term stay there, teaching English to a couple of young Hungarian refugees from the 1957 Budapest uprising, introduced me to a different world.

I always remember my shock when a young Californian boy came up to me, the budding schoolmaster in the British tradition where boys call masters 'sir', and said: 'Hey, Mike – are you ready for another day with *alart* of it?'

'A lot of what?' I asked, mystified.

'Well, *alart of fern*, of course!'

I was being educated into American fun, and American ways. Edward VIII once said: 'The thing that impresses me about America is the way parents obey their children.'[3]

Aunt Gertrude had a small business in church silverware, chalices and candlesticks and all that, which necessitated travelling all over to churches, monasteries – you name it. I was invited to go along. Off we went in their Lincoln, ever so grand, up to Montreal in Canada, and then along the St

Lawrence up to Quebec City. The next trip was down to Virginia and James-town, site of the first permanent English settlement in America in 1607.

I was getting to see America. And I was hugely happy. Perhaps John Updike was right: 'America is a vast conspiracy to make you happy.'[4]

Studying theology in the USA?

As it happened, while I was in New York, Billy Graham was conducting a three-month-long evangelistic outreach in Madison Square Garden.

The great man had already had an influence on me, but little did I realize how much he and his team would feature in my life in the days and years to come.

At this stage there was one question running around my mind. I had begun to wonder whether I might study theology in the USA. But where?

I knew only of Union Seminary in New York, but I felt its theology would be too different from my own. I decided to write to Billy to ask his advice, which I did – care of the New York mission office. It was of course a naive and unrealistic notion to suppose that Dr Graham would ever get my letter.

Anyway, among the thousands of letters coming in each day and handled in scores of postbags, my letter found its way into one particular bag which landed on the desk of a Japanese seminary student volun-teer helping out in the office, Harry Kawahara, from Fuller Seminary in California.

Michael at Madison Square Garden

I went nearly wild with excitement when Aunt Gertrude called me to the phone: 'I think it's Billy Graham!'

No such luck. Just a funny old student volunteer with a weird accent in the mission office!

'I've seen your letter to Mr Graham,' said Harry, 'and your enquiry about seminaries, and I'd like you to come down to the Garden one evening and we can chat.'

So down I went excitedly to Madison Square Garden where I knew my childhood hero, Joe Louis, had vanquished all challengers in many great boxing matches. But this was different. How could I have guessed that my life's destiny was to be determined by a letter landing somehow on the desk of one particular student volunteer? And in Madison Square Garden, of all places. It was a happening to put an extra dose of Calvinism into me!

The meeting, in a jam-packed arena, was exhilarating.

Cliff Barrow's thousand-voice choir took us into the heavenlies. African American gospel singer Ethel Waters sang out in her distinctive southern style, 'His eye is on the sparrow . . . and I know he watches me!' Then the big baritone voice of George Beverley Shea, backed by the choir, filled the arena:

> Oh Lord, my God, when I in awesome wonder
> Consider all the worlds Thy hands have made
> I see the stars, I hear the rolling thunder
> Thy power throughout the universe displayed
> Then sings my soul
> My Saviour God to Thee
> How great Thou art –
> How great Thou art.[5]

And Billy's earnest, passionate preaching of the gospel thrilled my soul. I was lost in admiration at the simple eloquence and persuasive power of public proclamation. How wonderful to be able to preach like that! Not that I would ever be doing anything like it, or so I thought.

After the service, Harry told me about a place called Fuller Seminary. I came to other services and, among the volunteers, I only ever seemed to meet Fuller Seminary students. And I liked them. Committed to the Bible. Passionate about the gospel. Eager to serve the Lord any way they could. And fun. Always laughing.

That sold me. That was that! I would write, as Harry suggested, to the college president, Dr Edward John Carnell, and say I wanted to come to Fuller. But that I would need a scholarship.

Carnell replied in due course. Yes, Fuller would receive me. And nearer

Billy Graham New York Crusade, 1957

the time of entry I should apply for a full scholarship, which would probably be given. I was over the moon.

*

One evening after one of the Madison Square Garden services, I drifted down to the basement where the many people who responded to the gospel message night after night were counselled.

I watched. Something awesome was happening here. I paced up and down, deeply pensive.

Then, a life-changing moment!

'I heard the voice of the Lord,' Isaiah said (Isaiah 6.8). And so did I. It was very clear, almost physically audible: 'Why not in Africa? I want you to do city evangelism in Africa.'

I think I began to protest: 'Lord, you don't normally mess up and make mistakes. But this time you are really fumbling the ball. You have the wrong man. I can't speak in public. Can scarcely manage normal social situations. All right with children. But nothing more. Not platforms. Or crowds of people. Or public proclamation. Evangelism. Challenging grown-ups. Come on, Lord. Not me. Send someone else.'

'I want you to do city evangelism in Africa.' The voice was unmistakeable.

My career and calling had become clear in a matter of minutes.

Family reactions

Back at 32 Whitewood Avenue, New Rochelle, my fervour went up a notch or two. Michael and Gertrude had to weather the storm – as reflected when they reported back to my folk.

Uncle Mike wrote: 'This dear boy of yours has got religion with a great big R. Nothing else counts, and, much as he dearly loves you, you are secondary.' Then he added:

> The subjects he is taking at Cambridge apparently do not interest him at all. I, of course, had no idea until he arrived here that he had given up Law, and changed his whole course to one which he considered prepared him better for teaching. He seems to have made up his mind that he wants to teach teenagers, but about the subjects he teaches he could not care less. His only objective is to be able spiritually to guide adolescents.[6]

As for Aunt Gertrude, she was more reassuring:

> We love Michael dearly and feel we have always known him. He fits in so easily into everything and is a perfect guest. Sweet and helpful at all times. He laughs and enjoys all our idiosyncrasies as happily as though he had been brought up amongst us. Not everyone can achieve this I assure you. We love having him and he seems happy with us . . . incidentally the lad looks like a different being since he arrived. It is hard to put into words. But everyone remarks on his changed appearance. He looks marvellously well now. Tanned, muscular, and happy with a twinkle that was lacking at the beginning.[7]

Of course neither Michael nor Gertrude could escape the clutches of my evangelizing endeavours on *them*. And I longed for them to come to Madison Square Garden. Michael refused, but also blocked Gertrude, in all likelihood a genuine seeker deep down. I was very cross about this.

Mum, however, would have been no candidate for a visit to the Garden:

> Sorry I can't enter more sympathetically, ducks [one of her pet names for me], into your account of Billy Graham, my only reaction being one of vexation that he has again crossed your path! I just cannot bear evangelism. It makes me simply curl up with embarrassment and revulsion inside.
>
> To me this public giving oneself to Christ seems almost indecent and everything in me rises up in protest at the awful exhibitionism of the whole thing, the mass emotion (not necessarily emotionalism), and the working up into a state of exaltation under the hypnotism of a young man like this. I suppose one should reserve judgement and I am quite prepared to live and let live. If people like that sort of thing, it is no business of mine, except when it touches something or someone who means a lot to me. Then of course, it does rouse me to antagonism. So probably the less I say the better.[8]

I loved her for her honesty. Her perceptions all had an important place in shaping perspectives later in my work.

Two different gospels?

While Billy was preaching nightly in Madison Square Garden, Martin Luther King Jr was marching and protesting in Arkansas and Alabama on civil rights issues, filling TV screens on and off all day.

Governor Orval Faubus was at the front end of the righteous wrath of Martin Luther King, whose rhetoric was deeply grounded in Christian principle.

Faubus's name became internationally known during the Little Rock Crisis of 1957, when he used the National Guard to stop African Americans from attending Little Rock Central High School as part of federally ordered racial desegregation.

Listening to Billy Graham at the Garden and Martin Luther King on TV set me thinking. Were these two different gospels? Two different Christian messages contradicting each other?

Clarity came quickly. No! These were complementary messages, the obverse and the reverse sides of the same coin and the same gospel. The one was addressing the vertical dimension of the gospel – and our relationship upwards to God – and the other, the horizontal dimension of our outward relationship to our neighbour.

First the vertical side. With every visit to Madison Square Garden the preaching of the gospel of Jesus Christ became more and more pivotal and central for me.

The eternal destiny of the human soul had to be kept central. And while I had become concerned about socio-political justice, I knew I couldn't embrace Christian labours for only a political kingdom. The Anglican Prayer Book had it right: 'We must live that we may so pass through things temporal that we finally lose not the things eternal.'

Then the horizontal side. I was daily hearing the thundering justice challenges of Martin Luther King. I couldn't but admire the huge courage and commitment of this man, all springing forth from his faith in Christ. I remember being very moved by King's words describing the arrest of Rosa Parks, an African American woman who sat down in the section of a bus reserved for white people and refused to go to the black section:

> You know, my friends, there comes a time when people get tired of being trampled over by the iron feet of oppression. There comes a time, my friends, when people get tired of being flung across the abyss of humiliation where they experience the bleakness of nagging despair. There comes a time when people get tired of being pushed out of the glittering sunlight of life's July and left standing amidst the piercing chill of an Alpine November.[9]

King went on:

> We, the disinherited of this land, we who have been oppressed so long are tired of going through the long night of captivity. And we are reaching out for the daybreak of freedom and justice and equality . . . in all of our doings, in all of our deliberations . . . whatever we do, we must keep God in the forefront. Let us be Christian in all of our action. And I want to tell you this evening that it is not enough for us to talk about love. Love is one of the pinnacle parts of the Christian faith. There is another side called justice. And justice is really love in application. Justice is love correcting that which would work against love.[10]

I watched all this develop on TV up in New York, and asked myself where such courage and commitment came from. The issues were the same as South Africa's. And these were the sorts of things Trevor Huddleston, Alan Paton and Albert Luthuli were writing about. And here too in the American South, just as in South Africa, were white Christians, millions of them, all Bible believers, yet supporting Faubus and all his works and propping up the segregationist way of life. Thankfully there were other Christian voices of protest from the black world, and some marvellous exceptions from the white.

Martin Luther King saw justice as love enshrined in structures, and all coming forth from the gospel, and I saw this afresh with eyes of fire as being profoundly relevant for South Africa.

So I resolved by the end of that summer that I would seek to embrace a balanced, holistic gospel, preaching faithfully that people needed to come to Christ for new birth and personal salvation, but then embracing the wider sociopolitical and horizontally focused message of compassionate concern for social justice, and the needs of the poor and marginalized.

A grown-up now!

In the middle of all this I turned 21!

I received the dearest letters of affirmation from my parents. But I remember being particularly glad, what with all my paralysing social fears, that being away from home in New York I would have no twenty-first birthday party and therefore would not have to make a speech.

I was still, somehow, working extensively on Latin and French. The critical home-straight at Cambridge was just ahead.

With huge gratitude to Michael and Gertrude for multiple kindnesses, and with doxologies to God for a momentous summer, I boarded our little charter plane, seemingly now satisfactorily repaired, and headed back over the Pond and into my final year at Cambridge.

What would it bring?

12

Facing brokenness

*I am sure that he who began the good work in you will
bring it to completion at the day of Jesus Christ.*
(Philippians 1.6)

'I should say three years in California will successfully wipe out all the
effects and influence of Cambridge as if they had never been!'

That was my darling mother's pronouncement on my thoughts of going
to Fuller once I finished at Cambridge.

Well, time enough to sort that out, but in the meantime I had a degree
to finish!

Mum and Dad and the family, not fully aware of the precarious nature
of my studies, were planning on coming over for my graduation. A faith

*Graduation day: sister Judy, Charles Cassidy, Michael,
Dee Cassidy, Olave Cassidy, May 1958*

Rubicon, for sure. But what if I failed? The prospect could only stir me to more gargantuan efforts at my desk. And to prayer.

Brave and intrepid Mum and Dad, Olave and Judy took to the high seas in faith, anticipating my passing and graduating.

And I did.

A second-class honours degree from Cambridge University finally came my way. My BA would also automatically become MA, because it was an honours pass. I would be C. M. A. Cassidy MA (Cantab). It sounded good.

Now I saw in a light-bulb moment that God *does* answer prayer. But in his own time and way. He can say 'Yes', 'No' or 'Wait.' In 1956 he said 'No!' In 1957 he said 'Wait.' And in 1958 he said 'Yes!'

And the No and the Wait times were for his purposes of disciplining and refining and purging to be fulfilled in me. He put me into fire – which for good reason I needed.

On my memorable graduation day my tutor Stanley Aston, all rigged up in doctoral academic dress himself, saw me and beamed: 'Well, Cassidy, we all had to put in a bit of prayer for this, didn't we?!'

London and teaching

As a family we then toured England and Scotland before they all left, Olave excepted, to return to South Africa. Olave and I took up residence

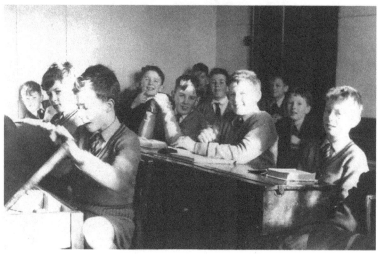

Holmewood School, London: one of Michael's classes, 1958

in the Victoria League students' hostel in London, Olave to settle into a secretarial course before going to Lausanne University, and I to enter my third school-teaching job before eventually heading back to South Africa.

The school this time was in north London, Holmewood School, where the legendary George Rich, a sort of latter-day Mr Chips, was the hilarious headmaster.

I had bought for £50 an old London taxi and called him Theodoric, after Theodoric, the sixth-century king of the Ostrogoths who conquered Italy in 567. (See, I did learn some Roman history at Cantab!) This, the ultimate vintage car, was the most magnificent and fun vehicle I ever owned.

All any of the boys at Holmewood ever wanted was to get a ride in Theodoric. One day, playing football with the kids, I accidentally kicked a little guy who leapt from nowhere into the swing of my kick, and I cracked his leg. I had to dump him hurriedly into Theodoric and get him speedily home to his mum, and thence to hospital.

As I carried the limp little fellow into his house, his mother exclaimed, 'But, oh, Mr Cassidy, how wonderful he got to ride in your car!'

Once when I was in London, sitting in Theodoric while waiting for someone, a woman walked boldly across the road towards me and to my utter astonishment asked, 'Are you engaged?' I wondered at a stranger thus prying into my romantic affairs, and the look on my face must have horrified her for sure.

Theodoric: Michael and Olave, London, late 1958

Holmewood School: the boys adored Theodoric

Facing brokenness

All I have been writing suggests that life for me was, at this stage, un-complicated and happy. In reality I was broken and fractured inside. The external was fine and dandy. The internal, anything but.

The reason was my omnipresent nervousness and sometimes paralys-ing fear in social situations. Maybe a modern psychiatrist might say I was suffering from a type of post-traumatic stress disorder – some things in my schooldays and in my academic struggles at Cambridge had indeed been traumatic.

When my uncontrollable blushes happened, with the blood rushing up from my toes to my trembling cheeks, I died a thousand deaths of shame. And this would affect my ability to speak or respond coherently.

Even saying 'Goodbye, Rector, thank you for your sermon' as I left church on Sunday evenings filled me with fear, and made my hands sweat, my throat constrict. I was a wreck. A mixed-up kid if ever there was one.

So my journal records:

> Bible Class in the afternoon. Felt far less nervous than ever before at one of these do's and found myself contributing easily and fearlessly to the dis-cussion. But after tea when Julian Charley, a curate, came up to me very nicely and asked me my name, I blushed, and felt overcome with confu-sion. Extremely annoying!
>
> However I put this 'failure' out of my mind and reminded myself of my far more numerous triumphs of late over my fear. So much of my bravado is only an act to keep the attention away from myself and on to someone

else. No doubt my Dear Lord can sort out the chaos of contradictions that is me! Indeed I feel this may be a God-given thorn in the flesh, like Paul's, 'Lest I should exalt myself above measure' [see 2 Corinthians 12.7]. However, I am not yet at Paul's advanced spirituality where I can say, 'I take pleasure in my infirmities'! Far from it, I hate them like the plague![1]

At the time, I was greatly inspired by the example of George VI, whose speech impediment gave him real determination and courage.

It didn't help when I was introduced to a 'tall girl' at a tea party. By then my slow physical development had been left far behind, and I was pretty tall myself, doubtless inspiring the hostess to introduce me to a few other young adults there. But as I confessed to my diary, 'I'm afraid I couldn't have impressed one young girl very much as I blushed wickedly and was overcome with confusion. Very annoying indeed because it so hurts one's pride.'[2]

Such was my anguish in these months that when I saw an advert in *The Times* for a psychological self-help course, run out of London University by correspondence, I paid the modest sum and signed up for it. My remote tutor gave me assignments each week, some written and some practical, and I had to report to him weekly on how I was doing with my nervousness.

One assignment required me, as I was going to sleep, to try to get my mind absolutely empty and then introduce a mental picture of myself doing easily something I normally feared. Thus, as I fell asleep, I would picture myself confidently entering a room full of people and moving around in a relaxed fashion, greeting them all with quiet and natural ease.

This course went on for several months. And whenever I could report to my tutor that I had pulled off the assignment in a real-life situation, he would compliment me and write 'Well done; you're getting there.' His advice was undoubtedly helpful and I always wished I could have met that wise, sensitive and anonymous man. But it was later that same year that a further measure of healing was granted me.

The fairer sex

Yes, I was waking up in more adult ways to the delightful reality of girls in the world. So there was something beyond Latin and French after all. And even beyond Bible studies. The realization was intoxicating. Not that I'd been totally unaware of girls before. After all, I'd grown up with two sisters. I had also had childhood crushes and some warm friendships with fellow female students at Cambridge – but there had simply been no time for more than that.

However, now that I was a young 23-year-old Cambridge graduate and aspired to be a man about town in London, things must be different. Others my age were even thinking of marriage. Would it be criminal to entertain similar thoughts? But my nervousness seemed to rule me out.

I remember going to a Hunt Ball weekend while staying at Hampton Court Palace, an invitation coming through a friend of Lady Baden-Powell, or Aunt Olave as we called her. I was astounded to get the impression that one young lady in our party, 'the belle of the ball', was taken with me, as I was with her. 'Found dancing with her a joy, and inevitably wanted to hold her closely.'[3]

But my sudden romantic stirrings in such situations filled me with guilt. What did my Christian faith sanction? What did it prohibit?

I was maybe being hard on myself, but my conscience was highly sensitized.

Olave

While negotiating my modest social activities in London, I was also seeking to witness to my sister Olave.

One Sunday evening I took her to a guest service at the famous All Souls Church in central London, when the equally famous rector John Stott was preaching.

And she got it. Suddenly, in answer to so much prayer, the gospel was crystal clear and she responded to Christ, and took him as her Saviour, Lord and Friend. And what a thumping good conversion it was! Deep, penetrating, life-transforming and permanent.

We were always good friends, but this took our friendship to a deeper level.

Europe and the Schaeffers

As the year ended, I planned a trip around Europe in Theodoric, the taxi of any young man's dreams, along with Tom Barlow, Olave, Richard Stevens, a fellow teacher at Holmewood, plus two Christian girls we'd met in London called Denise and Vicky. We would finish in Switzerland, at the home of Francis and Edith Schaeffer. Francis Schaeffer was a deeply committed Evangelical theologian and philosopher. His great commitment was to the truth of the gospel ('true truth' as he called it), and his profound concern was for the extensive distortion of biblical truth in many theological and church circles. To facilitate discussion and study of these themes the Schaeffers had opened their home, L'Abri (French for 'shelter'), so that people could come and meet there informally and find answers to their questions.

We all went in full merriment from Dover across the Channel to Boulogne, through France to Rotterdam, near which we had a breakdown, and skidded into a ditch, then on to The Hague, Amsterdam, Brussels and Cologne where a dear family spotted us on Christmas Eve and in pity took us home for a Christmas meal before we found our way to the youth hostel. In the public square in Cologne a few days later, a huge crowd gathered round Theodoric while we went to find somewhere to eat. A scrawled note and a few coins were also found in the driver's seat: 'Boxing Day, 1958. Dear Lads, just to wish you a very Happy New Year and also a very pleasant journey.'

We then travelled down the west bank of the romantic Rhine, decorated every few miles with magnificent medieval castles. Then into Switzerland – Zurich, Berne, Lausanne, always staying in youth hostels, and finally to Francis and Edith Schaeffer's L'Abri in Huémoz-sur-Ollon high up in the Alps, Theodoric creating a sensation in every village as we roared, minus silencer, up the steep and sometimes perilous Alpine roads.

I had written to Francis Schaeffer saying we would 'arrive at L'Abri at 23-and-a-half minutes past three on January 2nd 1959!' We got into Huémoz-sur-Ollon at ten past three and checked in the village how long we needed to reach L'Abri. 'Two minutes!' At 3.20 we fired Theo's engines and chugged deafeningly up the hill.

As we reached L'Abri, and turned up its precipitous drive, Francis, Edith, Susan, Franky and the whole family and all L'Abri were on the front lawn, Francis with stopwatch in hand to check our timing. It was 23-and-a-half minutes past three on 2 January, a lovely sunny afternoon.

Half an hour later we were snowed in.

In her book on L'Abri, Edith Schaeffer recalls the happening:

> It was during the Christmas holidays that the first group of Cambridge students arrived at L'Abri. A postcard had informed us that they would arrive at 3.23 and a half . . . in the afternoon! On the dot an old London taxi, with flowered curtains drawn back from the windows in ridiculous imitation of looped back kitchen curtains, drew to a rattling stop. Out poured a group of laughing young people, to show us proudly that the lights would even go on if you kicked the car in just the right fashion. They were an hilarious group, with a tremendous sense of humour, and personality, and brains![4]

Before arriving at L'Abri, December 1958

I used to tease Edith Schaeffer that my taxi rated an extended paragraph in her book, and my work of African Enterprise got nothing!

The days at L'Abri were blissful. I remember a wonderful sermon by Francis Schaeffer with the headline: 'All are lost. Jesus saves. Only Jesus saves.' I think this is the only outline of any sermon I ever heard which I have always remembered. And it's worth remembering: 'All are lost. Jesus saves. Only Jesus saves.'

But something else quite important took place – some further relief in my nervous struggles. I felt I was finally on my way to conquering them. It was God's healing on top of the gains from my correspondence tutorials.

In some way the Lord seemed to use this trip in an extraordinary way to heal me to a large extent of the illness in my subconscious from which I had been suffering so acutely. My fear of other people was very, very much less than it had been – and, blessing of all blessings, I learned to laugh at myself. That is something I had wanted to be able to do for ages, and at last the Lord began enabling me to do it. In all the playful abuse and banter that flies around when a group of people are together for a long time, each person comes in for his or her fair share of ragging. I was no exception – and I received as much as I gave.

The mutual ragging of the first part of the trip – when I was always with

Left: Michael with Ranald Macaulay, Switzerland: tobogganing near L'Abri
Right: Olave at L'Abri

people I knew well – prepared me for the bigger ordeal of the odd laugh at my expense in the company of people I didn't know so well. During my first evenings at the Schaeffers I was very nervous, but gradually this wore off and soon I felt able to contribute to the discussions and conversations without any nervous inhibition. And then suddenly I found myself succeeding admirably or laughing at myself on many occasions when before I would not have succeeded. The Lord, in his loving and gentle way, was rooting out of me the insidious curse of an inferiority complex. I spoke to Francis Schaeffer about it all just before we left – and his warm advice was that I should attempt to claim *moment by moment* victory over it rather than struggle to achieve a complete, exhaustive and once-for-all victory. This was good advice, which I sought with diligence to heed, and it threw me back on the Lord so much more.

Evangelism on the high seas

On 3 February 1959, I boarded the *Winchester Castle* ocean liner and took to the high seas and headed for home, sweet home.

The thing that was galvanizing me was the overwhelming urge to preach the gospel! I had South Africa in my sights, and my certainty that Christ was the answer to the country's turmoil had grown stronger the more I thought about it.

As I wrote to my parents:

> When I came up to Cambridge I had visions of returning to South Africa to hold protest meetings, wave banners, go to jail etc., etc. But the more I study the Bible, the surer I am that that is not the way at all.[5]

I felt that political solutions could only go so far, and were then often lost or frustrated:

> But within the framework of a great spiritual revival this would not be the case. Certainly Christ is the answer. But before He can be the answer to South Africa – the country, He must be the answer to South Africans.[6]

And I made good on this conviction by trying to evangelize the eager-beaver group of young South African students and academics returning home on the same ship. The voyage was basically one long evangelistic meeting with my witnessing right, left and centre, handing out booklets, sharing reading material, and finally tipping the stewards who had served me ten shillings each, and giving each one a Gospel of John!

I had a goal. Now it was time to 'press on toward the goal for the prize of the upward call of God in Christ Jesus' (Philippians 3.14).

At an on-board Bible study I met a couple from Mazabuka, in what was then Northern Rhodesia, Jack and Ruth Holmes. But crisis struck when Jack suddenly became ill, so much so that the ship had to put in to Freetown, Sierra Leone, for Jack to be taken in emergency to the hospital there. It was a desperate time for Ruth, who had no option but to sail on to Cape Town with her five children. I was staggered at her calm and courage. How intensely we prayed, and how relieved we were a few days later when a wire came saying 'Holmes out of danger and progressing well'.[7]

My bond to Ruth Holmes and her little tribe was quickly forged. Believe it or not, it continues to this day, though Jack and Ruth have gone to the Lord. Their son Tim (then aged four or five) would later be led into finding his wife through something in one of my books written in the early 1980s!

Ruth prayerfully engaged with me about my calling to the cities of Africa. Then she said she felt led by the Lord to give me an article, and one passage really stuck with me: 'When God desires to shake, shock, or shape any age in order to save sinners, He always chooses a man – not a system,

Ruth Holmes and her family

not a plan, not an organisation . . . but a man. Be that man!'⁸ Maybe these words fed into some worldly ambitions or illusions of grandeur on my part, but they inspired me. Better to dream too big than not to dream at all. In any event, the article brought a further sense of confirmation of my calling.

One young nurse from England, Jane by name, overheard me in combat with some young lecturers and asked me to explain more. About six months later I got a letter from her saying she had gone to All Souls in London as I had advised and was gloriously converted. She later married Maurice Taylor, a young churchwarden there, and my sister Olave, now married to John Snelling, became godmother to the first of their children. A sea-voyage witness had led to a sea change in her life!

Africa at last!

I had offered to drive the Holmes family up to Northern Rhodesia once we had docked, but they opted for the train and then accepted my subsequent offer to get their car up there for them. I would go via Basutoland, see Mum and Dad, and then hitch-hike back from the Holmes' home in

Mazabuka, Northern Rhodesia. I was single, footloose and fancy free, and could therefore do such intrepid things.

'Use the car to see people in Cape Town, and your family in Maseru, then drive north,' said Ruth Holmes. Which I did, intending to seek counsel for my plans from trusted friends along the way.

But I had no money, even for basic food, let alone petrol. 'I'll just trust you, Lord,' I affirmed in faith. As we were about to disembark from the ship, the ship's purser came up to me with two envelopes. One was a 'welcome back' letter from Pat and Cynthia Duncan. The other bore my name in Dad's handwriting. In it was £20! Thank you, heavenly Father. And thank you, my earthly father!

I was privileged to be able to arrange a meeting with Archbishop Joost de Blank, Anglican Archbishop of Cape Town, at Bishop's Court. I spent an hour in prayer beforehand. My journal says:

> I asked a rich blessing on what I thought might prove a very important time indeed. I hoped I would not leave Joost with the impression I was simply an enthusiastic young hot head.
>
> I got the impression Joost would support me in anything I did – with reservations of course! He mentioned the evangelicals' neglect of 'Incarnational Responsibilities' indicated in their failure to condemn social and political evils. I said I felt this to be a real failing on our part. Joost said that if only a man would rise who could confront the country with the necessity of synthesising the spiritual as well as the political and social responsibilities of the Gospel, then the church would make real progress here. He added: 'Perhaps you're the man to do this.' This was so flattering I could hardly feel he meant it. All the same it reiterated what I felt inside. I left after an hour, deeply impressed with the man, and his humility, and rather suspecting this was not the last Joost and I would see of each other.[9]

Next day I picked up two young men, Arthur and Ed, whom I'd met on the ship, and who needed lifts north through Old Rhodesia to Salisbury (now Harare). We set off up through Grahamstown, where I called on my old Cambridge friend Michael Nuttall, and then slowly up via Aliwal North, and 'a frightful mud road' that had us 'skidding all over the place', to Maseru.

After a week of connecting to the most precious parents in the world, and imbibing again the delicious elixir of home, I set off for Salisbury with my new shipboard friends, Arthur and Ed. As we got to Salisbury, we found Southern Rhodesia and Nyasaland in full political upheaval, and Prime Minister Sir Edgar Whitehead declaring a state of emergency.

The *Evening Standard* of Salisbury on 27 February 1959 editorialized:

The people of Southern Rhodesia heard with shock and deep concern the Prime Minister, Sir Edgar Whitehead, announce over the radio this morning that the threat to public safety and order in this Colony is such that a state of emergency has had to be declared. The announcement makes it clear that although disorder and violence have broken out only in Nyasaland, the threat from Congress embraces the whole of the Federation. That is the grim fact now apparent; and the measures taken by the Prime Minister here will have the undivided backing of every man and woman, of whatever colour, who has a respect for law and order and desires peaceful relations between the racial groups of our country.[10]

My folk were very aware of all this, and a telegram reached me care of Jock and Effie Macaulay, parents of Alasdair and Ranald, with whom I was staying: 'Please make full enquiries before travelling Mazabuka. Imperative not motor alone. Dad.'

The Central African Federation was to remain pretty much in political convulsion for the next two decades.

Anyway, disregarding my dear dad's counsel, I did indeed motor on to Mazabuka alone, and found Jack Holmes recovered and well and back at home. How we rejoiced! And how they all prayed with me about my future – and my call. They prayed for my getting safely home by hitch-hiking the thousand or more miles. One ride I got was with a diamond smuggler, who kept pulling his revolver from the cubby-hole and shooting out the window at some animal or other. Another ride of several hundred miles was atop a coal truck, and straddling the coal!

I remember my reading for the journey was the great Martin Luther biography *Here I Stand* by Roland Bainton. I got much inspiration from such biographies and autobiographies and read a lot. On the ship I had been reading the writings of Field Marshal Montgomery, a man I'd deeply admired since childhood. My journal records how I learned from him that 'resolute and immediate decision always wins the day'. 'I also admire his fearlessness.'[11]

In Johannesburg I visited Bishop Philip Morris, head of the Church of England in South Africa, who had me address his youth group. I also called on my darling sister Judy at Roedean.

Home, sweet home

Finally I was back in Maseru with my precious parents and doing all the things I loved so much to do at home. There was also Maseru's church life and some home Bible studies to get involved in. The rector, Francis Cull, was a strong Anglo-Catholic with an evangelical heart. We got on famously. At one home Bible study he urged on all of us the importance of witnessing for Christ, to which one of Maseru's leading socialites memorably declared: 'But, Father Cull, that sort of thing is just not done!'

Of course, uppermost in my mind was gearing up to go to Fuller Seminary, and the funds needed to make this possible. I had already received a letter from Fuller giving me a full scholarship 'for double the value of the one I applied for'.[12] God had provided! Now all I needed was the travel money to get to California. In faith I booked on a ship in the Farrell Line sailing in August from Durban to New York.

On Wednesday 5 April 1959 my journal records:

> Received a letter from the Fulbright [scholarship people] saying my application for a travel grant had not been successful. Not a blow as He is sovereign. But humanly speaking it is maddening to have a scholarship in US, but not be able to get there: divinely speaking it's wonderful to know that all things work together for good.[13]

Next day I wrote:

> Went down to the river for my quiet time and asked the Lord fervently to lead me with regard to the US. I still feel He wants me to go *this* year and I consider this just a test. It is quite a considerable one though, as I cannot for the life of me see where the money might come from. Anyway, He is Lord – and if He still considers me worth bothering about, I am sure He will provide.[14]

About that time I went with my sister Judy and two friends out to the Morija Mission Station and Printing Press run by the Paris Evangelical Mission Society. Its director, Mr Zurcher, showed us round both the press and the adjacent hospital. My journal recalls a particular event:

> A woman in the press told how her expected source of finance for overseas leave had suddenly ceased to be and she was praying hard for provision. I told her about the Fulbright business and as I left she gave me this little slip off her calendar with Philippians 4:19 printed on it: 'My God shall supply all your need.' I shall hold onto this verse for all I am worth.[15]

And I did. It became a life verse. An anchor. A guiding principle. For ever.

The date arrived for paying the Farrell Line for my sea-voyage ticket. But no money was in hand so I had to cancel. And the ship sailed.

God's provision

Then my diary notes:

Praise the Lord's great and mighty Name. I received today a letter from Robbie Footner saying he wants to give me £90. This is staggering evidence of the Lord's hand at work. Talked to Robin Whalley over a cup of tea about my confidence that the Lord would supply the needed £300. Then returned to the house just in time to receive a phone call from Tom Barlow, with the blessed, sacred, and unspeakable news that the Lord has put it on him to give me £300 he has just received for selling his polo ponies. Tonight I am too tired to write about this as it deserves. But, oh, my God and Saviour, and Father and Lord – let me never ever fail to glory in your unsearchable faithfulness and love. Lord, you really are alive. Please let me never forget this. And give me, Lord, wisdom in the next few days – particularly as far as telling Mum and Dad is concerned – because Tom wanted his giving to be kept anonymous.

Most mighty and unfailing Saviour, take me as I am and make me as You want me to be, that Your Name should be glorified.[16]

I was now going to the United States. And by October, no less. Of course I would have to go by air because there was no longer time to go by sea.

Mum particularly had lamented this, and shed a mother's tears several times. 'We are going to lose you. You will never come back. You will marry a girl from Hollywood and that will be that!' What made her think a girl from Hollywood would take even a second or third or fourth look at an impecunious, scraggy prospective missionary going back to darkest Africa, I can't imagine. But mothers' perceptions of their children are capable of distorting all the realities!

I remember walking with her behind our house as she sobbed and saying, 'Mum, darling. You must accept it. I am going to the States. And you must believe that I *will* come back.'

It was the moment when I finally snapped the psychological umbilical cord. I would always deeply love and honour my parents, but I had to live my own life, and follow my own dreams.

On Wednesday 26 August I journalled:

It was a difficult time as I had to wait till evening before telling Mum and Dad about the £300 – otherwise they would have immediately guessed it was Tom. But I do hope Tommy *will* let me *tell* them. When I told them they were truly wonderful about it and refused to badger me with unfair questions. They could not really approve my accepting the money and in their typically upright and generous way they insisted on paying the fare if

135

I was set on going. But they cannot really afford it and I therefore just *could* not accept their unbelievably self-sacrificing offer. However if God truly put this on Tom's heart, then I feel I can accept the money.[17]

Mum and Dad rose to the occasion in their marvellous graciousness. Mum said: 'All right, you accept the money from Tom. But I am going to give you £150 as half of your airfare – so that we can feel we are sharing in sending you.'

I never forgot that. That was Mum. Bless her.

Mum and Dad drove me to Johannesburg to meet up with my sister Judy and they all bade me a tearful farewell on a Bristol Britannia jet-prop aircraft flying to London via Salisbury, Nairobi and Khartoum, and then over the Alps, even letting me see the Matterhorn. Then it was New York, and catching the inaugural jet service of United Airlines to San Francisco – with red carpets and all for everyone as we boarded the aircraft.

I landed in Los Angeles the same day as a furious President Nikita Khrushchev of the Soviet Union flew out, apoplectic because he had not been allowed to visit Disneyland. He was gearing up to take his shoe off and bang it furiously on the desk at the United Nations, thereby ensuring that the Cold War between the Soviets and the West heated up.

Leaving for Fuller, 4 September 1959: Charles,
Dee, Judy and Michael Cassidy at the airport

13

Fuller Theological Seminary

Fuller Seminary was hoping to be a light on the hill . . .[1]
(George Marsden)

Mary Ashley, the registrar at Fuller Seminary, had been in the loop with me for about a year regarding all my dreams and plans to get to Fuller. She had tracked along in faith, urging me to trust the Lord for the funding.

Imagine the welcome she gave me when I walked into her office! She said I had been assigned 'Dorm 190' with two roommates, Alan Rosenberg and Bob Ives. The space was confined, three beds and three desks in a very average-sized room, with a shared bathroom.

But two more wonderful guys would be hard to find! Amazingly, we are still in touch, all of us having lived to ripe old age. Alan was older than Bob and me, having been in the military with US forces in 1945. He was from Brooklyn, New York, with an accent of note to prove it. A Jewish man, he had come to faith in Christ through reading the New Testament. Bob Ives was a born scholar and a man of deep piety.

First on our agenda was a five-day New Students' Retreat in the San Bernardino Mountains. It was a great time of getting to know one another and I was enjoying myself until I heard about plans for the final evening. It would be given to the sharing of personal stories and how we got to Fuller.

A nudge from the Lord came quickly: 'I want you to tell how I provided and brought you to Fuller.'

I was full of fear at the prospect. Even though I had conquered some of these difficulties, they still came back to haunt me at times. On the afternoon before the final evening, I cut out of the sessions and took myself off to the woods in solitude, protesting to the Lord that I couldn't do it. The Lord just quietly whispered: 'I want you to do it. And I will be with you.'

The evening session arrived, led by the ebullient Dr Carlton Booth, Professor of Evangelism. Student after student stood up and told their stories with boldness and confidence, plus wit.

At last I heaved myself up, feeling as if I was about to jump to my death off a high bridge. But another student was also on his feet and I sank back into my chair, convinced I could never rise to the occasion again.

The student stopped.

It was as if I was lifted to my feet by an Unseen Hand. Booth saw me and signalled. My throat constricted. My hands perspired. Every drop of blood in my body seemed to have gone to my face.

I squawked a tortured word or two. Suddenly a flow began. And I told the story of the Lord's call to me, his open door to Fuller, and finally his extraordinary financial provision at the eleventh hour.

I sat down. There was silence. Almost a holy hush. Dr Booth quietly announced: 'We can't have anything more after that. We must just pray and close the evening.'

I was bewildered and deeply grateful. God had seen me through.

But it wasn't over. Two students were then selected to give their testimonies the next week to the whole seminary, lecturers and all. And I was one of them.

Again the protests. But again the provision. It all went fine.

Then the seminary's Women's Auxiliary, a group that provided all scholarships, asked me to tell my story. Suddenly I was a sort of 'flavour of the month' and was being invited all over Pasadena and Los Angeles. The Lord was throwing me in the deep end and enabling me to swim, not sink. My confidence in speaking was growing. And they all said they just loved 'the cute accent'!

Another early challenge came when I was told by a delegation from the Student Body Council that the chairman of the Fuller Missions Fellowship (FMF), normally a fourth-year student, had dropped out. Would I take on the job? A daunting prospect! I asked for time to pray.

The FMF promoted overseas missions among the student body, but how could I promote 'overseas' missions if my call was to the continent of Africa, my home? Would I be willing, for example, to surrender that, and open myself to going to Asia? I wrestled with this for over a week.

Finally I said to the Lord, 'OK. Anywhere!' As the great Christian explorer David Livingstone said: 'Anywhere – provided it be forward.'

My destiny was now missions – 'anywhere' – but most likely Africa. So I could in good conscience try to lead the FMF and call on students to go *anywhere* the Lord sent them. I had a committee of five or six and would need to raise several thousand dollars each year from the students themselves for missions. That was good practice for future fund-raising as it turned out! My FMF position also put me in the Student Body Council.

Thus within a fortnight of arriving at Fuller I found myself in a leadership role.

Needless to add, there was also much study. I wrote home:

> I am finding my time very full indeed and any idea I ever had of Americans not working hard has been thoroughly and permanently exploded. We really are kept very hard at it and keeping up with the reading (two hours outside of class for every hour in class) and other assignments is a full-time job, but fine practice in getting one's life rigorously organised and thoroughly disciplined.[2]

Attending 17 hours a week of lectures meant 34 hours of reading, a total of 51 academic hours.

Greek was a particular challenge, with Hebrew to follow the next year.

Fancying myself as reasonably good at languages, I was pleased when I got an early Greek test grade back of 97.8 per cent. I was busy flushing with pride when I found to my alarm and horror that I was tenth in the class with a 'B'.

More alarming still was the fact that to keep my scholarship I had to maintain a 'B+' average across all my subjects.

I discovered that, unlike the English system of competing against an objective standard, here the grading was 'on a curve', with the top few students in a course getting an 'A', the next cluster a 'B+', then those lower down coming in with 'B's or 'C's. 'D' or 'E' meant you were almost on the way out.

Suddenly it was all about competition. I had to keep ahead of my mates.

Anyway my struggles were put in perspective by periodic reports from my darling sister Judy, now at Roedean School in Johannesburg. In one she wrote: 'We've still got eleven more weeks of this term left. Most depressing. Especially Latin. It is still absolute Greek to me! Have you perhaps any way of learning that will help me?'[3]

I chuckled at Latin being absolute Greek to her, and felt like writing back, 'Well, darling Sissie, I've got problems too. Because Greek is absolute Hebrew to me!'

Romance

Mum and Dad were worried stiff about my descriptions of the academic pressure, and Mum in her no-nonsense style soon expressed her views on the subject: 'The place seems to have an unhealthy, unnatural and machine-like atmosphere, and I think even two years of it would do more harm than any possible good, especially with this new complication which you cannot and must not underestimate.[4]

The 'new complication' to which my mother anxiously refers was a beautiful young Filipino girl, also a first-year student at Fuller. She had once been Miss Manila! A knockout, to be sure. And a lovely and godly person. I had fallen head over heels for her. And her feelings were reciprocal. She had a voice to bring out the angels in chorus, and we were both on the same 'Gospel Team', as they called the little foursomes of students sent out to preach in Sunday evening services around the Los Angeles basin. A certain electrical and electronics engineer from Princeton University, Chris Smith, was our leader. He worked part-time at Jet Propulsion Lab (JPL) on the Mariner space probe to Mars. Later, he became a founder member of the first African Enterprise team.

Oh my! Life suddenly became very complicated. Here I was – called, as I thought, to South Africa, but Miss Manila in South Africa would have been declared 'non-European' by the apartheid regime. Marriage would have been not just complicated, but illegal. Should I, after all, consider the Philippines for my mission field?

My mind was contradicting my heart and telling me it was all crazy, and that she was not in fact God's choice for me as marriage partner. But I just couldn't break with her. Nor did I really want to. So guilt now entered my life like a great Goliath. I even contemplated leaving seminary – I wasn't enjoying my studies.

My journal of 4 March 1960 says:

> Lord you must meet me, help me and show me your will. Moreover I am becoming so dry spiritually that doubts are ever present, and I often wonder whether it is worthwhile to go into any kind of Christian ministry. This indicates a considerable deterioration in my spiritual life since coming to Fuller. This cannot and must not go on much longer.[5]

Next day my diary records:

> I wandered the streets for a while in prayer. I besought the Lord to make me the man He wanted me to be through a dynamic working of His Spirit. I kept asking the Lord not to require something of me that in my own strength I could not accomplish. The more I look at this situation the less able I feel to change it. Could it possibly be that the Lord would have me marry this girl? Humanly speaking it would seem ridiculous – and the personal cost to me in terms of social and family reaction would be great. But if I am to be preaching about a Christ who breaks down racial barriers,

I suppose it is just possible that He might call me to demonstrate the fact in my own marriage and family relationship.[6]

Of course I shared all this with my parents, with friends like Ed Gregory and with my own Prayer Mother, Leta Fisher, as assigned to me by the seminary. Every new student was given a Prayer Mother to pray for him daily throughout his seminary career. Leta in fact prayed daily for me for decades thereafter until she died in ripe old age. Carlton Booth, my Professor of Evangelism, also knew my heart and soul, and sensed my calling hanging in the balance.

How I praise God in retrospect for friends and counsellors who then and down the years have held me steady in crisis times and given me wise and gracious counsel!

At the end of that first academic year, when the long vacation brought enforced separation and closure for me and her, we finally and painfully recognized we were not for each other.

African Enterprise (AE)

The notion of starting an evangelistic team was much on my mind during these early months of 1960. One of my friends was Murray Albertyn, also a South African, who was studying at California Baptist Seminary in Covina. He and his lovely wife, Marjorie, had taken me under their wing, perhaps sensing my lostness in southern California as well as knowing of my romantic turmoil.

I told Murray of my plans to start a new organization and how there already seemed to be a fair bit of interest in it.

'What are you going to call it?' Murray asked.

'Not sure. I've thought of African Leadership, because Africa and leadership will be its special focus.'

Murray was not wildly enthusiastic.

Then he said, and I can see it now with the desert dunes racing past our window as we drove out to an Easter service in Palm Springs, 'What about African Enterprise? It's the name of a ship in the Farrell Line that sails from Africa to the US.'

'Mmm!' I responded. 'Quite nice. Yes, I like it. Trips off the tongue easily. Good feel to it. OK. Let's go with African Enterprise.'

And that was that!

A couple of weeks later my journal has this entry:

After supper, Murray and Marjorie came over for an evening with new friends Don and Joyce Ehat. This was a useful time as we really thrashed

African Enterprise *ship: Farrell Lines*

through some basic matters as to what we are aiming to do in 'African Enterprise'. We came up with this, which I like: 'African Enterprise Inc. is a socially conscious, biblically orientated Christian service organisation. It is committed within the contemporary African context toward:

1 The furtherance of the cause of Christ, particularly among educated people of all races.

2 The advancement of social welfare among all people.

3 The promotion of understanding among people of all races.

4 The extension of learning by a carefully supervised scholarship programme of overseas travel and study for students of all races.'

Of course, sooner or later, money had to enter the equation. It made sense to open an account and begin raising money in a small way. Otherwise we were constantly going to be hampered by lack of funds. And once an account was open, the Lord could begin to work.

I was personally challenged at that time by the story in Matthew 26.6–12 about the woman who broke the very costly jar of spikenard ointment over the Lord's feet. This was a once-in-a-lifetime sacrifice, and it is highly likely that it was all this woman had. And the Lord was well pleased with her. I couldn't help but feel that, when an account was opened for 'African Enterprise', similarly he would be well pleased if I gave to him all of the very modest monies that I had set aside in savings. This I duly did.

On Monday, 9 May 1960, I sent off my first African Enterprise letters. My journal records my thoughts on this move:

> Once committed to this, it will be difficult to turn back. But I go forward sure of the Lord's ultimate sovereignty and not fearful of having Him block these plans if they are not in His will. I do not fear mistakes – because I know that he who made no mistakes never made anything.[7]

A few days later I had dinner with Charles and Honey Fuller, founders of the seminary. Dr Fuller told me of a businessman who wanted to start a new organization to support and undergird missionary work. He had been in the Fuller Missions Fellowship (FMF) Chapel where I had spoken a couple of weeks previously after spending a whole night in prayer with a friend of mine.

Spending nights in prayer was something we occasionally did in those days. We would choose some prayer points, read selected Scripture verses and meditate on them. Then we would discuss them and repeat the process. Sometimes we would spend up to half an hour on our own, walking up and down and around the church where we met.

The Lord had blessed and used my message, which flowed from that night of prayer, and many had apparently been affected, including this businessman.

My journal says: 'How unsearchable and past finding out are the ways of God!'[8]

I had spoken in utter weakness, but a connection was made with someone who, in the sovereignty of God, was to become a major source of funding for the infant African Enterprise.

First attempts at preaching

As to my studies, one of the subjects I studied in that first year was Homiletics, the science and discipline of preaching. Dr Clarence Roddy, a larger-than-life character, was our lecturer.

Once a week we had to preach a sermon of eight to ten minutes to a class of colleagues who marked our performance. We ended the classes inflated, deflated or chastened, resolved to do better or ready to give up the ministry and leave seminary! I always made it a point to have something encouraging for every fellow student whose talk I had been obliged to critique.

I heard from fellow students that they felt I had a gift for preaching, for all my lack of confidence. Even Roddy finally agreed and one day gave me a book on Charles Spurgeon, one of the most renowned preachers of the nineteenth century, by the great German theologian Helmut Thielicke. In the cover flap he wrote: 'Stir up your gift, work hard! Study hard! Pray hard! Preach the Word.'

Roddy drew my attention to Spurgeon's priorities. As Thielicke points out in his book, Spurgeon did not allow himself to become consumed with busyness. Instead he immersed himself in the quietness of prayer and meditation, and then poured himself out without reserve:

> The temptation of becoming the star preacher and enjoying the respect and adulation of men held no attraction for him. Neither did he become a 'soloist.' Instead, as a serving member of the church, he sought out the 'ensemble' in which to work.[9]

This was 'teamwork'. And a lesson I took to heart.

From Roddy I learned how 'the solemn task of preaching the gospel demands everything that a man can give, the very best'. For this reason we are responsible not only for what we say, but equally for *how* we say it. 'Our tools too must be kept sharp. Not only our spiritual knowledge but also the means of its communication are entrusted talents, meant to be used for service.'[10]

Clarence Roddy. Yes, I owe him the world for his encouragement.

Charles Fuller

And of course the ever genial and congenial Dr Charles Fuller himself was always there to ensure the primacy of faithful evangelism. How many times did I meet Dr Fuller at his office or in the seminary and have him exhort me with that great beaming smile: 'Preach the word, Mike, preach the word'?

Even back then Fuller had representatives from no fewer than 42 denominations. This made it hard for one ever to be a full-blown 'denominational' person. But what I do know is that the range of experiences of those years was both preparing me and frightening me about spending my days working 'in partnership with the church'[11] where we would be called to 'contend earnestly for the faith once for all entrusted to God's people' (Jude 3).

Carnell

The teacher whose influence and shaping was most key to me at Fuller was Dr Edward Carnell.

Carnell was Professor of Systematic Theology, a discipline in which theology is reduced to a number of doctrines and themes, such as conversion, sovereignty of God, redemption, second coming of Christ, assurance. He also taught Philosophical Apologetics whereby we were trained to defend the faith philosophically, not just historically.

Indeed, so intrigued and fascinated was I by Dr Carnell that I asked him occasionally if I could bring a bagged lunch to his office and share the lunch hour with him. These were deeply instructive times.

Edward John Carnell

The big debate of the day, which no student arriving at Fuller in the late 1950s could escape, was between the two extremes of theological liberalism and biblical fundamentalism. Coming from my CICCU background at Cambridge, this presented me with the challenge of seeking to bring grace and truth together, something which I certainly did not do. I was fearsomely judgemental and hard on anyone who did not see things as I did. But I also knew that we had to learn to resist the nonsensical liberal notions of a Christianity without a supernatural Christ, or a Bible without divine inspiration and authority, or morals without absolutes, thereby rendering ethics relative, variable or situational.

Calling himself an Evangelical, Carnell focused on the inspiration of the Bible, the sinfulness of human beings, conversion, sanctification and new birth by the Holy Spirit, and the ministry of God's word.

For attempting to address the Church on these assorted issues Carnell was roasted and castigated by extreme right-wing fundamentalists, while held in some suspicion by theological liberals. But he remained committed to the way of openness and graciousness. And it was this posture that Fuller Seminary sought to manifest.

Holding the line on a biblical theology but doing so with love and humility was held up to us new students as the ideal. The Augustinian watchword, we were told, especially by Carnell, was for us: 'Conviction on essentials. Liberty on non-essentials; and love over *all*.' It was a position and posture into which I would seek to lead the embryonic African Enterprise team. In fact it was this posture which we embraced as a ministry which would enable AE in due course to win the confidence of a very wide range of churches and denominations right across the theological spectrum. As I look back on this I see Carnell's influence as the key.

A light on the hill

The ethos described above was the heritage of the Fuller Seminary into which I had arrived. The seminary, as historian George Marsden had said, was hoping to be

a light on the hill . . . Yet the ideological hill on which the Seminary was situated had long, steep slopes and deep valleys on each side. One of the valleys was inhabited by strict fundamentalists, the other by Protestant liberals.[12]

The concern of Fuller remained to recapture what had once been the historic inheritance, tradition and balance of Evangelicalism, of biblical faithfulness, substantial scholarship, fervent evangelism, plus relevant and contextual social action. There was also a strong concern often articulated by Harold John Ockenga, whose razor-sharp mind so impressed me when I first arrived at Fuller, that the Church face the major cultural issues of the time and not withdraw into a separated or separatist community.

As John Stott said:

> All down history the church has tended to go to extremes. Sometimes in its proper determination to be holy, it has withdrawn from the world and lost contact with it. At other times, in its equally proper determination not to lose contact, it has conformed to the world and become virtually indistinguishable from it. But Christ's vision for the church's holiness is neither withdrawal nor conformity.
>
> In place of these two extreme positions, Jesus calls us to live 'in the world' [John 17.11] while remaining like Himself 'not of the world' [John 17.14], that is neither belonging to it, nor imitating its ways.[13]

In all, the aim of Fuller was to plant the evangelical flag in the middle of the road, taking a conservative theological position but a definite liberal approach to social problems. Name-calling and mud-slinging were also to be banished as *modi operandi* in theological debate.

This became my personal posture, DNA and ethos, which I then sought to bring into the ministry of African Enterprise.

Another big debate

My first tumultuous year at Fuller ended in June 1960. I then found myself, to my surprise, part of a five-person student evangelistic team to the eastern USA, with a Christian and Missionary Alliance evangelist called Eddie Jones.

A Pasadena businessman, Steve Lazerian (who also became a supporter of African Enterprise and remained so for nearly 60 years until his death in October 2018), had put up the money. Eddie Jones, a fiery evangelist of strongly held Arminian views, would be the main speaker in all the churches we would visit. This raised a big debate among us. Arminianism, deriving from Jacobus Arminius (1560–1609), a Dutch theologian, is a system of beliefs that attempts to explain the relationship between God's sovereignty and people's free will, especially regarding salvation. It stresses that we choose Christ for salvation, but if we move away from that choice we can lose our salvation.

Fuller Summer evangelistic team, 1960. Back: Russ Lance, Ed Gregory,
Bob Thomas, Michael. Front: Alex Aronis and Eddie Jones

Calvinism, to which the rest of us subscribed, stresses the sovereignty of God and his Holy Spirit in revealing Christ to the enquirer and enabling him or her to respond to the message. The Reformers called this the 'doctrine of illumination'. It also implied that, once truly saved, a person could never lose his or her salvation because 'no one is able to snatch them out of the Father's hand' (John 10.28–30). The Reformers spoke of this teaching as the 'perseverance of the saints'. In other words a genuine believer would persevere to the end. As the apostle Paul says in Philippians 1.6, 'He who began a good work in you will bring it to completion.' In our present context we speak of this as the 'doctrine of assurance'.

Ed Gregory was our Fuller Seminary team leader, while Alex Aronis, Bob Thomas, Russ Lance and I brought up the rear.

And so we set off in Ed Gregory's big old Pontiac with this big theological issue dominating our minds, to drive across the vast expanse of the United States of America.

14

Summers trying our wings

―――――•◆•―――――

We desire to bequeath two things to our children.
The first one is roots; the other one is wings.
(Sudanese proverb)

One of the beauties of being at Fuller was the summer vacation! It was long, and just asking to be filled with useful and exciting activity. For us it brought the opportunity to try our wings in organized evangelism, testing the waters for African Enterprise.

The first summer

As we all got to the other side of the United States, our first assignment was to join the Billy Graham outreach in Washington DC.

We were counsellors in the meetings for those who came forward in response to the evangelist's appeal, trained to have certain answers and Bible verses to share. Bob Thomas thought he was pretty good at this until one person who had responded said: 'I came forward to celebrate my tenth anniversary of becoming a deacon.' Bob couldn't think of a single Bible verse to fit the occasion, then suddenly blurted out, 'Well, I do know the Bible says somewhere "A deacon should be the husband of one wife."' The man looked thoroughly startled, registered that he was faced with a serious novice, and fled!

Russ Lance, very handsome, with wavy blond hair, was ecstatic one evening when someone mistook him for Billy Graham. He told us: 'You know, I have dedicated my hair to the Lord.' Alex Aronis and I chuckled over this for years and teased Russ mercilessly. And what could *we* dedicate? Alex had muscles, having come third in the 'Mr America' contest, and all I had was the gangly awkward frame of an overgrown teenager!

During the Washington mission I also met a young man called Doug Coe. He had come out of the Navigators ministry to work with Abraham Vereide, who had founded what was then called International Christian

Weightlifting with Alex Aronis!

Leadership (ICL), later to be known as the Prayer Breakfast Movement, which worked to bring a Christian witness to leaders, mainly political, initially only in the United States but thereafter worldwide.

Doug took me to meet Vereide, and God gave us an instant click. I shared my embryonic vision for African Enterprise and Vereide was eventually to play an important role in the development of AE in Africa.

'I want you to come to the National Prayer Breakfast next year' was his parting shot.

From Washington DC we went up into New England where, in assorted small towns, with Eddie Jones now fully in harness as the main preacher, we conducted a number of week-long evangelistic campaigns.

We spoke to youth groups, shared testimonies in the services, spoke at women's morning teas, and even sang here and there. Bob, Alex, Russ and I had formed ourselves into a passable quartet while Ed, who couldn't hold a note, was sidelined at this point. We basically had one song, 'Redeemed, How I Love to Proclaim It!' I carried the melody; Russ was tenor, Alex baritone and Bob bass. We sounded pretty good!

But in one church our musical exploits unravelled. We had successfully negotiated two or three verses, but at the fourth, our pianist set off on a musical extravaganza of flying notes and cascading chords, all set to lead to a change of key in the final verse.

I had somehow not been warned of this. So while the other three remained silent, I set off as a good leader in the fourth verse to get the melody under way, competing with the pianist. At which point Alex elbowed me violently in the solar plexus, knocking the air out of my lungs and forcing me to double up, gasping for breath. As the pianist completed her virtuoso transition with a spectacular sliding *glissando*, the other three struck up the tenor, baritone and bass parts without the melody, for which by this time I was incapacitated. The congregation finally collapsed in uncontrollable mirth. So did the quartet. And the song, sans finale, ended abruptly at that point – as Eddie Jones came on to pick up the pieces, rescue the evening and preach a fiery message!

Eddie liked the story of Arminian revivalist Charles Finney's response after being approached by a woman who said, 'Mr Finney, every day I sin in thought, word and deed.' To this Finney replied, 'Madam, you'd better stop!'

Eddie Jones's view was: 'You can't say "once saved, always saved" if you go on living like the devil.'

To which we aspiring Calvinists replied: 'But Eddie, someone who is truly saved and born again and knows salvation in Christ will *not* continually, deliberately and persistently keep sinning every day in thought, word and deed.'

In the end I concluded that both the sovereignty of God and the free will of the unprogrammed, non-robotic human are taught in the Bible. Both Calvinism and election as well as Arminianism and free choice are there. Both 'eternal security' and Arminianism stress the necessity of wilful perseverance in the Bible. Philippians 2.12 for me captured the paradox, non-resolvable in our finite minds but assuredly resolvable in God's: 'Work out your own salvation with fear and trembling [Arminianism]. For it is God [who works] in you both to will and to do of his good pleasure [Calvinism]' (KJV).

Always with an eye on how African Enterprise might develop, I was struck that summer by a notion from the life of Dawson Trotman, founder of the Navigators. The Navigators' stated aim was: 'To know Christ, make him known and help others to do the same'. They major in mentoring, discipleship and equipping Christians to make an impact.

Trotman was known for his way of praying for different parts of the world and claiming them for new Christian witness and discipling possibilities. I decided there and then to list 31 key cities of Africa and 'claim' them for Christ, one a day for each of the 31 days of the month, and for open doors into them for African Enterprise ministry. To this day in AE, we still pray for a city a day, each day of the month.

As I began to pray in this way, a word seemed to slip into my spirit from on high: 'I want you and Ed to go and visit those African cities next summer.' I was startled. An impossible idea, surely. But it stuck. I kept it secret for the time being.

Heading to the hills

At the end of our summer of itinerant evangelism in fancy churches, we were due to wind up in a huge and extra-fancy church in Louisville, Kentucky. But when the church heard our team had an *Anglican* on it, no less, and what's more a former *Greek Orthodox* (Alex), the invitation was withdrawn in the name of not compromising the gospel! Dr Booth back at Fuller did some fancy footwork. If the big city-slicker church would not have his team, then why not send the team into the mountains and valleys of Kentucky to the not-so-fancy backwoods folk? And, ever resourceful, he knew of a mission working with these mountain people called, if you please, the Beef-Hide Gospel Mission, so named because of the river creek (called Beef-Hide) where the first mission church had been planted.

We were intrigued. I reflected that if I wrote home to my folks and said 'Send your next letters to me care of the Beef-Hide Gospel Mission', my mother would be on the next plane coming over to pluck me from the dread clutches of America, even if it meant commuting their pension and selling the family plastic!

The mission was made up entirely of single women, because its members had found that men couldn't survive the strain of working with the mountain and forest people, most of them illiterate and inbred, many living in caves, some of them snake-handlers, and all blissfully cut off from the outside world.

'They couldn't tell you the name of the President of the United States, nor which is the right or wrong way up for a page of printed text, so don't ask anyone to read a verse of the Bible, which if they have one, they are probably holding upside down,' said the briefing ladies in deep southern drawl. 'And, remember, it's OK to preach against sin, but not specifically mentioning brewing moonshine or chewing tobakkie. Otherwise you could get ya-selves shot or have our house burned down, like happened when one visiting missionary last year preached against moonshine. There ain't no police here neither, nor law-enforcement officers. Too dangerous.'

No wonder we were not amazed that these women could drive us in off-road vehicles through the forests, along mountain tracks, over wickedly precarious little bridges swaying as we went over them, to our preaching assignments, with a Bible in one hand and a rifle in the other! Really, no kidding!

As for our venues and assignments for preaching?

'No, we can't use the town hall because it's covered in blood. You see, the Regular Baptists had a debate there last night, and a big fight broke out. A lot of stabbin', you know.'

We listened, unbelieving!

'Now, Michael, this Sunday evening you'll be preaching at Hell for Certain,' our lady leader went on.

'Where?' I expostulated.

'Oh, sorry, should have explained. Hell for Certain is the name of the church built on the river creek with that name.'

'Oh!' I mused inwardly. 'Something new for my CV. Imagine if one day I could write: Has preached in St James (Melbourne), St Johns (Cape Town), All Souls (London), Nairobi Cathedral, Christ Church Cathedral (New Zealand) and Hell for Certain (Jenkins, Kentucky)!' It sounds impressive enough.

That night Russ Lance preached in a little forest church, and to our enormous amusement and Russ's manifest discomfiture about 20 young people moved out of the second and third rows and left the church midstream in his sermon.

'That'll teach him not to be boring,' Alex whispered to me with a chuckle. But ten minutes later they all reappeared and dutifully sat down to listen to Russ's now supercharged Ciceronian eloquence.

'What was that all about?' we asked one of the lady missionaries afterwards.

'Oh, they all went out to go and get a few swigs of moonshine so they could manage the rest of the sermon.'

Mmm!

In another service four or five thugs appeared, apparently with the intent of breaking up the meeting. But when they saw four of us over six feet, and Alex, the muscular almost Mr America, they thought better of it, and sat down rather menacingly to listen to the message!

My journal for 2 August 1960 also records:

I preached last night in a little schoolroom some miles up a creek. There were about five adults present, about 10 teenagers, and a score or so of ragged and rugged little mountain children. Throughout my message there was talking, laughter and movement, with children coming and going and general ruction all round. But no one sought to break up the meeting, for which, I gather, I ought to be grateful, as this sometimes takes place, even to the extent of having stones thrown in the windows at the preacher. But how much I appreciate now what it means to labour in the regions beyond, in places where the true Gospel has never gone and where Satan and his forces are thoroughly entrenched. These women are staggering and the job they are doing is enough to make the hearts of many a sturdy man quake. More than ever I praise God for the lady missionary – but where are the men? Where are the men? This is the sort of job they should also be doing. I truly praise the Lord for the privilege of preaching in that place last night. It has taught me much.[1]

Lake Minnetonka

After our astonishing time in the back country, I went on to Mound, Minnesota, on the edge of Lake Minnetonka, to attend a three-week Campus Crusade Summer Training Institute to which its founder, Bill Bright, had invited me.

The African Enterprise vision was so challenging me that I felt constrained to ask Bill if I might spend the first week of the Training Institute just in prayer and quietness, walking by the lapping waters of the lake and seeking some word of clarity from the Lord.

After that week of spiritual interaction with the Lord and earnest prayer, something very special and determinative happened back at the lodge. Mary-Jane Smith, wife of the famous Fuller Seminary professor Wilbur Smith, handed me a tract which she felt had a message for me. It was entitled 'This Thing Is from Me'. It opened:

> My child, I have a message for you today; let Me whisper it in your ear, that it may gild with glory any storm clouds which may arise and smooth the rough places upon which you may have to tread. It is short, only five words, but let them sink into your soul and use them as a pillow upon which to rest your weary head. 'This Thing Is from Me.'
>
> Have you ever thought of it, that all that concerns you, concerns Me, too? For 'he that toucheth you, toucheth the apple of Mine eye' (Zechariah 2:8). 'You are very precious in My sight' (Isaiah 43:4). Therefore, it is My special delight to educate you.

The tract concludes:

> Are you suddenly called upon to occupy a difficult and responsible position? Launch out on Me – I am trusting you with the 'possession of difficulties,' and 'for this thing the Lord thy God shall bless thee in all thy works, and in all that thou puttest thine hand unto' (Deuteronomy 15:10).
>
> This day I place in your hand this pot of holy oil; make use of it freely, My child. Let every circumstance as it arises, every work that pains you, every interruption that would make you impatient, every revelation of your own weakness, be anointed with it. The sting will go as you learn to

see Me in all things. Therefore, 'Set your hearts unto all the words which I testify among you this day . . . for it is not a vain thing for you; because it is your life, and through this thing ye shall prolong your days in the land' (Deuteronomy 32:46–47).

The words which hit me overwhelmingly were, 'Are you called upon to occupy a difficult and responsible position? *Launch out on Me – I am trusting you with the possession of difficulties.*'

There and then I resolved, with no turning back, that I would launch out on him. And I took on board the fact that my task would be full of difficulties. Indeed, the Lord never told me the half of it. But what I *do* know is that hundreds of times over the years when the heat was really on, I have gone back to those words and found solace.

Writing to me *on that very same day* (10 August 1960) was Bishop Bill Burnett, now Bishop of Bloemfontein, and formerly my chaplain at Michaelhouse. My old mentor said: 'You will, of course, expect to encounter *many difficulties* in putting your plans into action.'[2]

Extraordinary. The same word. Coming from two continents. On the same day. The possession and encountering of 'many difficulties'. It has certainly been so.

Back at seminary

Back at seminary some weeks later a flurry of preaching assignments and activities engulfed me, including Greek assignments and theology, believe it or not, but also a miraculously sponsored trip to Seattle to a conference of the Christian Business Men's Convention. For me it was all about making contacts for African Enterprise.

But a new thought pressed itself in on me, echoing that whisper from the Lord in the summer. I should go all round Africa, north to south, the following summer and do a sort of 'Caleb and Joshua spying out the land' exercise. Quietly I made the booking. All in faith, of course, as there was no money! I decided not to tell Ed Gregory, who I thought should come with me, but instead see if the Lord would speak to him too. This would be a confirming sign.

A few weeks later Ed came to me: 'Mike, I feel we should go to Africa next summer.'

'We're already booked, Ed,' I replied with all the nonchalance and suppressed excitement I could muster.

Some weeks later a call came to me from Dr Charles Fuller's secretary, Rose Baessler. She told me that he wanted to get behind African Enterprise and 'take it under the wing of the Fuller Evangelistic Foundation till it gets going'.[3]

He would assign me three people to constitute a small initial board – two businessmen, Bruce Bare and James Gorton, plus his own secretary, Rose, a genius of an administrative assistant.

God was confirming, with signs following. My journal said: 'Now, Lord, I thank You for this new development, and again remind myself that this whole project is Yours, not mine. Keep me out of the way, and see that Your will is done [see Psalm 150.6].'[4]

In mid-December (1960) my journal entry captures the struggle:

> The last two days my soul has been much bound and my mind very heavy with regard to the step to be taken in launching African Enterprise. I do feel so utterly inadequate and dangerously frail that the whole idea of stepping out in this way fills me with alarm, hesitation and fear.
>
> What if this is not of God? What if I begin and then find it all too difficult? What if I take money from God's people and do not spend it satisfactorily? What if I let down Dr Fuller? And disappoint in his old age such a choice servant of the Lord? What if I fell into sin? For the leader of a work this would be cataclysmic. Lord, it is all too much – too big – too heavy – too serious for me. If you take it forward, Lord, you must equip me with new spiritual power and insight, new qualities of leadership and strength, new determination to go deeper with you, new hunger for the Word and prayer, new discipline in running my own life and studies. In short, Lord, you're going to have to do in me a pretty thorough job of renovation.
>
> Spent an hour with Dr Carlton Booth – such a dear, compassionate and patient servant of the Lord. He says he will serve on the African Enterprise Committee. And he has given me much encouragement to move forward into 'the possession of difficulties.'[5]

AE formally born

At the end of that first term of my second year, I went up to an Inter-Varsity Students house party at Lake Tahoe in northern California. About 10.00 p.m. one night, down at the water's edge, with the moon lighting up the snow all round, I felt the Lord give me peace formally to accept Charles Fuller's offer. I had asked him for six weeks to pray about it. Now I felt a freedom to say 'I accept.'

But I was aware that what was being birthed was birthed in fragility. On the last day of 1960, I affirmed:

> Through all the weakness and defeat of this last year God has worked to raise up African Enterprise. Never will I be able to say that I raised up the

First-ever AE Board meeting: Ed Gregory, Bruce Bare, Rose Baessler,
Honey Fuller, Charles Fuller, Michael and Murray Albertyn

work. For it was while I was pinned down by the darts of Satan and while I was fighting for my very existence that African Enterprise was raised up. As I was freed from Satan's clutches, the work, somehow already on its feet and moving, was thrust into my unsteady and faltering hands. Truly His grace has been made perfect in my weakness. More than ever I know that it is in spite of me rather than because of me that African Enterprise has come into existence. God forbid that I should ever boast of starting this work. The conception and development has been entirely His. The running of it must remain His. So also its consummation in glory.[6]

Twelve days later on 12 January 1961, the first formal committee or board meeting of African Enterprise took place.

I was launched on my life's work.

Second summer vacation

Prior to our big trip to Africa the following summer, John Stott from All Souls Church in London came to Fuller for a week-long lecture series on preaching. The timing couldn't have been better for building a foundation for our preaching efforts in Africa. The lectures were later published in *The Preacher's Portrait* (1961) – an invaluable collection. The key was as follows:

True evangelism seeks a response. It expects results. It is preaching for a verdict. Heralding is not the same as lecturing. A lecture is dispassionate, objective, and academic. It is addressed to the mind. It seeks no result but to impart certain information and, perhaps, to provoke the student to further enquiry. But the herald of God comes with an urgent proclamation of peace through the blood of the cross, and with a summons to men to repent, to lay down their arms and humbly to accept the offered pardon.[7]

This was an 'aha' moment for me. I learned from John Stott that I must tell the story, explain the meaning of the story and secure a response to the story. Or, in more theological terminology, I must make 'a historical proclamation, a theological evaluation, and an ethical summons'.[8]

This approach anchored my preaching. I recognized I had a gospel to preach, to whose content I needed to be faithful, and to which I needed to call people in response via repentance and faith.

African trip

I was not a novice in the ways of the Lord when it came to his providing needed finance, but even so, the funding for our big African trip challenged my faith until almost the zero hour.

A lady in Washington had told me to let her know if we needed money for the trip. But while praying about contacting her, I felt constrained by the Lord *not* to write. I could look only to him at that point.

Just two days before we left, and the day after my final seminary exams for the year, the major gift for the whole trip came from Dr Fuller.

Ed and I raced to a phone to ring travel agent Bill Lescher, by this time California's leading emotional wreck, because this total exercise was big dollars. We invited him out to lunch. He came, I suspect, with a sinking heart. These crazy boys were going to default and bankrupt him. Over lunch we handed him a cheque in full payment for the 50,000-kilometre (30,000-mile), three-month journey, covering Africa from stem to stern.

Bill's eyes goggled. Then he burst into tears and sobbed uncontrollably while other diners around us in the restaurant looked on in mystification! It was a good moment. Both he and we knew God was alive and well.

First stop for Ed and me was Washington DC where Abraham Vereide of International Christian Leadership (ICL) had convened in the Capitol a private luncheon of African ambassadors and ICL leaders.

The luncheon was co-chaired by General Merwin Silverthorn who had commanded the US invasion of Okinawa in the Second World War, and

Rear Admiral Robert Morris, a distinguished Second World War admiral in the Pacific theatre and, after the war, Operations Officer at Pearl Harbour.

Next to me on my left was the US Under-Secretary of State, and on my right the Ambassador of Ethiopia who was very keen that we should meet the Ethiopian royal family.

My journal says: 'I spoke without much nervousness, though a little incoherently, I thought . . . But reactions afterwards showed that the Holy Spirit had worked in spite of me.'[9]

Silverthorn and Morris, I gathered, had been asked to check me over to decide if Vereide and ICL could give me all their contacts in Africa, and especially African parliaments. I seemed to pass muster, as Vereide then gave me the most extraordinary list of governmental and even royal contacts across Africa. For the use of these I was given two days of intensive training by Doug Coe and Bill Bullard of ICL.

Then it was up, up and away.

We began in Tripoli in Libya. Then to Tunis in Tunisia, then via Algiers to Casablanca in Morocco, and on to Dakar, Senegal; then Conakry, Guinea; and Freetown, Sierra Leone; all the way connecting with contacts given us in Washington and then asking questions, questions, questions. What is happening politically in your city? What is happening religiously? How do you view South Africa? How is Christianity perceived? How could a Christian team of young people best contribute in Africa right now? The answer to the latter question was always: 'Come and do something major in our cities and in leadership circles.'

In Sierra Leone it was my privilege to meet the Prime Minister, Sir Milton Margai, and the Honourable Karefa Smart, Foreign Secretary of the country. When asked about South Africa he said all Africa was united in detesting apartheid, and Sierra Leone was joining the other African nations in cessation of all trade with South Africa and a boycott of South African goods and citizens. No South African citizens were allowed into Sierra Leone. Thankfully I had dual nationality and a British passport so could travel freely.

Then it was on to Liberia. While waiting for the ferry to take us across the bay to the airport, a young 16-year-old African and another older man about 35 saw an old Union-Castle label on my case with 'Cape Town, South Africa' written on it. They at once got very nasty and belligerent. The youngster fired at me with wickedness in his eyes.

'You like apartheid?'

'No, I'm English. The English do not like apartheid.'

'That is good,' he went on. 'We no like apartheid and those people down there.'

And so by a quick manoeuvre I got out of what might have been a very nasty situation, as they were definitely menacing. Had I mentioned my South African nationality there would surely have been an 'incident'. It was this sort of thing, needless to say, that made me tremble for South Africa. Africa was in no mood to tolerate South Africa's apartheid much longer.

The plane ride to Monrovia was rather fun as we flew very low to avoid cloud disturbance. Next day, while speaking in the morning service at Eternal Love Winning Africa (ELWA) radio station, I told the listeners I had written a stanza to celebrate my arrival in Liberia and how it might have been!

> A thinker of stature superior
> Took a plane that was bound for Nigeria.
> So a long swim at sea
> Didn't happen to be
> How he thought he'd arrive in Liberia!

Ray and Sophie de la Haye, directors of this famous and mighty missionary radio station, were wonderful to us, fully embraced the AE vision, and in fact followed and supported our work all the rest of their lives. They also gave opportunities for radio broadcasts there and then, and brought radio into our vision as very important for propagating the gospel across Africa.

Now I flip you back to Chapter 1, 'A walk on the beach'. It was here that I went down to the sea on a lovely early morning, made 50 footprints in the African sand and asked the Lord for one year of ministry in Africa for every footprint. So here I am now, 57 years later, penning these pages about the 50-plus years of our African ministry journey from that day to this. How utterly faithful God has been!

Accra, Ghana, came next. Here I saw a statue of Kwame Nkrumah, the country's first prime minister and president, which had quite an impact on me. The statue was inscribed with the words: 'Seek ye first the Political Kingdom and all other things will be added unto it.' I remembered back to childhood and as a 12-year-old having a big crush on Catherine Arden-Clarke, whose father, Sir Charles, went from Basutoland to Gold Coast, a former British colony, and saw it through its political revolution to become Ghana. But he was a devout man of faith, and I don't think he would have approved of Nkrumah's short-sighted slogan on his statue.

Next stop, Lagos produced more ICL contacts and conversations, but most especially a key word from the Lord to me in a thunderstorm as I huddled alone in a little rondavel (an African round hut). It came through Acts 18.10 with the force of a determinative word from on high, the word of the Lord to Paul as he stood before Corinth: 'Do not be afraid, but speak and do not be silent; for I am with you, and no man shall attack you to harm you: for I have many people in this city.'

The thrust of the word was this: 'My son, AE's focus is to be cities. Don't be overcome with fear. Because I am with you in this. And there is a great gospel harvest in the cities. Proceed.'

'Where first?' I asked.

'Pietermaritzburg,' came the Spirit's whisper. I wrote it in the margin of my Bible. Then I thought, Isn't that a bit ambitious to start off with? And to soothe my nerves I added 'Maseru', my home village. Pietermaritzburg, of course, was not my home then. Maseru was. So the identification of Pietermaritzburg for our first major city campaign came out of the blue, as something of a surprise.

Last stops were Brazzaville and Leopoldville, at that time overrun with United Nations troops because of the Katanga crisis.

Pierre Shaumba, head of the 46-denomination Congolese Protestant Council, informed us that missions here had not produced Africans of political calibre, and had not made an effort to relate Christianity to politics. Thus there were no political ethics that were both Christian and Congolese.

He saw this as perilous for his country's future. Little did he know.

Finally South Africa

Finally it was Johannesburg. Mum and Dad met us for some precious time in Maseru before Ed and I went on to Pietermaritzburg where I had been invited by Jenny Comrie, a friend from schooldays, to speak at Natal University.

For three days before the meeting I could scarcely take in any food, so terrified was I to speak in such a context. Besides, who would come? But when I stepped from backstage to confront a huge jam-packed lecture theatre, I almost had cardiac arrest. 'What is the matter with me, Lord?' I called into my soul.

However, as I launched into my address, I found words pouring forth in an eloquent flow on the need for Christ in the cities of Africa.

Afterwards I was horrified to find that Jenny and two other students,

Ivor Glass and Marjorie Watling, had barrelled down to the Pietermaritz-burg city hall and booked it from 12 to 24 August the following year (1962) for what they called 'a citywide youth mission'. A stadium was also booked for the closing meeting. I felt overwhelmed.

They had also rushed to Calvin Cook, effectively in due course to become the father of AE South Africa, whom they knew as pastor of the Presbyterian church and chairman of the City Ministers' Fraternal, to tell him of the university meeting. 'Will you preach in my church?' Calvin asked. I found myself agreeing.

Then to my further amazement Calvin went to the Ministers' Fraternal, whose members had been thinking of a citywide interdenominational mission. His message to them as they considered inviting John Stott or Canon Bryan Green, the great Anglican missioners of that day, for a city-wide mission: 'No, not these greats! I think the time has come for the Church of Pietermaritzburg to take a major risk and invite these young unknowns to come to our city.'

And you know what? The idea prevailed! A formal invitation to us arrived in Pasadena some weeks later. Our first citywide mission was set for the following August (12–25 August 1962), in the city hall of Pietermaritzburg, closing out in Jan Smuts Stadium – now Harry Gwala Stadium – exactly as booked and dreamed by those three crazy students, Jenny Comrie, Ivor Glass and Marjorie Watling.

I was much touched by my heart-warming welcome back to Fuller after some eventful further travelling. I arrived two weeks late for the start of term, and was greeted with much interest from everyone about our trip.

Third year

That academic year was hard work, but I also enjoyed a gentle, sweet ro-mance with a godly nurse in the seminary. But again we had to conclude we weren't for each other. Oh, the heartbreaks of youth and singleness!

I had my full scholarship and board, but for a little spending and pocket money I worked in the seminary library for four hours every evening (6.00 p.m. to 10.00 p.m.), for all four of the years I was at Fuller. Mercifully I could study much of the time.

With the Mission to 'Maritzburg set for August 1962, there was much work to be done on sermon preparation, fundraising, strategizing and getting our little AE team of five ready for the Big Adventure.

The other four special friends in our team were all Fuller Seminary students. Dick Peace was very knowledgeable on evangelism, discipleship

AE team in 1962 pre-Pietermaritzburg Mission. Back: Paul Birch, Michael,
Ed Gregory, Dick Peace. Front: Chris Smith and Don Ehat

and follow-up. Chris Smith was a great music coordinator and had a keen eye for administration and detail, as did Don Ehat, who had learnt about mission set-up from the legendary Jerry Bevin of the Billy Graham Evangelistic Association. Paul Birch was also a musician of serious note, and already had two degrees, one in English Literature and the other in Music, when he arrived at Fuller.

So that was my crew as we geared up for the Mission to 'Maritzburg in August 1962.

Just before we left on the first leg of our journey to South Africa, Mum and Dad went across to England, and Dad came on to USA and then out to California, while Mum stayed on in England with Aunt Olave.

My sister Olave had come out to California from New York where she had been working at the United Nations in the radio department, and the two of us met Dad at the airport. He appeared at the arrivals area absolutely bubbling, but obviously a little relieved to be out of the plane which he said had bumped around terrifically in flight due to poor weather. Nevertheless he was tickled pink with the aircraft and the thrill of crossing the continent at a mile a minute. Olave and I then drove Dad back to Pasadena via Hollywood (!) and put him to bed in my room, while I slept with a mattress and sleeping bag on the floor (very well too).

Frantic packing followed for two days before Dad, Olave and I set out to cross the continent in Chris Smith's car, taking also his wife, Barbara, with us. Barbie, as Miss Arizona, was majorly ecstatic to show us her home state's Grand Canyon.

The five-day exhilarating journey ended as we met the rest of the team heading out to Africa, with Olave and Dad staying on in New York.

My prayer as I set out was based on a verse I believed the Lord gave me at that moment, 1 Chronicles 4.10:

> And Jabez called on the God of Israel saying: 'Oh that you would bless me indeed and enlarge my territory, and that your hand would be with me, and that you would keep me from evil, that it may not harm me.' And God granted his request.

Curiously this has become a prayer I still use daily. I prayed it this morning – 56 years on from that day aboard the *Capetown Castle* in July 1962!

My journal noted that

> I have had some good opportunities to witness for [the Lord]. May they bear real fruit. I have also had some very wonderful times in prayer. Oh, I do so love to be used of Him and see my life count for His glory! I am also yearning more and more for 'Maritzburg and its people. I pray that this campaign may turn the city upside down and be a turning point in the history of South Africa.[10]

As our ship neared Durban, I opened my little *Daily Light* volume of readings. There at the head of the page was Acts 18.10 and the Lord's word to Paul as he faced Corinth: 'Do not be afraid, but speak, and do not be silent: for I am with you, and no man shall attack you to harm you; for I have many people in this city.'

It was *exactly* the same verse by which the Lord had spoken to me back in Lagos exactly a year previously (virtually to the day – 1 August 1961), and confirmed our call to the cities of Africa. Next to that verse in my Bible's margin back in Lagos, I had written 'Maseru' (my home town) and 'Pietermaritzburg'.

Maseru would come later. But now it was a deeply confirming word.

Only days later, on 5 August 1962, just outside Pietermaritzburg, Nelson Mandela was arrested. He would spend 27 years in prison.

15

Early lessons in evangelism

*God did not direct His call to Isaiah – Isaiah overheard God saying . . .
'Who will go for us?' The call of God is not just for a select few but for
everyone. Whether I hear God's call or not depends on the condition of
my ears, and exactly what I hear depends upon my spiritual attitude.*[1]
(*Oswald Chambers*)

About the same time as Mandela's arrest, we had our first-ever evangelistic meeting. We had been invited by the Christian organization Youth for Christ to the huge city hall of Durban.

Inauspiciously, on the way out of Pietermaritzburg, I was caught by traffic police doing 63 kph in a 60 kph (35 mph) zone! And issued with a ticket.

I had to go to the magistrate's office to pay for my speeding ticket on my return to Pietermaritzburg.

My picture had been plastered all over the city in anticipation of the 'Maritzburg Mission, so the magistrate recognized me.

'Aren't you the young man about to preach in the city hall?'

'Yes, sir,' I responded, head down and shamefaced.

'Well, young man,' he responded with a twinkle, 'may I suggest you do a talk on speeding and obeying the rules of the road?'

I'm not sure I promised to oblige, but I did have a new sermon illustration: 'Whoever keeps the whole law but fails in one point has become guilty of all of it' (James 2.10). I had been only 3 kilometres per hour over the limit. But I was held as guilty as if it had been 103.

So I paid my fine. And left promising to be a good boy!

Judging by appearances

The evangelistic meeting in Durban saw some 3,000 young people jammed into the city hall. It was terrifying! I preached my heart out and then launched into my first-ever evangelistic appeal.

Calling people forward as the sponsors had insisted, I had them sing 'Just as I Am' – that was how Billy did it! No one responded. Not a soul. Panic-stricken, I called on the choir to sing 'Just as I Am' again. We had done 11 or 12 verses of the famous song, with me feeling I was being hanged in public, when from the very back of the hall a drunk staggered forward. Along with a young boy. There and then I felt ready to give up preaching and slink back to a classroom of boys to teach Latin and French.

But God was to surprise and rebuke me for judging by appearances.

At a pastors' meeting at African Enterprise about 20 years later, a man came up to me and asked if I remembered preaching in the city hall of Durban in August 1962.

'Yes, I do,' I replied, 'but I never want to recall that disastrous meeting when the only people who responded were a drunk and a small boy.'

'I was that small boy,' said the man. 'I am in full-time ministry. And I *train* evangelists.'

I had thought that meeting was a great flop. But God made it fruitful. And who knows, maybe the drunk became a missionary!

And so I learned, nice and early in my ministry, never to judge evangelistic fruitfulness by numbers alone.

Looking to results

Back in Pietermaritzburg, our first citywide evangelistic mission opened on Monday, 12 August 1962, and produced 'Maritzburg's first-ever 6.30 p.m. traffic jam! And such were the crowds that, miraculously, it pretty much stayed that way for the whole two weeks. There was no precedent for it in the city's history. Not even up to now!

One incident taught me another valuable lesson.

The first couple of days had brought many people forward in response to the message preached. Traditionally at such gatherings, a specially trained team of counsellors is on hand to talk with those who come seeking God, offering support and prayer as needed. But as this week wore on, the responses tapered off and on Thursday, when the message was about the cross of Christ as I recall, the head of the counselling team came to me after the meeting.

'Young man, when are you going to produce? I have trained over 70 counsellors and some are in crisis because they are not being used each night. After all our work preparing for this thing, you now need to deliver.'

How very thankful I was that I had read James Packer's classic on *Evangelism and the Sovereignty of God*. In that volume he stresses that our task as preachers is to be faithful, not successful. We are called to proclaim the gospel faithfully and then leave results to the Holy Spirit. 'No one can say "Jesus is Lord" except by the Holy Spirit' (1 Corinthians 12.3).

Packer also stresses that if we see the Holy Spirit as sovereign in evangelism, it will prevent inflation when we see results, and deflation when we don't!

So I said to the Director of Counselling: 'This is the problem, brother, that you are looking to me and my team to "produce". And we can't. We can't just produce converts like rabbits out of a hat.'

Then I added: 'Why don't we all look to Jesus to bring the results we want? And why don't you and some of your counsellors meet me and my team at the Congregational church, and we'll have a night of prayer and really get our eyes off Michael and his crew, and on to Jesus?'

Bless him! He readily agreed. And the night of prayer was wonderful. Our eyes and faith refocused from the human realm to that of God.

The next evening, when I arrived at the city hall, it was packed beyond capacity. The atmosphere was electric with the presence of the Lord. I knew many would come to the Lord that night.

And they did. So huge was the response that the counselling director had a massive crisis on his hands with not enough counsellors to cope! It was a good moment. And a salutary lesson.

Mission to 'Maritzburg, 1962: Michael preaching in City Hall, Pietermaritzburg

167

We closed on 25 August with a full house in Jan Smuts Stadium, booked in faith one year previously by those three brave and visionary students.

Even to this day I still bump into people who were converted during that mission.

The way for South Africa is the way of the Master

After the mission we met in secret with the recently banned president of the African National Congress (ANC), Chief Albert Luthuli, and winner of the Nobel Peace Prize.

The South African government 'banned' over 1,600 people in the apartheid years in order to restrict their movements and silence their political opposition. Banned people were not permitted to enter places where large numbers of people met, nor to participate in political parties or to publish their writings.

According to the banning orders, we were meant to obtain permission from local authorities to meet with Chief Luthuli, so our meeting was in fact illegal.

We were deeply touched and profoundly impressed with this gentle giant of black South African politics. I remember him saying: 'The South African government must not think by banning me that they have destroyed the ANC. Far from it. The movement will just go on stronger

Meeting with Albert Luthuli in secret: Dick Peace and Michael

than ever, but maybe with leaders who won't have the same commitments to peace which I have.'

He encouraged us much when he affirmed with strong Christian conviction that 'the way for South Africa is the way of the Master'.

So here we were. Luthuli banned. Mandela arrested. The lid was being screwed down tighter and tighter. We knew that the law of lids thus screwed down was that they would finally blow.

Celebrity status?

It was so good, once everything was over, to spend a week in Maseru with my parents, who were modestly shell-shocked at what I had been up to in the 'Maritzburg city hall.

When I was on the train back to Natal, I remember weeping half an hour's worth of hot, convulsive tears of prayer for their full salvation in Christ. The conductor who came to click my ticket saw me in this state and fled embarrassed down the corridor!

The day after finally arriving back at Fuller, I was asked to report to the whole seminary community. Suddenly I was being made a bit of a celebrity. But my balloon of self-important pride was popped next day when I met my homiletics teacher, Dr Roddy, who I thought would hail me as a conquering hero and budding preacher, but he just said: 'Mike, I don't give a damn what you are at twenty-five. I want to know what you'll be at forty-five.'

Bang! That was all – as he strode off down the corridor!

It was a more than salutary word. Yes, my balloon popped. Perspective returned. And I never forgot the utterance. The test, I suddenly saw, was how I would do over the long haul.

Leaving North America

In my last year at Fuller, alongside intense studies and local preaching, I was gearing up for the full launch of African Enterprise.

As I wrote on New Year's Day 1963 to Mum and Dad:

I can't really take it all in . . . But I must say I am excited about the future and more eager than ever to get back to Africa which is where I belong. Most especially my concern is for South Africa and it is my fervent hope and prayer that circumstances will permit me to pull my weight there, at least in the initial years of my ministry.[2]

A month later I added:

> My guess is that unless something startling intervenes, my life will be spent presenting the Gospel in the various cities of Africa from Cape to Cairo. As I sense it, this is my primary call, one in all conscience which does not look like offering much security and tranquillity – either for me or a wife or family! But my blood and temperament seem to have destined me for the firing line and to turn now to anything less would be like shutting off the air I breathe. So time must tell what will become of the strange bundle of drives of which I am made up.[3]

In the summer after I graduated from Fuller, our little team got involved in the Billy Graham Los Angeles Crusade. We chauffeured team members, stuffed envelopes, licked stamps and got in on counsellor-training sessions. Anything, just to serve. And to learn. The closing meeting in the Los Angeles Coliseum closed out with 150,000 people present, and 20,000 responding to Dr Graham's appeal. I also remember praying that one day I'd get to preach to some big crowds! Oh, vanity of vanities!

I then flew to Fredericton, New Brunswick, in eastern Canada. The legendary riot of autumn colours in the trees took my breath away. I was responding to Leighton Ford, Billy Graham's brother-in-law, inviting me to join his team for a mission to the small city of New Brunswick. My assignment was the local university.

Local pastors were horrified to learn I was going on to the campus, reputedly the toughest in North America. It was known as Canada's centre of godlessness and, by one student's own boast, the campus with more fornication and intoxication than any other in the country! A challenge indeed.

On Tuesdays and Fridays I had a midday talk, and for six evenings I had a 15-minute slot on the university radio station. I remember giving one talk entitled 'Jesus Christ Died for Me and I Don't Give a Damn!' That shivered a few timbers.

Each evening after Leighton Ford's meetings in the city I had 'bull sessions', open discussion sessions, in the student halls of residence – eight in all. The reaction and response varied from extreme hostility (which later mellowed) to extreme friendliness, and numerically from 3 to 40. It was a fine intellectual exercise to defend my position against the sundry battering rams of psychology, science and sociology. I saw many areas where I needed to do some more reading. I was seldom in bed before 2.00 a.m.!

Actually very few students were hostile – most just wanted to live like the devil and find a reason to justify it. So junking Christianity was part of what the situation called for. The worst 'bull session' was in one house where I had to contend with a young Cambridge don plus the Professor of Logic. The latter was gracious and gentle, but the other was crude in his unashamed defence of free love in front of almost 60 students!

There were of course some wonderful rewards in terms of a few lives authentically transformed by the power of Christ. One young woman in particular told me she had considered suicide as a way out of all her guilt and wretchedness, but after her commitment to Christ she became a different person in a matter of days, finding for the first time in her life that she felt free of guilt and 'a real person'. Several others spoke of similar experiences, and many were provoked to the kind of serious thinking and evaluation which would in due time result in meaningful commitment.

I also managed to winkle many professing Christians out of their hiding places to stand courageously on the campus for their faith.

The experience gave me a new appreciation for my own home. I wrote to my parents:

> I must say, the longer I am out in the world the more I thank God with all my heart and soul for you, Mum and Dad, in the upbringing and standards and security you gave us. Never will I be able to express adequately all that 'home' has meant and does mean to me and if Olave and Judy and I can do half as well for our children we shall not have failed. I hope therefore that if bringing up a happy family means anything, you will never be tempted to think you have failed.[4]

A tempting offer

One day, Leighton Ford took me aside and said: 'Michael, I'd like to invite you to join me in the Billy Graham Association. I'll give you everything Billy has given me. And we can all work together.'

The offer rocked me. Imagine all that administrative support and highly professional capacity for mission set-up. Money no object. Worldwide opportunities and exposure. And I would be Billy's man, or one of them, for Africa.

'Oh, Leighton,' I responded, overwhelmed. 'Let me think and pray about this.'

But I knew what the Lord's word would be. And it came through quickly: 'No, my son. I want you to start from scratch. With nothing. No financial backing. Nothing. Just depending on me.'

Around the time of this key moment for me personally, America was rocked by the assassination of John F. Kennedy (the same day, incidentally, that C. S. Lewis died).

It was 22 November 1963 and I was in Kingston, Ontario, visiting my old friend of PTS teaching days, David Kepple-Jones. The announcement was made as we were lunching in a restaurant, and everyone just sat in shocked incredulity.

Into the silence a waitress asked, 'Do you want French fries or mashed?'

'Who cares?' I remember responding.

A petrol station attendant said that evening, 'Get your uniforms, boys; you're going to need them soon.'

A team for Africa

Back in Los Angeles there was a huge amount to do to get ready for Africa.

There was an office to set up, a director (a wonderful friend called Gene Parks) to appoint, a board to establish, money to raise, visas to work on, a mailing list to develop. Then there was packing and crating up all the team's possessions; team member and handyman Chris Smith built all the crates to save money. There were endless letters to write and a myriad friends to whom to bid tender and fond farewells.

Our team, some of whom had been part of the Mission to 'Maritzburg, was a diverse bunch. Chris was a preacher, teacher, song leader and choir trainer, carpenter and general factotum. His wife Barbara was

Barbara and Chris Smith

Judy and Dick Peace

an intercessor and prayer warrior. She and Chris loved old-time gospel music, had great voices and did duets together.

Dick and Judy Peace were mad C. S. Lewis fans. Dick, with his degrees in Electrical Engineering and now Theology, was a scholar and teacher of prodigious intellect. Judy was intellectually sharp as a razor, feisty and, like Dick, a prolific reader. On racial issues she was passionate, and saw South Africa, literally and metaphorically, in black and white!

Paul Birch swelled the bachelor ranks. Also intellectually brilliant, Paul could remember most of the world's useful information and much of its trivia as well. His special gifting was music – he was a marvellous accompanist and organist (classical), and a fine choirmaster. He always had oil to pour on any troubled waters within the team.

One or two others had considered the call to join us. Ed Gregory, who had come with me round Africa in 1961, had concluded that being long-term in Africa was not for him. Don and Joyce Ehat, who had been with us for the Mission to 'Maritzburg, had reached the same conclusion. They would all have been great additions, had the Lord led them our way.

As we prepared for departure, one enormous hurdle seemed insurmountable. We still had no residence visas for the Americans (Chris and Barbie Smith, Dick and Judy Peace), or for Canadian Paul Birch, to get into South Africa.

Our applications had been with the South African authorities for months. As a South African I was fine. Likewise Joan Gemmell, also

Paul Birch

South African, a lovely person and fine Christian, who had been working diligently in our Pasadena office and was returning with us.

We all prayed. And prayed. But nothing.

Finally, I felt God giving me a promise. Or at least an assurance.

It came from the life of Abraham. '*By faith* Abraham obeyed when he was called to go out to a place which he was to receive as an inheritance; *and he went out*, not knowing where he was to go' (Hebrews 11.8, my emphasis).

I told the team, 'We are going to go, regardless. We will leave without visas. We will act as if they have been granted. We will step out by faith.'

And we did, setting off first for New York, then to Southampton on the SS *United States*.

Shouldering responsibility

My journal as we steamed out into the Atlantic reflected conflicting emotions:

> This has been an exciting and significant day – yet my heart is heavy tonight and burdened. I fear much for our work and for our witness. It seems that we are all still spiritual babes – more worldly than spiritual, more inconsistent than consistent, more enamoured of ourselves than our Saviour, more dependent on our qualifications than on our God.
>
> For the first time ever, I think, I feel a real *spiritual responsibility* for the team – individually and corporately. I feel the need to pray as I have never done before for the individual members – and their wives – for their needs, growth, and strength. I feel an intense jealousy for the ministry that is ours, to guard it and see that it becomes all it could and should be. I feel

a deep determination not to tolerate that which could spoil or undermine our effectiveness. I am utterly resolved that we be a team comprised of men and women of God.[5]

A couple of nights later at sea I wrote:

I am still much concerned for the team, especially for our prayer deficiencies. Sometimes I truly wonder if I can ever hold this project together. I want to run away to something simpler and less exacting. Yet there can be no retreat.[6]

From Southampton it was up to Hampton Court Palace where we were to be staying with Lady Baden-Powell in her delightful, roomy annexe attached to her grace-and-favour apartment.

I drilled all the team on how to greet one of England's great aristocratic duchess-type ladies.

'You don't say "Pleased to meet you". That is definitely not done in English high society! You say "How'd you do, Lady Baden-Powell." Now got that, guys and gals? Don't let me down.'

We finally arrived at Lady Baden-Powell's apartment, knocked on the big, ancient door and waited apprehensively. Suddenly there she was in all her aristocratic grandeur, but beaming a warm welcome. I embraced her, and then turned to introduce the team, Chris first. In the apprehension of the moment, etiquette amnesia overtook him totally.

'Hi, Mrs Powell,' he beamed, holding out his hand like an American presidential candidate.

I could have slunk down a thousand feet into the slimy depths of the Thames flowing close by.

Once in our rooms I formally cast Chris to outer darkness, leaving Dick, Judy and Paul a story to dine out on ever after!

And still no visas. Anxiety was mounting. But my resolve to continue the journey regardless was firm. God would undertake to provide for us. Even if it meant committing the crates and Paul Birch's car to the high seas before visas were in hand.

The next port of call was the Schaeffers at Huémoz-sur-Ollon in Switzerland. Francis and Edith were so solicitous and caring for all of us. One big moment was my sensing the Spirit saying that I needed to be 'not only a proclaimer of the faith, but also a defender of it'.[7] In other words, Christian apologetics needed to enter my armoury more fully.

Our travel plans, visas or not, were that Paul, Chris, Barbie and Joan, crates and car would leave by sea from Venice, while Dick, Judy and I would fly down via Cairo, Khartoum, Nairobi and Salisbury (now Harare).

Another hurdle

But I got ill in Addis Ababa with typhus.

'I have never felt worse in my life,' recorded my journal.[8] I thought my last day had come, and so, I think, did the doctor and tropical medicine nurse at the Sudan Interior Mission Home in Addis. But I had to fly on to Nairobi to see if the visas were there. Time was of the essence with the crew on the high seas steaming south. What to do? Frantic phone calls followed to Archie Hart in Pietermaritzburg, former chairman of the Mission to 'Maritzburg, but his enquiries to Pretoria fell on deaf ears.

Leaving Dick and Judy in Nairobi, I flew on to Salisbury feeling like death warmed up. Jock and Effie Macaulay, Alasdair and Ranald's parents, rushed me from the airport to bed, so horrified were they by the emaciated ghost who stepped off the plane when he should have been in hospital.

Again no word in Salisbury from Pretoria. Dick and Judy followed me there to bide their time. Would I have to get the others off the boat in Beira, Mozambique? If they sailed through to Durban without visas, they would probably be turned back to Venice, their port of origin.

On 6 October I flew to Johannesburg and checked into a dumpy little hotel in Hillbrow. In body I was a wreck, and in spirit ready to toss in the towel.

Next morning, surprised to find myself still in the land of the living, I was prompted by something – I don't know what – to look at Deuteronomy chapter 8. I fell on this passage which speaks about going in and possessing the land, not ever forgetting that it was God himself who accomplished this.

I feasted on the words like a man dying of hunger and thirst.

God was bringing us into this South African land of mineral wealth and agricultural bounty. We would be mightily and even materially blessed. But we must never forget – it *all came from him*. I almost leapt from my bed like a rising Lazarus.

I knew God was promising we would get in. But there was an accompanying warning.

After breakfast I dragged my weakened self over to Pretoria to the Department of Home Affairs.

'Visas for African Enterprise?' said the Afrikaner official. 'Never heard of them. Never seen them.'

By now there was both faith in my heart and fire in my belly.

'Where are all your visa applications?' I boldly asked.

'In this big box,' he replied.

'Would you mind if I looked through it?'

'OK,' he grunted, probably wondering what kind of nutcase he had on his hands.

I spent the next two hours going through hundreds of visa applications while the official got on with his other work.

Finally, like a miner pouncing on the Cullinan Diamond, or a pirate unearthing an ancient treasure chest, I seized a jaded file: 'Applications for African Enterprise for Permanent Residence'. I had rescued it from the grave of a bureaucratic cemetery.

Even the slightly shamefaced official seemed pleasantly surprised.

'Sir,' I said, 'please process these right away. I have all these colleagues waiting in Salisbury and heading on the seas to Durban. This is really desperately urgent for me.'

He looked suitably startled. And said he would do something. At which I realized that had I not gone to Pretoria as militantly as I did, and searched as tenaciously as I had, those visa forms might not have ever surfaced. At least not for years. God had worked a miracle in the midst of the team's and my own desperate weakness. What a lesson in dependence on him!

I returned to Johannesburg and took a train that night to Basutoland. And home to my anxious mum and dad.

I alerted the team. We all needed to wait. Could the visas be issued before the boat arrived in Beira? If not, my colleagues would have to disembark there. Everything was on a knife edge.

These were not easy days. I spent most of the mornings down at the Caledon River, near our home, almost too worn out to pray. But my soul was directed towards God and I felt confident that my phone call to the officials in the Immigration Department would produce a favourable reply. But they had not decided yet. So I had to contact the ship and get the others off at Beira. I had a wire from Chris saying 'Send instructions immediately.' However, the telegram office seemed unable to get hold of the ship and I started to find myself involuntarily anxious over the situation . . .

On 9 October I journalled:

This is perhaps the deepest test of my life to date – and being so physically down I don't feel I am weathering it frightfully well. May He deliver me from anxiety, fatigue, doubt and confusion. Oh, how I need Him! I still have just enough faith to believe for a miracle on these visas. 'If Thou wilt, Thou cans't.'[9]

Next day I wrote in my diary: 'Sent telegrams to the ship and to Dick and Judy in Salisbury: "I am weary with His chastening. I seem alone and far from Him. I don't like it."'[10]

The seafaring team now disembarked, in Beira, disconsolate. Our crates went into dockside warehouses.

Then two days later, this entry: 'Had a wonderful, free time in prayer last night. The team is going to get in. And what's more South Africa is going to listen.'[11]

My sad entry on 13 October recorded:

> The ship docked [in Durban] today *sans* African Enterprise. But I am assured that all will be well. Am reading J. C. Pollock's biography of D. L. Moody – and I am encouraged. In seeing a life like Moody's I see that I am as far from being a real man of God as the earth is from the sun.[12]

My own next port of call was Pietermaritzburg where I sought the help of National Party MP for the city, Mr Howard Odell. Though a 'Nat', as we called National Party MPs, he was a believer and became enthused about us. And he was a great friend ever after.

He sent word through to Parliament to Honourable Minister Jan de Klerk, father of F. W. de Klerk, later to be President of South Africa. On my side I was already giving thanks to God, 'for this is the will of God in Christ Jesus concerning you' (1 Thessalonians 5.18 KJV).

Once in Pietermaritzburg I phoned Archie Hart. The Special Branch of the security police had visited him to enquire about African Enterprise.

The wait is over

'News of news,' said my journal. 'They are apparently now satisfied with our *bona fides* and are ready to recommend to Pretoria the issuance of visas. Now, Lord, make it final. I look to you and you alone.'[13]

Howard Odell, who always remained so warm to us, shortly thereafter burst in to see me.

'The visas have come,' he exulted jubilantly. 'Final permission has come in, signed at cabinet level by Minister Jan de Klerk.'

I later told President F. W. de Klerk that his dad had let us in. He seemed to approve!

The team, plus the next ship from Beira with our crates, headed to Durban and Pietermaritzburg. African Enterprise was open for business.

Faith in the God of Abraham had finally prevailed. His inspiration had reached us because 'no distrust made him waver concerning the promise of God, but he grew strong in his faith, as he gave glory to God, fully convinced that God was able to do what he had promised' (Romans 4.20–21).

God had once again proved himself faithful.

Part 2

LIFE AND MINISTRY
IN FULL FLIGHT

16

Taking a stand against racism

*There comes a time when a moral man can't obey a
law which his conscience tells him is unjust.*[1]
(Martin Luther King)

African Enterprise opened a little office in Braemar House, Longmarket
Street, Pietermaritzburg. Everyone looked for homes or lodging. Mine
was a spare room in the home of Chris and Barbara Smith. I bought a
bed, a cupboard and a desk. The omni-competent Chris made me some
bookshelves, which I still have. The cupboard is still in our garage! Esther
Kuhn joined us as team secretary, receptionist and general factotum. The
complement of our full team and staff was five souls.

We set up a board, and our first chairman was Dr Edgar Brookes, who
had sat in Parliament as one of two whites representing black interests.
That was an example of antediluvian politics, of course. But no other
options were open for someone like Brookes. He was Professor of History
at Natal University and a champion of human rights, especially black

First two AESA chairmen – Edgar Brookes and Alphaeus Zulu

rights, and also a founding member of the South African Liberal Party along with Alan Paton, Peter Brown and Patrick Duncan.

Our board was appalled that we said we couldn't have budgets because we didn't know what God would be asking us to do, so naturally we couldn't anticipate costs! Faith would have to see us through. This resulted in us appointing and losing a slew of finance chairmen who rather naturally resigned under the strain.

The big thing now was to pray for open doors of mission opportunities for gospel proclamation.

Naively, we all thought it would be fairly straightforward. But plain sailing, we quickly found out, was never going to be our lot.

We were, after all, in apartheid South Africa.

Christian nationalism

I once asked a leading Afrikaner how, politically and theologically, South Africa got to the place of apartheid. He responded at once, saying, 'One must start with the theological side, because what has happened in our country is due more to a theological development than a political one.'

The Boer War had left Afrikaners shattered. In effect the Boer War, and especially the loss of 28,000 women and children in the British concentration camps, was to Afrikaners what the Holocaust is today to the Jews. After all this loss of Afrikaner identity there emerged a desire to regain their honour and national pride. A small anonymous group of young intellectuals called the Afrikaner Broederbond (brotherhood) formed to try to address Afrikaner interests.

Young Afrikaner theologians studying in Amsterdam came under the influence of the Dutch neo-Calvinist theologian Abraham Kuyper, and formally adopted and adapted his ideals to their South African context. The idea of 'isolation for survival' emerged and the belief that Afrikaners, like the Israelites in the Bible, should not fraternize with foreigners or break down the walls of separation instituted, they believed, by God. Meanwhile, a group of young Afrikaner political scientists were studying in Germany and were to be inspired by ideas of German nationalism.

Many other influences were of course being processed by the Broederbond think tank, but the convergence in South Africa of these two overseas streams was like the bringing together of fire and methane: there was spontaneous combustion. Here was what seemed to be a morally valid, theologically justified and politically legitimate way not only to secure survival for the Afrikaner *Volk*, but to triumph as a nation. In fact it became 'the Christian duty of the whites to act as guardians over the non-white races until such time as they have reached that level where they can look after their own affairs'.[2]

From the time of the Nationalist victory in 1948, the Dutch Reformed Church (largely, although there were exceptions among its members) began to pour itself into the task of justifying apartheid and seeking to reconcile it with Scripture.

Basically the leaders of the Dutch Reformed Church were trying to coalesce the gospel with their nationalistic priorities, but they effectively put ideology over biblical theology. Ideology was lord.

I was to get a glimpse of Christian nationalism early in January 1965. One of my Washington contacts from International Christian Leadership was the English Christian Conservative Party MP, Sir Cyril Black, whom I had met in his House of Commons office en route back to Africa in late 1964. Knowing I was keen to start a parliamentary prayer meeting in South Africa, he introduced me to the Honourable H. J. K. Klopper, the Speaker of the Houses of Parliament in South Africa, and we went to meet him together when Sir Cyril was in South Africa.

Klopper was a diminutive man, with white hair, white goatee, aquiline nose and sharp, piercing eyes. The pleasantries behind us, I explained our errand and my delight at Sir Cyril's support, and at the Speaker's willingness to see us.

'A prayer group in Parliament, Mr Cassidy?' he replied. 'No, not necessary because we are all Christians. We all pray every day. Our Cabinet are all in church every Sunday. I myself teach a Sunday school of Bantu children every week on my farm. So, I don't think we can think of any new and special prayer group you might want to set up.'

And that was that.

Afterwards Sir Cyril and I reflected on this piety which brought forth cruel racial segregation under the rubric of Christian nationalism.

It made me think very 'thinky' thoughts. I began to realize that if theology provided the clue to the genesis of apartheid, so must theology provide the clue to the process of its dismantling. Thus Afrikaners and the Dutch Reformed Church, who put it together ideologically, must be the primary and humble agents under God in dismantling it.

To those Afrikaners who were the chief architects of it all, the grand design of apartheid policy was a beautiful building ushering in peace and prosperity for all; it was too bad about the ugly but necessary scaffolding which had to go up beside the building to get it into place.

Collisions with the system

The Mission to Ladysmith, in early 1965, our first-ever combined churches outreach in the town, produced our first collision with the system. Set-up and planning had all gone swimmingly well. Except the Dutch Reformed Church refused participation because we insisted on non-racialism and were pushing for our major evening meetings, set for three weeks in the town hall, to be interracial.

We were trusting by faith for permission to come through for multiracial attendance. The mayor was warm to us and we proceeded with confidence. Publicity went out. Counsellors were trained. Multilingual follow-up material was prepared. Excitement mounted among both white and black pastors.

Then *bang*! Just before our meetings were to get under way, we heard from the town council that permission for interracial meetings had been declined.

Regrettable decision

Now followed a decision which to this day I regret. The Mission Committee felt we just had to proceed, regardless of the circumstances, and do our best. We couldn't turn back and cancel now.

And we as the AE team agreed. Here was our first test in facing the state system. And we failed. Thankfully we never again sanctioned such a happening. The main mission meetings in the town hall went ahead without our black and brown brothers and sisters.

I was personally sick at heart, and little assuaged by the compromised arrangement set up by the Mission Committee of having a landline from the town hall to the Methodist church close by where Africans, Indians and Coloureds could come and listen.

A pitiful bunch came each night. For my part I went over to the church to sit with them until it was time for me to go to the town hall and preach. The mission took place over three difficult weeks. One night I spent the whole night in prayer with a Pentecostal pastor, praying for hearts to soften and a breakthrough to come.

God works regardless

But there were some positive stories, by God's grace and mercy.

One morning at the mission office an older woman came barrelling in and insisted on seeing me. How could I decline?

As she spoke, I remembered something from the previous evening. As I was giving the message, a verse had come flying into my mind: 'Eye has not seen, nor ear heard, neither has there entered the heart of man the things God has prepared for them that love him' (see 1 Corinthians 2.9). It wasn't in my prepared material, but it kept coming back to me.

Finally I found a place to bring it in and quote it: 'Eye has not seen, nor ear heard, neither has there entered the heart of man the things God has prepared for them that love him.'

The woman was telling me with great excitement that she had found Christ the night before. 'Tell me about it,' I said.

'Well,' she replied, 'I grew up as one of four siblings. The others were all Christians. But I was the rebel. The prodigal. I had no time for that stuff. But my mother kept praying for me. All her days. Finally on her deathbed she called me and said she wanted to give me her Bible. But, she said, before I give it to you I want to inscribe it with a very special verse for you. And with shaking and wobbly hand she wrote in it: "Eye has not seen, nor ear heard, neither has there entered the heart of man the things God has prepared for them that love him." When last night you spoke out that verse, all the prayers of my mother for me for decades came back. And all her longings for me to find Christ. And I knew at last – tonight is the night after all these years of rebellion for me to let my mother's prayers be answered and to give my life to Christ. And I did. I am overjoyed. He has come to me. Praise his name. I have been born again!'

Now imagine if I had not obeyed the Spirit's word to speak out that particular Scripture.

The broken-down car

Another story touched me. This time it was a praying wife. A man began coming each night to the town hall. He was from Rhodesia, and while passing through Ladysmith on his way to Durban, his car had broken down. The required spare part would take a week to come from Johannesburg. So he was stranded for a week, with nothing to do in the evenings except come to the town hall to the mission meetings.

The messages began to touch his heart, and his seeker instincts were aroused. So he kept coming. Also over coffee one day he said his wife was a Christian and had been praying for him for years. But he had been very resistant. Finally he said to me, 'I've heard everything you have said, but I just don't get it, can't grasp it, don't understand what you're saying.'

I said, 'Just keep coming. You need the supernatural work of the Spirit in your heart to reveal Christ to you. It will happen!'

On the last night of the mission he rushed up to the front: 'I see,' he exulted, 'suddenly I see. I understand. I'm giving my life to Christ tonight!' And he did. Nor could he wait to tell his wife how her prayers had been answered. Imagine her rejoicings.

Years later I was invited to speak in Durban to a Christian business-men's luncheon sponsored by the Full Gospel Businessmen's Association. Guess who the president of the group was? My stranded friend from the Ladysmith Mission. Yes, God works in mysterious ways, his wonders to perform. He even has control of motor-car engines!

After the mission we went to the black township, pitched a giant tent, and by God's mercy and grace had a packed-out series of evangelistic meetings for a couple of weeks until the tent was blown down in a huge thunderstorm! There was a great response to the gospel as we preached it night after night.

We pressed on with further missions, including the nationwide pre-independence mission to Basutoland, where the local communists said we had been sent by Dr Verwoerd and the Nationalist government. Sometimes you just can't win! And it seemed we were even under suspicion from the government and the security police!

Berlin

But there was no going back and I was soon to be making my stand against racism on a worldwide stage, which brought me personally into conflict and collision with the South African Dutch Reformed Church.

I found myself headed to Berlin for the first World Congress on Evangelism, sponsored by the Billy Graham Association. I had been in-vited to speak in one of the major workshops on 'Ethics of Political Nationalism: Political Nationalism as an Obstacle to Evangelism'. A précis of my paper, among others, was put in every congress participant's pigeonhole.

As I arrived at the congress hall two gentlemen, who turned out to be South African Dutch Reformed leaders, fell into step on either side, each taking an elbow and sort of frogmarching me to a seat.

'We have seen your paper,' they said, 'and we demand that you with-draw it and not deliver it, as it will set back race relationships in South Africa by twenty-five years. If you go ahead we will also tell five million people in South Africa that you are a traitor to the country.'

Berlin Congress: Michael with famous Zulu preacher Nicholas Bhengu, Berlin, 1966

'Five million people in South Africa?' I almost replied. 'I thought there were twenty-five million.' But being combative at that moment seemed counterproductive.

I told them I did not see my way clear to withdrawing my paper, but would pray over what they had said. They left like two thunderclouds gearing up to produce some lightning bolts.

Just after this I bumped into Robert Birch, father of Paul on our team, and told him of my encounter and its accompanying threats. I had about two hours to make up my mind.

'Would you like to pray about it?' Robert asked.

'Oh yes, Bob, I surely would.'

We found a secluded corner amid the throngs of congress participants. And Bob launched into fervent prayer, opening up by quoting Isaiah 54.17, which unbeknown to him was a life-verse the Lord had given me at the beginning of the AE call:

> No weapon that is fashioned against you shall prosper, and you shall con-
> fute every tongue that rises against you in judgment. This is the heritage
> of the servants of the LORD and their vindication from me, says the LORD.

The moment Robert uttered that lifetime verse, I knew he need pray no more. I had my answer. I would proceed with my paper regardless.

And I did, to a packed congress seminar hall.

Among other things, I noted that the temptation for people on both sides of the racial fence in South Africa was to subordinate Christian principle to political expediency, and to begin to equate their own political progress with the divine will.

I called this idolatrous and anti-Christian:

> The Church dare not permit itself to be aligned with the corporate self-interest of any state or race group within it. Consequently, a difficult part of the evangelistic task in South Africa is to woo people from the idea that God is concerned primarily with the promotion of the interests of their group, whether black, white or brown.[3]

The Dutch Reformed people, whom I could see across the room, were looking thunderous at my challenge to the apartheid system. I was definitely letting the South African side down.

I was in hot water and it was going to get hotter:

> Nationalism remains a legitimate force only as long as it operates within the ethical limits prescribed by the New Testament. It is never to become its own master. It is always to be under the authority of the Word.
>
> And, of course, if we start to say this, we find ourselves in collision with both the white philosophy of self-preservation without reference to the African, and the African philosophy of self-realisation without reference to the European. True evangelism must confront both these philosophies, modifying both and being seduced by neither.

I concluded:

> Evangelism's task is thus to help people, through Christian commitment, to work through the dilemma of whether they can in fact dare to love, and leave the consequences with God, whether they can dare to lose their lives in order to save them. This is no easy task when politics seem to advise realism about human nature and a selfish protection of life, so as not to lose it . . . The body of Christ is not a pretty idea, but an authentic spiritual reality uniting all kinds and conditions of people. The church in Southern Africa must therefore beware of national identifications. In crossing racial boundaries, it must also demonstrate within itself that sort of society which it desires to see in the body politic.[4]

I was no sooner done than the senior NGK (Dutch Reformed) official, face puce-red, leapt in fury to his feet and demanded my paper be expunged from the congress record. It was unfair, inaccurate – and racist. 'Yes, racist, because he calls African people blacks instead of Bantu.'

Their tirade met with no sympathy. (No! The congress would *not* expunge my paper from the congress record.) And one after the other, congress officials plus people from around the world, including senior

African American leaders from the USA, came to my defence. My antagonists were made to feel isolated. Especially when Canon King, Dean of
the Anglican Cathedral in Jamaica, said: 'If you are thrown out of South
Africa, you have a job next day in my cathedral!'

The Congress Symposium volume, when published, reported with
some understatement: 'Discussion of the explosive subject of political
nationalism provided some tense, frank and open disagreement and a
sharp clash of opposing opinions.'[5]

I left the hall feeling both battered and affirmed. As I did so, I saw the
other Dutch Reformed leader – probably an informer, I concluded – at
the exit and said, 'I'm sorry you're feeling this way. And I know you are
very angry.'

'I just want to vomit and go home,' he spat out with angry venom.

As I walked away, I bumped into Carl Henry, the great American
Evangelical theologian: 'Michael,' he said with sympathy, 'I knew you had
problems in South Africa but I didn't know the half of it.'

John Stott put his arm round my shoulders and said, 'Maybe, Michael,
there are some people in South Africa whose support you just should not
have.'

My antagonists then went to the world media, but found no joy there.
Some papers claimed they wanted to take up my cause. I declined. 'Let the
Lord work it out,' I said.

As the Congress proceeded I found myself feeling bitter towards these
Afrikaans brethren. Then one morning Dick Halverson, pastor of a great
Presbyterian church in Washington DC in which I preached some years
later, spoke about Acts 2 and how the mission of the Church, reflected in
verse 47 which records that people were added to the Church daily, was the
spontaneous, effervescent overflow of the fellowship and togetherness of
the believers recorded in verse 44: 'All [who] believed were together.' And
in verse 42: 'They continued . . . in the apostles' doctrine and *fellowship*,
and in breaking of bread, and in prayers' (kjv, my emphasis). Fellowship
and unity were integral and central to everything else.

The Lord's people, Dick then added, needed to be in reconciliation.
And he recalled how Jesus said: 'If your brother has anything against
you, first go to him and be reconciled and then bring your gift' (see
Matthew 5.23–24). I was immediately convicted that I needed to confess my bitterness to the Dutch Reformed brethren, and seek forgiveness
and reconciliation.

Exiting the congress hall for a tea break, they were the first people
I bumped into. I confessed my bitterness, asked for forgiveness and

Berlin Congress: Haile Selassie and Billy Graham; crowd shot

extended the right hand of fellowship. The senior man accepted it. The other refused. I was beyond the pale.

The older one said, 'Young man, I am so sad for you because I see a young man of potential throwing his life away.' The other brother, the one I assumed was our informer, looked set to go about his informing business.

Under suspicion

I think that is exactly what happened because while I was away, my parents, now just retired from Basutoland and living in Hilton, Natal, were visited by a Mr Piet Viljoen (not his real name), supposedly from the Durban branch of the South African Broadcasting Corporation, saying he had heard of their son's presence at the World Congress on Evangelism in Berlin and would like to interview him. And he had some questions. For example, what passport does he travel on, how is he financed, what are the aims of African Enterprise, why did he travel overseas and what was he really doing there? And what are his links to the United States?

Dad, naive, dear man that he was, was taken in. Mum smelled a rat at once. She got his name and contact details and said she was sure her son would just love to be interviewed on radio on his return.

I duly phoned Mr Viljoen in Durban on my return and set up an interview time. I acted totally innocent and, following his peppering me with questions, I flooded Mr Viljoen in an elegant soliloquy as to what AE was about, its vision, history to date, purposes, evangelistic aims in South Africa, and how we got our finances from prayer partners and individual churches and believers.

I could see him registering me as something of a nincompoop! But while I had the floor and the ear of the South African Special Branch in the guise of a radio interviewer, I kept up my monologue, giving him everything I could about the work as he furiously took down notes.

I'd rather he has the truth, I thought, than his own bunch of surmised conspiratorial and seditious guesswork.

I finished up by asking him when I should be there for the radio interview.

'Oh well, Mr Cassidy,' he replied, 'I think the Berlin Congress is old news now, so we won't proceed with an interview. I am so sorry!'

I put on my most crestfallen look. After all this disclosure and giving so much information, and now no interview. I had to act devastated!

But I came away realizing what it was like to be under suspicion by the security police.

This was not quite the end of the story with Mr Viljoen. Years later, my assistant, Lois Stephenson, was approached by the said Mr Viljoen, who offered to have her salary doubled if she would try to listen in on all my conversations with overseas visitors, and copy to the Special Branch any letters I received from overseas.

Lois, like my mum, put on a good act, pretended to be interested in his proposition, asked for his details and said she would get back to him. Then she came immediately to me.

I rang Mr Viljoen and asked him to come to see me in my office and roasted him good and proper. 'If you want, sir, to know what I'm on about, don't go behind my back to my staff. Just come to my office with your photostat machine, go through all my files, and copy whatever you wish.'

The following Sunday, about 6.45 a.m., just as I was preparing to rise for church, the phone rang. Mr Viljoen!

'Mr Cassidy, I just want to apologize. The Lord has convicted me about what I was doing to you.'

I thought: Only, but only in South Africa, land of mixed-up religion and politics, and of contorted Christian Nationalism, could such a bizarre phone call happen.

I thanked him and asked him to visit me at my home the following week.

This was another bizarre conversation of cut and thrust. 'Were you tape recording me in my office last week?'

'Yes, Mr Cassidy,' he replied somewhat shamefacedly. I shook my head. He looked nonplussed. Then he commented, 'And I gather you're going to Australia next week.'

Well-informed guy, I thought. I then told him how I would be sharing information about the AE work in churches, preaching, and asking prayer partners and little old ladies to support us financially.

His eyes widened. 'Thank you, Mr Cassidy, for telling me what you will be doing in Australia. It would have been very expensive to follow you all round Australia!'

Yes, only in South Africa!

Our resolve to resist the system

We recognized that over the centuries the Church had embraced three different postures vis-à-vis the state: *withdrawal* from the state (as many South African Evangelical and Pentecostal churches had done), *active identification* with it (as the Dutch Reformed Church had done) and *active resistance* to it (as for example the Catholics, Methodists and Anglicans in South Africa). We resolved, with most of South Africa's mainline denominations, to adopt the latter position, even if on occasion it might require civil disobedience.

This position, incidentally, in South Africa had an interesting pedigree on the Afrikaner side.

Back in 1914 there was a rebellion among numbers of Boers against the South African government for going into the First World War on the side of Britain. The official position of the Dutch Reformed Church then was non-condemnation of the rebels. In the furore of post-rebellion debate, according to a Dutch Reformed theologian, Carel F. A. Borchardt, the Dutch Reformed Council, manifestly sympathetic to the rebels, 'allowed that it is only permissible to resist the state should the state act in contradiction to God's laws'.[6]

As an Afrikaner, David Bosch, who became a very strong supporter of the AE ministry, brought forth an interesting observation on this episode:

> Today the sons and daughters of those same Afrikaner rebels of 1914 denounce any form of Christian support for liberation movements and armed rebellion as anti-Christian and ungodly. Most are solid supporters of a theology of the status quo, whereas their fathers supported a theology of revolution.[7]

This reality prompted Bosch to 'venture a thesis that the more a church supports a violent revolution in the pre-revolutionary period, the more that same church will become a captive of the new regime after the revolution'.[8] In fact, this is what we see happening in South Africa today. Many who fought in the struggle against apartheid have failed to stand up to the widespread corruption within our current government.

As far as African Enterprise was concerned, moving forwards in the racially convulsed and politically convoluted context of South Africa, we formally embraced the posture of Francis Schaeffer, at whose wells of conviction we had already drunk for some years:

> When Jesus says in Matthew 22:21 'Give to Caesar what is Caesar's, and to God what is God's', it is not:
>
>
>
> GOD and CAESAR
> It was, is, and always will be:
> GOD
> and
> CAESAR
>
>
>
> The civil government, like all of life, stands under the Law of God ... When *any office* commands that which is contrary to the Word of God, those who hold that office abrogate their authority and they are not to be obeyed. And that includes the State. God has ordained the State as a *delegated* authority; it is not autonomous. The State is to be an agent of justice, to restrain evil by punishing the wrongdoer, and to protect the good in society. When it does the reverse, it has no proper *authority*. It is then a usurped authority and as such it becomes lawless and is tyranny ...
>
> *If there is no final place for civil disobedience, then the government has been made autonomous, and as such, it has been put in the place of the Living God*, because then you are to obey it even when it tells you, in its own way and time, to worship Caesar. And that point is exactly when the early Christians performed their acts of civil disobedience, even when it cost them their lives.[9]

A final and telling point that we in African Enterprise had to take on board was that a proper biblical submission to the state meant living under its penalties when one chose to defy it. Martin Luther King, at whose wells we had also drunk, had taught us clearly:

> There comes a time when a moral man can't obey a law which his conscience tells him is unjust. And the important thing is that when he does that, he willingly accepts the penalty – because if he refuses to accept the penalty, then he becomes reckless, he becomes an anarchist.[10]

All this meant that if the South African authorities banned me, or put some sanction on African Enterprise, we had no option but to submit to it.

But on the race issue we knew that we could not embrace apartheid with one hand and hold the Bible in the other. Ne'er the twain could meet.

And on that, in spite of some initial failures, as in the Ladysmith Mission, we took our stand. There was really no option.

17

In the days of our youth

Remember your Creator in the days of your youth.
(Ecclesiastes 12.1 NIV)

It was fun being young and in ministry! We were all in our late twenties, with everything before us.

And our young team was expanding. We added to our ranks Abiel Thipanyane, who turned down a job offer as official interpreter for the Lesotho government to join our team, and theologian Ebenezer Sikakane, both as evangelists; and John Tooke in charge of publicity and youth activities. John and his wife, Rona, had both been converted during the Mission to 'Maritzburg in 1962.

We also sensed the need to expand the work into independent Africa. After all, our calling was to the cities of Africa, not just of southern Africa.

During our 1969 Nairobi mission, shared with my friend Festo Kivengere, a great exponent of the East African Revival, I asked him to

Ebenezer Sikakane

195

Abiel and Jemina Thipanyane and family

join us as leader of an East African AE team. Although Festo had been approached by other ministries, he and his wife Mera said they felt called to African Enterprise.

'All the overseas offers are attractive,' Festo said to me, 'but God is telling us, we need to be part of an indigenous, African ministry. We want to join African Enterprise.' This opened many new doors for ministry all over Africa. (More about this later.)

Back in Natal our young team were caught up ministering to the young, for example our mission to Natal University in Durban.

On campuses we needed to appeal to students with the gospel on the basis of academic integrity, and so our modest training in apologetics came to the fore. Here we were reaching opinion-makers and future leaders.

Although we were told to expect much apathy on the Durban campus, thankfully we did not encounter this. There was no apathy, only excitement and interest. Inevitably, some of it was hostile, which was a bit unnerving.

Thus I did feel very nervous participating in the first university symposium I'd ever been in – this model being one where a guest spoke with two or three others of different standpoints, and then was grilled with questions from the floor.

I remember walking around in the dark outside the hall and saying, 'Lord, I can't think of any place on Planet Earth right now where I want to be less than in this place at this moment, facing this audience.'

Team: Chris Smith, Abiel Thipanyane, Michael, Ebenezer Sikakane and John Tooke

All I got back from the Lord was a Scripture promise, a life-verse in fact, which he had given me at the launching of AE: 'My son, as I was with Moses, so I will be with you. I will not fail you or forsake you' (see Joshua 1.5).

The theme was 'The Resurrection of Jesus Christ: Fact or Fairytale?' To my real astonishment I felt suddenly unafraid, and went on to answer questions confidently, and in a closing word at the end of the evening carried the day! No one was more amazed than I. Nor more thankful, for I had seen the faithfulness of God coming through on behalf of such a weak vessel.

I remember a student, Alan Chattaway, who had been converted in the run-up to the mission, rushing up to me first thing one beautiful morning and saying, 'Guess what? Something amazing has been happening to me these last few mornings.'

'Let me tell you,' I responded. 'You've been noticing Nature for the first time!'

'Yes!' he exulted. 'However did you know? For the first time ever, I've been seeing the signature of God wherever I look.'

So we were on our way with university missions. It was exhilarating. And we had a philosophy of university missions in place, even as we started out. This I later articulated in the Lausanne Congress on Evangelism in 1974 where I was assigned the seminar on University Evangelism!

John Tooke and Abiel Thipanyane get some exercise!

Our approach in campus missions must focus on presenting one basic conviction: that Christianity is true and that the historically risen Jesus is indeed the Truth meeting man's needs.

Truth is personal and not simply propositional. It lies primarily in a person, not a system, although the Christian system as such is the one best able to make sense of all the data of life.[1]

Spearhead

The Basutoland nationwide pre-independence mission of 1966 had lots of incidental youth ministries in both high schools and the university, but our next focused mission for young people was the Spearhead Youth Mission in 1967 to the southern suburbs of Cape Town.

We were there for six months and had a ball! In those years we invested a huge amount of time and energy into preparation and also follow-up of those who responded during missions. Of course this kind of extended time away was certainly much easier before team members had children, and while we were all still very young.

Young people from all the churches, plus outsiders, thronged in. All the meetings were packed. Our so-called CHUM (Christian Home

Spearhead, 1967

Unit Meeting) groups were a smash hit. And our evening rallies on the Plumstead cricket grounds were a crowded riot of fun, fellowship, revival and spiritual response.

I recollect the struggle in finding a venue where the meetings could be interracial. We were faced with vigorous obstruction all round.

In the police station I asked the commander, 'May we meet in the open air, whites and blacks, in Wynberg Park?'

'No, sir.'

'May we meet in the Wynberg cinema?'

'No, sir.'

On and on we pressed through an assortment of venues. Negative every time. Finally I said, 'What about the Plumstead cricket ground?'

'We don't have authority over sports fields,' said the station commander.

'Right, Officer,' I responded. 'That's where we'll go. And our meetings will be interracial.'

He and his colleagues stared as I left rejoicing.

John Tooke and son Lance at Spearhead Mission

However, our team continued to be closely watched. John Tooke remembers:

> It was with some surprise that my wife, Rona, and I discovered that our phone was being tapped. The innocence of our activities I had always understood as obvious. Persuading people to come to Christ through word or deed could not be a more benevolent and gracious act toward another person, bringing as it does inestimable good and eternal hope through the Gospel. Having this perceived as subversive to the state put us in the crosshairs of the security apparatus. It was our insistence that we regard all those we cooperated with and communicated to without racial categorization or distinction that had now made us suspects and, in the view of the security police, as probably associates of revolutionary agendas.[2]

Anyway, we pressed on regardless. And we remember it all with such joy and huge thanksgiving for the hundreds of young people who came to Christ. And people like Christine Milligan and Joan Evans who became AE supporters still are today, with their regular prayer group whose members meet in Kenilworth to pray for our ministry.

Wits University

Next up was Wits University (University of the Witwatersrand) in late 1967. There was huge prayer all over the world for this strategic mission in Johannesburg, the commercial capital of South Africa. The prayer was astonishingly widespread. We were not to know then that the Wits Mission would spawn a citywide mission to Johannesburg two years later, which

Wits University Mission discussion group, 1967

in turn spawned in the Lord's mysterious economy the great coming together of South African church leaders in the historic South African Congress on Mission and Evangelism in Durban in March 1973.

Almost all Christian societies (Anglican, Baptist, Methodist, Evangelical, ecumenical and even some Catholics) threw their weight behind the Wits Mission.

The meetings were all well attended, many students coming to Christian commitment, and our team, guest missioners and interns fanned out into the student halls of residence to meet and counsel students at a personal level.

David Bliss, a Princeton student and one of two American interns who joined us, made quite a hit (basically by being hit!) in an unexpected arena.

Some students from the university boxing team approached him, big fellow that he was, and said the Wits University heavyweight champion through illness had just dropped out from a boxing tournament against some big-shot opponent, set for that night, and would David step in for him and top the bill for the final fight of the evening?

David, ever spiritually alert, saw the invitation as a chance to connect for the Lord to the students!

'Well,' he replied, 'I've never boxed before, but I have seen it on television. Look, I have a Bible study to lead in one of the halls of residence this evening, but yes, sure, I'll come to the boxing arena after that.'

Needless to say, had I as Team Leader known of this deal, I would have stepped in to prevent what was clearly a very risky exercise!

Anyway, Dave arrived at the tournament ready to settle its outcome. He had on an old vest and running shorts and a pair of antiquated tennis shoes.

The opposing Goliath smelled blood. And as the bell rang he leapt like a panther across the ring and delivered the only blow of the fight, a sledge-hammer uppercut to the face and jaw, and knocked Dave out stone cold!

So Mission '67 at Wits left quite a mark on Dave. And he carries it on his lip to this day!

But this brave and sporting gesture from one of our mission team spread round the campus, with students saying, 'If this Christian guy from the mission team could do something as sporting as this, we'd better turn up to find out what these guys have to say!'

And they did. In force.

Mission '67 at Wits was also determinative for Dave Bliss's future, in that it birthed in him a call to return to South Africa for a lifetime of missionary service here.

Private school access

Early in 1968 I received a momentous letter from the Revd Harold Clarke, chaplain of Michaelhouse School, asking if I would come and do a mission to my old school.

I call this letter momentous because the Michaelhouse Mission, conducted later that year, opened up almost all the senior private schools of South Africa to African Enterprise for years and years thereafter.

I find it hard to believe I did that mission on my own, as the invitation was to me only, and not the team. So I was preacher in the morning and evening (voluntary) chapel services to which nearly the whole school came, teacher in all the Divinity classes throughout the week, counsellor (all afternoon every afternoon), song leader in the services, plus general cook and bottle-washer. But I suppose I was young!

The mission was later described by the rector, Tommy Norwood, in both written and public utterance, as 'the greatest week in the history of the school',[3] and on Speech Day that year as 'one of the most important events I have witnessed here'.[4] It saw some 25 or 30 per cent of the whole school come to Christian commitment, including, in the weeks after the mission, a dramatic, deep and lasting conversion of Tommy Norwood himself.

All down the years I have met men who say the Michaelhouse Mission was determinative for their lives. Somehow the Lord just owned the whole thing, and the Holy Spirit did a deep work.

Notable also among those who came to faith were Derek Morphew, who later headed up the whole Vineyard denomination in South Africa, and is a prolific author of theological books; Garth Collins, who gave his life full-time to an amazing Christian ministry to South African parliamentarians, and to parliaments in wider Africa; Jeremy Wex, who went into the Anglican ministry; Peter Twycross, also going into Christian ministry; and David Hotchkiss, who first in AE and then in several radio stations gave his life to Christian radio.

Looking back on that mission some 47 years earlier, David Hotchkiss has written:

> Chapel was mostly just boring . . . worse than some lessons. But I believed in God, and it seemed that his requirements were demanding, and church services, or chapel seemed to be one of the demands, so I tried to make the best of it.
>
> Then in my matric year came the mission to Michaelhouse. These were mostly voluntary chapel services – an opportunity to earn extra 'God-points'. I was there reluctantly on the second day . . . and heard a different message. This was not about what I had to do for God, but about what He had done for me! This was life with a different perspective! I was there every night for the rest of the week, just to try to get my brain around this new concept. It was almost unbelievable! By the end of the week, I was convinced that I had nothing to lose by surrendering my life to God who had made me and who loved me. I came away filled with a peace and purpose I had never before experienced.
>
> I was one of many in the school who had taken that step, and it was exciting then to grow in fellowship with others, and in understanding the Bible in a new way. It was the start of a walk with God that continues . . .[5]

There is one counselling encounter I particularly remember. The smallest boy in the school, I'll call him Frederickson, came to see me. He said he was dreadfully unhappy.

'Why?' I asked.

'Well, you see, sir, I wear toe-bangs and everyone teases me.'

'What's a toe-bang, son?' I enquired.

'Well, sir, it's my type of shoe, and it has leather threads over the front end of the shoe. Look! It's so old-fashioned.'

'Well, Frederickson,' I went on, 'would it help if somehow you got new shoes?'

'Oh, yessir!'

'Well, son, let me ring your dad.' Which I did.

Mr Frederickson, a Durban businessman, was deeply concerned to hear his son was so unhappy at Michaelhouse. 'Is there anything that can be done?'

'There is,' I replied. 'I need you to get him a new pair of shoes in the latest style.'

Relief. Relief! Mr Frederickson responded beautifully. A pair of new shoes, not toe-bangs, duly arrived at the school. And young Frederickson lived happily ever after!

Later the boy wrote me a letter expressing 'undying gratitude'. And I was enthroned at the top of his pops for ever and a day!

Hilton College

Shortly thereafter came a mission invitation from Raymond Slater, head-master of Hilton College, the big rival school in the area to Michaelhouse. That mission also saw some 25 to 30 per cent of the school responding to Christ.

I realized these school missions constituted an oil strike, and they emerged as some of the most significant ministries AE would ever undertake. The results were always very far-reaching, as numerous testimonies confirm.

One fun story comes from prominent Baptist minister, Gavin Sklar-Chik:

Here is my unforgettable memory of the 1968 Mission. I was a new boy at Hilton. I was one of the shortest boys in the school. I more than made up for this by being Jewish and having a lot of chutzpah.

As Michael was on his way to preach on the first evening of the mission I stretched out my hand and wished him 'Good Luck Sir.'

During the mission I was searching for meaning in my life and went for a one on one chat with Michael. He said to me: 'One day you will be a light to your Jewish people.'

Years later, by this time a young Baptist minister in Durban, I visited Hilton College to share my testimony of how Jesus found an insecure little Jewish boy from a divorced family. On my way to speak I arranged to have afternoon tea with Michael. As I was leaving Michael put out his hand and returned the compliment: 'Good Luck Sir,' he chuckled.

So you just never know what will happen when Gospel seeds are sown in young lives. Forty one years later I am still following Jesus and have been a Baptist pastor for 32 years – and still enjoying ministry.[6]

Hilton opened up again four years later in 1972 and we had what I consider maybe our greatest private school mission ever. Some 45 per cent of the school professed commitment to Christ, and 1,500 Christian books were purchased, some of the boys even reading books at night via torches under their blankets. Scores of boys came for counselling, and on the final Sunday I counselled non-stop for ten hours.

Every late evening we chatted over hot chocolate with the headmaster, Raymond Slater, and his wife Charlotte about the day. His pastoral concern for the lads was awesome. I consider him possibly the greatest headmaster I ever worked with, and we became the deepest of lifelong friends until he died. And Charlotte still follows AE and prays for us faithfully.

Alan Smedley, who became the chaplain of Michaelhouse, was one of many boys deeply affected. Already a Christian, he writes later of the mission's impact:

> The mission to Hilton became a watershed event. For the first time boys heard that Christian faith involved a relationship with Christ. It was a revolutionary concept and when Michael made the appeal for boys to make a commitment to Christ as Saviour and Lord, many responded, including most of my friends. In fact a large proportion of the matric class became Christians. This had a profound effect on the school. Overnight Bible Study groups sprung up in the boarding houses and the Christian faith became real and relevant. The ongoing domino effect, I believe, changed the nature of the school. It moved from being a fairly harsh hierarchical environment into one where there was much more caring and compassion. Today, virtually all of my closest friends will trace the start of their Christian pilgrimage back to the AE mission to Hilton in 1972. I personally am deeply grateful to God for what it meant in my life. I am not sure if I would have ended up being the Chaplain to Michaelhouse for the past 25 years, if that mission and its influence on myself and many others had not taken place![7]

Actually on many South African campuses in the years after that Hilton mission, student Christian leadership came from these Hilton converts.

University of Cape Town – and Carol

One of our greatest student missions was to Cape Town University.

The main initiative came out of the Student YMCA, its director Mick Milligan, and his wife Christine (still, as mentioned above, an ardent prayer supporter of AE). An awesome publicity campaign, one of the best we ever had, preceded our arrival, and the university was abuzz as our team stepped on to the campus.

A day or so before the mission opened, Chris Smith and I were with a group of YMCA students stuffing envelopes for final publicity mailings when into the room stepped a stunningly beautiful young woman.

Chris Smith's eyes were alight as he came over to me. 'Mike,' he said, 'just look at her. If you fumble the ball this time you have really had it!' This was Chris all over, forever the incorrigible matchmaker. I discarded his remark without a thought.

But who was she? Chris's rapid-fire investigation revealed that she was Carol Bam, brought in by the Milligans and Student YMCA leaders to be an assistant missioner in one of the women's halls of residence, replacing a lady missioner, Joyce Scott, who had had to drop out at the last minute because of contracting malaria. A sovereign mosquito bite had landed Assistant Missioner Carol Bam on the team!

Chris remained captivated. 'Mike, you must date that girl,' he pleaded all week. I ignored him, as I'd done in all previous missions when he'd tried to pick some lovely choirgirl or pianist for me. There was a job to be done. And besides that, I had a policy never to date anyone during missions. It had stood me in good stead thus far.

The mission meetings began with a packed-out multimedia show exposing the barrenness and lostness reflected in the popular songs of the day. Our US interns, Eric Miller and Don Andreson, had put this together with professional skill. Our lunch-hour symposia involved two or three

Enter Carol Bam

206

non-Christian exponents of an issue alongside the Christian view. It was always my view, and still is, that Christian truth authenticates itself when set alongside the non-Christian alternatives.

Coming away from the 'Sex: Rules or Free Love?' symposium, one big-time lover boy was heard to say to his friend, 'You must admit Cassidy's line on things made more sense.'

One evening, Assistant Missioner Carol Bam asked if I would go with her for coffee with two atheist friends who had asked if she would line up such an encounter with me.

It was the first time we sat side by side in the cause of the gospel. It would not be the last.

By God's grace many students came to Christ. For example, Andrew Judge, who went into the Anglican ministry, Rod McDade and Mike Patton who went into medical missionary work, and Paddy James, who has followed the Lord all his days since then, and we are still in touch.

On the Saturday after the formal mission ended, the whole team plus the assistant missioners went on a picnic. Chris Smith continued pounding me to date the mysterious Carol Bam. She seemed totally preoccupied looking after Mick and Christine Milligan's children. Very distant, in fact. Though she did tell us in small talk that she was being interviewed early in the new week for a teaching job at Westerford High School. Fine – so what?

Finally at the end of the afternoon I asked Assistant Missioner Bam if she would join me for a game of tennis the following Tuesday. To my astonishment she agreed.

Next day Chris and I went hiking on the north side of Table Mountain. All the way up, Chris maintained a relentless bombardment about dating Carol Bam. I told him that the more he pushed me, the more resolved I was to do no such thing.

Finally, when we were well up the flank of the mountain, Chris said, 'Mike, won't you just pray with me about Carol?'

I relented. 'OK – if it will make you feel better.'

So we sat down on the edge of a ledge with a spectacular view of the southern suburbs of Cape Town.

Chris prayed and we then headed down the mountain.

I had only gone about ten paces when I heard within me a compelling and unmistakeable Voice: 'My son, this is the girl I have for you. Go right ahead.'

I was stunned. We reached the car with my secret intact.

That Sunday night I was due to preach in the mission's first follow-up service in Rosebank Methodist Church. There from the pulpit I saw, halfway back in the church, Assistant Missioner Carol Bam.

And I loved her.

The service over, I was heading back to the hall for tea when up the path came Carol Bam. Apparently some students said to each other as we entered the hall, 'They look good together.'

That night I went to bed with my heart racing.

In the early hours of the morning I was almost shaken awake. It was the Lord on the line again.

'You must stop Carol taking that job. Because she will be with you in Johannesburg and the States next year.'

A strange word. Could it mean we would be married by then?

There was a sense of urgency in the Spirit's word about arresting Carol's process of accepting the teaching job at Westerford the following year.

After breakfast I acted fast and phoned her home. Her mum said she had already left for Muizenberg where she was teaching in the local high school. But she would convey the message that I had phoned.

Late in the afternoon Carol rang back.

'Would you come out to dinner with me tonight?' I asked nervously.

She hesitated. 'Well, I have a lot of marking to do tonight, so we would have to be quick and get back early.'

She may have a surprise coming, I thought to myself.

Thus did universities and schools across South Africa, and later across Africa, open to us. And thus did something very special open for me!

Oh, yes, nothing ever did come of that tennis date!

18

Romance

―――――――・◆・―――――――

Let her be the one [you have] appointed.
(Genesis 24.14)

Though some people can be called to be single, I had not felt that would be God's calling for me.

In fact, at the time of my conversion in October 1955, when I got my prayer-life going, I had begun praying daily for the woman God had appointed for me to marry. No, I wouldn't pray for a wife, but for the particular girl, now presumably alive somewhere, whom God had marked out for me.

In my prayer diary for years, next to my daily prayers for 'Mum and Dad, Olave and Judy', was the cryptic code entry 'My D'. That stood for 'My Darling'. Whoever she was, and wherever she was, I wanted to remember her daily, praying she would be 'kept for me, and me for her'.

Certainly I never guessed at that point that she was a little 12-year-old, with bulletproof stockings, cycling off to school every day in Cape Town!

Cambridge had not allowed for romantic escapades, and while a couple of little flutters followed in the months after leaving university, they were not enough for serious romantic contention.

Fuller Seminary was different, as I have already told. One day in late 1964, when I was feeling particularly challenged about the whole relationship thing, I was driving out to speak to a women's group at Bel Air Presbyterian Church in west Los Angeles. I was early and found there was time to pull my old car (the Chariot of Fire, as it was known at Fuller) off the road in the countrified hills near the church, so I could have a little time of prayer.

As I began praying, the story of Isaac and Rebekah came into my soul. Sitting in my car in that deserted spot in the Bel Air hills, I read the story in Genesis. Isaac was wanting to get married. And his father Abraham knew it and called his servant, Eliezer, to him and made him swear by the LORD, the God of heaven and of the earth, that you will not take a wife for my son from the daughters of the Canaanites, among whom I dwell, but will go to my country and to my kindred, and take a wife for my son, Isaac.   (Genesis 24.3–4)

The servant duly goes back to Abraham's ancestral home in Mesopotamia, seeking the maiden and praying, 'Let her be the one you have appointed' (see Genesis 24.14).

The story hit me: I would not meet 'the one appointed' for me in the United States but back in 'my country' (Genesis 24.3). I needed to wait until I was back in South Africa.

In some ways I had lived in Genesis 24 ever after. And prayed accordingly.

Now here I was, five years later, in my own country, and seemingly about to connect a few hours later to this one whom God had appointed.

My excitement knew no bounds. I was nearly 33. I had waited quite a while.

Carol

I duly tracked down the Bam home in Paradise Road, Newlands. Meeting her parents, lovely as they were, scared me to death. But I survived!

Carol suggested an inexpensive little restaurant close by. While walking from the car to our appointed eating place, Carol said: 'I had a very strange experience today. I went to see the head of Westerford High School and he said he had adapted his programme for next year to give me exactly the job I wanted – teaching Matric Biology. But I suddenly felt the strangest and strongest feeling that for some reason I just could not accept the job there and then. He's given me three days to decide.'

The job! The job! That was the early hour's message to me that same morning: 'You must stop Carol taking that job. Because she will be with you in Johannesburg and the States next year.'

That could only mean, I realized, that we would be married by then. It was confirmation. I resolved in my heart that I would propose to her that very night. My strategy would be to get the meal over as expeditiously as possible and then go to some romantic spot for the main business of the evening! Which certainly wasn't eating.

I don't know whether Carol queried the speed at which I gobbled my food before suggesting we take a quick drive down to the beach at Hout Bay. Brave, unsuspecting soul, she agreed.

Leaving my little car at the waterfront, we stepped out in the moonlight to walk along the beach.

We must have gone only about 300 metres when I stopped the polite small talk and cut to the quick with the Biggest Question I would ever put to anyone.

'Carol, you are just the kind of girl I want to marry. Will you marry me?'

She looked shocked, to say the least!

'Uh, well, I can't say yes. And I can't say no.'

I paused a few moments. One can't let these girls procrastinate, you know!

'Well, Carol, which is it to be?'

'Yes,' she replied. And we threw ourselves into each other's arms.

Later, Carol, who is the most cautious and considered and deliberate person I know, told me that the Lord just miraculously took her over at that moment. She had had a very traumatic previous engagement and had vowed to herself she would never marry anyone unless she had known them for two years. Now all this was happening in about two hours!

'Michael proposing on our first date was certainly a miracle,' she said much later, 'but I tell you, my accepting was the biggest miracle of all. The Lord somehow just flooded into my soul, took me over completely and said, "This is going to be fine. You can say yes!"'

And thus it was. We walked back to the car hand in hand and light-headed.

In the car on impulse I turned on the radio, which I did not often do. And out from it soared that magical romantic song from *South Pacific* about meeting a stranger on 'some enchanted evening . . .'

We agreed we should not tell anyone – not her parents, nor mine, nor the dear, doggedly persistent matchmaker, Chris Smith. Not just then, anyway.

'Well,' said Carol, 'you will certainly never again be able to talk to young people responsibly on "Love, Courtship and Marriage".'

'Mmm,' I replied. 'What I'll tell them is: "This is the deal: you can only propose on your first date if you have prayed daily for fourteen years for the right girl." That'll slow 'em down!'

I'm not quite sure when we got in. But I suspect it was too late for Carol to do much marking. I had destroyed her teaching tasks for that evening. And her job for the following year!

*

The next days were halcyon indeed. We were both on a cloud. But we had to keep our secret intact for the moment and therefore meet in private. It was a challenge.

Meanwhile, Chris Smith was harassing me daily that I really needed to date Carol Bam. How I kept a straight face I will never know! Never had I thought I could lie, prevaricate and dissemble as I did that week. I had to honour Carol's request that we not tell anyone until she was ready. Chris even produced his prayer diary and showed me with a flourish an entry he had written in it – 'that God will bring Mike and Carol Bam together in Christian marriage'.

At one point Chris exclaimed as we drove somewhere, 'Mike, goodness, how did you get all this beach sand in your car?' Hout Bay beach had left its trademark. My pathetic pleading of ignorance almost undid me. But I pulled it off. A close call!

Carol and I secretly planned that the following weekend we would go away to Franschhoek to the farm of her close friends, Bronnie and Mike Pickering. But first of all on the Saturday morning Chris and I had an appointment in Cape Town with a visiting board member from African Enterprise USA (AEUSA).

All the way into town Chris pleaded with me to date Carol Bam. I said I wouldn't consider it unless he stopped hassling me. But he had one last card to play. 'OK, Mike. But I want to make one final request. I want you to read Genesis 24, the story of Isaac and Rebekah, which the Lord put heavily on my heart this morning for you.'

Of course I nearly flipped. The dear man did not know I had been living with that chapter, day and night, all the previous week. Inside, my heart leapt for joy. It was further supernatural confirmation from the Lord.

'Well, Chris,' I replied casually, 'I'll think about it.' And that was that! Chris bore all the marks of a defeated man.

In the late afternoon, out in Franschhoek on the Pickerings' beautiful fruit farm, Carol said she'd like to show me some of the farm, with which she was already familiar.

'We'll come with you,' said innocent Bronnie.

'Oh, don't worry,' replied Carol. 'I can show him myself.'

As we went off together, Bronnie smelled a rat.

When we got back, a bottle of champagne was on the dinner table and Bronnie and Mike were quizzically beaming. 'May we propose a toast?' came the loaded question.

'OK,' said Carol shyly, as the Pickerings both exploded in delight.

Our secret was out.

Sharing the news

Very early next morning I went into the vineyards to pray and walk. My world, like the world around me – the exquisite mountains of Franschhoek – was luminous with doxologies. Then suddenly I had the very strangest sense, almost spooky, of Charles and Honey Fuller beaming down on me in approval from heaven and saying: 'Mike, we are so happy and thankful for Carol. We rejoice.' They were so close I felt I could reach out and touch them.

Later in Pasadena I saw their son, Dr Dan Fuller, then lecturing at Fuller Seminary, and told him of this mysterious experience. 'Yes, Mike,' he responded thoughtfully, 'very strange things can happen in life.'

Back in Cape Town that evening there was another mission follow-up meeting in one of the big churches. I dropped Carol off a couple of blocks away so she could walk into the church solo. By then we had agreed we could tell our parents and I could tell Chris. I then raced up to the University of Cape Town (UCT) to Chris's room, seized his prayer diary, found the marriage prayer-request entry and with a red marker scribbled across it: 'Answered: Genesis 24:48'. This verse says: 'Then I bowed my head and worshipped the LORD, and blessed the LORD . . . who had led me by the right way to take the daughter of my master's kinsman for his son.'

Then I tucked the little diary in my pocket and raced back to the church to preach in the follow-up service. Afterwards Chris asked if I'd like to go out for a bite. I said, 'No, let's just go somewhere quiet where we can have some fellowship.' So we drove up Signal Hill and parked the car near the top, looking down on the spectacular view of the darkened harbour and the twinkling lights of Cape Town outlining the curve of Table Bay.

After a bit of small talk, I put my hand in my pocket, pulled out Chris's prayer diary and tossed it nonchalantly into his lap.

'What's this?' he exclaimed. Then, as I stared casually into the distance, he raced through the diary to the Michael–Carol prayer entry, where he saw in the dim light: 'Answered: Genesis 24:48'.

Well, talk about a Mount Vesuvius explosion! Chris with a shriek of unbelieving laughter almost went through the roof of the car. To be sure, this was one of life's most special moments.

On 24 September, my thirty-third birthday, at a small party at the Bams', we publicly announced our engagement and sent shockwaves through Cape Town's Christendom!

Days later we set off in my little car for Natal so that Carol could meet my overwhelmingly excited parents, my sister Judy and her family, and the

AE team. All were, needless to say, ecstatic. At AE, streamers and colour-ful bunting decorated my office and a huge sign said: 'A cedar of Lebanon has fallen.' An engagement party at my home had everyone 'oohing and aahing' at the assistant missioner I had brought home as my future wife.

Not long thereafter, Carol had to return to Cape Town to her teaching duties. I had four or five recuperative days away at a cottage of dear friends, Garnet and Joan Venn, in Salt Rock on the Natal north coast, before having to go to Johannesburg for extensive preparatory labours on Mission '70, our huge citywide mission planned for the following year.

From Salt Rock I wrote my first two love letters to Carol. In the first I said:

Hullo, my dearest Darling,

It is certainly a new joyous experience to have a love to write to – and I do not cease to praise God for you. Actually I still cannot quite credit that it is all true – but it is, and my heart rejoices with joy unspeakable. The last days with you up here have also been very special as I have started to catch a glimpse of what married life with you is going to be like.

I anticipate such a richness that I know I will wonder how on earth I ever lived so long without you. Yet I did – by the grace of God, and I know I was learning many things which will make life more stable and satisfying with you.

For one, I discovered the genuine richness and reality of the Lord Jesus and

Carol meeting the AE team in Pietermaritzburg, October 1969

His friendship. Thousands of times He was my Friend, and my only friend and I have learned to know Him as one who never fails. That Friendship I bring with me to marriage – as I know you do – and our firm resolve must be that this deepen and develop into the richest possible Love Triangle. The Lord must always be first to us individually and first as a married couple. Indeed my constant prayer is that by His grace we may truly have a marriage worthy of the name – and one that will be a blessing, inspiration and example to others. Naturally this will take faith, love, honesty, courage, humour and work – but I firmly believe it can be done. Not only that but I believe it is the destiny of our marriage to be something special. Let's hold on to this vision.

After leaving you yesterday, my heart was full of joy and thanksgiving for you and although separated from you by distance I nevertheless felt you very close – as I do today.[1]

I won't tell you how I signed off!

In the second letter from Salt Rock I wrote: 'I have just described you to my sister Olave as "the all-round, supersonic, atomic Christian bombshell". How do you like that?' I concluded: 'Words are hopeless to convey how much I love you – and thank God for you.'[2]

Mission '70 preparations

Up in Johannesburg, again now with Chris, we were at full stretch preparing for the mission.

One episode I remember was going to visit the mining magnate Harry Oppenheimer. What struck me most was how humble and gentle he was; in fact he was grace and charm itself. He made me feel like a million dollars, though I wasn't sure I would get that much! He later gave Mission '70 a generous gift which got us launched.

Then our team in the USA asked if I could go over to do a little fundraising tour. I felt torn as I seemed to be needed in several places: Johannesburg, 'Maritzburg and Pasadena. And of course ideally I should have somehow been in Cape Town. Thus was developing the kind of clash that Carol and I would forever know between work and family.

There was also a South African general election brewing for April 1970.

The autumn session of the Parliamentary Assembly in the previous year was the last to be attended by three white representatives for the South African so-called Coloured population. They were only allowed to elect representatives to the Coloured Persons Representative Council, which consisted of 40 elected and 20 appointed members drawn from the Coloured community, mainly in Cape Town.

Shockingly, of course, black Africans were excluded from the vote for the white Parliament and could only vote in their so-called homelands, which were self-governing areas in South Africa during apartheid.

Anyway, whites were urged into rapid voter registration.

In terms of claims on my time, our US office won out and I had to head over there. I wrote to Carol virtually every day.

It was a very full and demanding time, but in the middle of it I, along with Ed Gregory, visited old friends in Pasadena, Paul and Elisse Larsen. Naturally they asked all about Carol. After lunch while we were chatting, Elisse, who had a strong prophetic gift, suddenly looked as though she wanted to say something urgent.

Ed said, 'Mike, let's just be quiet for a moment.'

Then Elisse, who knew nothing at all of my Isaac–Rebekah history, suddenly, with eyes closed, burst forth: 'Son of Abraham – son of Abraham – son of Abraham – I have called you Isaac. And I have brought a Rebekah unto you, Isaac, my son.

'I have snatched her out of a snare and a trap of Satan and have given her unto you.

'And as you heard in this thing and were obedient, so you will hear even again my voice, and regularly in other things, like a bell.

'I will cause you to ride on the highways of the earth. Trust that which I am putting in your heart.

'And there are some shakings that shall come upon you. Yea, everything around you that can be shaken will be shaken, and what remains will be of my Spirit.

'In the midst of the battle, stand still in quietness and peace, for this day I have kindled my fire within you.'

In my book *Bursting the Wineskins*, which I wrote many years later about my journey relating to the work of the Holy Spirit, I shared this story as an example of the contemporary operation of the gifts of the Spirit, in this case prophecy:

> My reaction after this was firstly one of awe, for I had said nothing at all to Elisse about the years and years of Isaac and Rebekah background with its climactic significance in recent months when both Chris Smith and I had independently felt so powerfully led again into the story. Of course I was also greatly excited at yet more confirmation about Carol. On the other hand I was fearful about the shakings. Unbeknown to me our team was due in the following two years to enter such a set of convulsions as would leave the ministry almost destroyed.
>
> During this time of convulsion all I had to hold on to were these

prophetic words plus the accompanying assurance that God was somehow in it all for His purpose. Otherwise I might have wanted to give up. But on November 23rd 1969, in the Larsens' home, I was not to know any of that. My preoccupation was with the marvellous word of confirmation about Carol, and the utter mystery of its being couched in the Isaac and Rebekah categories with which I had been living so intensely throughout that time.

Later Elisse told me that every time I mentioned Carol's name in the post-lunch discussion the name Rebekah leaped overwhelmingly into her mind until finally she had to burst forth in that prophetic word.

Inevitably, of course, apart from the personal side, was the theological. For here incontrovertibly to my mind, was the operation of yet another supernatural, charismatic gift. And if it could happen once authentically, it could happen again. Not only could but should.

One of the things which intrigued me was that this sort of prophetic utterance was not something I expected and was not part of my pre-suppositional world, as it were, in any significant way. My exposure to such things had been modest, to say the least, and I was not therefore spiritually pre-programmed to be favourable. It was therefore another big surprise. But not one I could ignore.

I then reflected on the modern Church's attitudes to this kind of prophecy: 'Was not the modern Church often short-changing itself, screening out

Cassidy wedding, 16 December 1969

by presupposition, pride and prejudice aspects of the fully supernatural heritage which was not only part of its birthright but should be part of its normal life?'[3]

So this prophecy was hugely significant for me. And I still have it pasted into the flap of my Bible.

Also in my *Wineskins* book, I used the way I had come to know that Carol was the woman for me as an example of the Charismatic 'gift of knowledge' referred to by St Paul in 1 Corinthians 12.8.[4]

Back in South Africa there was only time to gather my goods and chattels and drive to Cape Town for our wedding on 16 December 1969. In a lovely service in the Congregational church in Claremont, I married Assistant Missioner Carol Bam.

And we lived happily ever after.

19

Marriage and ministry

*A happy man marries the girl he loves, but a
happier man loves the girl he marries.*
(African proverb)

We had a wonderful honeymoon, partly going up the coast of the Western
Cape and partly with the extended Bam family and friends at Kenton-
on-Sea. We had decided that a good honeymoon required not just private
love-nest time, but social time as well. This was good.

Leaving Kenton, we were headed up towards East London and a few days
in a hotel there. En route, near a tiny Eastern Cape town called Peddie, a
red warning light suddenly glowed on our dashboard, signalling generator
problems. We put in to Peddie, but the local garage owner told us that, being
a Sunday, the mechanics were off and could only start work on the vehicle
the next day. But the car would be 110 per cent safe, locked in the garage
overnight. So we left it and checked into a scruffy little local hotel.

Honeymoon

First thing next morning I went down to the garage. The manager met me looking glum and disconsolate. His garage had had the burglary of the century. Our car had been broken into and the whole back seat, piled high with Carol's luggage and many of our wedding presents, had been rifled. Everything was gone. The boot of the car with my own beaten-up suitcase and some old clothes was fine. Lament! Lament!

I trudged back heavy-hearted to the hotel and broke the awful news to Carol. All her stuff was gone. Plus four months of her mother's work on a magnificent trousseau of dresses; also her collection of recipes and records.

Carol was numb with shock and dismay. But she summoned up her bravery, saying, 'Well, it could have been worse. We might have had a serious accident. Or been injured. At least we are OK, and together.'

This is one tough dame, I thought to myself. And surely I have the right woman for my wife.

Although Carol now had only one dress, the one she stood up in, she just soldiered out into the new situation.

'Well,' she chuckled, 'I guess the Lord knew I was marrying a missionary and I needed from the start to make do with the minimum. Fortunately the dress is drip-dry and it's summer!'

Later, as a mother, Carol said, 'At the time I never really thought how sad it must have been for my mother who had worked so hard by sewing all those lovely dresses; but she never said a word.'

Marriage and ministry: Carol and Michael taking time to relax and be together

After a short spell in our home in Hilton we had to go to Johannesburg to prepare for Mission '70. Accommodation for newly-weds was trying and we would live in seven different locations that year. I suspect Carol often wondered if being married to a missionary wasn't asking her to cross one bridge too far.

On top of that, Carol was scheduled to go into hospital in Cape Town for major knee surgery, her right knee having given her trouble for years. We had been married only two and a half months.

Checking into the hospital, she had to fill in the hospital form, including 'Husband's Salary'. When her father saw that her husband scarcely earned enough to pay income tax, he freaked out, wondering who on earth his daughter had got saddled with!

We were separated for over two months but made up for it by writing almost every day.

Mission '70, Johannesburg

As for the mission, it was moving full steam ahead.

In the year leading up to the mission we had sent out thousands of questionnaires to get the personal involvement of as many Christians as possible.

About 250 churches and thousands of volunteers across racial divides signed up to be equipped to conduct evangelism and discipleship groups in homes all over the city. And our numbers increased daily.

These volunteers were mobilized into action with spectacular results. Youth events were held at our Narnia Coffee Bar, established by AE intern Don Andreson, in Hillbrow where many young people were converted. Dinners were held for sports and business people, and teams were sent into schools, businesses, boardrooms and factories. The response was always warm and open.

In Soweto (South Western Township), the major black township outside Johannesburg, we faced many problems because of the enormous difficulties with lack of transport and communication and so on. Very few ministers and church members had telephones, for example. We also found that there was little inter-church work, and many people thought that Mission '70 was just another attempt to form yet another church.

Some great things came out of that mission. Dick Peace's eight-week evangelistic and discipling course, called Witness, caught on as hundreds of groups formed all over Johannesburg. In fact this Witness course pretty much launched the home-group movement in South Africa which had scarcely been evident until then, but thereafter spread throughout the nation. Such groups prevail everywhere to this day.

Then there was the story of the disillusioned husband. One day a man came to the mission office and asked to see me.

'Mr Cassidy,' he expostulated, all hot and bothered, '*that woman!* I am sick and tired of her. She is driving me crazy. Messing up everything at home. So I've packed my bags and I am leaving her. It's finished. Now I want to come and work for the Lord full-time.'

'Well, brother,' I replied, 'I love people who want to work for the Lord full-time!'

He beamed.

'But now I've got your first assignment.'

He was eager to hear what that was.

'I want you to pick up your suitcase, go back to your car, and go home to your wife and say, "Sweetheart, I am so sorry I behaved so childishly this morning. Please forgive me."'

'Oh, you can't ask me to do that,' he protested.

'Well, my friend, you are now working for the Lord full-time. And that's your first assignment.'

He left, looking sheepish. Disconsolate. Pole-axed.

Then in the final mission meeting in Ellis Park tennis stadium, after I'd given the appeal for response, I saw this man and his wife coming across the arena. They were beaming – two lovebirds if ever I saw any!

Now that they have a testimony, I thought, they can certainly go and work effectively for the Lord full-time!

I also recollect in those Ellis Park stadium meetings how a distinguished scientist from Wits University, Dr Mary-Jean Silk, responded to the gospel. She went on to shine her gospel light ever more brightly in academia for the rest of her life – even towards the end doing a theological degree and getting ordained. She kept in touch with me from 1970 onwards until she went a few years ago to be with the Lord.

Discouragements

But that mission in Johannesburg was also an uphill struggle.

Many churches stayed away for the usual absurd reasons. One reason was new, however: 'Michael smokes!'

At first I was mystified at this complaint because I don't smoke. I gave up smoking when I left school, remember? But this story arose from an interview published in the Johannesburg *Star*. The chain-smoking columnist had offered me a cigarette, which I politely declined. The article opened: 'Brushing aside the offer of a cigarette with a wave of his hand, mission leader Michael Cassidy said . . . [etc.]'

One denominational leader saw 'cigarette' and my name juxtaposed, and as a result a whole denomination took a stand on principle!

Then there was the simple inertia of the local church. As I wrote in my book *Prisoners of Hope*:

> Ministers gave the impression of being tired, bogged down and trapped in the web of ecclesiastical machinery. Some had despaired of moving and motivating their laity to active witness; others were simply down on mass evangelism, but had little idea of alternative methods. Others admitted having lost their message. Here and there clergy spoke of leaving the ministry. The flight from the parish looked like taking hold on South African soil. Many felt alone and isolated. On top of everything was the overwhelming complexity of the race problem. Should one be protesting about injustices? Or was it enough to restrict oneself entirely to presenting a personal gospel? How did the roles of prophet and evangelist relate to each other? Was the Christian task over when the decision was recorded and the soul saved? Our hearts went out to clergy and we became committed to them as never before.[1]

This sort of thing made numbers of us lament and weep over the divided state and spiritual health of the South African Church. And had not the Lord spoken to us, even at the inception of our work, saying: 'Gather my saints together unto me' (Psalm 50.5 KJV)?

This word of course had been on our hearts for a number of years and we had more than once felt prompted to set up some kind of nationwide congress. I, in particular, had felt the Lord's clear call to do this, but it wasn't until Mission '70 that we finally got it together – over a cup of coffee!

John Rees, the mission chairman, and soon to be appointed General Secretary of the South African Council of Churches, was the one having coffee with me on that occasion. John, a prominent Methodist layman, often found himself in Soweto because of his work in a government department, and he had a huge heart for the plight of blacks in the country. He also was anguished about the divisions in the Church between English and Afrikaners, Evangelical, ecumenical and Pentecostal, but above all, black and white.

Midstream in what for us transpired to be a momentous conversation because of all that flowed from it, the South African Congress idea, which had come to us a few years previously, surfaced again and led me to blurt out to John: 'Hey, John, why don't we have a party? You invite all your ecumenical friends from all round South Africa and beyond, and I'll invite all my Evangelical ones, and we'll put them together in a Congress and have a party for the Lord.'

The idea of a South African Congress on Mission and Evangelism, co-sponsored by African Enterprise and the South African Council of Churches, suddenly gripped our hearts. We both fell on the prospect of gathering the South African Church, helping it to find new unity, be renewed in mission and evangelism, and develop a united front against apartheid.

Race

The many complexities caused by racial injustice we experienced during the mission fuelled our determination to get the Congress together.

It was exceedingly difficult, for example, to go into Soweto for a special series of evangelistic meetings, but it was virtually impossible, and certainly highly unrealistic, to expect blacks to come into the Johannesburg city centre for evening meetings.

Beyond that, how could we go into the township and declare God's love for the people when it was a white supposedly Christian government that had segregated all those citizens to Soweto, well away from the white areas? This put an albatross of destroyed credibility around the necks of any white preachers, for sure, and even around the necks of amazing black preachers, such as Abiel Thipanyane and Ebenezer Sikakane, on our team.

One story stands out from our time in Soweto: I was walking one day in the heat of noonday traffic down in the city centre of Johannesburg. Suddenly, above all the din of traffic noise, I heard my Sesotho name, shouted out loud – 'Mojalifa!' I looked up and saw a beaming black face high up in the driver's seat of a coal lorry stopped at the traffic lights. I assumed he must have known my Sesotho name from our Soweto meetings. This name was given to me by a wonderful old Mosotho lady who did the cooking in our home when I was still a child. It speaks of the 'first-born son and heir of the father's fortune'. This always highly amused my father as there was no fortune to inherit!

Anyway, I bounded between bumper-to-bumper vehicles as the lights turned green, reached high up into his cab and clasped his hand as he shouted, 'Praise Jeesas!' And I yelled back 'Hallelujah!' And dodged back, risking life and limb between already moving vehicles! Another high-point memory.

Carol Cassidy, Jemina Thipanyane and Emily Sikakane, Mission '70, Soweto meeting

But the more we were in Soweto, the more we felt the place was cooking up, and about to blow. Especially among the young people in schools.

We therefore sought to get a communication to this effect to Prime Minister John Vorster, and other authorities. The word we got back was that 'Soweto is fine, and everything is under control'.

We knew this was self-deceiving nonsense, but we could not convince the myopic authorities otherwise.

In the event, they kept things 'under control' for a further six years until June 1976 when the lid did blow in the famous uprising of youth protesting over so-called 'Bantu Education'. This policy was there to ensure that blacks did not aspire to equality with whites, but instead understood that any skills they had were to serve their own people in the homelands, preferably, or else in 'certain forms of labour' in the white world. Also it ensured that Afrikaans, seen as the language of the oppressor, would soon become the major medium of instruction. Over 170 young people were killed in the uprising, and South African history changed for ever.

If race was a key issue for us in the mission, it was even more key in the upcoming election. And I said as much in my weekly column in the Johannesburg *Star*:

> We are blinding ourselves to inexorable spiritual laws by imagining that peace and security can be built upon discrimination and injustice. I believe that white South Africa is sowing a wind, and it is our children who will reap the whirlwind, unless we come to our senses and start putting principle above expediency and Christian truth above ideological tenet.[2]

I noted in that pre-election article that there was 'one issue. And that [was] race.'

It was true – and even more depressingly evident when once again the Nationalist government was returned to power, albeit with a slightly reduced majority.

Only four political parties contested the elections. The number of registered voters was 2,028,487 (out of a population of 25 million); the number who voted was 1,503,284; void or blank ballot papers totalled 10,524; and 1,497,760 was the number of valid votes.

As Mission '70 came to an end, and along with it our first year of marriage intertwined with mission, Carol, who had been used to a structured schedule as a teacher, was bewildered. She said, 'Seven different abodes, seven different shopping areas, all in our first year of marriage! Is this what urban missionary life is all about?'

Pregnancy and overseas travel

In the latter part of the year Carol became pregnant and suffered badly with morning sickness. Though this was not part of our plans, we nevertheless rejoiced. Oh, but we were so excited. We would become parents!

But there were other things to attend to as well, not least an extended ministry tour to the United States with Festo and Mera Kivengere, this really being the first time since our 1969 mission to Nairobi that we had teamed up together for ministry.

We began in November in Boston and found ourselves spontaneously, both of us, drawn to Paul's word in 2 Corinthians 5.18: 'All this is from God, who through Christ reconciled us to himself and gave us *the ministry of reconciliation*' (my emphasis). And this became the theme song of that tour, and indeed of our ministry together ever after.

In fact, between us we were well placed to address this theme and testify to its reality in our lives.

After all, Festo was black. I was white. He was older. I was younger. He would in due course become a minister, then a bishop. I was a layman. He came from independent and free black Africa. I came from apartheid South Africa. Festo came from the background of the very freewheeling Anglicanism of East Africa, whereas I came from a very staid, traditional Anglican background in South Africa. My experiences of renewal, such as they were, came out of the Charismatic Renewal, with its stress on the Holy Spirit and the gifts of the Spirit, whereas Festo came out of the East African Revival where the focus was on the cross, and the Calvary Christ, and 'walking in the light', which meant open, even public, confession of sin.

All this meant we had a lot to say out of our own relationship, our background differences and how we found each other which could address the needs of many individuals in our audiences. In any event, we seemed to connect quite deeply with people wherever we went.

We also followed the East African preaching style of preaching in tandem in one sermon. Thus I might take the prodigal son to the far country and bury him in a hole out there, and Festo would dig him out and bring him home. Or, for example, with Mark 1.15: 'Repent, and believe in the gospel', Festo might take 'Repent', and I would follow on with 'Believe'. It was certainly fun, and it worked.

While in New York, Carol began to have some worries related to her pregnancy. These intensified. And we both became pretty worried. At one point I was scheduled to preach up the west coast in Seattle and Vancouver, while Carol remained in LA with a dear friend who cared for her.

On a Sunday morning at the huge Seattle Presbyterian church, I was preaching on Paul's famously declared ambition – 'that I may know him, and the power of his resurrection, and the fellowship of his sufferings' (Philippians 3.10 KJV). When I mentioned the sufferings of Christ, I had such a funny feeling in my spirit. A sort of premonition of a suffering time to come.

As I stepped down from the pulpit, the church secretary came up to me and asked me to ring Pasadena urgently. My heart sank. I called and got the message I dreaded: would I please come back at once? Carol was threatening to miscarry. She was four months along.

Trauma

I cancelled my meetings that evening and those for the next day in Canada, and took the next plane back to LA. There I found Carol in such a state of touching bravery and sadness that my heart almost broke. But we were melted together in new love and faith.

Carol was taken to hospital with labour pains and delivered prematurely a baby girl. Sadly we lost our first child. And it was hard. We felt stricken as we saw jubilant mothers and fathers coming out of the labour wards with big rosettes displayed across their chests announcing 'It's a girl' or 'Bravo for a boy'.

After getting home at around 1.30 a.m., I was praying about the next steps and had the deepest sense of God saying, 'Take her to Kenton!' It was very clear – and I decided there and then to do just that. Next morning I took Carol a birthday present – a precious necklace from Athens, bought en route to the USA, and then handed her a big birthday card which I said was her main present! Inside, in unobtrusive letters, I said I'd have her in Kenton in three weeks' time. She almost flipped with unbelief and joy, and I told her the only other time I'd seen her so startled was the night I proposed! That afternoon the nurses brought in a little birthday cake with a lone candle on it, saying 'Happy Birthday', and gave her a card too.

It was a dark and difficult time. Nevertheless, in the following days the Lord, through his people and lovely friends like Festo and Mera, and our hostess, Marjorie Gorton, ministered to us most wonderfully. As we anchored ourselves in the Lord, and his sovereignty, and in his word, light returned to our souls and the sun began to shine again. While we did not understand his ways, we did understand his character.

Carol manifested a serenity, bravery and faith that left everyone gasping – not least me. Her spirits became more cheerful and her physical strength increased, and three weeks later after fulfilling a few ministry chores, and leaving Festo and Mera to soldier on alone, we left for England and Christmas there, and then by 31 December, as promised, we were at her folks' seaside home in Kenton-on-Sea.

Carol's parents and family were loving care personified, and those holidays were precious times of recovery and closeness.

Moving on

The year 1971 was a funny, rather raggle-taggle time, coping with both the ministry and marriage. A number of shakings came upon AE, as prophesied back in October 1969, especially when Dick and Judy Peace, such kingpins in our work, decided it was time to return to the States. I experienced a deep sense of loss. But maybe God was slowly transforming African Enterprise South Africa (AESA) into an indigenous African team.

That year also saw the coming to fruition of the first East African team in Uganda under Festo Kivengere's leadership. Carol and I went up to Limuru in Kenya where numbers of Festo's friends from Uganda, Tanzania and Kenya gathered together to dream and plan for our East African team.

Meanwhile, a new leader had come to power in Uganda called Idi Amin. We went to a ceremony commemorating Uganda's martyrs where he spoke. He sounded so good and on the side of the angels that numbers of locals thought he might be a new Cyrus of Persia who would bring new freedoms. Little did anyone know.

Carol and I, for our part, had been invited by the great Bishop Stephen Neill, then lecturing at Nairobi University, to go up and spend three months of sabbatical under his inspired tutelage.

The following year, 1972, raced by as well. Above all, plans went full speed ahead for the South African Congress on Mission and Evangelism to take place in Durban in March 1973. Acts 2.44 says: 'All who believed were together.' Could it really happen in South Africa for all racial groups to come together? We would soon find out.

Catherine Louise Cassidy

But absolute pride of place must go to 2 May 1972 when our precious Catherine Louise Cassidy, with no hitches this time, arrived on Planet Earth to make us truly proud parents.

I decided in her young life that I could never love another human being, besides Carol, as much as I loved her. She was a treasure, to be sure. Of course, in the way the Lord works things, one does love each of one's children equally as they come along.

Baby Cathy; Michael with Cathy

229

One of the things I loved when Cathy was a baby was putting her on my lap when I was playing the piano. Her uninvited banging on the keyboard made every piece a duet of her own composing!

Carol proved immediately to be a wonderful mother, as she was to all of our three.

20

Prisoners of hope

―――――▬▮▬―――――

Return to your stronghold, O prisoners of hope:
today I declare that I will restore to you double.
(Zechariah 9.12)

The South African Congress on Mission and Evangelism in Durban in March 1973 was, I believe, a turning point both in our own ministry and for South Africa. It involved a collision between secular and spiritual powers, and the outcome proved that the spiritual way can vanquish and triumph. It did then. And it can do so now.

The great sadness was the lack of participation of the Dutch Reformed Church. We saw this as crucial and sent an early invitation, but we had no response. Over many months we tried vainly to secure the formal involvement of the Afrikaans churches. Numbers of individuals from their ranks did join the congress, but the DRC as a whole stood back, which we felt was tragic.

We had consulted many people around South Africa and overseas as to the shape and content of the congress programme. There was a strong sense that the congress should be on both mission and evangelism, with the primary focus on evangelism, but not ignoring the wider mandate of mission and social concern. We resolved to address the real problems facing our country and to confess our real failures thus far.

Dr Calvin Cook, then Professor of Ecclesiastical History at Rhodes University, and a member of our Congress Committee, and also the person who got our AE ministry launched in South Africa, pleaded that we take into account what the Holy Spirit had been doing in others, for example on the issues of justice and reconciliation. In other words, we needed to be open to being challenged and changed by the Holy Spirit through our encounters.

In the end our congress aims came together as follows:

1 to hear together the proclamation of the gospel;
2 to discover together the relevance of the gospel and the meaning of mission and evangelism in present-day southern Africa;

South African Congress on Mission and Evangelism, Durban: John Tooke planning

3 to face up to the urgency and priority of evangelism;

4 to access the resources and potential of all Christian churches and agencies for mission and evangelism;

5 to give stimulus, inspiration and encouragement to Christians as they face this task.

The aims were worthy. Would we succeed in fulfilling them?

As to venue, we became so desperate that someone suggested the use of a ship! He thought this would solve the multiracial problem. The ship could sit out at sea or perhaps cruise. Calvin Cook's wry comment was: 'The Church more at sea than ever!'

The new Elangeni Hotel in Durban, reasonably priced, finally emerged as a possibility.

We sent invitations out to 110 local and 25 overseas speakers. In spite of the openness of the Elangeni Hotel to housing delegates on a non-racial basis, the one challenge was the securing of written permission from government authorities for blacks and whites to use the same accommodation. Letters went to department after department. Local authorities said: 'Apply higher.' Higher authorities said: 'Apply lower.' Middle authorities referred us in both directions. The Department of Community Development, as we were informed, handled matters relating to Indian and Coloured people, while the Bantu Affairs Department said that all applications relating to Africans should go to them.

Then we were told that the interracial use of a licensed hotel required special permission from the Department of Justice in terms of the Liquor Licensing Act. This act stipulated that the sale of alcoholic beverages to racially mixed groups was forbidden. But what if we weren't interested in alcohol? No matter. The permission was still needed.

Not only that, but the mixed use of toilets was also forbidden! That particular obstacle, as we were informed, was well-nigh insuperable. For quite a number of nightmarish weeks the congress looked like foundering on the imponderable combination of liquor, toilets and justice.

I was now becoming very frustrated and on 8 November wrote to the Prime Minister, John Vorster, outlining for him the complications and difficulties involved for us if permission to use the Elangeni Hotel was not forthcoming from government authorities. Shortly thereafter two letters reached us, one from the Minister of so-called Bantu Affairs saying that his department could not cooperate 'as the government disapproves of this congress'. The other one came from the Secretary for Community Development saying that he was not going to grant us permission for the use of the Elangeni Hotel. This was quite devastating because we had scoured the country from stem to stern for over a year trying to find somewhere to meet. On 14 November I wrote again to the Prime Minister, who had not yet responded to my earlier letter.

Our letter to the Prime Minister concluded by observing possible repercussions from obstruction which we were most anxious to avoid:

1 If we are unable to find a suitable venue this will *reflect very adversely* and negatively on South Africa. It would make it appear that this country is unable to provide the proper facilities to conduct and house an international conference.

2 Above all we want to *avoid the possibility of the local and world press exploiting* the predicament of the congress in a way which would adversely affect South Africa's name at home, in the rest of Africa, and abroad.

3 We also want, at all costs, to *avoid polarising* the South African situation further.

4 We are also eager to *minimise possibilities of Church–State confrontation.* It is hoped that the congress will rather ease misunderstandings and help all parties in South African life to understand each other's viewpoints with greater patience, love and sympathy. With some of the top Christian leadership from South Africa and the world present in the congress, we run the risk of serious alienation if legal obstructions are put in the way of what is a peaceful religious gathering . . .

We will be genuinely praying, Mr Prime Minister, that God will guide you and your colleagues as you seek to do the right thing in the matter of this congress which we believe could affect our country very positively and significantly for the years ahead.[1]

We also sent the substance of the above letter to the Revd J. D. Vorster, brother of the Prime Minister and Moderator of the Nederduitse Gereformeerde Kerk (NGK), the largest of the three Dutch Reformed churches.

A couple of days later another blow came. We heard from the Department of the Interior that all overseas speakers to the congress had been barred entry to the country.

I couldn't believe my ears. Clearly there had been a cabinet decision against the congress. Curiously enough, I did not fall off my perch in despair, but immediately felt the constraint to turn in my Bible to a promise from the Lord which had already meant much to us in the past. This comes in Isaiah 54.17 where the Lord says (my emphasis):

> No weapon that is fashioned against you shall prosper, and you shall confute every tongue that rises against you in judgment. This is the *heritage* of the servants of the LORD and their vindication from me, says the LORD.

I then went out into a forest near our home and claimed this Scripture with new and fresh intensity for what was our promised heritage and our natural birthright, our blessing in the Lord and protection from weapons formed against us, and with the assurance that we could leave our vindication to come from the Lord himself, provided we were moving in his will. During that forest walk I became convinced that the Lord would come through. I likewise became convinced that there was a serious misunderstanding on the government's side which had produced a cabinet decision of this forcefulness.

Grappling with government obstruction

The whole AE staff then went into intercessory prayer. Interestingly enough, there was not one person who was discouraged or depressed. We all felt buoyed up in our faith and eagerly expectant as to how the Lord would work it all out.

Charmian Tracey (now Le Feuvre), an AE intern, expressed everyone's faith in a memo circulated to all of us entitled 'God is able'. It included quite a stack of Scriptures (my emphasis):

The LORD is *able* to give you much more than this.

(2 Chronicles 25.9)

Now to him who by the power at work within us is *able* to do far more abundantly than all that we ask or think, to him be glory . . .

(Ephesians 3.20–21)

He is *able* . . . to subdue all things unto himself.

(Philippians 3.21 KJV)

These and many other Scriptures assured us that the Lord was able to pull down all obstacles and prevent the prospering of any weapon formed against those working in his name.

I wrote a third time to the Prime Minister. Our Congress Committee met a few days later in Johannesburg. It was decided that John Rees, David Bosch and I would, as a delegation, seek an appointment with the Prime Minister. Accordingly we rang his office. Would the Prime Minister be willing to receive a small delegation from the congress? We considered this important, indeed imperative. The reply to us was a very polite but quite categorical no. But a letter from the Prime Minister was on the way to me, we were told. At last.

A couple of days later it came in, as from the Prime Minister's secretary:

I have been instructed by the Honourable Prime Minister to acknowledge receipt of your letters dated November 14th and 17th 1972 and to say that your representations should in the first instance be taken up with the Honourable Minister of Information, Dr Connie Mulder. In view of your mission's connections with the World Council of Churches . . . you will

South African Congress on Mission and Evangelism Committee meeting, 1973: John Rees (centre) with Ebenezer Sikakane and Michael

appreciate that the Prime Minister cannot be associated with your efforts in any way and he, therefore, regrets that he cannot, under the circumstances, be of any assistance to you.[2]

Some sense of light relief came that same day in the form of another letter from the Department of Justice telling us that after very careful consideration of the matter it was now granting us permission to 'supply liquor to non-whites at the Elangeni Hotel', though the Elangeni had long since fallen through as a possible venue!

When our team met once again that night for prayer, we were strongly affected by a communication from Dr Ted Engstrom, a senior member of our AEUSA Board, in which he gave us the Scripture of 1 John 3.20, which has these three titanic words: 'God is greater . . .' Yes, we believed exactly that. God was greater than governments, greater than cabinet decisions, greater than apartheid, and greater than any or all attempts to frustrate the purposes of his kingdom.

After a series of determined efforts to make contact with Dr Connie Mulder, we got word back that he was open to receiving a memo from us on the congress before he went on leave on 11 December, and a delegation at the end of January. We decided that this was far too late. Somehow, by God's miraculous grace, it had to be sooner. After all, the congress was in March. But word had reached us that government departments do not reverse decisions quickly, and the Cabinet, never. Besides that, there was no possibility of getting the members of the Cabinet even to consider the matter as they had met that very afternoon for the last time before going into recess over the Christmas season.

Someone asked whether the congress could not perhaps be postponed a year. No! Seven hundred delegates and speakers were geared up for March. An Afrikaner friend in Pretoria phoned us and said he would try to make contact with Dr Connie Mulder and encourage him to meet with us, but said he didn't hold out much hope, 'barring an outright miracle'. But that was exactly what we were looking for – an outright miracle. And that, we resolved, is what we would have.

On the way home on the evening of 28 November, I put on my car radio for the seven o'clock news.

'It has been announced in Pretoria today that because of incomplete business, the Cabinet will sit once more this year on Friday morning.'

My heart leapt. The Cabinet to sit once more! Surely this was the outright miracle for which we were looking. 'Lord,' I resolved, 'the congress is going to be on the agenda of that meeting if we have to die to get it there.' This was now Tuesday evening. We had just over 48 hours.

In a phone conversation John Tooke, John Rees and I decided in faith to get a memo on the congress done and ready for the Cabinet on Friday. We worked feverishly on the document all the next day and most of the next night. At 2.00 p.m. next day, a call came to John Rees from a senior official in Pretoria: 'John,' he said, '*Ek moet gou praat* [I must talk quickly]. *Alles sal regkom. Totsiens* [Everything will come right. Goodbye].'

At 3.00 p.m. a call reached us from Dr Mulder's office saying we should have the memo on the Minister's desk by 8.00 a.m. next day, Friday, along with 18 copies. The congress was on the cabinet agenda for 9.00 a.m. At 6.00 a.m. next morning, John Rees drove to Pretoria with 19 neatly pre-pared folders. The next afternoon a summons came from Dr Mulder's office that a congress delegation should go to meet him at 2.00 p.m. on the following Tuesday, 5 December. The assignment had fallen to Rees, Bosch and myself.

Dr Connie Mulder

By 2.15 p.m. on 5 December, we were in Dr Connie Mulder's office. We found him to be polite, and graciousness itself. He asked about each of the overseas speakers and the genesis of the congress. 'No,' we said, 'it has nothing whatever to do with the World Council of Churches.' This was a South African-initiated project. Mulder explained that the government for obvious reasons could have nothing to do with the World Council. However, he told us, the government was indeed concerned for change and knew that change must come, but the problem was timing. 'Maybe,' he said, 'if it had been five years down the road you could have had the Elangeni Hotel.'

Finally, in quite a congenial atmosphere, Mulder said:

> You know it makes a difference to sit down and look a man in the eye. I would like to work this way in the future. Let's talk man to man. It prevents misunderstanding, because we have been misunderstanding this congress all along. Anyway, I have been asked by my colleagues in the Cabinet to convey to you that we have reversed our decision. You played open cards with us in your memo and we appreciate that. You may proceed with your congress. Outside speakers should apply for their visas in the normal way. No one will be blacklisted. We will inform our Consulates abroad. I will inform my Cabinet colleagues of our talk and ask them to cooperate. Secure one of Durban's international hotels for over-seas speakers and outside delegates. Local blacks will have to use Durban's African hotels.[3]

Amid our rejoicing spirits, we of course choked on his final stipulation. That was a challenge we would still have to face and a bridge we would still have to cross. But, we thought, let's in the meantime get on with the job of getting the congress to happen. The accommodation challenge would then be faced in faith and with resolution.

Christmas came and went and January 1973 was well advanced before there were any new developments. Of course we were exceedingly anxious, and time was running out. We had whites and outsiders housed all right, but could not find adequate room in Durban for all the congress blacks, even if we took over all the black hotels. We kept pressing the authorities. Finally, on 26 January Mr T. N. H. Janson, Deputy Minister of Bantu Administration, phoned us and said, 'You must be getting anxious about this accommodation business, so I thought I would ring. I just want to tell you that we are granting permission for you to house all congress delegates at the Lonsdale Hotel. The physical set-up of the place fulfils government's requirements.'

The Lonsdale Hotel was one we had been working on, when things had seemed either blocked or doubtful with the Elangeni. So I thanked Mr Janson and rang the Lonsdale Hotel managers, telling them that government permission had come through.

Their reply was like a body blow: 'Very, very sorry, but we have changed our minds. It has been decided by our management not to make the hotel available.'

I gasped and said, 'You must be joking.'

'No,' they said, 'the decision is firm.'

We were back to square one!

The last hope

A thought then came to us. Why don't we go back to the very first hotel we had investigated many months before, the Athlone Gardens? It was inadequate in size to take everyone in the congress, but if it could take a substantial proportion and could be non-racial, then it was a possibility. It was the last fragile and precarious hope. We rang the hotel managers and asked if they would house the congress. Yes, they would, but they informed us that there were no middle walls of partition so that blacks could be in one section of the hotel and whites in the other, as the government had previously stipulated. (These government regulations were nonsensical and so very wrong.)

Anyway, I got on the phone again to Mr Janson and told him that government delay and other factors had now lost us the Lonsdale. So there was only the Athlone Gardens Hotel but there were no middle walls of partition, and beyond all of that, we actually wanted and were committed to being together. Janson asked me to put my request to him right away in a cable and said he would get back to me. Forty-five minutes later, Janson phoned back and told me that he had not received our cable yet. 'Well, it has gone,' I told him. He then asked me to read him the text.

He then replied, 'OK, my colleagues and I have decided to let you have the Athlone.'

'May we eat together?' I asked him.

'Yes, you may.'

'May we share the same bedrooms?'

'Ah, Mr Cassidy, you know the situation,' said Janson ambiguously. 'Let me say simply that you will not be policed. Proceed with your congress and God bless you.'

We rejoiced. We had interracial housing, under one roof, in a South African hotel for a historic first time. And all in the name of Jesus Christ. It was a cause for many doxologies.

But one detail remained and that was transport. Local Durban bus authorities said the races could not be bussed together to and from the hotel and the congress venue. So back I went to the helpful and long-suffering Deputy Minister of Bantu Affairs: 'Mr Janson, the bus people say we can't ride on mixed buses. Now, sir, we can't eat, sleep, discuss and pray together, morning, noon and night, and then ride to and from the hotel to the Central Methodist Church in separate buses.'

'No, indeed not,' Mr Janson replied, and gave me the names of several people to ring. He said I should phone them and he would work on things from his end. An hour later we had permission for integrated bussing.

The breakthrough precedent had come. The edifice had been breached. The wall had cracked, and through the cracks could be faintly seen the distant light of a new day dawning.

And so on the evening of Monday, 12 March 1973, delegates arrived from all over South Africa and indeed from around the world and other parts of Africa at the Athlone Gardens Hotel. The atmosphere was euphoric. In the lobby that evening, in the middle of an ecstatic bevy of pastors and ministers from every race and background, I bumped into John Rees beaming irrepressibly like *Alice in Wonderland*'s Cheshire Cat. Our eyes met and sparkled with delight and emotion.

I also noticed that he was sipping a coke, in spite of the fact that during the afternoon word had come through again from the Department of

Justice that, just in case we wanted it, which we didn't, liquor could be served to everyone!

Next morning, as John Tooke and I awoke in our shared room high in the hotel, we looked down and saw two Africans delightedly run across the lawn and jump into the swimming pool of this so-called all-whites hotel.

'Let's join them,' said John. Down we rushed and jumped into the pool. And into a new day.

21

Heaven is opening

If people of all shades of theological and political opinion can get together in a spirit of cooperation to discuss mutual problems, then why can't politicians follow suit?[1]

(Natal Mercury)

The opening service of the South African Congress on Mission and Evangelism saw everyone in high spirits, and press cameras flashing all around.

Emotions were evident as we sang:

> Let every kindred, every tribe,
> On this terrestrial ball
> To Him all majesty ascribe
> And crown Him Lord of all.[2]

I remember seeing the Mayor of Durban begin to weep.

It was extraordinary for once in South Africa to feel the spread of the South African Church. Delegates were there from far left to far right on the religious and political spectrum. And we were certainly experiencing new levels of fellowship, even if we were a fellowship of strangers coming from 31 major denominations, 35 Christian service organizations and 15 countries.

While two smaller Dutch Reformed churches participated officially, the largest body, the Nederduitse Gereformeerde Kerk, kept aloof. Roman Catholics were present as observers. Tom Houston of Nairobi Baptist Church noted that we represented 'the fundamental, the sacramental and the sentimental!'

Part of the problem was getting real with each other, shedding tentativeness and finding courage to break through racial mythologies. But the Lord was working in our midst.

An elderly Indian waiter at the hotel said with tears in his eyes that it was the first time he had seen people of all races mixing together so happily. Another waiter commented on how good-natured and patient everyone was. 'Ordinarily the hotel has only a handful of guests, but they demand more attention than this whole crowd.'

The spirit of unity was wonderfully manifested in two other incidents recorded in my book *Prisoners of Hope*, in which I chronicled the congress:

> A young African girl at a local Durban school went to the congress centre searching desperately for her father from Pretoria. Reunited later that day with him, she was hesitant to board the same bus with whites. 'Won't they push me out, Daddy?' she had asked. 'No,' said her father, 'apartheid is dead at the moment. Come in.' In great and pathetic excitement she travelled on an integrated bus. Later it was all she could talk about to her school friends.
>
> The other phenomenon was spontaneous singing on the buses going to and from the hotel to the venue. One driver announced each day: 'If you want to praise the Lord, ride my bus.' Mrs Gill Tracey of Rhodesia [as it was then] said later: 'One morning on the bus we had not started singing yet. To my surprise the bus driver popped his head round the cab and said: "What's stopping you praising God in song?" What could we do but respond to the challenge? Then he popped his head round again and asked whether we could have "What a friend we have in Jesus"? The hymn rang out around the bus and down the highway. However, I was a little startled when, peeping into his cab, I saw him singing away while following the words in his own hymnbook! The driver's safety and that of the passengers had obviously been commended into the hands of a sovereign God!'[3]

We arranged for regular meetings of fellowship in groups of four during the congress. These were times of deep sharing. And all through the week we were challenged by messages from a wide range of speakers. For example, Bishop Alphaeus Zulu, the second chairman of African Enterprise, noted that if the members of the body of Christ were not in fellowship with one another it meant that there was something wrong. And that they had forgotten that Jesus is the foundation, and that 'blood, race, colour, tradition and culture may never be substituted for Him'.[4]

Canon Michael Green, then of St Aldate's Church in Oxford, set this principle in biblical context by reminding us about the huge inequalities of wealth and opportunity faced by the early Church, and how the believers ironed these problems out:

> Acts 2:24 tells us that after they had been preaching about repentance and faith in Christ, they were 'together' and had all things in common. They sold their possessions and goods and distributed to all men according to their needs. They continued daily with one accord in the temple breaking bread from house to house and praising God together with singleness of

heart. And the Lord added to the Church daily people who were being saved. Of course He did. This sort of love has got to mark us as we go out from this congress, or else what happens here will have been sheer window dressing, escapism and holy talk.[5]

Key issue – the nature of the gospel

Of course the big issue, beyond finding fellowship, was the very nature of the gospel.

In South Africa at that time the differences between Evangelicals and ecumenicals, between pietists and activists, were considerable. For many Evangelicals the gospel was simply a matter of getting someone 'saved' or 'converted', through receiving Christ as Lord and Saviour, and then confirming it or ratifying it by filling out a decision card or something like that in a meeting. Relating the gospel to the social, political, economic contexts of South Africa seemed unnecessary, even slightly worldly.

On the other hand there were the hyper-activists, many of whom relegated the idea of the Great Commission (Matthew 28.16–20) to the periphery and redefined the gospel as working for justice, humane re-lationships, the ending of apartheid, and national development. In this paradigm (how we relate to one another) the horizontal dimensions of the gospel were made to overshadow totally the vertical (the way we relate to God). Commitment to Christ is thus considered a pietistic periphery, where the Church's non-intellectuals reside, while the more serious and relevant work of the Church is performed by those who step into the social and political arena to demand its moral adjustment to biblical principles.

The reality was that each section of the church, as we in African Enter-prise had strongly believed, had much to learn from each other. And that is exactly what happened at the congress. Many Evangelicals found so-called ecumenicals to have real gospel commitments as well, and genuine experiences of Christian conversion. And they also began to realize that not having a deep concern for justice was actually a compromise of the gospel. Many ecumenicals found something powerful and refreshing in the Evangelical commitments to the priority of bringing men and women into a personal relationship with Christ.

The issues were encapsulated in the story David Bosch told of 'a fellow found in a gutter. The Pentecostals saved his soul, the Reformed Church taught him some sound theology, the Anglicans introduced him to high society. Then the Salvation Army picked him out of the gutter.'[6]

We all got the point.

Although the congress had many local speakers, both black and white, we were often helped out of our theological prisons by some of our less hidebound overseas speakers. Thus one particularly insightful word came from Canon Douglas Webster of St Paul's Cathedral in London:

> Evangelism is part, albeit a primary part, of God's total mission to mankind. Jesus sends His church to do many things. Their totality is the Christian mission. Of these things evangelism has its unique importance. But healing, teaching, baptising, liberating, protesting, working for peace and justice, feeding the hungry, reconciling those at variance, are all essential parts of mission, as we see it in the New Testament. They all arise from the Gospel; nevertheless, however closely we may associate these activities with evangelism, the New Testament does not identify them with it. Evangelism is the *proclaiming* of the Gospel, particularly to those who have not heard it, or who have not understood it, or who have not responded to it, or who have forgotten it.[7]

Billy Graham

This sort of insight helped pave the way for open and unprejudiced listening by all to the message of Billy Graham, whom we had invited as one of the major overseas speakers.

When word hit the press that Graham was coming to South Africa that year (1973), there was a frenzy of interest and enquiries, plus rejoicing from Evangelicals and much rumbling and mumbling from more liberal clergy.

John Rees, Dave Peters, Ebenezer Sikakane and I met Billy Graham at the airport on Friday, 16 March. Ebenezer formally welcomed him to South Africa, Dave Peters garlanded him with a gorgeously coloured Indian garland, and the press interview got under way. It was quite a hectic affair, and Billy answered well.

'How did I do?' asked Billy afterwards with boyish simplicity and characteristic humility after the intense grilling.

'Fine,' said John Rees, 'just fine.'

'Well, I didn't want to embarrass you people,' he replied. 'I know the situation here is very touchy and I've got to feel my way.'

For the rest of that day, I had the privilege of being alone with Dr Graham, briefing him on South Africa and trying to answer his voluminous questions. We had room service brought to us, although we would both have far preferred to go for a walk outside or on the beach and stop at a little restaurant. But it was out of the question, of course. 'You don't

*Billy Graham
arriving in Durban,
with Michael
there to meet him
at the airport;
Billy Graham in
Inanda outside
Durban; conference
registration; delegates*

have to be behind bars to be in prison,' Billy commented reflectively and poignantly.

The next day, Saturday 17 March, thankfully dawned bright and beautiful as people from all over Natal and other parts of South Africa began arriving at the Kings Park rugby stadium for the great evangelistic rally.

The stadium began to fill with every kind and description of person, some in fine array, others in garbs either poor or simple or both – the white man in his safari outfit, the African in his Sunday best, the Indian in her sari, schoolchildren in their uniforms. An army of police, arriving to be on standby with their dogs in case of trouble, surveyed the orderly, happy and buoyant crowd, then packed their dogs into vans, and drove off. Garnett Venn, a Pietermaritzburg lawyer, and a 25-year veteran spectator of rugby at Kings Park, sat in the stands, staring in unbelief. 'The most orderly crowd I have ever witnessed,' he said to his neighbour. 'In fact the whole thing's more thrilling than a test match.' Kathleen Sutherland, a psychiatric nurse, said later, 'One sensed God's presence and felt he was well pleased.' Prince Mntambo, an African pastor, said, 'Black alone looks dull. White or yellow alone look pale and empty – but black, brown, yellow and white look like beautiful flowers planted by God. That was the beauty of Kings Park with Dr Billy.'

'It was beautiful too,' said one observer, 'to see Bill Burnett, a bishop, serving as an usher.' That said something.

At three o'clock, the members of the platform party moved out and took up their seats. The stadium, now jammed beyond capacity with a record audience of between 45,000 and 50,000 people, presented an unprecedented spectacle. Here was South Africa as it should really be – a glorious kaleidoscope of racial beauty and diversity. In fact, never did the segregationist way seem more unnatural and grotesque than in those moments.

Just before getting up to preach, Billy leaned over to me: 'Should I give an invitation today?'

'You bet, Billy,' I replied. 'Our counsellors at least are all planning on it.'

Dr Graham's message was straight down the line, speaking on the sinfulness of human beings, and then exalting the person and deity of Jesus, explaining his atoning work on the cross, and affirming the historic resurrection of Christ, and the need for repentance, faith and response.

This was the familiar Graham invitation. It had worked in London's Harringay Arena and New York's Madison Square Garden, but what about in conservative and racially convulsed South Africa?

Billy Graham rally, Kings Park Stadium, Durban, March 1973

My thought was scarcely formulated when I stood to my feet, incredulous. A sea of humanity was surging towards the platform like a tidal wave. A Methodist minister in the grandstand broke down, overcome by the whole thing. He was not the only one. A Catholic priest stared in unbelief, and then prayed, 'May this be a milestone for South Africa.' Quite forgetting her shoes, which remained on the grass, a teenage girl moved forward. A schoolboy walked forward, stopped, turned, then turned again and almost ran to the platform.

A Coloured family – husband, wife and four children – slowly wended their way to the front, hand in hand. In the grandstands, Nan Hopkins, a doctor's wife, said to herself, I hope none of my friends see me, but I'm going forward. Eighteen African schoolchildren from one school moved forward together. Later they would bring a spiritual revolution to their school. Andrew Losaba, from the Free State, bubbled, 'Oh, heaven is opening!'

The staggering response of more than 4,000 individuals, with many unable to get near the platform area, reduced all our carefully laid plans for counselling to a shambles. All we could do from the platform was throw bundle after bundle of follow-up booklets to the gesticulating forest of counsellors' arms, all waving frantically for attention. Blacks counselled whites. Whites counselled Indians. Coloureds counselled blacks. And so it went, for an hour or more, as the stadium slowly began to empty. This was South Africa. The Beloved Country. The country to weep for. And pray for. And work for. Here it was in an identity crisis, and trying to find itself. And here was the Spirit of Jesus on the job, proclaiming good news to the poor, release to the captives, recovery of sight to the blind, and liberty to those who are oppressed.

Newspaper banners screamed in hyperbole: 'Apartheid Doomed'. Beyond that, multitudes in that stadium and around the country via the media caught a vision of what South Africa could become.

Billy Graham's address to the congress two days later stressed the vital necessity of a strong socio-political witness in the arena of justice, plus compassionate acts of caring and kindness for the poor, marginalized and oppressed.

'This kind of commitment to the total needs of human beings is vastly more effective than simply preaching from an air-conditioned pulpit.'[8]

At the end, congress delegates leapt to their feet and erupted in prolonged applause. At least one Evangelical in some ecumenical minds had been demythologized.

The following days focused on the nature and theology of evangelism,

Billy Graham addressing the conference

the need to contextualize the gospel, and also how practically to face and end institutionalized racism. White racism was also seen as intricately coupled to economic exploitation.

One important contribution was due to come at this point from black Lutheran theologian Dr Manas Buthelezi, but he had suffered that nightmarish and cruel South African penalty of being 'banned'. This involved forbidding him to leave the area of his home, or meet with more than two other people, as this would constitute a political meeting. No public statements were permitted. So his powerful and penetrating word to the congress was not possible, and in the first edition of *Prisoners of Hope* the space for his essay was left blank. But we had the text and later took the chance of allowing it to see the light of day:

1 The future of the Christian faith in this country will largely depend on how the Gospel proves itself relevant to the existential problems of the black man.

2 The whites in as far as they have incarnated their spiritual genius in the South African economic and political institutions have sabotaged and eroded the power of Christian love. While professing to be traditional custodians and last bulwarks in Africa of all that goes under the name of Christian values, the whites have unilaterally and systematically rejected the black man as someone to whom they can relate with any

degree of personal intimacy in daily life and in normal ecclesiastical situations. They have virtually rejected the black man as a brother. Love can never be said to exist where normal fellowship is banned.

3 For the sake of the survival of the Christian faith it is urgently necessary that the black man must step in to save the situation. We should now cease playing the passive role of the white man's victim. It is now time for the black man to evangelise and humanise the white man.[9]

Courageous Afrikaner theologian and activist, Dr Beyers Naude, affirmed:

Whites will have to face their deep-rooted fears, their material selfishness, their false sense of superiority, their sinful complacency to the terrible sufferings of people of colour; this will require that the blacks will have to face their deep frustrations, voice their suppressed anger and fears, discover and spell out their bitterness, admit and bring into the open their many subtle psychological attitudes and techniques of subterfuge and false subservience. Only when this new honesty replaces so much of the unreality and duplicity of our human relations, will worthwhile change take place.[10]

Several of us had anticipated a crisis, and felt it would be both necessary and healthy. We couldn't skirt or erode the issue.

Finally it came to a head when the blacks said they wanted to caucus separately, leaving whites to meet on their own. But there were interesting consequences. On the black side there was division as to the way forward. On the white side there was the first taste of being discriminated against. But on both sides there was a new awareness of the unnaturalness of the South African norm.

To be separated from one another seemed an ungodly rupture of that which relationally belonged together. In any event, we were all being stretched. Someone said we all felt a bit like a fellow who had for years ridden a bike with crooked handlebars. When someone straightened them, he fell off. We saw we were all accustomed to a spiritually 'crooked' way of living. Could the Spirit of God straighten us out? The sense of needing to move forward together was deepening.

In the end a number of significant words came through to all of us:

1 Let the gospel be declared and heard everywhere.

2 Let the layperson loose. Ministers and pastors need to train and equip laypeople (Ephesians 4.11–12) to carry forward the work of holistic witness and evangelism.

3 Let the Bible speak. Holding a high view of biblical authority, we should unleash the Scriptures in a new way into all society.

4 Let forgiveness flourish.

I need you

On the final morning of the congress, East African Presbyterian leader John Gatu concluded his address by asking everyone to turn to his or her neighbour and say, 'My brother/my sister, I need you.'

It was an emotional time as delegates reached across all barriers, real and perceived, and gave this greeting with feeling and sincerity. And often with tears.

It was as if we all got a new vision of a renewed and recommitted Church – a Church committed to Jesus and the Bible, to prayer and the gospel, and to the ending of apartheid and injustice. The fellowship of strangers had become the fellowship of brothers and sisters.

Suddenly it was all over. The Church gathered had now to be the Church dispersed. Now we needed to go out and make a difference, and I think we did.

The *Cape Times* wrote: 'The South African Congress on Mission and Evangelism is the biggest gathering for straight, frank talking across barriers ever to have been organised in this country.'[11]

The popular black magazine *Drum* said: 'South Africa will never be the same again.'[12]

Pietermaritzburg's daily, the *Natal Witness*, posted its editorial in these terms:

> We may never be in a position to judge the outcome of this congress, but one thing seems certain: If this is how the Church in this country can get down to its problems, then there is a lot of hope for everybody for they have demonstrated dialogue in action.[13]

I give Dr John de Gruchy, scholarly theologian and church historian, the last word here:

> Five years as an ecumenical globe-trotter has provided me with a reasonably wide experience, but I have never experienced or imagined possible what occurred in Durban from March 13–22nd 1973.
>
> I do not believe that any cheap victories were won at the congress for I believe that the experience of living together, praying together, and wrestling with the issues together, was an intensely demanding exercise. The triumph is that it was not an exercise in futility but in repentance, forgiveness and conversion in totally unexpected ways. Without drafting, debating or passing one resolution (surely a record in itself), I have seldom experienced the sense of resolution that was present during the final few

days. No evaluation dare be made at this moment for reality is here and now. All I know is that some black brother has offered me his eyes and ears so that I might see and hear things to which I have previously been blind and deaf.[14]

Of course, history would prove that we still had a long way to go. But a start had been made.

Almost all had moved from being prisoners of history to being prisoners of hope.

And some had even moved into the glorious liberty of the children of God.

22

Family

———◆◆◆———

A family tie is like a tree; it can bend but it cannot break.
(African proverb)

In the year after the Durban Congress, we made Focus on the Family the basis for four missions in the Durban area. In all this we sought to establish the centrality of the relationship with God out of which happy and productive family relationships could come.

James Irwin

In Pinetown, Durban, we closed out the mission with a big public rally where we heard the testimony of James Irwin, there with his wife, Mary.

Jim was the first American astronaut to drive a moon-buggy on the

Focus on the Family mission: Ebenezer Sikakane,
James and Mary Irwin, and Michael

253

moon. Imagine! He told us how, in his family, his mother was the great prayer warrior and prayed deeply for him to come to Christ. James did feel a deep emptiness, but filled it with flying, which was his passion. So from light planes to small jets to bigger ones, to testing the fastest plane ever built, he sought vainly to fill that gap. Then he thought being an astronaut would do it. So into the lunar programme he went.

Meantime his mum kept praying. Jim told us how he was then assigned to drive the first moon-buggy on the moon.

On the moon, as he saw the heavens and the breathtaking beautiful earth over there in the distance, he was overawed by the majesty of the Creator's creation and a sense of the presence of God. This transposed into an awareness of the Christ his parents had taught him about. And there and then, Jesus became real to him as Lord and Saviour and Friend.

A couple of years later I saw a huge framed picture of James Irwin driving his moon-buggy on the lunar surface. Beneath it James had written: 'Man walking on the Moon is not nearly as significant as God walking on the Earth.'

James's early family influences, and especially his mother's prayers, had borne fruit, showing the importance of godly family life and parental prayers.

This prayer commitment had been embraced by Carol and me in our married lives together, in our praying for and nurturing our little Cathy, then two years old, and also for the new little baby Carol was carrying.

Debbie's birth – Carol introducing Catherine to Debbie, September 1974

It was just as I completed the final talk in the Focus on the Family mission that a policeman came to the back of the church and informed me (there were no cell phones around in those Neolithic times) that 'the baby is coming!' The timing was perfect.

I had loved being in on Cathy's birth, and I wasn't going to miss this one. I think it's a blessing and comfort for mums to have their husbands there – provided they don't faint!

Debbie and Martin

Deborah Maria Cassidy announced her arrival with a lusty bellow.

'*Ntombazana!*' (Zulu for 'little girl'), said the obstetrician with a flourish, holding the little creature upside down by her legs.

Oh, what a moment!

Then came our son Martin John Charles, arriving two years later (1976), but not before giving us fearful frights when Carol's waters broke three months prematurely due to violent coughing after contracting viral pneumonia.

Three months of medical gymnastics in hospital by a specialist in prematurity staved off the birth, but at one point it began to look as if we could lose both Carol and the baby. One doctor suggested abortion. This was not an option for us as Carol felt the baby was very much alive, what with all the strong kicking!

The treatment given to Carol, to arrest premature labour, was drastic and involved racing the heart to double its normal speed. At the start she seemed fine, but 15 minutes later she looked as if she had had several rounds in a boxing ring. As she sustained these assaults on her system, her

Carol with Martin Cassidy, Disneyland, Los Angeles, 1980

dad said to me, 'It's almost sinful that someone has as much courage as Carol.' But our Anchor held. Praise God! After Marty's arrival, a month early, we were told there was only one other recorded case in medical history of what Carol had had to go through to get our son into the world.

I was so very proud of her.

Family of three

Now we had a family of three to raise. So, yes, let me focus on our family.

The biggest thing for us was trying to raise this little tribe 'in the nurture and admonition of the Lord' (Ephesians 6.4 KJV). From the time each child was conceived we prayed for two things – that he or she would find Jesus Christ as Lord and Saviour, and that God would at the right time bring to each 'the one appointed' (see Genesis 24.14, 44) as life partner.

Then from their earliest years we prayed with them together at bedtime, maybe after a Bible story or a children's tale – such as Beatrix Potter's *Squirrel Nutkin*, which starts out, 'This is a tale about a tail, and the tail belonged to Squirrel Nutkin!'

Of course the children's prayer times were precious. One evening Debbie had her little friend Sarah Bliss over to the house to play in the afternoon and stay for the night. At supper Carol and I noticed that the box of chocolates on the piano was seriously diminished.

'Now, kids, who's been taking the chocolates?'

Sarah stared out of the window. Debbie, all innocent and pure as the driven snow, said: 'What chocolates?'

Martin's first day of school, Hilton, Natal, 1983

Expanded family: Cathy, Debbie, Martin

The positions were firmly and irrevocably taken. Then came bedtime prayers.

Sarah began: 'Dear Lord Jesus, I think Debbie has something to tell you about the chocolates . . .'

Silence from Debbie. End of prayer time!

I heard of one spiritually diligent family who lived in New Haven, Connecticut, and who were teaching their little girl to say the Lord's Prayer. In she launched: 'Our Father who art in New Haven, how did you know my name?'

Anyway, everyone was trying! But my point is that praying daily with one's kids is a lot of fun. It is also deeply formative. And finally deeply transformative.

Dad's absence

All through the kids' childhood, we tried to make Jesus a natural part of everyday life, and a participant in all we did. Before any long car journeys we prayed for angelic protection. If anyone was sick we prayed for their healing. We prayed for friends, little or big, or in trouble. And of course they prayed for Daddy when he was away on ministry assignments.

This latter was a big challenge in our family lives. I was not a local pastor who would be giving all-year stability to the home. I was an itinerant preacher, a ministry fundraiser, and an activist caught up in the traumas and challenges of a country and continent constantly in crisis. This was all very time-consuming.

A missionary friend once told me that he had concluded, through much experience, that a married man with children should not be away from home for more than 90 days a year.

Imagine my guilt! In the early years of my married life I was probably away 150 days each year on assignment. This was a hugely inappropriate ordeal to place on Carol and the kids. One ministry tour in the States, I remember, was eight weeks long. Others there, or to Australia or wherever, lasted five or six weeks. And communication was very difficult – with no emails, video chat, text messaging, or even phone calls, which in those times were too expensive.

Carol remembers: 'More often than not, Michael was stretched to capacity. I remember one Christian leader once saying to me that Michael was spread so thin you could see right through him! This usually was the case, and I quickly realized that much of my role as his wife needed to be to relieve him of some of the home responsibilities. So along with being a mother, teacher and school counsellor, it was also up to me to decide on which lawnmower to buy, when the brake pads needed changing and when to prepare to submit tax returns.'

How I ever inflicted this on Carol I will never know! Yet she took it, bore it, coped with it and ultimately triumphed way beyond what could be imagined.

'I made these sacrifices', she would say to me, 'so you could do the Lord's work. It was my contribution. I knew from the outset that marriage to you was never going to be "normal", but I also knew with absolute certainty that God had called me to serve him through our marriage.'

Indeed Carol kept a marvellously stable ship at home. The fact that we remained living in the same place – the same town and the same house – also gave the kids stability. They never had to move schools and, while they were at home, they went to the same church that we attend even now.

In due time I cut the absences back to 120 days, and then 100. We also concluded that if I was away for more than three weeks at a time, it began to be emotionally destructive for us all.

I really sought to be a good dad. If working at my office in 'Maritzburg, I always tried to be back by the kids' supper and bedtime, to read stories to them, tickle their backs and say prayers together.

To any young fathers I would say with conviction: 'However late you may be home from work, don't miss your kids' bedtimes and prayers with them. Otherwise they grow up thinking, This Jesus thing is just for mums and not dads. And later they may forsake their developing little faith if it seems only a girlie thing.'

Failure

Once, at a leadership breakfast, I told a story relating to the famous Boswell, of Boswell and Johnson fame. He tells of being taken as a child on a fishing outing with his father, and describes this as one of the happiest and most memorable days of his entire childhood.

Later his father's journals were found, and in them he had recorded: 'Went fishing today with my son. A day totally wasted.'[1] To the father, a day totally wasted. To the son, the highlight of his childhood. When I told this story there was an audible gasp, as if I had struck a hard blow straight in the solar plexus of scores of people.

One painful memory of my own failure is of a day, when Cathy was about seven, when I said I'd go for a run with her when I got home from work. When I got back, there she was, eyes alight and delighted with excitement, and decked out in little running shorts and tennis shoes.

I still remember her stricken face when I said, 'Sweetheart, I am *so* sorry. But Daddy has a lot of work I must do right now.'

Her face fell with disappointment. Oh, shame on me! I'm so sorry, Cath. I really am.

More successfully, I sought with Carol to be at any school concerts, sports occasions or whatever in which the kids were participating. If I was home, it didn't matter what team Martin was playing in; he knew Carol and I would be there, watching with keen interest and fun.

Imagine our gratification when Martin on his wedding day, getting married to our lovely daughter-in-law Samantha, said in his wedding speech that 'although Dad was gone a lot, it never really felt like it'.

But what I do know is that if my kids have turned out as well as they have, Carol must take the major credit for a deeply sacrificial job of parenting.

Table talk

One of our little institutions was family mealtimes together and family 'Pow-Wows'. In her book *Chai Tea and Ginger Beer*, our Debbie looks back on these:

> Home was also about food and nourishment – in every sense of the word! Mom is a great cook and meal times are always an event. We had dessert every night of my childhood! It was usually fruit salad, which came from the trees in the garden and became known as '365'. But it was the ceremony of it all that I still remember. Bowls, serving spoons and material napkins.

I can't recall ever eating a meal in front of the television set. It was around our big dining room table that much of my learning was digested, and over platefuls of food these thoughts, values and ideas began to take root.

Debbie continues:

> Around this table more than just eating took place. It was also here where we held what we called our family 'Pow-Wows'! I was appointed as the secretary in charge of taking minutes. The Pow-Wows were the forum where we would discuss anything from our monthly goals, our suggestions for an upcoming holiday or even our bad table manners! Mom and Dad were equally obliged to share with us their own personal goals and I remember listening very intently when they spoke. I felt that I was getting a glimpse into their grown-up worlds and I liked that.[2]

Actually, Carol and I always believed that mealtimes were exceedingly important and special occasions for togetherness, communication, conveying values in a low-key way, and plain fun and laughter. For breakfast and dinner we all sat down together, and even did so for lunch if or when we were all home. We also had a good few years when we were able to have brief and crisp family devotions after dinner, together with Ntombi Ndlovu, our domestic helper.

One of Carol's and my commitments to the Lord in our marriage was to open our home to whomever he brought through our door. As a result, we have had the joy of offering hospitality to hundreds of wonderful people from all walks of life. Carol has managed this amazingly well, and her homemade soups, lemon syrup, ginger beer and homegrown salads have become legendary.

Carol certainly has the gift of hospitality and has said: 'I am grateful that Michael's ministry opened many doors for me and also encouraged me to explore my own gifts and how I could best use these to serve the Lord.

'Our home became a constant hub of hospitality, and maintaining a beautiful garden, offering good food and meeting the varied needs of those passing through became *my* offering to the Lord. Other doors that opened were opportunities to serve in areas within AE and also in a weekly ministry in our local disadvantaged community. I have done this for nineteen years and am grateful for the privilege to make a difference.

'So it has been a rich life of sharing travel and meeting some of the finest people in the world. I have loved learning from Michael about theology, politics and the application of Christian living. Yes, sometimes I longed for times of less responsibility and more carefree fun – with Michael, but there was no time for pity parties, and our special planned family holidays provided memorable times for filling up our emotional tanks.'

Outings

As Carol has said, memories constitute a rich treasure of emotional input into children's lives. And our memory bank was often enriched by our camping holidays!

One of the first of these was in Kenya, where I was on assignment. Carol and Cathy, who was still pretty much a toddler, had joined me. Friends lent us a camper-van for a weekend and we went to Amboseli, a spectacular game park under the shadow of Mount Kilimanjaro. We pitched camp and Carol began, in very cramped quarters, to prepare supper while I played outside with little busy-bee Cathy. Suddenly, perilously close by, we heard the loud roar of a lion. Whereupon I seized our little bundle of treasure and leapt back into the camper-van where somehow, between Cathy and me, we managed to knock the cooking supper on to the floor. While contemplating divorce proceedings, Carol wondered why I had

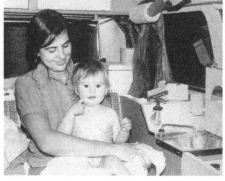

Camping in Amboseli

not learnt to manage our child better! But as the evening sun bathed Kilimanjaro in a glorious pink glow, and our rescued meal was thoroughly enjoyed, all was forgiven and we camped happily ever after.

In South Africa our camping trips happened in our unsophisticated second-hand camper-van, otherwise known as 'Campie'. It consisted of a rather precarious canvas tent roofing which opened up out of a trailer. But we could all squeeze in. Then came all the infuriating arguments about who would wash the dishes!

After breakfast one day, we set off on a hike into the spectacular Amphitheatre in the Drakensberg Mountains.

On the way back from this 22-kilometre (14-mile) excursion, there was a huge cloudburst, which turned one stream we had previously crossed into a raging torrent. But with Victoria Cross-type bravery we formed a human chain, clinging to each other for dear life, and negotiated the hazard.

Nearing Campie, Debbie announced: 'My feet are giving me a heart attack!'

Outings, holidays, camping trips

Back at camp all the other, top-of-the-range caravans seemed to be soaked, but Campie looked the worst for wear: its canvas had sunk into huge bowls of rainwater, so heavy that all the metal poles had bent beneath the weight. But not a drop inside! After an hour of emptying water from the sagging canvas (Debbie's cardiac condition now on the mend), we roasted marshmallows around the fire. We were the proudest campers in the camp that night!

Holidays

Christmas holidays with Carol's folks, and her three siblings and their children, at Kenton-on-Sea and their lovely seaside home, provided great memories for over 30 years. We all packed in, and the children bonded with their cousins like brothers and sisters; they are all today among each other's very best friends.

Sea and surf and river fishing occupied us daily. Once Martin got interested in fishing, he allowed me to manage his bait department. I had to catch live mullet with a throw-net, bait up his line, and let him catch the fish and shower himself with glory. On one of these throw-net expeditions, we were trudging through deep mud on the edge of the river. Suddenly Marty burst out, 'Daddy, I'm following in your footsteps and I'm getting stuck!'

Bam family at Kenton-on-Sea

I laughed. Then reflected: Hey, Michael, just think of that. He's following in your footsteps in real life. And what if you so live and behave that your bad example makes him get stuck?

There's a moral here for all dads.

Adolescence

One of the most significant assignments Carol and I had was preparing our kids for adolescence and coping morally and spiritually with its multiple challenges.

We carefully navigated this space with the help of tapes recorded by James Dobson and Focus on the Family. One suggestion I found particularly helpful was for dads to take their daughters on a daddy–daughter date on the day they turn 13 and enter their teen years. Just make it very special and an awful lot of fun. He also suggested that parents give their daughter a beautiful necklace with a silver heart-shaped locket symbolizing a commitment to keep her heart and body for the man she would marry. Both these dates on Cathy's and Debbie's thirteenth birthdays were memorable and moving to each of us.

Another idea from Dobson, for when the kids were on the edge of puberty, was for dads to go away for a fun weekend with their sons, and mothers with their daughters. Book a special place, take the recordings

Debbie stands next to a sign on the beach: 'Strand [beach] exclusively for the white group'

Debbie, turning 13, and Michael on a daddy–daughter date, 1987

and listen to them together. These tapes covered not just the 'birds and bees' stuff but also subjects like peer pressure; self-esteem; temptations around sex, drink or drugs; coping with depression; emotional and physical changes; the nature of real love; thinking into one's future occupation, and so on. The faith and spiritual sides also came in strongly, of course.

Carol took our girls to beach resorts on the Natal coast at the appropriate times. I took Marty out to Sani Pass Hotel, just under the Drakensberg Mountains. We listened to the tapes in-between plenty of fun time spent swimming, playing squash or tennis, and climbing small mountains. Part of the fun was taking a four-wheel drive up the precarious and spectacular Sani Pass to the very top of the Drakensberg. Wow! The views!

The beauty of the tapes – which allow Dobson to do the hard yards on each subject – was that one could stop them, interject, and say, 'You know, son, just to illustrate the point Dr Dobson is making, I remember once when I was in my mid-teens, and I faced a situation just like that. Let me tell you what happened and how I coped.' (Or it could be 'how I failed, and learned from it'.) Or Martin could say, 'Hey, Dad, what does peer pressure mean?'

Each of these experiences set the children up with principles to help them navigate the turbulent teenage waters they would soon be facing. I think Dobson's counsel to do this just before puberty was good, in other words, before all the hormones and new emotions kicked in and the kids were emotionally involved! If one had tried it once they were midway through the billowing storms, it could have been like throwing a lifebelt when they were already drowning in mistakes and follies. It would risk making the exercise too little, too late. And also, as kids get into the teen years, parents don't carry quite the same authority. Someone once said, 'A teenager is a person who doesn't realize that one day he'll be as dumb as his dad!'

For Carol, being home much of the time gave many opportunities to be alone with the kids, while my extensive absences forced me to be innovative. So I decided with the girls in their last couple of years at school to go out with each one on a monthly daddy–daughter date. This was usually just a meal or a milkshake. Not too long. Not too heavy. However, virtually every time, there was an opportunity to check out how my daughter was doing, or make a brief input on this or that issue of real importance.

One of the girls, I forget which, as a young adult once wrote to me: 'Oh, Daddy, those dates! We will never forget them.'

And even when the girls were older, I tried as far as I could to keep up these occasions, whenever possible even having to negotiate past their husbands!

With Marty the occasions were easier and more obvious: tennis or squash games, or fishing together; playing with him at junior school in the father–son cricket match, and once winning as a twosome; or going with Carol to watch him play football (soccer), cricket or rugby.

Once, I hatched a little plan for Martin – I would ride into mountainous southern Lesotho on horseback with him. Shortly before I did so, I was invited to speak at the same time to a very significant group of leaders in Pretoria. I declined, saying I was already committed. They remonstrated. But I stood firm. Finally one asked, 'What kind of commitment would keep you away from this strategic opportunity?'

'Well, if you must know,' I responded, 'I am riding on horseback across southern Lesotho with my son.'

Big silence at the other end. Then a grunt of approval!

And what a magical week Marty and I had, riding the mountainous bridal paths, crossing rivers, sleeping in Basuto huts, waking to the mist over the mountains. Then I let him drive back in our car, under my tuition and coaching, even through a torrential thunderstorm. And he did it!

And surely, speaking at the leaders' meeting in Pretoria would soon have been forgotten as it vanished into oblivion along with many such meetings I had spoken at.

One other thing I did for a couple of years, this time with the girls whenever I was home, was to go with each of them to modern piano lessons together. We all got quite good actually! And driving to and from the lessons invariably gave us time to natter, or even touch on something moral or spiritual.

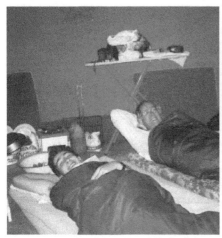

Father–son trip, Lesotho, 1988

Young adults

Amazingly, a way opened up for Cath to go on a scholarship to Covenant College, just outside Chattanooga, Tennessee, for a couple of semesters. I accompanied her partway to the United States, stopping over in the UK with some special time in mind.

In London we had the weekend of a lifetime with my sister Olave and her family, plus my mum who was visiting at the time. I introduced Cath to old friends. Olave also took us up to my haunts in Cambridge, where we walked her around the university, paying a visit especially to my college, St Catharine's. The view over the River Cam across spectacular lawns towards King's College Chapel was as hauntingly lovely as ever.

Saying goodbye to Cathy as she flew on to the USA and Covenant College rent my emotions asunder! Little did I guess that the few brief months would turn into four years as Cath was offered a full scholarship until graduation. My visits to her while on AE assignments were always bittersweet experiences. Sweet because of the fun, but poignant in the partings, which had me weeping all the way to the airport!

There too she met her husband Jonathan Scott, a splendid, highly capable and godly fellow, marrying him in 1994. Jonathan's whole family came out to South Africa for the wedding, which was held in the Michaelhouse chapel; Jonathan's dad, a Presbyterian minister, married them, and I preached the wedding sermon. After some days of 'private' honeymoon,

Cathy and Michael – Cathy going to the USA, 1990

the honeymoon then went 'public' as the bridal pair joined the two families in a magnificent shared adventure up to the famous Kruger National Park. Jonathan is mad about the outdoors and nature, and his company is all about equipment for nature activities like mountaineering, kayaking, skiing, and adventure walks. So a Kruger experience fitted in here really well for him. A local church in the park had said that we could use the church house and its grounds to base ourselves in, and even sleep in, if I would preach on the Sunday morning. I think that was the only time I ever peddled a sermon commercially! But it was fun. Sleeping in a church vestry was definitely a novelty!

On one of the nights, the game wardens said they would like to let us have a free night in a big treehouse in the middle of the bush. This was a long single room in which all of us, including the bridal couple, settled down for the night! I told Jonathan's dad, Arthur Scott, that this was the cultural custom in Africa – that all the families sleep in the same place for one night along with the bridal pair! The startled look on his face spoke volumes.

Cathy and Jonathan are still in Chattanooga 25 years later with their dear boys, Andrew and Cameron.

Sometimes when one sets up something for one's kids, however apparently inconsequential, one never knows the consequences which will follow. Cath is now the CEO of a non-profit organization in Chattanooga called Bible in the Schools, and in 2017 we proudly attended her graduation for her master's degree in Leadership and Education.

Debbie, like Martin, went to the University of Cape Town, where she studied primary school education. Debbie had a scholarship for her final master's year, and Marty had one nearly all the way through. How faithfully did God provide!

Once when I visited Debbie at UCT and she fetched me from the airport, I noticed her petrol gauge gyrating violently. When I expressed alarm, she said, 'Don't worry, Dad. When it does that, there is still fifteen kilometres' worth of petrol to go, and to town is only twelve.' My stress level rose dramatically and I said, 'Pull in at the first garage,' which she did. I told the attendant to fill it up.

At this my child looked at me with that pathetic look impecunious daughters reserve for softy dads. What could I do but hand the attendant my credit card?

As we drove off, Debbie said: 'Oh, Dad, I knew that trick would work!'

While at UCT Debbie met Gary Kirsten, a legendary and great South African cricketer who had opened the batting for South Africa for some 12 years. They married in 1998 and Debs switched her teaching career to journalism to allow more flexibility to accommodate their travelling lifestyle. In 2015 she published her first book, *Chai Tea and Ginger Beer*, quite a bestseller, and now, along with her writing, works as a motivational speaker. The Lord has blessed them with a trio of lovely children, Joshua, James and Joanna.

I always told Gary, whenever he got a century, that he should give me at least partial credit for praying him through!

In fact, once while returning from the USA following a ministry tour, I stopped in London where Gary was playing at Lord's; I had a ticket for the next day. But Gary was opening the batting that same day against England. I watched it all on TV, and I think I prayed him through every ball, until he got his century, and his name inscribed on the great oak panel-board in the pavilion at Lord's. I always felt my name should have been there as well! In heaven the Lord may take me aside and do some adjusting to my theology of prayer about sport!

Likewise in 1999. Gary hit a bad patch, and there were mutterings he should be dropped from the side. But in his second innings – again with his father, mother-in-law and wife praying up a storm – he batted for two days and made 275, thus equalling the then highest Test Match score by any South African cricketer! Now that was fun. And his place in the team was assured for another five years.

In 2001, Martin married his lovely Samantha Anderson, whom he had met at UCT. While at UCT, Samantha was doing her degree in Primary School Education and she is now a very fine teacher. I remember that while they were still courting, Martin thought he could score points with her by having a 'number one' haircut which made him look like a convict. I was shocked by his appearance, to which he responded, 'Dad, the chicks really dig this!' Sam, always very much her own person, quite firmly responded, 'Actually, the chicks don't dig this at all!' I was gratified to see a young woman coming into Martin's life who really had the measure of him! Sam and her family are also wild about the bush, and visits there had always been a major part of her life. This clicked well with Martin, who has developed a passion for wildlife photography. And by the way, Samantha has had him grow his hair again!

Their three children, Jessica, Emma and Matthew, light up any day for them and for all of us. And their main aim whenever I visit them is to push me as vigorously as possible into the swimming pool. I oblige, to their ecstatic delight, by somersaulting in with such a splash the little pool is almost emptied. We have been incredibly proud of Martin as he graduated with a Bachelor of Science degree, and later a Master of Business Administration from the University of Cape Town, and then, after a good few years in mining concerns, he became CEO of a company producing rubber products for mining. He takes it in his stride to travel the world on business. But our greatest sense of gratification lies in the fact that he married someone who would be a wonderful mother, while he himself is a deeply committed father and family man, as are my two sons-in-law. At the end of the day these are the things that mean most.

Oh, but I must say, our eight grandchildren have been a rave and a delight for Carol and me. The Bible says: 'Grandchildren are the crown of the aged' (Proverbs 17.6). Certainly the joy of the aged. And they have fulfilled a promise the Lord gave me back at Fuller Seminary in about 1962 when I felt pretty desperate about finding a wife:

> Your wife will be like a fruitful vine within your house [and we do have one at home!];
> your children will be like olive shoots
> around your table . . .
> thus shall the man be blessed who fears the LORD.

> (Psalm 128.3–4)

The psalm ends: 'May you see your children's children' (verse 6).

Whole Cassidy family on holiday at Kenton-on-Sea, January 2016

Something not lost on the grandchildren, nor on me, is Carol's omni-competence, from which I have benefited all our married lives. I remember one Christmas when the grandkids were performing a little play they had devised; the plot involved me taking them into a forest to cut down a Christmas tree. In the sketch my car gets a puncture and Joshua Kirsten says comfortingly, 'Don't worry, kids. Granny will fix it!'

Carol

Never, ever, can I adequately thank the Lord for bringing Carol, my Rebekah, so miraculously into my life back in 1969. I never deserved such a one who is not only beautiful on the outside but also on the inside – and surely one of the most godly, capable and practical people I've ever known.

In 2015 I wrote in my journal about Carol:

1 My wife

2 My friend

3 My love

4 My lover

5 My children's mother

6 My grandchildren's granny

7 My home-keeper

Carol

8 My household manager

9 My administrator

10 My financial manager and director

11 My carer

12 My guardian

13 My guide

14 My advisor

15 My counsellor

16 My home-maker and dietician

17 My garden-creator and supervisor

18 My spiritual director

19 My ministry sustainer

20 My medical superintendent

21 My unique gift from God

22 My all in all.

Thank You, O thank You for her, Lord. And I love her.[3]

Hassles

Did we ever have unhappiness, difficulties or traumas as a family?

Of course we did. We were blessed with a lovely family life, but we were not the perfect, no-problems type of family. We had our ups and downs.

Sometimes these involved coping with disappointments (e.g. poor exam results, or failures in promotion or recognition), or financial struggles to make ends meet, though the Lord always came through in the end. Then of course there were the occasional family rows with tears, anger, or rough and regrettable words. These particularly happened on long car journeys. The kids would fight and hassle each other, until finally in desperation I would pull the car up on the side of the road, get all the kids out, remove my shoe and give each one of them a hiding just south of the equator where it makes all the difference! Thereafter if the hassles started again, I would just put my foot on the brake, slow the car down . . . and from the back came cries of petition: 'Oh, Daddy, no, we promise to be good!' This method is not legal now, of course, in South Africa, but it sure worked well back then!

As for Carol and me, do we ever have hassles?

You bet we do. We are both strong characters and can on occasion meet head-on, steel on steel. But we have learned to talk things through and forgive. The late Ruth Graham, Billy Graham's wife, used to say, 'A good marriage is made up of two good forgivers.'⁴ It is true; mutual forgiveness is the oil that lubricates the wheels of a good marriage. More often than not, I am the one at fault, and, such is my pride, I often struggle to acknowledge this. But finally we claw our way back into closeness and press on.

Forgiveness is interesting. It is the one thing which, along with apology, can change any situation. Unforgiveness, on the other hand, inflicts pain both on ourselves and on the unforgiven.

To be sure, Carol and I find that if we harbour grudges, or brood on hurts inflicted, intentionally or unintentionally, we are both left miserable. And even our relationship with the Lord suffers. It is important to air these hard feelings at an appropriate time and in a way that does not aggravate the situation. Of course the Bible does say: 'Don't let the sun go down on your wrath' (see Ephesians 4.26). One comic paraphrased this as: 'Don't go to bed angry; rather, stay up and fight!'

We do both surrender our life-and-death destinies to the Lord and know that in his hands all is well.

Meanwhile we celebrate the family God has given us, both immediate and extended, and feel that, next to Christian salvation, the greatest gift God has for humans is the Christian family.

Thank you, dear Lord, thank you.

23

Leadership as the possession of difficulties

———◆———

I press on towards the goal to win the prize for which
God has called me heavenwards in Christ Jesus.
(Philippians 3.14 NIV)

Besides my biological family, one of life's greatest blessings has been the gift of the wider Christian family and being part, quite often a leadership part, of the body of Christ, although this has often been challenging and full of difficulties.

Some of my greatest friends have been those whom I have worked beside in ministry. And I have had the privilege of walking alongside and learning from some wonderful Christian leaders along the way. I can confirm that taking part in any form of Christian leadership is to become caught up in very demanding situations. The challenges are immense.

We saw and experienced this in 1974 when Billy Graham called together 3,800 Evangelical Christian leaders from 150 countries for the first-ever Lausanne Congress on World Evangelization. It was a very difficult assignment but worth all the struggles because it has shaped Evangelicalism and the cause of evangelism worldwide ever since. Out of the Lausanne Congress came the famous and landmark Lausanne Covenant, again very difficult to draw up, but one of the finest and most comprehensive faith statements in the history of the Church, and one which AE adopted and enshrined in our constitution, and to which it still holds firmly.

While the Swiss city of Lausanne was a furious hustle and bustle of final preparations before the congress started, our own AE leadership team met in nearby Glion, high in the Alps. We were discussing the need to gather the Christian leadership of Africa together to face very specifically the difficult challenges of our own continent.

Festo Kivengere spoke up amid enthusiastic discussion as the pan-African idea increasingly gripped our imaginations. 'What I think we should do', said Festo, 'is share the vision with as many leaders as we can gather during the Lausanne Congress this coming week.'

Lausanne '74: Festo in the foreground

And the following week, Festo and I did indeed share the vision with a group of some 45 African leaders, who responded with unanimous enthusiasm. 'You know,' chuckled Festo to me later, 'I think we've landed ourselves a little job!' But he saw that we had embraced a task involving enormous difficulties and challenges.

Leaders of the Pan African Christian Leadership Assembly (PACLA), as we called it, needed to grasp this.

Nose to nose

For sure, in the run-up to the assembly there were indeed many challenges. For example, as we began to plan, major resistance came from far-right Evangelicals and from far-left ecumenicals, as we had reached out in both directions. Each side saw us as compromisers if we included the other!

Besides the theological sensitivities, there were also political chasms. But despite these divisions, as our PACLA chairman, Gottfried Osei-Mensah, said, there was 'the glorious sense that God was in PACLA. He was overcoming the obstacles.'[1]

As leaders we had to lead without losing our nerve. We saw that if one is truly sure a venture is of the Lord, one can press through the most severe challenges and come out on top.

We saw pre-PACLA that confronting the problems head-on was the only way to go. So we flew here and there across Africa to sit down with the protagonists on both sides. Bruce Bare, the first chair of AEUSA, used

275

to tell me: 'Mike, if there is a major problem, there's no way to solve it other than nose to nose.' Slowly, both ends of this ecclesiastical spectrum came together and people began to sign up from all over Africa.

Then we found out that, due to Africa's communication difficulties, hundreds we had invited had not replied or their replies had not been received by us. Were they coming? Were they not? This was nerve-racking because from West and Central Africa we had booked out a Boeing 707 to bring delegates to the conference, an action that had taken faith from PACLA's leaders. So we sent out a couple of colleagues, Titus Lwebandiza from AE Tanzania and John Wilson from AE Uganda, and what troupers they were, going from city to city and capital to capital!

When the PACLA date finally arrived, the plane filled up at its various stops with laughing, witnessing delegates. Seemingly most of the stewards and stewardesses on board were evangelized before the plane landed in Nairobi!

Visa challenges

Meanwhile, in apartheid South Africa we faced another major problem in getting Kenyan visas for the over 80 delegates who were signed up. The Kenyan government seemed downright resistant. And South African delegates were getting very anxious. What should they do? Cancel or come?

Our faith, like Abraham's, kicked in, and 'no distrust made [us] waver concerning the promise of God, but [we] grew strong in [our] faith as [we] gave glory to God, fully convinced that God was able to do what he had promised' (Romans 4.20–21).

Finally, an immigration official reported to us that we had been granted visas for the black delegates, but not the white. But we could not accept this. Kenyan Dan Serwanga said: 'How can we accuse South Africa of discrimination, if we discriminate?'

All we could do was pray. Into my own heart, three days before the flight was to leave South Africa with our delegates on it, came a very strong sense from the Lord: 'Don't cancel. Let events take their course. Let the process roll. Have faith. I haven't brought you thus far to fail you now.' So we kept the South Africans in blissful ignorance of our dramas, and left them to proceed to Johannesburg airport.

Back in Nairobi, Immigration said the matter now had to go to Foreign Affairs. Then Foreign Affairs said it had to go to the Vice-President, but he was away upcountry and would not be back until Tuesday. The 80 South Africans, with a booked plane, were to fly on Monday night.

In desperation, and with only three hours until the plane's departure, it suddenly occurred to us, 'What about the Attorney General of Kenya, Mr Charles Njonjo?' We knew he was married to a white South African who, we were told, was keen for the South Africans to come.

'Let them in,' said Njonjo with authority.

And that was that. In a jiffy we telegrammed South African airport officials. Two hours later, the plane was on its way.

Together in one place

In an unprecedented display of African Christian togetherness, 800 leaders gathered from 49 out of 51 African countries.

Though we had arranged a diverse programme, not everyone was happy. As programme chairman, I was approached by a number of African leaders saying they objected to an Afrikaner missiologist, David Bosch, speaking on the second night of the congress.

'He is your brother in Christ, brethren,' I remonstrated. 'You must receive him. Besides, you won't have heard an Afrikaner like him before.'

In the event, David's message was the interracial breakthrough moment for the congress. David took us all to the cross with his challenge of reconciliation and forgiveness. Most in the congress were in tears. The Spirit of Jesus was breaking barriers down and bringing healing as people came together in repentance.

And thus it was throughout those momentous ten days.

Not that the congress was without its challenges for me personally. I must say, as a white South African I felt pretty insecure, especially when I was due to speak at one of the main plenaries of the conference. But Festo, who had huge credibility around Africa, insisted on introducing me. He shared with the audience his thoughts on how we had ministered widely together as a black Ugandan and a white South African and how this had become possible through our discovery of ourselves as 'miracle brothers' through the reconciling love of Christ.

He then gave me a great embrace of love.

Sitting in the assembly, Simone Ibrahim of Nigeria said he was deeply touched by this demonstration of brotherhood: 'In that moment the Holy Spirit worked in my heart and I began to feel that perhaps after all violence was not the way in Southern Africa. Maybe we could really bring an answer by the power of Calvary love.'[2]

Indeed, PACLA set up a network of key and precious relationships all across Africa that remained in place for a generation.

Titus Lwebandisa, top left, and delegates at PACLA, December 1976

John Wilson at PACLA

A memorable moment

One evening during PACLA Billy Graham, who was one of our speakers, was not feeling well and remained in his hotel room in bed. I went to find out how he was doing, and we shared what was for me a memorable evening. I remember asking him, 'Billy, if you were to live your life over again, what would you do differently?'

'First,' he said, 'I would study more. When I hear Michael Green preach I realize how inadequately I have studied. Second, I would cut out everything secondary. For example, when I get back to the USA I have to go somewhere to lay a foundation stone. I shouldn't be doing things like that!'

Yes, leaders work hard to know their field and focus, and maintain priorities. Second things should not become first things.

I also shared with Billy that night that I was very depressed and despairing about South Africa. The non-racialism of PACLA accentuated South African racism as endemic. Unchangeable. I told Billy that in my secret heart I sometimes felt like leaving the country.

'Michael,' Billy responded, 'you know, it is your context that makes your ministry special. Almost unique. You'd lose that if you left South Africa. Beyond that, you must grasp that there is a very special blessing attached to those who endure unto the end, even unto death.'

It was a determinative word to my spirit. Billy was saying that good leaders face difficulties, and don't give up. It was a word I much needed.

There are many other ways in which Billy inspired me to keep going, and I continue to bless the Lord for bringing him across my path, even as he has now gone to be with the Lord. When he died at the age of 99

Billy Graham with Festo Kivengere in the background

in February 2018, I felt that a great era and season of church history had closed. I wonder if that voice can ever be replicated?

In fact Billy Graham and the late John Stott have been my main leadership inspirations in terms of my ministry throughout the years.

Janani Luwum

Another poignant and memorable moment was a challenge to the congress from AE Uganda Chairman, Archbishop Janani Luwum:

> The Church must always know that in the process of witness and service to the world, either individually or collectively, she is sometimes called to a life of suffering for Christ and His Gospel. Paul was not afraid when he said he completed in his body the suffering of Christ. And it is through such suffering that the seeds of the Gospel are sown, scattered abroad and nourished. Thus Peter and John were not afraid when they were taken before the Council as recorded in Acts 5:41: 'Then they left the presence of the Council rejoicing that they were counted worthy to suffer dishonour for His name.'[3]

Was this a mere theory? A nice religious platitude? An airy-fairy dream? Was this just sentimental conference talk? For Janani Luwum, at least, the answer was just around the corner.

Gottfried Osei-Mensah, Billy Graham and John Wilson

As we spent time together at PACLA, he knew that Church and state were on a collision course in Uganda. And as the key Christian leader there, he grasped the personally perilous nature of this fact, as I gleaned from him one morning when we had breakfast together. Here was a man of prodigious moral and spiritual courage.

Just a couple of months later, back in Uganda, he and his bishops, as leaders of the Ugandan Church, in a very strong letter (dated 8 February 1977) challenged Idi Amin, whom they were obliged to address as 'His Excellency Alhaji, Field Marshall Dr Idi Amin Dada, VC, DSO, MC, Life President of Uganda'.[4]

The letter expressed the strongest protest yet to the President about the desperate situation in the country, and declared that the state was now going way beyond what the Church could tolerate.

Some ten days later Luwum was arrested, almost certainly tortured, and was praying aloud for his captors when he, along with some others, was shot dead. According to Festo, 'prison vehicles were driven over the bodies to make it look like a car accident'.

Janani Luwum (centre) at PACLA

Janani's death sent shockwaves through our PACLA family. A more gracious, peaceful and saintly man you could hardly imagine. A giant indeed in spiritual stature, and the kind of Christian leader of which any nation could be justly proud. In fact, so influential was Janani's contribution that since 2015 Uganda has declared a public holiday on 16 February every year in celebration of his life.

Of course the tragedy of Uganda had its poignant but important lessons. The first was that no government and no one person should ever be allowed to become too powerful. Power corrupts, and absolute power corrupts absolutely.

Second, sin is all-pervasive in black hearts as well as in white, and the doctrine of selective depravity must be banished to the heretical outer darkness where it belongs. Bishop Lawi Imathiu of Kenya, who was also with us at PACLA, said: 'Unless the Church in Africa condemns black sin as well as white sin, it is doomed.'

Third, when tyrannies or potential tyrannies arise, they must be resisted, especially by the Church, when the first signs of totalitarianism appear. Thus the German Church awoke too late from its slumber in the 1930s, and likewise the Chinese Church in pre-communist China. To be roused at the eleventh hour is too late.

Finally, I believe Uganda showed the world that New Testament faith and courage, to the point of martyrdom, have not yet fled this earth. Amin did not destroy the Church there. For it is founded upon Jesus Christ.

I love Idi Amin

After Luwum's death, Festo was number one on Idi Amin's enemy list. Amin was after him. Indeed he and his wife Mera were in great danger. Very reluctantly they took the decision to flee into exile. They were tracked through Ugandan forest roads towards the Rwandan border, where they took to small paths over the mountains and into Kigali. Festo's welcome was huge, but he knew he had to hurry on to the AE office in Nairobi.

Already there were scores of exiles seeking AE's help to escape overseas. This very quickly included scores of university students who wanted us to try and get them university scholarships wherever available. This finally led to our forming RETURN (Relief, Education, Training, for Ugandan Refugees Now). In the end AE placed some 300 such students in universities across the world.

As Festo now headed towards our US office and the prospect of fundraising for our stricken team and Ugandans generally, he himself was struggling hugely with the Everest-sized challenge of forgiving Amin. En route, it was the Easter weekend and Festo went to All Souls Church in Langham Place, London, where John Stott was Rector. The message included Jesus' anguished Good Friday prayer, 'Father, forgive them; for they know not what they do' (Luke 23.34).

Festo felt the Spirit of God speaking to him and saying, 'If all those people around the cross at that time had included Idi Amin, would Jesus have said, "Father, forgive them all except that big Ugandan"?' Festo realized that could never be. And there and then he decided to forgive Amin, at which point his spirit leapt into freedom and joy. This in due course

Michael and Festo Kivengere, top of Table Mountain, relaxing during ministry tour, 1980

led on to his writing his penetrating and blockbuster little book, *I Love Idi Amin.*[5]

'You love Idi Amin?' said some sceptical journalist in a press conference.

'Yes,' replied Festo. 'Because Christ loves him and died for him, I am obliged to love him and want God's highest and best for him. But that does not mean I like him or have to like him.'

Another sceptical journalist asked, 'If you were with Amin and he handed you a revolver, what would you do?'

'I would hand it back to him and say, "Sir, this is your weapon. Mine is Jesus and the Bible."'

Yes, leadership is the facing of challenges and the possession of difficulties!

Leading in Africa

Of course in Africa today there are still many difficulties and pressures pushing us Christians apart. But as we get a vision of the functional rather than the merely theoretical or theological nature of the body of Christ, as we saw at PACLA, we begin to see that we are not intended simply to think lovely thoughts about our unity in the body of Christ. Rather we are to function together as a body. We have to move away from the 'you do your thing, I'll do mine' approach, and resolve to be mutually and practically supportive of one another.

The huge task in Africa cannot be tackled, let alone accomplished, unless we do it courageously together.

Africa is like an enormous lion and we are like tiny insects in the face of it. Yet we are not powerless, because as the old Ethiopian proverb says: 'When spiders' webs unite, they can tie up a lion.'

24

Reaching for the rainbow

Any Christian leader, or indeed any Christian working for the Lord, will tell you that it is no surprise to feel downhearted or even depressed after a big initiative. Physical and mental exhaustion is part of it, of course, and it is necessary to recognize this, give it time and if possible take a break!

Such moments are times also to lean harder than ever on family, friends and colleagues. One comfort for me was that AE South Africa could continue as strongly as ever because our administrative genius Malcolm Graham, and his mega-capable wife Bertha, were there. Malcolm came into the work in 1974 and became for decades afterwards the admin glue holding our whole ministry together. So I could not only slow down and rest but face new and fresh challenges which were around the corner. Sharing one's thoughts and feelings with a spouse, friend or colleague such as Malcolm can often be a crucial first step out of the Slough of Despond, as described in *Pilgrim's Progress*.[2] I have also used my own

Malcolm and Bertha Graham – administrative kingpins of AE for decades

journal to great effect in this regard. It's a place where, like the psalmist, I can let it all hang out, and write down my most anguished cries.

After PACLA, that's where I was. I was as bruised and battered as I had ever been. I took some days out, and rescue came when I found myself reading in the Old Testament book of Numbers (chapters 13 and 14) and hit again on the story of Moses sending out the 12 spies to spy out the land of Canaan.

The 12 men returned. First there was a minority report of faith from Caleb and Joshua: 'Let us go up at once, and occupy it: for we are well able to overcome it' (Numbers 13.30). Then the majority report from the ten declared: 'We are *not* able to go up against the people; for they are stronger than we . . . and all the people that we saw in it are men of great stature . . . and we seemed to ourselves like grasshoppers, and so we seemed to them' (verses 31–33, my emphasis).

But Caleb and Joshua hung in there:

> [They said:] 'The land, which we passed through to spy it out, is an exceedingly good land. If the Lord delights in us, he will bring us into this land and give it to us, a land which flows with milk and honey. Only, do not rebel against the Lord; and do not fear the people of the land, for they are bread for us; their protection is removed from them, and the Lord is with us; do not fear them.' But all the congregation said to stone them with stones.
>
> (Numbers 14.7–10)

Then the Israelites 'murmured' and said they would prefer to return to the less perilous haven of Egypt. A faithless slap in the face to both God and Moses.

I read on and saw the anger of the Lord for this faithless posture: 'According to the number of the days in which you spied out the land, forty days, for every day a year, you shall bear your iniquity [in the wilderness], forty years, and you shall know my displeasure' (14.34).

Caleb and Joshua put on the spectacles of faith. God could do it: 'If the Lord delights in us, he will bring us into this land' (Numbers 14.8). The ten wore the spectacles of unbelief: 'We are not able to go up' (13.31).

I went, early one morning, on to some sand dunes overlooking the magical Kenton coast and brought this passage before the Lord. It seemed to me as if the Lord put a penetrating question to me: 'My son, are you with the ten, or the two?'

'Well, Lord, I guess if I am honest I am with the ten.'

Then sternly came the Lord's word: 'Now move over to the two.'

There and then I did. And I have never gone back to the ten. My resolve was to look at South Africa and its giants with the eyes of faith. Indeed, 'we are well able to overcome' (Numbers 13.30).

In my journal I recorded a simple prayer:

> Give me, O God, the spirit and faith of Caleb and Joshua. Do we not need then to gather the South African Church together on a far more ambitious scale than in Durban '73, *to discern together what it means to be witnesses to Jesus Christ as Lord and Saviour in South Africa today?*[3]

My memory tells me that before I left Kenton, I phoned my friend David Bosch to share this vision with him.

'Michael,' he said, 'this is exactly what I also have been thinking.'

So was born the South African Christian Leadership Assembly (SACLA)!

And there was so much confirmation. The Student Christian Association sent me a letter at that very time, saying they wanted to get a national student leadership gathering together *à la* PACLA.

Then there was a second letter from the Revd Douglas Bax of Grahamstown, urging that we organize a mini-PACLA for South Africa. 'Is it not possible', he wrote, 'that such an event, by the grace of God, might yet open the way toward reconciliation, justice, peace, and away from the judgement and anger of God that threatens our society because of our profound alienation from and discrimination against, each other?'

Next was a letter from Keith Jesson (our capable USA Office Director), saying our US Board wanted my thoughts regarding AE's role in bringing 'a contribution to the total peace effort in Southern Africa'.

Then came a letter from Professor Elaine Botha at Potchefstroom University, talking of a small group she was gathering to think how to apply biblical principles to the political and economic situation in the country. Once more, the nation theme.

As we shared the idea, people caught it and we began our planning.

Moving forwards

A committee was formed with David Bosch as the logical chairman, plus a representative non-racial and interdenominational group of leaders from around the country. I was asked to be Programme Chairman as I had been for PACLA.

Just as downheartedness can follow initiatives for the Lord, so it is that obstacles often precede them! Such was the case with this major undertaking. Trumped-up rumours, assorted character assassinations

David Bosch

and fearmongering seemed to meet us at every turn. I had a call from a senior Pentecostal minister in Port Elizabeth who said, 'Michael, I need to give you some information. One of my parishioners, who is in the Bureau of State Security [BOSS], came to me the other day and said he needed to confess something that was heavy on his conscience. He told me that BOSS had been mandated to destroy SACLA.

'It explains a lot, my brother,' I replied with gratitude, and then rang David Bosch with this information. David seemed unsurprised.

'Michael, we must redouble our prayers and vigilance, and try not to lose heart.'

Of course, while setting up SACLA, David had to continue with his lecturing and other academic responsibilities for the University of South Africa (UNISA). And I had to fulfil my AE responsibilities; we couldn't let our Main Thing ministries in evangelism falter because of the SACLA task.

Steve Biko

One of the invitations at that time to Maurice Ngakane, a good friend, and myself was from the Christian students in the black university of Fort Hare to lead a mission to their university. As it turned out, permission from the university authorities for that mission was withheld for fear of a riot – a sad reflection on the state of affairs in South Africa. But going to Fort Hare for our initial discussions gave us a significant opportunity as we stopped in King William's Town to meet in secret with the brilliant black consciousness leader, Steve Biko. He had been banned, which meant he was confined to that magisterial district, required to report weekly to the police, and not allowed to meet with more than one other person at a time or it would be constituted 'a meeting' according to the banning order. Sickening restrictions, each one.

In my ignorance, I had previously got a bit frustrated with Biko when I was trying to set up some non-racial university missions. He would resist these, saying, 'We blacks need to find each other first, and establish our own identity.' His line was that blacks needed first to build themselves into a position of non-dependence on whites. This way they could move themselves towards a deeper realization of their own potential and worth as self-respecting people. So, in his view, sharing non-racial activities with whites, even in missions, was at that moment premature. After all, if blacks left white liberals to speak for them, no black spokesperson could ever develop for the blacks.

I was being educated.

Consequent upon his banning, Steve Biko was arrested on 6 September 1977 and taken by South African political police to room 619 of Sanlam Building in Port Elizabeth. There he was handcuffed, his legs were put into leg irons, and he was chained to a grille. He was subjected to 22 hours of interrogation, tortured, and beaten, especially with severe blows to his head. These fatally damaged his brain, resulting in his lapsing into a coma. Six days later he was dead.

All this seemed sickening beyond the telling. An overflowing expression of national insanity. A case of 'Whom the gods wish to destroy, they first make mad.'[4]

Anyway, while Minister of Police Jimmy Kruger notoriously said of Biko's death, '*Dit laat my koud*' (It leaves me cold), the temperature of everyone else in the country rose by many degrees. The police responsible for this heinous crime were never indicted.

For me and many others, Biko represented the last best hope for a peaceful accommodation of black aspirations to resolve the growing South African race crisis. In condoning Biko's death, the apartheid government was forcing black resistance into dark and violent channels.

Spiritual renewal

Such dreadful realities in our rainbow nation toughened our resolve to do all we could to bring hope in the name of the Lord. We had faith that SACLA would bring something significant, but in the face of all that was involved, I found myself in need of fresh resources from the Lord.

I was searching for a new experience of the Holy Spirit. This was, first, to deepen my personal prayer-life; second, to empower my ministry; and third, to give me emotional fortitude to cope with the many pressures around us.

Early in the year I had had the sense of the Lord saying: 'In August I want you to go to that Renewal Conference in Milner Park in Johannesburg. But first you must get right with A and B [two friends and former colleagues] from whom you are alienated.'

It was a sobering word.

As to the latter injunction, I postponed it and procrastinated until just a few days before the Renewal Conference when I was in Nairobi for meetings with Festo and our Kenyan team.

This ruptured relationship had lasted many years. After dreaming a lot about my estranged friends, I decided to write them a letter:

> I have woken, having had yet another of a myriad dreams about you both which I have had down the years since you left AE. All of these have been warm, affirming and reconciling and I have felt increasingly over the last months that God was speaking to me through these and other means to re-establish contact with you. I feel as if in my own heart and attitudes there has come a healing from on high along with both a capacity to forgive and forget the past and an ability to face more fully and realistically my own contribution to its pains and complications.
>
> If it is also in you to forgive and forget, and if it is indeed the Spirit of God who moves me at this moment, then I wonder if there is any let or hindrance why we should not re-extend the hand of fellowship to one another and at least set our feet upon the path of re-entry to real relationship. I am conscious that the cost of such re-entry might be not inconsiderable, for sometimes such healings are not cheaply bought, but the cost to our souls and to the Kingdom of an ongoing alienation is almost certainly much greater. In any event, I am fully conscious of the yearnings of my own soul. Dare I ask if there are any reciprocal yearnings in yours?

I signed off, 'Still yours because His'.[5]

At breakfast I told Festo of my early morning conviction and action.

'My brother Michael,' said Festo, 'you have now entered the Calvary arena.'

That arena, for now, involved the conference and my own plenary address. God had given me a difficult message: 'Remind them Soweto is only eight miles from here. And the fullness of the Holy Spirit must also bring forth justice.'

On the day of my talk I was overcome with weeping as someone read out the Scripture: 'Unless a grain of wheat falls into the earth and dies, it remains alone; but if it dies, it bears much fruit' (John 12.24). Many friends rushed to gather round me and pray and comfort me. The fact was I had seen that a new dying to my sinful self was a prerequisite of new Holy Spirit life.

That night in trepidation I gave my talk. My subject was 'Hope for South Africa'.

I indicated in my opening comments my concern that in the excitement and euphoria of the conference we should not allow ourselves to dangle too far above the complicated and ravished soil of South Africa today. If we did, we would 'allow the intoxication of these days to open up an unbridgeable gulf between this great and glorious conference and the tortured tragedy of a city eight miles away called Soweto'.

I went on:

> At the outset I have to say this, that humanly speaking I see no hope. Humanly speaking, I believe that we have through our political lifestyle sown a wind and we must, if human events take the normal course, reap the whirlwind. Every human law of history tells me that this is so. Humanly speaking, if we live in a moral universe, as I believe we do, then the judgements of history must surely overtake us. Humanly speaking thirty years of official discrimination cannot but produce a political convulsion of shattering and mind-boggling proportions. So humanly speaking I feel the situation in our land today is absolutely hopeless . . .
>
> And yet, I want to say before this gathering that *I am hopeful*. I am full of hope in my heart tonight . . . because of two tiny but atomic words that we see throughout the Bible . . . *But God* (e.g. Acts 2:33; 10:28; 10:40).

'In those two words', I continued, 'I see the tremendous hope we have for this land because they speak of Divine initiative, a Divine intervention in history.'[6]

I ended with a strong plea not only for repentance but also for reconciliation between husband and wife, between race and race, tribe and tribe, denomination and denomination, nation and nation, friend and friend.

While the other talks had been greeted with huge amounts of laughter, clapping and regularly interspersed eruptions of 'Hallelujah' and 'Praise the Lord', mine was received with quietness throughout and then silence.

I can't deny I felt pretty stricken and a failure. And I went to bed heavy-hearted, though sharing a room with Bishop Michael Nuttall, my dear friend of Cambridge days. Our time of shared prayer over, we said goodnight and turned to the business of slumber.

But I could not get to sleep. Instead, quite out of the blue, the Spirit of praise, release and freedom came upon my soul. Hour after hour I praised my God in unrestrained rejoicing. And I did not grow weary. All my senses were vibrantly alive to God. The Holy Spirit was blessing me. Wave upon wave, it seemed. He seemed to be bubbling up from within, surrounding from without, ascending from below and descending from above!

I kept praising until Michael Nuttall's alarm clock went off at dawn, and I told him of my experience. We began praising the Lord together until finally the insistent calls of bacon and eggs were allowed to intrude upon the delights of the soul. It had been a monumental night. I had never had one like it. Nor have I had a comparable one since.

I think, next to conversion, this was perhaps the most important spiritual renewal experience of my life. Not that I have manifested or walked in the Spirit since then as I should have. But definitely something new happened which has affected my life ever since. And it certainly strengthened me to cope with the desperate challenges of mounting SACLA and facing upcoming ministry demands.

Crazy busy!

In 1978 we had 30 major ministry invitations to fulfil!

These included setting up the National Christian Leadership Assembly (NACLA) in Rhodesia; Festo and I conducting our first major mission in Sydney, Australia, to that great city's southern suburbs (all part of an AE ministry tour); and our first Egyptian missions in Cairo, Assuit and Alexandria; and finally a third mission to Hilton College in South Africa. I was also writing a book on the PACLA conference and editing another – a collection of all the assembly papers.

Really, I don't know how we did it.

I was also constantly being challenged as SACLA programme chairman to deliver the programme for scrutiny and interaction, but I had to reply that the Lord had not given it to me yet. I kept praying and seeking the Lord. Then in the very early hours one morning, in my sleep, a programme outline rolled out in vision before me, like a scroll.

Before my experience at Milner Park I could never have visualized or entertained such a prospect. I leapt from bed, rushed to my study and wrote it all down. Then a week later I presented it to the SACLA committee. David Bosch and the others all said unanimously, 'Yes, that's it. Praise God. We'll go with it.'

The SACLA programme handbook has it still recorded, just as I got it.

Smelling a rat

At one of the SACLA Council meetings an Indian brother came up and badgered me to let him have the draft programme. But I smelled a rat. Some of us sensed he might be a government informer or spy.

We then found out that he was working for an extreme right-wing, so-called Christian newspaper. We also gathered somehow that they were producing an anti-SACLA booklet.

One of my AE colleagues, very naughtily, and not at my instigation, went all innocent into this newspaper's offices and said, 'I've heard you are producing an anti-SACLA booklet. I too am anti-SACLA and I'd love to see it.'

'Brother, we only have it in draft form, but I could give you a photocopy of it.'

'Fine,' said my colleague without a trace of remorse!

Then while he was waiting, the phone rang at a desk behind the screen. And he heard the voice of our Indian brother from the SACLA Council, who had so wanted the programme, responding to his caller: 'SACLA, madam? SACLA comes from the pit of hell.'

The document, maybe 20 pages long, was handed to me by my smiling and slightly guilty detective colleague. It was a diatribe, particularly singling out David Bosch and me as the main villains of the piece. In the bibliography, I noted that 23 of the 26 quotes used were from my own writings. David and I were branded as 'liberals and communists'.

Next day John Tooke called in at the newspaper and asked to see our SACLA Council friend.

'Listen,' said John, taking him outside, 'we know who you are and what you are up to. If you come anywhere near the council again, or set your foot in the Pretoria Show Grounds for SACLA, we will publicly expose you.'

And that was the last we ever saw of him. In fact, not long after SACLA itself, that paper collapsed and closed down, and its editor fled overseas.

Thus was one of the promises the Lord had given us fulfilled: 'If any one stirs up strife, it is not from me; whoever stirs up strife with you shall fall because of you' (Isaiah 54.15).

In fact we saw this happen several times.

This tied in with that other promise, already referred to, which we stood on, time and time again in our AE ministry, a few verses later in Isaiah:

No weapon that is fashioned against you shall prosper, and you shall confute every tongue that rises against you in judgement. This is the heritage of the servants of the Lord and their vindication from me, says the Lord.

(Isaiah 54.17)

David Bosch and his wife, Annemie, also faced vilification from within sectors of the different Dutch Reformed churches. They were considered betrayers of the Afrikaner cause. This was incredibly painful to them, coming as it did from their own people.

But for me personally the worst strike came with a story put out by the security police, and picked up by a Dutch Reformed mission leader in then South West Africa (now Namibia). It was almost laughable in its desperation, but it didn't seem so at the time: 'Michael Cassidy is a terrible chap, has left his wife, and is living with a black woman in South West Africa!'

I felt awful telling Carol, and thought she might collapse.

'Don't worry, darling,' she replied. 'I once worked for the Christian Institute with Beyers Naude, and the security police were always putting out stories like that on him.'

A strange journey

A very fine young man called Vusi Khanyile, now a prominent businessman, went around South Africa to encourage black participants for our conference. We were insisting, as in Durban in 1973, on non-racial accommodation. This time, though, blacks were to stay in white homes. And whites in black homes. This was scary and upset lots of people!

The smearing of my name began to get to me, particularly that of the Dutch Reformed mission leader in then South West Africa.

Preparing my talk for the conference on 'The Person and Work of the Holy Spirit', I felt a nudge inside: 'How can you work on this talk with such bitterness in your heart towards your brother? You need to go and get reconciled to him.'

'But, Lord, he's in another country,' I wailed.

'I'm well aware of that,' said the Spirit.

'But, Lord, it will cost money. I can't use AE money.'

'You have some savings, don't you?'

If the Lord knew about my savings, he should have known they were very skimpy!

'Now, my son, I want you to go. And don't tell him you are coming.' That last bit was very clear.

As my plane took off some days later from Johannesburg airport, I said, 'Lord, this is the weirdest errand I have ever been on. *Help!*'

I found my way by taxi to the Dutch Reformed headquarters in Windhoek and asked to see Dominee Petrus Louw, as I shall call him.

'May I say who's calling?' said the receptionist.

'No,' I replied. 'I'll tell him myself.' And at least now, I knew he was in!

In a few moments I was ushered in. The Dominee's face went ashen. I imagine he recognized me.

I duly explained my errand, and said I wanted to ask his forgiveness for my bitterness on account of all the things he was saying about me. And I had flown here especially to say that.

He sat there thunderstruck.

Then he began to open up about all his fears of SACLA and his hostility to me.

Our sharing became deeper. And warmer. We were each demythologizing the other. And he found I wasn't so off the wall as he thought. And I found he wasn't so racist as I had imagined.

Then he confessed something interesting.

'You know, Mr Cassidy, I have connected with the security police here who want to put up money for you to be charged with high treason against our country. But I will stop that now.' Then he added, 'I would like you to come out here sometime and speak at some of my mission stations.'

Shortly before we ended and prayed together, he blurted out: 'You know, it's lucky you didn't tell me you were coming, or I would have left town.'

I chuckled and flew back to South Africa on the wings of praise. And, for sure, my preparations for my SACLA talk on the Holy Spirit went better after that!

Great is thy faithfulness

We had decided the conference would start and end each day with everyone together, and thereafter break into five sub-conferences: one for pastors and lay leaders; one for church youth-group leaders; one for university student leaders; one for leaders from high schools (teenagers, in other words); and one for government, civic and business leaders.

Then, before supper, we would break for an hour into assigned groups with representatives from all these different sub-conferences meeting in groups of 10 or 12 to dialogue, relate, communicate and find one another.

We would also take the bulk of the weekend before the assembly opened to train a thousand facilitators in conflict resolution.

Things looked bleak when only seven weeks before SACLA we had only 800 delegates. We were familiar with this pattern, so we redoubled our prayers. We told people we didn't want bridge-builders. We wanted people to be bridge-crossers, because Jesus was the bridge and all we had to do was cross over to each other through him.

Suddenly it was as if a stronghold was pulled down. A week before SACLA, 5,000 had signed up. And other leaders were applying to come. From Kenya, Uganda, Angola, Zaire (as it was – the Democratic Republic of the Congo (DRC) now), Nigeria, Ghana, Botswana, Malawi, Lesotho, Swaziland, South West Africa/Namibia. From overseas too they applied – from Germany, the UK, USA, Switzerland, Holland and Austria.

Dr Piet Koornhof, the Minister for Plural/Bantu Affairs, whom we knew as a professing Christian, summoned me to his office. He seemed very agitated.

'Brother Cassidy, this thing is very dangerous. So we have the army ready to move in if it explodes. And we will hold you accountable.'

'Dr Piet, it won't explode. I assure you. Because God is in it. Your army can relax!'

I went over to the Pretoria Show Grounds Main Hall to hear our sound system in operation under the skilled supervision of AE's Mike Odell. Suddenly the auditorium burst into magnificent stereophonic sound as the hymn came forth:

> Great is Thy faithfulness, O God my Father,
> There is no shadow of turning with Thee,
> Thou changest not, Thy compassions they fail not,
> Great is Thy faithfulness, Lord, unto me.[7]

My tear ducts opened and, high up back in the stands, I wept profusely. I sensed the Lord's affirming word and embraced it. It was all going to be fine. SACLA would not explode.

At last SACLA opens

Our excitement knew no bounds a week or so later as we all headed back to Pretoria for the assembly. En route, Carol and I stopped in a little Free State town for petrol. I duly picked up a leading Afrikaans newspaper. There was a whole full-page of negative press on SACLA, David Bosch and myself.

Of course final logistics were something of a nightmare. One of my young AE Indian colleagues, Derek Bruce, and his brother, found a mix-up on their accommodation, and seemed stranded. A white woman nearby offered to help: 'You could come to my house.'

Our registration helper said with relief, 'Your name, madam?'

'My name is Strillie Oppenheimer. We'd love to have them.'

So Derek and his brother found themselves in one of the most lavish and magnificent homes in all South Africa belonging to the world-famous Oppenheimer family.

'It was like going from Bethlehem's manger to a palace,' said Derek afterwards, chuckling!

Other episodes were less comfortable. The Singhs, an Indian couple, found themselves assigned to an Afrikaner home. They were shown their room, and then told they could use the outside toilet in the garden.

'No,' said the Singhs very firmly, 'we are all brothers and sisters in Christ and all SACLA delegates.'

Their hosts acceded. And these two couples became devoted friends.

SACLA opened that night with worship; then Bishop Desmond Tutu spoke on 'The Lordship of Christ'. At that stage most whites were very hostile to Desmond, and to smooth the way we had John Staggers, an African American from the USA, sing, 'real southern style', 'Jesus Loves Me, This I Know', accompanying himself blues style on the piano.

Desmond caught the spirit of the moment and was more than equal to both the occasion and its mood. He started right on in, launching that other lovely African American song: 'A-a-a-men, A-a-a-men, A-a-men, Amen, Amen'. Not too hard to get the words, of course. Everyone joined in, raising the roof.

Many whites who didn't know Desmond other than as a human rights and anti-apartheid activist were captivated.

I whispered to someone sitting next to me, 'If Desmond doesn't mess up in the next few minutes, he will get a standing ovation, even from all the whites here.'

And that is exactly what happened: everyone on their feet, clapping and shouting for a couple of minutes.

The assembly moved from high point to high point, all the speakers excelling themselves on the overall theme: 'What It Means to Witness to Jesus Christ as Lord and Saviour in South Africa Today'.

As people left the arena that night, they went out to find the tyres of hundreds of cars slashed, and communist 'hammer and sickle' signs spray-painted on cars and banners.

The devil is getting really worried, we thought.

Dialogue

But there was pain too, and many tears were shed in the pre-supper dialogue groups when wounds and hurts and prejudices were shared – maybe

SACLA conference

SACLA participants David and Lesley Richardson (with daughter Nicky), who out of SACLA were called to AE

a teenager from Soweto with a Cabinet Minister or MP, a black housewife from a poor background with a rich white businessman from a wealthy white Johannesburg suburb, an Afrikaner dominee with a politicized Anglican priest.

The transforming chemistry of these groups was remarkable. A Harvard University social science professor who had come to research the 'change processes in SACLA' wrote, after doing a random survey, that in his entire career he had never seen such transformative change in so many people in so short a time. And it happened in the main in the dialogue groups.

As Tom Houston of Nairobi once said: 'Nothing happens till people meet.'

Beyond that, everyone seemed concerned to help everyone else. Some participants were astonished and humbled to see Philip Russell, Anglican Bishop of Natal, helping to clean the public toilets.

The experience of the 500 Dutch Reformed leaders who finally came was revolutionary. And in their eyes the much-maligned David Bosch was mightily vindicated, and his courageous faith recognized and saluted.

One such Afrikaner leader, the retiring head of the prestigious mission department of the Church, came up and apologized for how I had been handled by his fellow NGK leaders. Then he added: 'As to Dominee Petrus Louw out in South West Africa who had greatly coveted succeeding me as head of the Department of Mission, he was finally declined the position because of what he did to you.'

Interesting.

In any event, many of those Afrikaner leaders were seeing the birth pangs of the rainbow nation emerging. Even Afrikaner newspapers changed their tune. It looked as if we were rounding a corner.

One person deeply affected was Professor Johan Heyns, Professor of New Testament at Pretoria University, and Moderator of the largest Dutch Reformed church.

We were unaware then that he would shortly go out and launch a theological commission to ascertain if apartheid and the Bible were compatible. Also unbeknown to us then, the commission would report six years later to the Synod with the landmark conclusion: 'Apartheid is a sin.' This ruling, in my mind, did more long-term to undermine apartheid than all the violence, boycotts and economic sanctions which came later. The fact was that once the Dutch Reformed Church had said apartheid was a sin, the theological skids were under the government. And the end of the iniquitous system would be in sight. Interestingly enough, former prime minister of South Africa and chief architect of apartheid, Dr Hendrik Verwoerd, had once said that if the DRC stopped justifying apartheid theologically, the system would be finished. The state was dependent on the Church to keep legitimizing its policies.

Also unbeknown to us at that moment was the terrible fact that Heyns would some months later receive an assassin's bullet through the back of his head while reading Bible stories to his grandchildren.

Change

There is no doubt that SACLA birthed change.

Moss Ntlha, now Secretary General of the Evangelical Alliance in South Africa, was a student at SACLA and notes:

> SACLA helped me understand that God had not abandoned His creation to the forces of evil. Rather, the power of God transforms people at their very core, and makes them restless and impatient with the sinfulness of the world. They become part of God's transformative influence in the world. SACLA framed a language and a paradigm for witness that clarified the challenges that faced my generation of evangelical student leaders.[8]

An Anglo-American businessman, David Richardson, who shortly thereafter joined African Enterprise, reflects:

> My wife Lesley and I were also challenged at SACLA to face our growing wealth and began to think about ways we could share it. We decided also to sell our home in Kloof, near Durban, as we felt this money was needed by others. So we soon gave all that away.[9]

David went on to serve in the AE ministry for 37 years with distinction.

The first phone call I got on the afternoon SACLA ended was from Cabinet Minister Piet Koornhof: 'Thank you, Michael. This is the miracle we have been praying for. This is the breakthrough for South Africa.'

As for the South African army he had alerted, it had been a lazy week!

What next?

It was a very good question.

25

Open doors to Africa

I have set before you an open door, which no one is able to shut.
(Revelation 3.8)

Mercifully, as 1980 opened, our South African and USA boards had granted me and the family a six-month sabbatical to the United States. The fact was that I was more than exhausted after SACLA in every possible way. And I was in crisis about my ongoing calling to urban Africa.

Younger leaders have from time to time asked me how I kept going strong with ministry well into my seventies. The key, I believe, lay in taking annual holidays, as well as these invaluable sabbatical times which AE gave me approximately every ten years. I think without these I could

On the way to the USA: Cathy and Debbie excited about the aeroplane food, 1980

have run myself into a couple of nervous breakdowns. They varied in length from a few months to one of ten months.

We all arrived as a family in Pasadena, California, where our AE office was, on the evening of 12 January 1980. This Support Office and others existed in order to raise funds and prayer support for the AE ministry in Africa.

Jet-lagged Debbie asked next morning, 'Is this breakfast, lunch or supper?'

After a week in a missionary home secured for us, we found ourselves in an embarrassingly splendid huge white American car, loaned to us by George Rowan, a great AE supporter, and driving up to Santa Cruz in northern California.

We stopped a number of times to admire the gorgeous views on that coast and explore a few beaches. Back in the car, four-year-old Martin admonished me: 'Daddy, if we keep stopping like this we'll never get to America!'

The purpose of this excursion was to speak at the beautiful Mount Hermon Christian Conference Center and share ministry with Luis Palau, the great Argentinian evangelist, and Presbyterian pastor Earl Palmer, in a pastors' conference. Sabbaticals don't let you off the hook entirely! In the opening dinner Luis and I were asked to give a few words of greeting.

Sabbatical in the USA: Catherine, Carol, Martin
and Debbie with luxurious American car

Afterwards Cathy said, 'Daddy, are you always asked to speak when you go out to restaurants?'

The following evening, Luis spoke powerfully on the letter to the church at Philadelphia in Revelation 3.7–13. I was riveted not only by Luis's message generally, but more specifically by the verse 'Behold, I have set before you an open door, which no one is able to shut' (Revelation 3.8). Jesus seemed to be saying: 'I am the one who opens and shuts, and I can open Africa to you, regardless of your colour or origins.'

Next day Luis, such a dear friend, and I walked and talked in the lovely woods surrounding the centre, and I shared with him my thoughts about my vocation and the impact of his message the previous evening.

Luis said: 'That's amazing. When I was reading that passage, I thought of you. Then I looked up and saw your head bob up above all the others in the crowd. Look, Michael, the Lord has called you and given you the cities of Africa. Nothing must deter you from answering that call. Nothing. Certainly not your skin colour. Or country of origin. No! Follow your calling.'

Next day, an African American from San Francisco asked to have breakfast with me. The conversation was very ordinary, not seemingly significant. But then he handed me his business card. Inscribed on it were the words: 'I have set before you an open door' (Revelation 3.8). Yes, the door that could not be shut. Again something exploded in me.

When we came to leave southern California, Carol and I felt we should call on Leta Fisher who had been my Prayer Mother when I first came to Fuller back in 1959, and continued to pray for me ever after.

After tea with Leta, and before we left, she said, 'Let's pray together. But before we do so, I want to give you a Scripture the Lord has given me for you. It is Revelation 3.8: "I have set before you an open door, which no one is able to shut."'

Imagine! The Lord was certainly making the point!

From Pasadena we went to Washington DC to spend a month with the Washington Fellowship and Prayer Breakfast Movement led by my old friend Doug Coe. It was a special time over the next few weeks, meeting many congressional leaders, plus people like the chaplain to Congress.

Then we headed for the UK, and on to Tyndale House in Cambridge where I was scheduled for a month of writing. Finally, I enjoyed a month of supervised reading and tutorials with my long-standing mentor Bishop Stephen Neill at Wycliffe College, Oxford. These were exhilarating days with lovely memories of cycling as a family along the banks of the River Isis, and staying in the Bonginkosi home of our friends, Tonia and Stephen Bowley.

Then it was time to set our sights towards home. We had decided to go via Switzerland and Israel. In Lausanne we visited our dear friend Sylvie Annen and also called on the elderly de Benoit sisters, Claire-Lise and Elizabeth, who had been our translators/interpreters at the Nairobi PACLA Conference in 1976.

'Michael,' said Claire-Lise, 'have you seen my French translation of your book on PACLA?'

'No,' I replied with eager interest. 'But I am thrilled you've done it.'

'Well,' she went on, 'I want to give you a copy. But first let me inscribe it with a verse God has given me for you. It is Revelation 3.8: "Behold, I have set before you an open door, which no one is able to shut."'

I guess by now the message, given four times, was getting through to this hard-of-hearing sinner! Open doors to the cities, towns and townships of Africa had been sovereignly given to us.

Doors opening

The word we had received from that verse in Revelation certainly proved to be true. Over the years, the Lord graciously opened doors for the AE family to expand, and today we have ten teams across Africa. In addition to the South African team we now have teams in Malawi, Zimbabwe,

*Meetings under the trees: Mike Odell of the media
team talking to a little girl in a rural community*

*David Hotchkiss of the media team making
sure the sound for our preacher is all in order*

Kenya, Rwanda, Uganda, Tanzania, Ethiopia, Ghana and the Democratic Republic of Congo. And support offices in Australia, the United Kingdom and Europe, in addition to our USA–Canada office. There are many people across the globe who faithfully support us in prayer and financial giving, and by volunteering their time.

A team of AE's size and diversity can be a challenge to manage and operate, but the Lord has kept us together through it all.

*Taking seriously the social implications of following Christ:
a volunteer ophthalmologist helps a little girl during a mission*

The Lord has opened doors for hundreds of missions to take place and our footsteps have truly trodden the ground of the continent. Missions have ranged from small meetings under the trees in rural communities to projects involving hundreds of evangelists preaching in our modern African cities and among our leadership circles. And the gospel message has touched the lives of all kinds of people, from murderers in prison to presidents and members of royal families.

AE's aim has been not just to 'convert' people, but to make disciples of Christ, disciples who will take seriously the social and political implications of following him.

Back in South Africa

Back in South Africa, the first 'doors' to open for new missions were the townships of Imbali and Edendale on the edge of Pietermaritzburg.

Then came Elsie's River on the edge of Cape Town. I stayed in the home of a young Anglican minister, Njongungkulu Ndungane, later to be Archbishop of Cape Town. We closed out with an extraordinary rally of 10,000 people.

Doors also opened for Festo Kivengere and me to tour South Africa as a duo, holding 17 rallies with audiences totalling some 20,000 in Soweto, Johannesburg, Durban, Pietermaritzburg, Cape Town and Pretoria.

While we were in Cape Town an astonishing door opened to Stellenbosch University, a major Afrikaans campus and a Dutch Reformed

Festo preaching to a packed city hall in Pietermaritzburg, 1980

stronghold. A huge throng turned out. I was at first surprised to find myself as an Englishman in such a context. But Festo's address, winsomely delivered with love and compassion, was a knockout. A black Ugandan conquering Afrikaners!

In Pretoria, though I can't remember how it happened, maybe through Cabinet Minister Piet Koornhof, Festo and I found ourselves sitting in the Union Buildings office of Pik Botha, then Foreign Minister of South Africa. Festo gave his testimony of being liberated by Christ from his hatred of whites. Botha seemed very moved and said his government wanted to change, 'but we will do it in our way and our time'. He was also much touched when we prayed for him at the end.

Botha was very emphatic about his government controlling the change processes. Nothing would happen haphazardly. Afterwards, Festo said with a twinkle, 'Now I have met a *real* Afrikaner!' A few years later, when my book *The Passing Summer* came out, we were gratified to hear that Foreign Minister Pik Botha was reading it!

Kimberley and its Galeshewe Township came next, and our Ambassador Youth Team was occupied for weeks ahead of the mission, working among the angry youth of the township. But it all boiled over; there was rioting in some of the schools over so-called 'Bantu Education', and some class-rooms were torched.

The police cordoned off the township and dropped propaganda leaflets from the air. Our AE youth team was stuck there for three weeks. So although that door was formally closed to us, nevertheless our youth workers were already in there before it closed!

When we arrived for the Kimberley city preaching mission, we found that the youth leaders of Galeshewe wanted to meet with us. We learned of their very valid grievances and laments over so-called Bantu Education. So while the front door of the township was closed, the back door was secretly opened, and these youngsters came to us that way! We put together a document on their grievances which we promised to try and get to government.

In the mission's final rally, hundreds came from the township, because the cordon was by now lifted, they were free to come, and we at the end were able to go in there. God proved himself faithful. Not even govern-ment police could close doors that God wanted to open.

The apostle said: 'A wide door for effective work has opened [for ministry], and there are many adversaries' (1 Corinthians 16.9). Yes, the doors were open and opening, but for sure there were many adversaries. Nothing was easy.

Juba, southern Sudan

One of the open doors was in Juba in southern Sudan, an area which had been almost completely closed to Christian outsiders, not least because of the civil war. Some of the worst crimes against humanity were committed by northern Sudanese Arabs against the southern Sudanese black peoples.

An invitation had come to us in early 1982 to conduct a major Christian mission to the capital. The team would consist of Festo, Gershon Mwiti from AE Kenya and myself.

But the big question was how on earth I as a South African resident could get in, given that South Africans, especially white ones, had been declared *personae non gratae* in Sudan. On the Sunday before leaving, a lady in our home church who had a mature prophetic gift, and who knew we were going to southern Sudan, came up to me after the service and said: 'Michael, the Lord has brought to me that as he can open the eyes of the blind to see, so too he says he will make those with seeing eyes blind so that they will not see you are from South Africa!'

Blind eyes

It was a reassuring word. On previously checking with officials at both the British and American embassies in Nairobi, we had been told that my getting into Sudan was a lost cause: 'Don't even bother.' The British High Commission officer said that even in normal circumstances, it could 'take up to six weeks to get a visa, even on your British passport, let alone with the complication of your South African birth and residence. Some people sit in that embassy waiting room every day for three weeks before getting attention.'

I replied that my schedule required that I could only allot one morning of three hours, the morning after arriving in Nairobi, and before taking our charter flight to Juba at 2.00 p.m. that same day.

I arrived at the Sudanese Embassy in Nairobi at 9.00 a.m. as it opened, and informed the officials I needed a visa for southern Sudan and would be leaving in five hours' time.

No one seemed put out by this request.

I filled out the application form with all the details required, including place of birth – 'South Africa' – and place of residence – 'South Africa'. I also in my heart claimed again Revelation 3.8!

'Come back at noon,' the official said.

I duly complied. And was handed my passport, plus visa for entering Sudan! It had taken three hours.

'Thank you, Lord. Your promises hold true!' I prayed silently. 'And you can indeed seemingly blind the eyes of those who see!'

We had a quick bite, then headed out to the Wilson Private Airport where our little charter plane was waiting, plus Gershon Mwiti and the rest of our AE crew, but without Festo. He, in a mysterious twist, had been denied entry – because he came from Uganda!!

As we flew low into Juba I prayed again: 'Lord, blind the eyes of the immigration official who will check my passport so that he does not see the reference to South Africa.'

We landed at the little makeshift airport and went to passport control. The official, with, in my imagination, his eyes glazed over, took less than ten seconds to glance at my passport and stamp it with approval for entry. Our hearts rejoiced. How faithful is our God!

The town of Juba was devastated by war, with only one functioning petrol pump. The hospital had been declared almost a no-go area. Our mission there was a precious time of preaching and proclamation, with many responding to the gospel. Our outreach included a Governor's Prayer Breakfast, with the Governor and other political leaders present.

In one church service, I remember, when it came time to take up the collection, a woman came forward carrying a live hen. Though difficult to put in the offering bag, the feathered creature was deposited at the front of the church where it was entrusted for safekeeping to some brave deacon!

Something else I remember in that mission was visiting a small Anglican theological college which had 14 ordinands. The principal, an Englishman, told us that 12 of the 14 had been called into the ministry through a dream in the night.

'The Lord often speaks to the people here through dreams,' he said.

Most wonderfully, that first Juba mission opened the way for others. Then in 2007 we conducted their first National Prayer Breakfast. In 2010 was another citywide mission. Recently we have held other missions with the new political leadership, led by our International Team Leader, Stephen Mbogo of Kenya. Southern Sudan finally got its independence and became the world's newest nation, South Sudan, on 9 July 2011. Stephen Mbogo's reconciliation endeavours were widely hailed in South Sudan. And they are part of ongoing AE ministry projects there. In fact, we have now set up an AE associate office there with one staff member.

Blantyre, Malawi

Blantyre, Malawi, was a very special open door.

The origins of this opportunity went way back. In my 1961 tour of Africa, Ed Gregory and I stopped in Malawi where we met up with Jack and Ruth Holmes, then posted as government servants to Nyasaland; this was the family I had met on board ship when going to South Africa in 1959.

Now they invited us to meet in their home along with a few other concerned Christians, including two missionary ladies, Marjorie Cranage (who died in 2018 at the age of 100) and Cora Vines. We shared the vision of AE, and these two ladies and the others started a prayer meeting for Malawi, and the whole of Africa, which ran for about 25 years.

Their prayers and these other contacts opened up the way for me to speak at the Blantyre Keswick Convention. In that convention I was assigned a brilliant young interpreter and explosive preacher called Stephen Lungu. I think my preaching ended up playing second fiddle to my fiery translator! We overnight established a firm friendship which there and then led me to invite Stephen to join AE, and he has served the ministry with huge distinction until now. He became our first Team Leader in Malawi and then succeeded me as International Team Leader, and his preaching ability took him all over Africa and around the world.

Stephen's story of his transformation, from being a bomb-throwing 'terrorist' in Old Rhodesia to a passionate Christian evangelist, is known all over the world, especially through his bestselling book *Out of the Black Shadows.*[1]

Anyway, these links opened the door to the citywide mission to Blantyre. Its success led the Blantyre newspapers to describe it as a 'born-again city'. Eight thousand follow-up letters were sent out to those who had professed commitment. Even the level of crime came down.

One story I especially remember related to one of our Zimbabwe team members, Chris Sewell, preaching to a crowd of 15 or 20 people at a bus stop. Following his message, he asked all who wanted truly to respond to Christ to put their hands up. Everybody did.

'I'm not sure you understand me,' said Chris. 'You aren't just committing your life to Christ for today or tomorrow, but for all the rest of your lives. This also means repentance from all the bad stuff in your lives. If you still want to take this Jesus, put your hands up again.' They all spontaneously did so. Still wondering if some of this reaction was superficial,

*Stephen Lungu, Songe Chibambo and Yeremiah
Chienda; Stephen Lungu translating for Michael, 1983*

Chris said, 'If you really, really want to come to this commitment, I want you to kneel down on the pavement.' All 100 per cent went down on their knees.

At this point the bus arrived. The eyes of the startled driver almost burst from their sockets when he saw all his potential passengers kneeling on the pavement! He opened the bus door with a whoosh of wind, then called out, then closed it again and opened it again; but none of his passengers moved from their knees. Utterly bewildered, the driver closed the door and moved on. The passengers, who had missed the bus to town, but caught the bus to heaven, now listened to Chris's counsel about discipleship and received the gospel literature he handed out.

A few days later a young African man, his face shining with New Testament glory, came to the mission office. Our staff asked him who he was and where he came from. He gave his name and then added with a beaming smile, 'I found Jeeesas at the bus stop!' All in our office roared in delight and gathered round to pray for him.

Also helping us in that mission was a very energetic and able young intern called Songe Chibambo. We were all struck by his giftings and invited him also to join AE, where he rose in due course to become AE's Pan African Missions Director. And he remained in the ministry till his retirement at the end of 2018. A remarkable, dynamic fellow.

In the Blantyre Mission, not only were we able to bless Blantyre, but Blantyre blessed us with two amazing Christian workers in Steve and Songe, and opened the way for us to plant a full-time team in Malawi.

Monrovia, Liberia

The Anglican Archbishop of Liberia had been with us in a Renewal Conference in Nairobi and during that time was given a vision from the Lord of a citywide interdenominational mission to the country's capital, Monrovia.

'But the churches are very divided,' he said. 'I represent the Christian Council of Churches in Liberia and then there is the Evangelical Fellowship of Liberia. But between us is a great gulf fixed.'

'Let's see what we can do,' said David Richardson, our irrepressible 'never say die' Pan African Missions Director.

David had demonstrated his unifying, diplomatic and reconciling skills in many situations, so he knew his way around the process of getting the churches of a city together.

On one of his many trips to bring people on board, David was arrested for photographing a public building. The police officer, who might have locked him up – and such things happened then in Liberia, and people were 'disappeared' – was unpleasant and aggressive. He finally told Dave he could be freed if he paid $100 to the officer's 'Presbyterian church'! Mmm! David thought that discretion, even if a bit morally dubious, might be the better part of virtuous valour, and the contribution was duly made. At least David's wife, Lesley, would see him again!

Finally, an invitation came in July 1984 from the Combined Churches of Liberia for a citywide mission in March 1985.

With no direct flights, travelling to Liberia from South Africa was exceedingly complicated, and involved going via London. Tickets were exorbitant, costing our media team and two others no less than R50,000. And those were the days when the rand meant something!

I was sitting in my study at home a week later, doing some final preparation for the mission, when there was a knock on my door, and in walked all our media team, plus Abiel Thipanyane. I nearly fell off my seat.

'I thought you guys were in Liberia!' I expostulated.

'Well, you must let us tell you the story,' they replied.

Apparently, after an exhausting overnight journey via London and Freetown, Sierra Leone, they arrived in Monrovia, were checked through immigration and customs along with all their AE sound and PA equipment ($340 worth of excess baggage!), and emerged into the Liberian sunlight.

At this point they were suddenly approached by plain-clothes officials saying there was a problem. Yes, Home Affairs had given permission for the South Africans to enter, but Foreign Affairs had overruled it! The five were shunted back to the airport lounge to await deportation.

While local mission representatives raced back to town – a full 50 kilometres (30 miles) – in an attempt to chase down government officials and appeal to them, our crew waited prayerfully in the airport. The mission reps returned at 3.00 p.m. that afternoon with a new verdict.

'The black South Africans will be let in, but the white South Africans must be on the next flight out.'

At this my colleague, Abiel Thipanyane, who had been on our team since 1966, spoke up: 'I have spent my whole life fighting against this kind of discrimination in South Africa. We are brothers in Christ on this team, black and white. And if you refuse my white brothers, we blacks also refuse to enter your country.'[2]

And that was that!

While our guys waited for a flight out, they wasted no time. As David Richardson later reported:

> we formed a prayer group right in the middle of the airport concourse. Many locals and airport staff joined us and a huge group locked arms and prayed for the mission, the city, the country, for Africa, and the trip home for the whole South African group.[3]

And they took the next flight home, going via Addis Ababa this time.

As I heard this story, I was never more proud of my team. This extraordinary witness, which reverberated around Liberia, was far more valuable than setting up sound systems for the mission.

But now our minstrel, Brian Gibson, and I, both residents of the hated South Africa, had to gear up for our own departure. Again we had to fly overnight to London, then overnight again back to Freetown, Sierra Leone, and then on to Monrovia. Flying there from Freetown Airport, where no sandwiches could be acquired ('bread has run out'), and no washing or shaving was possible ('we only pump water in the afternoons'), we headed prayerfully towards Monrovia, claiming Revelation 3.8! Hours later we were through immigration and customs – South African residence and all – and rejoicing with the jubilant locals and AE team members who met us.

'Togetha'

At the opening meeting, the thousand-voice choir under Timothy Thomas (Tamas as they called him), who twirled his fingers and hands like a furious windmill to get certain notes held, lifted us to the heavens. I remember thinking that if I could take these one thousand voices to London, we would fill the Albert Hall for a month!

In spite of living in a convulsed country, the people of Liberia were buoyant and full of laughter. I remember one lady called Ellie who came into our mission office every day to help. We used to say, 'Good morning, Ellie, how are you?' And she would always reply with her delightful and typical Liberian Creole: 'I's togetha', with an upward lilt on that final 'a'! She certainly was always 'togetha'!

It is a good word, especially as Paul says of Jesus: 'In him all things hold together' (Colossians 1.17). Ellie's testimony should be ours. We need to be 'togetha'!

An appointment was made for us to meet the President, but while we were waiting for him, and he for us, the secretary said she had misplaced the letter of invitation. This meant the interview had to be cancelled! Oh, well, you can't win 'em all!

Responses to the gospel in these two weeks were awesome, such was the spiritual hunger, and some 8,000 people professed commitment to Christ.

The final stadium rally, with some 10,000 people, I always remembered as one of the most lively, fun and spirited I was ever in. It began inauspiciously for me with a sudden violent Liberian tummy attack which required me to be raced across town by the Archbishop's chauffeur in a fancy car to his office and toilet at the Cathedral. 'The stories behind the story, hey Mike,' chuckled Gus Marwieh, a Liberian church leader.

'The best crusade ever in Liberia', said a purple banner presented to each AE team member by Archbishop Browne. Hundreds of precious people had committed their lives to Christ after Festo and I had preached.

When the time came to leave, I couldn't but reflect on what a far cry all this was from the quiet beach 24 years previously when I had made 50 footprints in the African sand of Liberia and claimed 50 years of open doors into the cities of Africa.

God was surely fulfilling his promise to us.

Kampala, Uganda

I conclude with one other very remarkable opening door. This was our June 1986 citywide mission to Kampala. Forty-seven city church leaders, representing hundreds of congregations from over 30 denominations and 28 para-church organizations, had committed to the venture. And what a topsy-turvy and traumatic ride we had had in preparing for this great endeavour! First of all, Festo Kivengere became critically ill and unable to join us. Then, our amazing ambassador at large for AE, also our Set-up Director for this mission, and Deputy East African Team Leader, John Wilson, one of the very finest men I have ever known and one of my most loyal friends, was assassinated. A cruel blow.

John had been an outspoken critic of the government of Milton Obote, whose atrocities after he had supposedly liberated Uganda from Idi Amin had equalled or maybe even exceeded Amin's. John was also trying as a Christian leader to bring warring factions in Uganda together. Victoria, John's most wonderful daughter, who came from the USA to do a memorial film on her father during the mission, believes firmly that John was not just assassinated but martyred for his principled Christian stand at that time.

Victoria said later:

There is no light brighter than the one that is lit from within. A father's primary function on this earth is to be a reflection of our heavenly Father. He is to love and nurture his family. He must be there for them, provide for them, protect them, and guide them in the ways of righteousness. By being a reflection of God to his children, a man gives his children the greatest gift of all, a love for God that is natural, exciting and revolutionary. He lights a beautiful fire within each child. A light that never burns out. A light that keeps on shining even after he's gone and the world around seems dark and bleak. A light that gives them the courage to stand alone even as the world around them rewards immorality and selfish ambitions.[4]

The next blow was that Steve Mongoma, one of our greatest and most effective evangelists, was stabbed in Nairobi by a thief, thankfully not fatally, and was ordered to give Kampala a miss.

Having already once been thrown out of Uganda by Idi Amin back in 1973, I wondered how I would fare in terms of travelling to the country, as I was once again with another South African resident, Brian Gibson. But as we know, God can handle immigration officials! Just as Brian and I reached Immigration at about 8.00 p.m. and proffered our passports, all the lights in the airport building went out and we were plunged into near total darkness. The official, seemingly not wanting to hold up the long queue, took our passports and stamped them pretty much sight unseen.

Then, as Brian and I stepped away from his counter, all the lights in the airport suddenly came on again! And we registered that the God who normally brings light can also sponsor darkness when necessary!

Michael burning witch-doctor paraphernalia

Again, our multiple meetings of stratified evangelism happened in schools, colleges, the university, marketplaces, factories, in civic offices – you name it, we were there. I preached daily for a week in an open-air expanse of grass near the city centre. One day a man came forward in response to my gospel appeal, bringing all his witch-doctor paraphernalia, and tossed it all on the ground below the platform to symbolize giving up that way of life. The big crowd shouted and ululated in delight. But a hush came when I said I would burn all his witch-doctor bits and pieces publicly in the meeting next day to show Jesus was more powerful than witch-doctor spirits.

This I did! Someone secured the lid of an old metal rubbish bin into which we placed all the bones and feathers and medicines. As I held it from beneath and lifted it up, now all aflame, we proclaimed the power of Jesus over the forces of darkness.

As the crowd went crazy, one soldier on guard around the edge of the gathering turned to another soldier and said, 'That man is a dead man by tomorrow.' After hearing this, I rejoiced to tell them all next day that I was very much still alive! And I've been fine ever since!

In total, 3,500 people professed commitment in that mission and were diligently followed up by local churches.

Thinking back on John Wilson's assassination, I am reminded of what the great third-century Church Father, Tertullian of Tunisia, once said in commentary: 'The blood of the martyrs is the seed of the Church.'[5]

Victoria would certainly agree with this.

A witch doctor comes to Christ

26

Reconciliation

⬤◆⬤

God . . . gave us the ministry of reconciliation.
(2 Corinthians 5.18)

Amid the tragedy of John Wilson's death and also the stabbing of Steve Mongoma came the sad news that our beloved Festo had been diagnosed in London with leukaemia, which was to take him to the Lord in May 1988. And of course he had missed the mission to Kampala.

As recorded earlier in this tale, from the very beginning God had placed into the hearts of both Festo and me the theme of reconciliation. It wasn't by our deliberate design. It just happened. It came naturally. And what a blessed natural happening!

Also, from the very beginning when we first preached together, Festo and I worked to stay close, and sought, as the East Africans always urged, to 'walk in the light' and be very open and transparent with one another.

I remember back in 1969 in the Nairobi Mission falling prey to what I call the preacher's sin of 'envy'. Ministers, pastors and evangelists can sometimes have competitive postures towards one another, usually rather

Michael and Festo Kivengere, Crossroads Mission, 1969

well concealed, and become envious if someone else is doing better than they! It sounds awful, but it's so.

In that Nairobi Mission when Festo and I preached on alternate days to crowds of many thousands, I always felt that Festo communicated much better than I, and his gospel appeal at the end of each talk secured a substantially larger response. In my eyes he was succeeding and I was failing! And I got envious. In fact it really got to me. Shame on me!

Finally I decided to confess this to him over a cup of coffee. When I had done so, he began laughing.

'Come on, brother,' I expostulated. 'What's so funny?'

'Well, Mike,' he responded, 'you know I used to travel the world with that famous East African revival leader, William Nagenda. Wherever we went, he seemed always to get all the success, the favour, the prominence, the applause, the limelight. Till finally I got really jealous and upset. So I felt I should go and confess this to him.

'At this William began to laugh. I was upset and mystified,' said Festo.

The story went on: '"Well, you know, Festo," William said to me, "when I was younger I used to travel the world with Joe Church, one of the initiators of the East African Revival, and wherever we went, he got all the praise, applause and favour. Till finally I got so envious and jealous, I had to go to him and confess. And Joe roared with laughter. 'Well, you know, William,' he said, 'when I was younger . . .'"'!'

By this time both Festo and I were laughing helplessly. And Festo knew how to laugh.

Suddenly we were free, and embracing each other. With 'no smog between us', as he used to say. It felt good.

A humorous sequel followed. That afternoon Festo was due to preach. As usual, great crowds came, numbering in thousands. And there was a tiny response! Next day was my turn. And we were overrun with a huge throng responding!

Again we laughed uproariously. But we were both sure the Lord was laughing loudest and saying: 'Oh, you funny little children of mine, I love you! But just let me bless how, and when, and where and whom I choose. Leave it all to *me*!'

I remember too how, when I was preaching with Festo in subsequent years, he often told a story out of his testimony just after he came to Christ. He had found the Lord convicting him of bitterness, even hatred, towards a particular white British missionary. The Lord said to him: 'Go and get reconciled.'

Festo told how he cycled eight or ten miles through the Ugandan mountains to make this confession. The missionary wept. And they became the firmest of reconciled friends and colleagues in the gospel ever after.

Thus from AE's early days, the 'ministry of reconciliation', especially in a context ravaged by divisions and alienation, became one of our central pillars.

Of course, in apartheid South Africa this ministry was sorely and desperately needed. In 1985 things were coming to a head. President Botha in his famous so-called 'Rubicon Speech' in August 1985 had completely failed to cross the Rubicon and decide to release Mandela from prison, unban the so-called 'liberation movements' and remove the army from the townships. In fact, fearing he would be drowned in the river, Botha had scarcely dipped his big toe in the water. The disappointment around the country and especially in the black townships was palpable.

National Initiative for Reconciliation

At AE we felt we urgently needed to launch a National Initiative for Reconciliation (NIR). The aim was to facilitate encounter, communication, understanding and fresh cooperation in the Church.

We started out by calling together church leaders at the AE Centre – at three weeks' notice.

We didn't want all church leaders, but just the senior ones, including a contingent of 56 from the Dutch Reformed Church, including Moderator Professor Johan Heyns. We also invited some politicians and Members of Parliament.

Malcolm Graham went to work and we convened in 'Maritzburg in September 1985. The gathering was opened with the moving cry of Psalm 130, selected by veteran activist Alan Paton. He chose these words as an expression of his deep cry for South Africa:

> Out of the depths I cry to you, LORD;
> Lord, hear my voice.
> Let your ears be attentive
> to my cry for mercy.
> If you, LORD, kept a record of sins,
> Lord, who could stand?
> But with you there is forgiveness,
> so that we can, with reverence, serve you.
> I wait for the LORD, my whole being waits,
> and in his word I put my hope . . .

NIR: Michael with Alan Paton, October 1985

> Israel, put your hope in the LORD,
> for with the LORD is unfailing love
> and with him is full redemption.
> (Psalm 130.1–5, 7 NIV)

Then came the indomitable Desmond Tutu. To the blacks he said: 'In spite of everything, we are nevertheless called to the business of forgiveness and reconciliation.' To whites he said: 'How can you ask forgiveness from someone when you still have your foot firmly planted on his neck?' He concluded:

> True reconciliation, my brothers and sisters, is costly. It involves confrontation because the Cross was confrontation with evil. The Cross showed the evil of evil. Are we ready even to die? Are we ready to die physically, to die to our popularity, to die to our security? Are we ready to be made fools for the sake of Christ?[1]

At one point my heart sank a bit when the very powerful black contingent decided to caucus on their own. They emerged proposing a five-day work 'stay-away' or strike, which would bring the whole of South Africa to a standstill, unless President Botha agreed to certain demands. These included taking the necessary steps towards the elimination of all forms of legislative discrimination, the ending of the state of emergency, the release of Mandela and the removal of the army from the townships.

That night I was very troubled about this threat of a five-day nationwide strike. A Scripture then came to me, describing the attitude of Jesus: 'When he was reviled, he did not revile in return; when he suffered, he

Michael and Desmond Tutu, October 1985

did not *threaten*; but he trusted to him who judges justly' (1 Peter 2.23, my emphasis).

I felt in a bit of a tremble when I shared this the next morning at the conference, underlining that threats were surely not the gospel way. Mercifully, the Spirit seemed to commend this approach to all. Our decision instead was to call for a one-day national 'Pray-Away' on a working weekday, not a Saturday or public holiday, and ask all of South Africa to stay at home that day and pray for our country and for reconciliation and justice.

The date was set for 9 October 1985.

Visit to the President

It fell to me to go privately and prayerfully to President Botha to pave the way for the delegation which would put forward the concerns coming out of our NIR gathering. My understanding was that we would meet alone. I was sure if we did, I could make headway, and the Lord would grant favour for our NIR delegation to visit him.

But when I entered his office the day before the 'Pray-Away', I was met not only by a gruff and surly-looking President Botha, but also by another Cabinet Minister, plus a man who was going to monitor proceedings and take notes. The atmosphere was freezing.

I handed the President a gift for him and his wife of Oswald Chambers' devotional volume: *My Utmost for His Highest* (in Afrikaans). I also told Mr Botha that I had tried in vain to secure for him a different book called *Abraham Lincoln: Theologian of American Anguish*, speaking of Lincoln's

NIR meeting, Pietermaritzburg, October 1985

spiritual life and calls for seven or eight different national days of prayer.

At this the President went off pop: 'Misterrr Cassidy,' he thundered, 'do you not think that I am already the Lincoln of South Africa? And the servant of the Lord?'

As I obviously reflected some modest doubt about that, the President rose to his towering height, picked up a Bible and read the first few verses of Romans 13 to me – about 'the powers that be' being 'ordained of God', and therefore requiring obedience and submission.

'Yes, Mr President,' I replied, 'but the passage says the state is "God's servant" for the good of *all*. Not just some. The state is not autonomous. It has a transcendent accountability to God.'

Botha glared at me. 'As for this NIR thing in Pietermaritzburg, those are fourrr hundred nothings, Mr Cassidy. Fourrr hundred nothings.'

I replied, 'On the contrary, Mr President, those four hundred people represent a very large slice of the Church's top leadership in South Africa, and you need to hear them in terms of their pleas about our country.'

By now the President was on a roll and warming to the skirmish.

'As to this so-called Pray-Away tomorrow, Misterrr Cassidy, it will be, I assure you, a total failure. A total failure.'

'Let's wait for tomorrow, Mr President,' I replied, 'and we will see.'

Then out of the blue: 'Now, Misterrr Cassidy – what do you think of the Kairos Document?'

This was a very weighty and powerful theological document which had come out the previous week from another cluster of mainly black theologians, some of them quite strong on so-called liberation theology.

Thankfully, I had read it, not without some reservations.

'Well, Mr President,' I replied, 'I think it's like the parson's egg – good in parts.'

This set off another tirade. How could anything be good in parts? It was either good or evil. What nonsense to say something could be good in parts!

Of course, people trained in theology are accustomed from their perspective to weigh up degrees of truth and error. But theology had clearly not been part of the President's training. It was all black and white. Right or wrong. Good or evil.

Then he added menacingly, 'Misterrr Cassidy, I know tonight you are due to be on national television about the Day of Prayer tomorrow. And I will be watching. Unless you denounce the Kairos theologians, I will fix you *perrrsonally.*'

'Mr President, I am not going to denounce the Kairos theologians, because that is a cry from the black world which you need to heed. You really do.'

Our interview, with its two silent wide-eyed onlookers, was clearly going from bad to worse, including the President's incredulity when I answered positively to his question about whether I was really a South African. To him, being South African and opposing the status quo was a contradiction in terms.

Finally, after an hour or so of getting nowhere, Mr Botha got to his feet to terminate the tense encounter.

'I suppose now, Misterrr Cassidy, you want your book back.'

'No, Mr President,' I replied politely. 'On the contrary, I want you more than ever to have it.'

Brisk, cold handshakes – as he walked uncomprehendingly back into his hermetically sealed fortress, cut off from South Africa's tortured realities, while I stepped out from that claustrophobic atmosphere into the sunny and fresh air outside. My mission to the President to pave the way for the NIR delegation had totally aborted.

My personal assistant, and wonderful friend, Nellis du Preez, comforted me on the way back to Johannesburg, but also insisted on my recording on tape there and then what had transpired, so that we had a record of it while my mind was still fresh. This we did. But some weeks later, in what seemed like a raid on my offices at AE, the tape and a file on the President went missing – presumably the work of the security police.

Before the TV interview that evening, I called Carol and told her that if

I went missing or vanished the next day, she should know it was the work of the President.

'Darling, don't you be intimidated by that bully,' she responded with characteristic grit and forthrightness.

In the event, the TV interview on the Pray-Away went well, although the interviewer had menacingly primed me that I would be getting 'a very hard time'. Needless to say, I did not denounce the Kairos people. Many around the country later told me they were praying for me throughout. One African lady said, 'I fell on my knees when I saw you on the screen.'

After the interview a young white Afrikaner lass from the TV control room called me up into the studio from where the programme and cameras had been controlled. 'We were all praying for you, Brother Mike,' said she and her colleagues.

Then it was down to the basement for a late-night interview on the Pray-Away with South African Broadcasting Corporation radio. The interviewer said beforehand: 'I have been asked to give you very tough questions about the Day of Prayer. But I want to pray with you that you will be able to answer well.' And he did. And I did!

Next day, in broad terms, the country stayed at home – to pray. Businesses were without workers. Many miners cut loose, to the point where an Anglo-American boss later roasted me!

A newspaper photographer in the rush hour had photographed 'the busiest road in South Africa', the one from Soweto into Johannesburg. In the paper the next day, the picture showed just one lone cyclist.

Pray-Away: spot the lone cyclist!

I wondered what the President was feeling about it. The Pray-Away was not such a failure after all. At least we knew the nation was praying for healing, for the end of injustice, and for reconciliation in a new South Africa.

As for reconciliation between the President and me, that appeared to be impossible. Yet history in time would have a strange turn of events. It often does. (More on that later!)

NIR ministries

One of the most useful outcomes of the NIR was the development of reconciliation teamlets which would travel the country to bring the message of justice and reconciliation through the gospel. The genius of these teams lay in their composition – blacks, whites and browns, Anglicans, Baptists and Dutch Reformed, and so on. These teams manifested reconciliation just by being who they were, in bringing together for ministry the 'impossibles' of South Africa.

I participated in several of these. One was particularly memorable. Several of us, including Adrio König, a Dutch Reformed theology professor from Pretoria, were due to minister together in the Port Elizabeth (PE) township of New Brighton, which was in convulsive political turmoil.

We got to PE and set off to look around one of its townships, called Soweto like the Johannesburg one.

Suddenly we were aware of a couple of police cars following us. We were soon pulled over to one side and told we were being 'detained for questioning'.

Why were we in a township without a permit?

And when they heard the reason we were in Port Elizabeth, the response was firm: 'No, we will not allow you to enter or preach in New Brighton tonight.'

'Officer,' I politely replied, 'we never got our mandate to preach from you or the South African state. We got it from the Lord, and we will be preaching in New Brighton tonight.'

More threats followed as we were released some two hours later.

That night at the appointed hour we drove into New Brighton. As we did so, two armoured vehicles, each laden with half a platoon of soldiers armed with assault rifles, slipped in behind us and followed us to the church.

'Why come with armoured cars, soldiers and guns for half a dozen preachers with their Bibles?' asked König. '*Dominee, ons is bang.*' (Pastor, we are frightened.)

As it turned out, the armed men had nothing to do that evening. Some may have even heard the message of reconciliation as a few came in to the back of the church and listened.

Mamelodi Encounter

We were, of course, not the only ones working hard at the reconciliation process. Dr Nico Smith, former Professor of Missiology at Stellenbosch University, moved boldly with his wife Ellen into Mamelodi Township on the edge of Pretoria where he launched a ministry called Koinonia (Greek: fellowship). He arranged a series of conferences, called Encounters, where concerned whites were invited to come and stay in black homes.

My participation in the Mamelodi Encounter, which AE co-sponsored, was an eye-opener for me. I stayed with as fine a Christian family as could be found anywhere, the Sawas. The father had to get up every day at 4.00 a.m. to have breakfast and then take a train into Johannesburg to be at work by 7.00 a.m. And he would only get back at about 6.00 p.m. Here was our system placing an incredible strain on African family life. Yet he and his wife and children bore it bravely.

Our conference was rudely interrupted by the arrest of one of our African participants, Sandy Lebisi, who was detained for being found sleeping in a shared bed with a male friend. He had doubled up because there was no other bed in the house. How the police knew, I don't know. But in any event, their suspicions regarding the reason were needless to say of the worst kind.

Mamelodi Encounter: Michael with the Sawa family,
Mamelodi Township, on the outskirts of Pretoria, 1984

I was asked by the conference at once to seek an appointment with Mr Adriaan Vlok, the Minister of Law and Order. Thankfully, Mr Vlok agreed that the police action was excessive. He also allowed me to visit Sandy in the Pretoria Central Prison and tell him he would be released. And he was, much to the joy of the conference when he returned the next day.

ANC exiles

AE's David Richardson and I were privileged to go to Zambia and not only have extensive time with President Kenneth Kaunda, including a mini-mission to his cabinet, but also meet up with some of the senior ANC exiles in Lusaka.

We spent an afternoon in the home of exiled Thabo Mbeki, later to become President of South Africa following Mandela. We were deeply impressed with Mbeki's intellect and gracious spirit.

'How on earth,' Dave and I asked each other, 'can the South African authorities banish such a man and deprive the country of his astonishing gifts and intellect?'

We also met a number of future ANC government leaders. And how special to encourage them that we believed change was coming!

We often took messages from exiles back to the South African government. Once, at a highly confidential meeting, we relayed information from the exiles to Mr Louis Le Grange, head of the police and the South African state security machine.

I went with Bishop Mmutlanyane Mogoba, later head of the Methodist Church and parliamentary leader of the Pan Africanist Congress (PAC), and a 'graduate' of the infamous Robben Island political prison, having been there for many years with Nelson Mandela. He deeply moved Le Grange by telling of the dreadful suffering of that experience, plus the present sufferings of all black people, and yet doing so in the spirit of love and forgiveness. We were trying to persuade Le Grange not to screw the lid down further on black aspirations nor to send police into black community gatherings. Le Grange seemed very touched when we prayed for him at the end of our time.

Intimidation

We did quite a few of these trips to Zambia, and on one occasion a phone call from the South African security police went to St Anne's College, Hilton, where our daughters were at school. Carol, who was teaching there, intercepted the call and read the riot act to the policeman concerned. But we realized that the call was intended to convey a message of intimidation: 'We know where your dad is going tomorrow, and who he will be seeing and, kids, we know where *you* are.'

AE also had a black African informer posing as a youth worker planted into our youth intern programme. This rogue was cleverly unmasked by our resourceful intern director Dennis Bailey, and he fled the AE centre within minutes of his exposure. Just before that, Dennis had had the brake-fluid pipes of his car cut and sabotaged, as confirmed by a traffic policeman who rescued Dennis plus vehicle from an arrestor bed off the freeway; fortunately it had been possible to navigate the car on to the escape ramp to avoid a fatal accident. We assumed this sabotage was the work of some in the South African security police, commonly known as a sort of dirty-tricks brigade. They performed nefarious acts for the government and were later exposed publicly after the country's first democratic elections.

These sorts of episodes, some very serious, and some mere pinpricks, made exercising the ministry of reconciliation very demanding. Several detractors came to me after 1994 and asked for forgiveness. Thankfully, I could honestly say, 'I forgave you before you even asked me.'

Eastern Cape

In spite of the best efforts of thousands of concerned citizens and socially aware Christians, South Africa lurched from crisis to crisis. In June 1986 we were ministering again in the Eastern Cape and I remember a couple of the days very well.

My colleague Neil Pagard and I were heading to two clergy meetings, one in the black township of Zwelitsha, near King William's Town, and the other a luncheon with white clergy in the centre of town.

Residential apartheid demographics and anomalies of this kind constantly frustrated all who laboured to get people together. The default position therefore was for people to meet in their segregated residential areas. This geographical separation is still something that has a negative impact on South Africa today.

As I was introduced to one black pastor, I asked him how he was.

'Positive,' he beamed back at me, rebuking my own faithlessness and pessimism and making me salute black resilience afresh. The major lament of the black clergy was the separation and distance between them and the white clergy 'in town'. One pastor said he wanted to 'cry, stamp or yell'. 'When in heaven's name will white South African Christians get their act together and stop betraying the gospel like this?'

Later, at the lunch for white clergy, I relayed this challenge to them. The chairman, an Afrikaner called Johann Neethling, conveyed his own agony in the situation. Whites were also traumatized. Johann's grief and frustration finally led him a few months later to leave the country, thus joining the 50 or more whites leaving South Africa per day at that time.

That night in King William's Town we managed a combined rally of blacks and whites. The challenge was for whites truly to feel and understand black pain, and for blacks to be encouraged in their quest for freedom and human dignity to discover that there were indeed some whites who wanted to be part of their quest as well.

Whites also had to try to grasp their own culpability. I once met Paul Oestreicher, whose father had died in a Jewish Holocaust camp, while Paul survived. Before he died Oestreicher's dad said: 'We all have to face the Hitler in our own hearts.' As whites and blacks, we all had to face such realities.

State of emergency

The next day a messenger of bad tidings arrived. All the black leaders in Duncan Village and Mdantsane, East London's major black townships, were being 'picked up and detained'.

The full import of this only reached me later in the day, as I alighted at Durban airport en route home from East London. South Africa had once again been placed under the strictest and most stringent state of emergency. It was Thursday, 12 June 1986.

A thousand people had been detained but we knew nothing yet. The number would climb to over 29,000 before the end of the year.[2]

The terms of the emergency were draconian. They included the following:

- The security forces may enter any premises without a warrant and seize anything they deem necessary; arrest any person whose detention is deemed necessary; interrogate any person arrested or detained.

- No civil or criminal proceedings may be instituted against the State, the State President, cabinet members or force members acting 'in good faith'.

- The Commissioner of Police may ban comment on news in connection with any conduct of the force or any member of the force.

- It is an offence for any person to make, write, print or record any subversive statement.[3]

How does one work for justice and reconciliation with these stipulations overshadowing everything? Soweto Day, 16 June 1986, commemorating the day ten years previously when police gunned down some 176 protesting black young people, dawned a couple of days later with the country in sullen silence.

In AE, in spite of the risks of going into Edendale, a black township on the edge of Pietermaritzburg, we went with a cluster of other whites to identify with black folk, plus some of our AE black colleagues, and met in a church. Armoured vehicles lined the roads. Would we be arrested? Injured? There did seem to be some risk.

Carol said to me, 'I think only one of us should go in.' Her thoughts did not have to be further verbalized. I got the point.

One of our colleagues, quadriplegic Allan Peckham, who had agonized about the decision to go, said, 'It didn't in the end seem to matter whether I lived or died. In a sense I had died already.'[4]

Another AE colleague, Jack Garratt, later recorded: 'It affected my sleep in those days. The thought of going into that township on June 16th really scared me.'[5]

At the church hardly more than a dozen individuals met us. Outside was the silence of suppression, not the buoyant crowds of black people we normally met there. Governmental force and military might had temporarily prevailed.

But we were not to be daunted. A little symbolic cluster of whites and blacks had met together in reconciliation and mutual care, and we could accordingly sing, pray, preach and dream of a New Day coming. Astonishingly, each white there, as we sought forgiveness, felt loved, welcomed and indeed forgiven.

Thus once again we saw the amazing depth of the black capacity for forgiveness.

Requirements of reconciliation

Our various attempts at reconciliation seemed pitifully inadequate and weak. But perhaps one day they could add up to something.

We launched what we called Bridge Building Encounters (BBEs) when we would get sizeable groups of black and white young people together for weekends of sharing and encounter. These events usually began tense, angry and scared, but then, as enemies were humanized, the kids were all exchanging addresses and phone numbers with a view to keeping in touch.

True reconciliation could never be cheap, and often for us whites that was how we wanted it. Justice concerns had to be constantly faced. Systemic change was something we all had to work for.

We all needed to meet at the cross.

Professor Klaus Nurnberger noted at the time:

> The suffering involved in reconciliation can be substantial because the stronger section has to forgo the advantages it derived from the structural imbalances and maladjustments of the past while the weaker section has to forgo its claim to the advantages it could gain from revenge or restitution in the future.[6]

Nurnberger was also concerned that white Christians in South Africa in particular keep front and centre of their minds the fact that

> all chances for genuine reconciliation will be destroyed if such fellowship appears to be designed to appease the wronged party or to cover up the cause of the conflict. In other words, any serious labourers for reconciliation in a society of conflict must be unambiguously and explicitly committed to dismantling unjust structures.

Otherwise, observed Nurnberger, 'it will make no contribution to a solution of the problem but only undermine the credibility and influence of the Church of Christ further'.[7]

Of course, the quest on the side of black Christians was to keep godliness central in such an ungodly environment. The quest for liberation is perilous without the controls which spirituality brings. We daren't become bestial while battling the beast. As Carl Ellis, a black American civil rights writer, once wrote:

> We saw that the closer a people get to liberation, the more their own ungodliness and God's judgement will show. Liberation is insufficient if it is not accompanied by a quest for godliness in every area of life. Liberation alone will lead to self-oppression because a liberated ungodliness will always do its thing, and that thing is sure to bring death (see Romans 6:23).
>
> Indeed, the quest for righteousness in every area of life must be on the top of the black agenda if we are to become the people God created us to be (cf. Matthew 6:33).[8]

Amazingly, distinguished black leaders like Albert Luthuli, Desmond Tutu and Frank Chikane were able to maintain their spirituality and moral equilibrium, in spite of being banned, like Luthuli, or being castigated and demonized by whites (as in Desmond's case), or even being tortured by a white member of his own denomination (as in Frank's case).

P. W. Botha again

Let me now pick up the good news story about President P. W. Botha.

I was writing about our reconciliation efforts in South Africa in my book *The Passing Summer*, when somehow the Spirit convicted me that I could not write the reconciliation chapter without seeking to get right with President Botha.

I accordingly sat down and wrote to him, confessing my bitterness towards him following our traumatic encounter. It was a costly letter, written from the foot of the cross.

Shortly thereafter I got a reply from the President's secretary: 'Thank you for your letter to President Botha. The contents have been noted.'

The rascal, I thought. If only he could have known what that Calvary communication cost me.

Anyway, I had done from my side what I could. And I felt free to get on with the chapter.

However, while walking through the KwaZulu-Natal hills around Nottingham Road one afternoon, while staying with Lynn and Derryn Hurry, I heard the Lord's voice saying to me: 'I will one day give you another chance to reconcile with the President.' I tucked this away in my heart to remember.

Jump forward now 13 years to 2000, the year in which South Africa's cricket captain Hansie Cronje was nailed for 'match-fixing', and barred from the game, leaving both himself and the country shattered.

One day I felt the Lord prompting me to go and minister to Hansie Cronje, and his wife Bertha, who lived in the Western Cape coastal beauty spot of George. I went and was all the more glad I had visited, bringing a message of encouragement, for Hansie was tragically killed a few months later in a plane accident.

When I was thinking about this visit, another word came to me: 'My son, someone else lives in George. And I want you to go see him too.'

My heart sank. Surely not *him*! The Lord could only have meant one person, P. W. Botha, now retired and living on the outskirts of George.

The visit was arranged through friends in George, not least Sandy Gush, a local doctor who knew and liked our ministry, and kindly said he would take me.

We arrived at the door. And there he was. Still an imposing figure of a man, and his wife Barbara (married after Botha's first wife died) was charm and warmth personified.

'Sir, I'm not sure what to call you. I want to say "Mr President", but

Sandy says I must call you "Oom P. W."' (pronounced Pee-a-Vee-a. *Oom* is a polite and respectful Afrikaner word for Uncle).

'*Ja*, of course, Mr Cassidy, "Oom P. W."!'

Botha began reminiscing extensively! I dearly wished I'd had a tape recorder going, as it was mega-interesting stuff.

'Now, Mr Cassidy, I don't know about Tutu. In this newspaper [headline] Desmond Tutu says "P. W. Going to Hell". I don't think so because I trust Jesus as my Lord and Saviour. What do you think?'

'Well, Oom P. W., I don't think any of us can say definitely of other believers they are going to hell!'

He looked relieved!

Then he added: 'As for Mr de Klerk, he be-trrr-ayed me, Mr Cassidy. And when he came to see me recently he was smoking all the time and I said to him, "Mr de Klerk, I never permitted smoking in my cabinet meetings. And I won't permit it in my home."'

The reminiscences were fascinating. But finally I said: 'You know, Oom P. W., I didn't come here just to be social. I came to ask your forgiveness for the bitterness I had in my heart after our last encounter on October 8th 1985 in your office. You told me amongst other things to denounce the Kairos document and people—'

Botha cut in: 'And I still think it's a terrible document.'

'Anyway,' I went on, 'you said that if I didn't denounce the Kairos people on national television where I was due to appear that night you would fix me personally.'

'Surely you didn't say that, P. W.,' burst in his wife. 'That's terrible.'

Silence for a moment. Then he smiled: 'But I didn't fix you, Mr Cassidy, did I?'

It was time to laugh.

'No, Oom P. W.,' I chuckled, 'you didn't. But I felt very bitter towards you, and especially when your office responded to my letter of apology by just saying its content had been "noted" – with nothing from you personally . . . Anyway, I want to apologize for all that.'

'Misterrr Cassidy, it's not you who should be apologizing to me, but . . .'

And then he sort of choked up.

Later Barbara showed me to the bathroom and in the corridor quickly whispered: 'Michael, this is amazing. I haven't ever heard him listen to anyone as he has listened to you today. But you saw how he couldn't quite get out that apology, but he wanted to. I feel the Lord has led me to marry him to try and help him amongst other things to say sorry – especially to the country. But it's coming!'

*P. W. Botha blowing the shofar during a visit by Michael
to the ex-president's home in George, Western Cape, 2001*

I was very touched. 'Barbara, let me pray for you.' And there just outside the loo I prayed one of my more unusual prayers!

Back in the sitting room, Barbara said, 'P. W., I think you should blow
the shofar horn for Michael as a symbol of spiritual victory.'

Michael kneels in front of P. W Botha just before he prays with him and his wife Barbara

She went to fetch that ancient Jewish instrument, blown at moments of spiritual triumph.

My camera click synchronized with P. W.'s blast on the shofar, which almost blew the roof off. Just to show it was no fluke, he blasted it again! And beamed like a little boy.

I suggested we close in prayer. Our little foursome formed a circle and held hands. As we prayed I opened my eyes to register the huge hand that had prosecuted apartheid's horrors firmly held in my own.

Lord, I said within, only *you* could have orchestrated such a moment. *Only* you.

On Christmas Day that year I phoned Oom P. W. to wish him and Barbara a happy Christmas.

'The trouble with our world,' said P. W., 'is that people don't know the Lord Jesus Christ and what Christmas is all about.'

I couldn't agree more with that.

Yes, reconciliation – it can happen between the most unlikely people.

*AE Centre South Africa, scene of much learning
about reconciliation, mission and evangelism*

27

The Mandela moment

Mike, come and meet Mr Mandela.
(Archie Gumede)

In these years from 1988 to 1994 in South Africa, all was struggle. For myself I fought off despair by clinging in faith to the Lord's Old Testament word through Jeremiah at the darkest and most desperate moment in Judah's history as Nebuchadnezzar was storming Jerusalem, pulling down the walls, destroying the Temple and taking the people of Judah to exile in Babylon.

Then, like a shaft of light into this darkness, came the word of a sovereign God: 'I know the plans I have for you, plans for welfare and not for evil, to give you a future and a hope' (Jeremiah 29.11).

I clung in faith to this promise for dear life when the darkness and despair about apartheid clutched at my soul. Of course, all of this tended to drag the AE team down into the depths as well, but for me the key was to reach a secure and unshakeable spiritual conviction that God could and indeed would bring us through. This posture began to pervade the whole team and we stood solid as a rock in hope and confidence. And when a group of people share a commitment like that, it becomes very hard to break down. I think AE definitely became known as a ministry of hope.

Of course, however battered and bent the team felt by the assorted pressures around us, probably affecting black team members more than white, there was always the healing balm of the tranquillity of the AE Centre which constantly washed over us as we worked and shared our lives together. Nature is ever the restorative medicine from God to us.

Charlie Bester

It was inevitable that apartheid would also clutch at the throats of our own family. This was particularly true in the case of my nephew, Charlie Bester, son of my sister Judy and husband Tony. Charlie refused, when

Charlie Bester with parents Tony and Judy

summoned, to serve in the South African Defence Force (SADF) which at that time among other things was screwing down the lid ever more tightly in the black townships.

Between the years 1957 and 1994, the SADF performed the dual mission of countering possible uprisings of any form (often supporting the South African Police) and continuing a conventional military arm to defend South Africa's borders. It was made up of mainly white South African males (aged between 17 and 25), who were subject to conscription for a period of 9 to 12 months, later extended to two years. There were times, especially in the late 1980s and early 1990s, when SADF troops were deployed to suppress opposition to Nationalist rule.

Charlie's refusal was based on the following motivations:

> My basic motivation for refusing to serve in the South African Defence Force is that I am a Christian, and as a Christian I must follow Christ. Christ's way is the way of love, and so in every situation I must try my best to follow a path of love. I want to break down the barriers which divide us and I reject violence as a means to do so. If I were to serve in an institution such as the SADF (South African Defence Force) which I see as perpetuating these divisions and defending an unjust system, it would be contrary to all I believe. I see it as incredible arrogance that eighteen-year-old boys like myself, most of whom have never previously been to a township, let alone been involved in its life, are ordered to enter, armed, on the back of a military vehicle to impose 'law and order' on a community they neither know, nor identify with.

The only way which I see that we, as white South Africans, can liberate ourselves from our spiritual oppression is humbly to seek reconciliation. Central to this is repentance before both God and man for the wrongs we have done. Only then can we begin to build a society on the firm foundations of justice, freedom and love.

I am fully aware that I am breaking the law of the land, and have no guilt in doing so. After studying Christ's commandments and seeking God's calling in prayer, I personally cannot be obedient to this law and to God's calling. I shall submit to the authority of the State and stand trial.[1]

Along with Robin Briggs, Dean of the Anglican Cathedral of Pretoria, I had the opportunity to testify before the court when the trial finally came up. In those days many clergy became involved in standing alongside people on trial for conscientious objection.

At the end of the morning the Bester family, my daughter Cathy and I lunched at a nearby restaurant. We were curiously cheerful and at peace, though we knew that after lunch the dread sentence would fall.

I remember the trial well.

At one point close to the end of the proceedings, as the judge withdrew to deliberate, I was asked to say a prayer right there in the courtroom. First Robin Briggs and then I prayed. We prayed for the judge, the prosecutor, the state, the government, Charlie, the situation, and for the healing of South Africa. My sister Judy looked up and saw tears streaming from beneath the cap of one bowed young white policeman.

Cathy and Michael with the Bester family for lunch on trial day: Caroline (Charlie's sister), Tony, Judy and Charlie

In the end, the magistrate took about 45 seconds to pass the merciless sentence and close the case. He said, 'Six years is your sentence.' It was the only moment in the trial when he appeared to have the initiative. It was the only moment in the trial he seemed to be in charge.

As he announced the sentence, cries and shouts came from the gallery. Some blacks led the singing of 'Nkosi Sikelel' iAfrika'.[2] The title of this song means 'God bless Africa'. It was originally a nineteenth-century hymn used as a pan-African liberation song, and was later adapted to form the national anthem of post-apartheid South Africa. A police sergeant barked out that the whole court was under arrest for contempt of court! All of us were duly shepherded down into the cells. Robin Briggs slipped out a back door to the colonel to ask him what on earth he was doing. The colonel replied, 'They sang a freedom song.' Robin Briggs pointed out that 'Nkosi Sikelel' iAfrika' is a prayer. Moreover, how could people be in contempt of court when the sentence had been passed and the magistrate had left the courtroom?

Anyway, some 150 of us were ushered to the cells. Charlie was over in a corner, already behind bars. The little bag he had taken down with him with clothes, Bible and toilet bag had been confiscated. Charlie pointed out that a friend of his in the Cape in similar circumstances had been allowed to keep his toilet bag. The policeman replied, 'This is the Transvaal. You can't have the bag.'

Eventually we prevailed upon the colonel to let Charlie at least keep his Bible, and handed it to him through a little window in the wall of wire. The last picture I had of him that day was behind those bars, clutching his Bible to his chest with a big grin on his face. He appeared to be undaunted to the last.

As Charlie was taken to a maximum security prison in Kroonstad, my sister Olave in England and a group of MPs set up an appeal to the British Parliament signed by some 60,000 people in support of Charlie and calling for his release. On Charlie's birthday Olave pushed a large metal cage on wheels, representing prison, festooned with balloons plastered with photos and captions saying 'Free Charles Bester', up to the Houses of Parliament! She also took a huge birthday card, about five feet by three feet, and presented it to Parliament, asking parliamentarians to sign it for her to take to Charlie in prison in South Africa. It was signed by hundreds of MPs and peers. When Olave and the Bester family finally took it to Kroonstad Prison to present to the warden for Charlie as a token from the British Parliament, the warden responded, 'That's a helluva big birthday card,' and reluctantly undertook to get it to Charlie!

Judy reflects back on that time:

I find it very difficult to go back to that traumatic time. For the most part I keep it covered like plaster over a wound. I haven't as yet acknowledged how much it still hurts me.

My memory of the lead-up to the trial and the very dramatic trial itself is shrouded in a fog of shock. One would have thought that we should have been prepared, as the sentence was a mandatory six year sentence for refusing to serve in the SADF, so the outcome was not in question. And yet it was like receiving hammer blows to the head and to the heart as they pronounced sentence and led him away to the cells. This lovely boy that Tony and I had raised was receiving a long custodial sentence for refusing to be part of an armed force which was at that time being ordered to act against its own people.

For the next twenty months as our lives changed into a new unfamiliar routine of prison visits, meetings of supporters, and occasionally being the target of police harassment, I was consumed by a primordial rage, like a lioness whose cub had been captured. I fuelled my rage with books on every conceivable topic relating to the politics and the injustices of the country at that time, and this was the method I used for my survival. There was no room for fiction or light-hearted entertainment as that would have diluted the energy required to stay sane.[3]

I also wrote to President de Klerk, who had by this time ousted President Botha, urging him to release Charlie and urgently amend the legislation which could send a young man of conscience like this to prison.

When Carol and I and our three children went to visit Charlie in prison, we experienced the bizarre and depersonalizing sensation of talking to him through glass. The kids found this very distressing and of course very difficult to understand. In some ways, one felt sorry for the prison guards, who were almost as much victims as they were victimizers.

Anyway, a lot of other people were praying for Charlie, and he got a thousand letters in prison. This support meant the world to him and was in stark contrast to the experience of thousands of young blacks incarcerated in South Africa with no trial and with minimal support of any kind.

Thankfully, by God's grace, President de Klerk reduced his sentence to three years, the Appellate Division of the South African Supreme Court having paved the way for a further review after declaring the law under which Charlie had been sentenced to be 'draconian and repugnant'.

Hope filled Charlie's heart on 11 February 1990 as he started to watch on TV the ecstatic and historic moment as Nelson Mandela walked free from Victor Verster Prison in Cape Town. Just before Mandela was seen on television, wardens sent Charlie back to his cell. Probably they couldn't bear the sight of Charlie's rejoicing at the new day dawning, which the said wardens of the old dispensation would find very difficult to swallow.

Finally, after 19 months Charlie too walked free.

Lutando Charlie

Another young prisoner/detainee also came into our lives at this time.

He was a black ANC youth leader called Lutando Charlie who was gloriously converted to Christ during our mission in Kimberley in 1980 – in fact in the first few days of our follow-up discipling conference at AE with some 30 young people from the Galeshewe township. He then helped us significantly in finalizing the document on Educational Grievances which I then took to Pretoria to the Minister of Education, Mr Ferdi Hartzenberg. I was sympathetically received and we seemed to be making progress.

But then, after the youngsters got back to Kimberley, we were called by the local Anglican bishop to ask if we could help as 19 Kimberley kids had been arrested on charges of vandalizing schools. Lutando and a friend were also incarcerated but only to act as witnesses. The prison sentence was two years. Our extensive efforts with the authorities were in vain as we were stone-walled, even in the case of Lutando and his friend. The law, so-called, had to take its course. Its dubious, desperate course.

At the end of 24 months they were released. Lutando and his friend were never charged or called on to be witnesses. He was also put into solitary confinement for six months and tortured quite often. I learned about this horror story, and more, after inviting him to come and stay with us after his two years in prison. His mother was dead, and he never knew who his father was, so he was very alone.

In the end I got 19 sides of taped testimony from him which we transcribed, summarized and then put into a legal affidavit. Then we informed the Minister of Justice that we were going to sue him. At this point, word was conveyed to us by phone (security police, presumably) that if we pursued this course, Lutando would be killed. We dropped the case.

Then I said to Carol: 'We can't take responsibility for all detainees in South Africa. But we do know one. Let's try and be responsible for him.'

The door on his further education had been banged shut. Could another open? I accordingly phoned Richard Todd, headmaster of close-by Hilton College, one of the finest schools in the country. I asked Richard to

*Lutando Charlie with Carol, Rona and John Tooke, and
Martin, Hilton College rugby match, first 15 rugby team*

fasten his seat belt and listen to this story – because I wanted him to open
the door for Lutando to Hilton on scholarship.

Next day, I had my answer: full scholarship for two years. So Lutando
had two years at Hilton, then two years at Natal University (for which
we found the money), and then, after a hiccup, four years at the Mango-
sutho Buthelezi Technikon in Durban where he ended up as head student,
before being taken on to the staff as its public relations officer. He married
a great Christian girl, Ayanda.

The Mandela moment

On 1 February 1990, I was in Philadelphia with the black civil rights leader
John Perkins, and we were hooked up to a New York radio station for a
one-and-a-half-hour talk show.

A listener who called in to the programme asked me what I was
expecting from the opening of Parliament next day in Cape Town. Might
Mandela be released?

My response:

> We've had lots of rhetoric in the past about government intentions. So
> I'm not too excited. And to be sure, Mandela won't be released tomorrow
> because he will not allow himself to be released into a vacuum. The ANC,
> PAC, SA [South African] Communist Party and other liberation move-
> ments will have to be unbanned before he'll agree to come out. And it will,
> you know, take more than a miracle for the government to do that.[4]

An overnight flight to London hardly set me up for what I would hear next morning in a transit hotel at Heathrow while waiting for my flight that night to Johannesburg.

I snapped on the TV for distraction, and the unthinkable miracle was unfolding. President de Klerk was speaking from the South African Parliament:

> The prohibition of the African National Congress, the Pan Africanist Congress, the South African Communist Party and a number of subsidiary organizations is being rescinded . . .
>
> The media emergency regulations as well as the education emergency regulations are being abolished in their entirety . . . The restrictions in terms of the emergency regulations on thirty-three organizations are being rescinded . . .
>
> These decisions by the cabinet are in accordance with the government's declared intention to normalize the political process in South Africa without jeopardizing the maintenance of good order. They were preceded by thorough and unanimous advice by a group of officials which included members of the security community.[5]

I sat thunderstruck.

De Klerk went on to describe the aims to which the country needed to aspire:

> A new, democratic constitution; universal franchise; no domination; equality before an independent judiciary; the protection of minorities as well as of individual rights; freedom of religion; a sound economy based on proven economic principles and private enterprise; dynamic programmes directed at better education, health services, housing and social conditions for all.[6]

But I was asking: 'Come on, Mr President, what about Mandela? What about Mandela?'

I didn't have to wait long:

> I wish to put it plainly that the government has also taken a firm decision to release Dr Mandela unconditionally. I am serious about bringing this matter to finality without delay. The government will take a decision soon on the date of his release.[7]

The Mandela moment had come. And F. W. de Klerk and his colleagues had crossed the Rubicon from which P. W. Botha and his crew had shrunk four years previously.

Nine days later, on 11 February 1990, Nelson Rolihlala Mandela and all South Africa stepped out into the sunlight.

Yes, it was indeed a turnabout, and the road to freedom had opened up.

But it was to be a bumpy one. There was a lot more lurching to do. It is perhaps hard for those who were not part of this experience to realize just how huge and momentous this moment was. For black people, Mandela was someone who had dominated their hopes and imaginations for nearly three decades.

But many whites were very anxious, some fearfully so; others, despairing of a so-called 'Black Future', began leaving the country.

On the far right, one hyper-conservative group said: 'Give us a million guns, and we will solve the problem.' On the far left, the Pan Africanist Congress still held to its slogan, 'One settler, one bullet'. And black political groupings began contesting for supremacy, sometimes violently. Especially in KwaZulu-Natal where we were based.

None of this boded well for the future.

But the big thing was that Mandela was out, and criss-crossing the country to inspire one and all with his message of hope and imminent liberation for South Africa.

Meeting Mandela

Not so long after Mandela's release, I had a request from Ben Nsimbi, a black pastor friend in Edendale, a black township on the edge of Pietermaritzburg, saying an ANC leader was asking through him if we in AE could lend a public address system to him for some meetings Mandela was having in our area that very day! Ben was a great guy, and his wish was our command.

After a high-speed scramble, several of us from AE found ourselves plus PA system racing after the Mandela cavalcade up into the hills and then down to Mpophomeni, near Howick, where there was to be the first of several rallies.

As we passed through one area where there were gutted houses, after a fearsome battle between Mandela supporters in the ANC and Minister Buthelezi's supporters in the Inkatha Freedom Party (IFP), Ben told us: 'I am often called out at night, like last night at 2.00 a.m., to identify bodies and minister to their families.'

I was lost in admiration for Ben and the sacrificial way in which he and so many other black pastors were at the front end of caring for unimaginable needs hitting them day and night. I just couldn't imagine myself coping with anything like that.

Once we reached the township, we caught up with Mandela and his entourage at a damaged church which Mandela was about to inspect. Disciplined ANC marshalls ushered Dr Mandela, Archie Gumede (co-president of the United Democratic Movement), plus ANC stal-warts Walter Sisulu and Harry Gwala (head of the Communist Party in KwaZulu-Natal at the time), as well as Ben and us, towards the church.

Archie Gumede, whom I had known as a good friend and a co-belligerent in fighting apartheid for some years, suddenly called out to me: 'Mike, come and meet Mr Mandela.'

Suddenly we were meeting the man of the moment on whom so much seemed to hang. Tall, erect, impressive and strong.

'I hope you got my book in prison, Mr Mandela,' I ventured as I shook his hand.

'Yes, indeed, and thank you very much.' Then to my colleagues: 'I have heard good things of AE's work.' Pause. A twinkle. 'But perhaps they only tell me the good things!' Perhaps.

As I came face to face with these impressive men, I wondered to myself what they had suffered to come to this place. Loneliness? Despair? Deprivation? Crushing depression? Regret over lost and wasted years? Emotional agony in separation from family and loved ones? Anguished wonderings if they would ever see the outside of a prison and the fruit of dreams and sacrifice?

Mpophomeni: meeting with Nelson Mandela, February 1990

But now for Mandela here in Mpophomeni was adulation. Possession. Adoration. More, surely, than any man could manage. And longing looks of hope from a people wearied beyond the telling with oppression and despair. Ben's people too.

Then the rally. Ben again was the ticket to our travelling in reflected glory as his car was ushered by marshals to follow those of the big men. 'They must know you, Ben,' I said. Wild shouts and cries of 'Viva this' and 'Viva that' greeted Mandela and his party as they took their places. Women ululated. Efficient and disciplined marshals controlled it all. My colleague, Mike Odell, head of our media team, chuckled to see a PA of sorts already in place. Our AE sound system's big moment had been missed!

Mandela's speech was brief and to the point: continue in the struggle till it's won. This was the music of political ecstasy to many ears.

And then the fanfare, fire and passion of it all!

As we left the stadium behind the big ones, a radiant black lady, who must have seen us in our mission to the area the previous year, called out, 'When are you coming back to Mpophomeni?' This touched my heart. What a land of gospel openness and need!

We remained, thanks to Ben, in the Mandela cavalcade and party for several more stops and heart-warming encounters, including a final meeting in Ben's packed church hall in Edendale where people had been waiting for over 24 hours to see and hear their hero.

What became clear to us through all of these different encounters, whether with senior or junior people, whites or blacks, was the crying need for communication, encounter and understanding. One of the compelling questions before us was whether we could facilitate this in some way.

Nelson Mandela, Neil Pagard (AE), Michael and Harry Gwala

28

Life at full stretch

--------•+•--------

*The pressure! It goes on from stage to stage, pressed beyond
measure . . . it changes with every period of your life.*[1]
(D. E. Hoste)

As I reach beyond life's normally allotted span of three-score years and
ten, I wonder just how on earth we kept up the pace in the late 1980s
and 1990s.

Pacing, in life, is always a challenge. It requires balancing the demands
of family, work and Christian responsibility to our neighbours near and
far, while trying to get the guidance of God right.

Part of the problem when it came to pacing was living on a continent
that was so challenged politically and socially. Passengers and crew on
the *Titanic* could hardly have a normal relaxing afternoon sipping cock-
tails when the ship was going down. Everyone was put under extreme
stress.

In those years we continued to conduct missions all over Africa in
fulfilment of our call. We were always aware of the Lord's challenge
in Jeremiah 23.21–22:

> I did not send the prophets, yet they ran; I did not speak to them, yet they
> prophesied [i.e. wasted religious activity]. But if they had stood in my
> council, then they would have proclaimed my words to my people, and
> they would have turned them from their evil way [i.e. effective spiritual
> ministry] . . .

The danger of going where we had not been sent and speaking what we
had not been given to say was real. We kept this in our sights, along with
the importance of seeking the Lord's guidance for what should be done
next.

We had to remember that our primary calling and challenge was to
preach the gospel in the cities of Africa and we were not to be inappropri-
ately distracted from that.

Sometimes we found ourselves in hilarious situations, such as that in Mbabane, capital of Swaziland.

A royal sermon

During an extensive mission, which saw many people coming to Christ, we were invited to speak in the Royal Kraal of the King's wives, both those of the late King Sobhuza and those of the new young king, Mswati. Sobhuza had had over 100 wives; the young king was just getting going!

Presiding over the open-air gathering in a reed enclosure was the senior and oldest Sobhuza queen, sitting on a sort of throne. No one was allowed to sit higher than she, and we were all ordered to sit on the ground, watched over by either modern-dressed soldiers with rifles, or semi-clad Swazi warriors with feathered headgear and loincloths, plus a shield and spear. A clash of cultures, you might say.

My AESA colleague, David Peters, sat down on a fallen tree to spare his suit from the dust of the ground, but a sharp prod from a rifle butt quickly had him seated on *his* butt!

After some formalities, I was invited to speak. I got to my feet with, to my relief, no threat of rifle butt or spear.

My address completed, the Queen apparently broke protocol and signalled that she wanted a microphone. At this a black-suited official from the Swaziland Broadcasting Association crawled, yes crawled, on his tummy through the dust (can't be higher than the Queen, remember?), dragging a long TV cord plus microphone which was handed to the Queen.

Then to everyone's astonishment the Queen gave about a 40-minute exposition of a chapter from Isaiah, which certainly knocked spots off my talk and stole the day!

During the talks, one of the young brides of the new king managed to pass a note asking if we could help her escape from the royal clutches in which she was imprisoned. Circumstances rendered us powerless to help.

Later on, another young Swazi girl secretly alerted us that she was to be taken into the royal harem, and one of our team helped her escape and find a place in a local Pietermaritzburg private girls' school. This was of course an irregular thing to facilitate, but knowing the girl's desperate plight we decided to cooperate and it was a plan which worked.

Thus are the sideshows of evangelism in the cities of Africa.

Prayer brings healing – and rain

Of my many memories of those years, a healing in the Zambian Copper Belt, in Ndola, stands out.

David Peters has an amazing healing ministry in terms of the gifts of the Holy Spirit. A young child of 12 or so brought her elderly and blind grandfather to David to be prayed for. David laid his hands on the old man and prayed for him. Nothing seemed to happen at the time.

But after they had gone a hundred metres or so, a cry rang out which the whole Copper Belt must have heard – 'I can *see*. I can *see*. I can *see*!'

Imagine the rejoicing all around.

I often wonder why one doesn't see more healing and the miraculous in the Church. It all seems to be very mysterious. Perhaps partly we need to be more expectant and full of confidence. Sometimes the miraculous involves another of the supernatural gifts, namely, the gift of knowledge (see 1 Corinthians 14.6). This refers to occasions when God reveals something supernaturally which could not otherwise be known. David Peters also has gifting in this area.

For example, in another situation a farmer just outside of Pieter-maritzburg had his brilliant young athletic and intellectual son suddenly become unaccountably ill with something no doctors could diagnose. When David was called in, he sensed that a curse had been put on the boy. David requested that all farm workers be summoned to the front of the house and asked whether any witch-doctor curse had been put on the boy, which was of course robustly denied.

David Peters and Stephen Lungu

He then asked that a spade be produced, and one of the workers was told to dig beneath the window of the lad's room. Sure enough, a mass of witch-doctor paraphernalia of feathers and bones was unearthed, which set the whole group of workers trembling.

David prayed, called for repentance and confession, and broke the curse. To the astonishment of the doctors, the farmer's son recovered immediately and was back at school in full strength 48 hours later.

Then there was the occasion we prayed for rain – and got it – in Bulawayo, Zimbabwe.

Zimbabwe had been in the grip of a desperate drought. In a well-filled welcome meeting I suddenly found myself emboldened to declare to the Mayor and all present that we would be praying for the drought to break before the end of the mission.

Ten days later, after a very hectic and fruitful mission, we were in the closing rally. I was sitting on the platform next to the Mayor, who was pretty focused on my comment about the drought coming to an end. As I began my talk, clouds gathered and, believe it or not, the heavens opened! I was quickly soaked, and in my sermon files I still have the rain-splattered notes of that talk.

While the startled Mayor beamed, much of the crowd fled for cover to nearby houses, thankfully returning when the rain eased!

After many came forward in response to my appeal, another 57 came after a second appeal I made for volunteers for full-time Christian service. A year later, when we went back to Bulawayo for follow-up, all 57 volunteers turned out for further encouragement and counsel.

Even more satisfying than the rain! And the drought broke countrywide!

Breakfast with Mugabe

In all our major missions in capital cities, we tried to have at least one major event for the senior leadership of the country. In Harare, Zimbabwe, this was the Presidential Prayer Breakfast for President Mugabe and his leaders – a couple of hundred in the event.

Mugabe arrived late, looking flustered, and told us he was quite unwell and had called for a doctor and nurse. When these did not turn up, we prayed backstage for the President with the laying on of hands as referred to in Hebrews 6.2.

With no medical personnel in sight, we then headed to the huge dining room.

When eventually a rather shamefaced doctor and nurse arrived, Mugabe gave them a casual wave and said, 'You can go. I'm fine. I've been healed!'

After my own address, it was Mugabe's turn to speak. He started rather awkwardly from the little tuft of notes he had requested from me, and obviously decided that Cassidy wasn't quite up to scratch! He then held forth spontaneously, telling us the whole story of his spiritual and ideological quest.

His oration went on for well over two hours, his time allocation having been 20 minutes! He told us how he had been raised in a Catholic environment and struggled to come to some sort of faith, and how he had then become disillusioned with Christianity, which didn't seem to meet his needs. He then turned to Marxism, and although he had pursued this most of his life he was still not spiritually satisfied. 'Perhaps I'd better look at Christianity again,' he reflected.

I was delighted when Mugabe agreed to our organizing an annual Presidential Prayer Breakfast for him. I wrote to him a couple of times in the following months about this but got no reply. Nor could my local Zimbabwean colleagues break past Mugabe's protective henchmen. I always felt very sad about this.

Feeding programme in South Africa

In South Africa, with the country's preoccupations so intensely political in those years, all we could do was hold small missions in schools, colleges or suburbs, alongside some of our practical ministries. AE's mission statement said we existed 'to evangelise the cities of Africa in word and *deed* in partnership with the Church'. Our concerns and commitments were holistic.

Thus back in the late 1970s we bought into the vision of Daphne Tshabalala, the head of Nichols Primary School in Edendale, and AE's Barbara Davies, who teamed up together to launch the programme of Bonginkosi (Zulu for 'Praise the Lord'). This was a child enrichment and feeding programme whereby we linked the need of hungry, malnourished children in township schools with financial resources in local, mainly white, churches. This project grew from feeding a few hundred kids a day to the point where, by the end of 1980, we were feeding thousands a day.

By 1990 the small seed planted in 1972 with 30 children had grown into a large venture whereby 10,500 children a day in 51 schools around South Africa were daily receiving a mug of protein-enriched soup and a thick slice of bread. We then extended the ministry to provide healthcare,

Bonginkosi: Daphne Tshabalala and Barbara Davies, 1972

blankets and clothes. Beyond that, wherever possible, the gospel was meaningfully shared with these kids.

I was proud of Carol when her additional commitments to evangelism, ministry holism, practical care and reconciliation led her 20 years ago to join friends in our church in a weekly Bonginkosi ministry to the poorest of the poor.

Looking for peace

In December 1989 President de Klerk made an appeal to South African believers and church leaders to develop an imaginative strategy for reconciliation and change. In June 1990 a number of us met to spearhead this and we chose Dr Louw Alberts, a Dutch Reformed scientist of note and a man who had the ear of de Klerk, and Dr Frank Chikane, the courageous General Secretary of the South African Council of Churches (SACC), to lead us.

There was method in our madness because these two very fine and powerful Christian men represented two ends of the political spectrum as far as the Church was concerned.

We met from 5 to 9 November 1990, in the dusty little right-wing town of Rustenburg in what came to be known as the Rustenburg Conference. We found we had succeeded in drawing together from 85 churches some 250 Christian leaders of perhaps the widest range ever to meet in South Africa, from farthest left (including liberation theologians) to the farthest-right conservatives.

Bonginkosi: little girl bringing out the bread for lunch

We needed to come up with a declaration to all the political players which would carry the full weight and force of the united voice of the Church.

On the first morning of the conference, Professor Willie Jonker, a Dutch Reformed theologian from Stellenbosch University, made a remarkable confession on behalf of Afrikaners.

Jonker said:

> I confess before you and before the Lord, not only my own sin and guilt, and my personal responsibility for the political, social, economic and structural wrongs that have been done to many of you, and the results which you and our whole country are still suffering from, but *vicariously* I dare also to do that in the name of the Dutch Reformed Church (DRC) of which I am a member, and for the Afrikaans people as a whole. I have the liberty to do just that, because the DRC at its latest synod has declared apartheid a sin and confessed its own guilt of negligence in not warning against it and distancing itself from it long ago.[2]

Right after this, Archbishop Desmond Tutu, with characteristic generosity and deep emotion, went up unannounced to the podium and said:

> Our brother here has asked for forgiveness for his sins and those of his Church and people, and I believe it appropriate at this time that I should on behalf of black people who suffered so much under apartheid, express that we have heard this request for forgiveness, and from our hearts we extend our forgiveness and we say that we love you and we receive you and we put the past behind us.[3]

Rustenburg Conference: Mmutlanyane Mogobo, Frank Chikane and Beyers Naude, 1989

Rustenburg became a conference of confessions, with much repentance and many reconciliations. And out of it came what would be called the Rustenburg Declaration, sent to church leaders all over South Africa. With its challenges to confront violence and injustice particularly, it represented for once the Church of South Africa speaking with a single voice.

National Peace Accord

Another major outcome of the Rustenburg Conference was the National Peace Accord which brought together church leaders and major figures in business.

In fact around the same time as our church initiative, a number of bold and progressive business people from many corporates had formed what was known as the Consultative Business Movement (CBM) to try to come up with an informed response to the deteriorating situation in South Africa.

It was logical that these two groupings of Rustenburg and CBM should converge, again with Louw Alberts and Frank Chikane playing a key role along with businessman John Hall, ably assisted by Val Pauquet. John was Chairman of the South African Chamber of Business (SACOB), which gave him tremendous clout.

John said:

> though Church and business seemed to be strange bedfellows, it was felt that they constituted the two poles of non-political power in the country. Therefore, it made a tremendous amount of sense for them, with their collective power, to play a role in influencing the politicians. Because, first,

you did not publicly defy the Church very easily and, second, with business you had to keep on the ball. So together we had a powerful leverage over the politicians.[4]

A Peace Secretariat was formed under the leadership of a Dr Antonie Geldenhuys, who testified: 'I see it as Christian duty to do what your hands find to do wherever you are placed. I believe by doing that you serve God.'[5]

When the Peace Accord was publicly signed in September 1991 at Johannesburg's Carlton Hotel, we had succeeded in capturing the attention of South Africa's leadership. Political leaders from 26 political parties and trade unions were present, plus financial, religious, philanthropic and media organizations. Nelson Mandela, Buthelezi and the Zulu king, Goodwill Zwelithini, were present.

In the next two years Peace Accord representatives worked tirelessly to prevent violence escalating. John Hall later commented:

> We saw divine intervention and the positive influence of the Church on the process the whole time. There are no coincidences; it was all a great tapestry which was being woven by God. I am not a deeply religious man but I know that it was not all my doing, that 90 percent was with assistance from Somewhere Else.[6]

All these experiences emphasized to us in letters of fire the importance of keeping adversaries talking.

From Africa with Love

In 1992 we celebrated the thirtieth anniversary of our first mission to 'Maritzburg, and people came to South Africa from all over the world to give praise with us.

It was an ideal opportunity to invite our AE brothers and sisters from wider Africa to join in an initiative we called From Africa with Love. From their experience in many broken African countries, they knew what shattered economies were, how difficult it was to fix things politically, and what part the Church could play. Their presence in prayer for our beleaguered political leaders would be powerful. So we arranged some strategic visits.

We set out around the country in seven teams.

Emmanuel Kopwe, our Tanzanian Team Leader, went to the Eastern Cape and met with both ANC representatives and Ciskei homeland's leadership, who were in conflict with one another, putting the National Peace Accord agreements at risk.

From Africa with Love team from all over Africa

Emmanuel tried without success to prevent an ANC march of 40,000 protesters. Shooting left 200 wounded and 28 dead. At least he had tried in Jesus' name to get the two sides communicating.

Some of us went to Ulundi, in KwaZulu-Natal, to meet and pray with Prince Mangosuthu Buthelezi and his leadership. Their enmity towards the ANC was palpable. At the end of the discussion time Buthelezi moved to the middle of the room, knelt down and asked us to pray for him, which we did with the laying on of hands.

Dr Andries Treurnicht

Next we were in Pretoria visiting one of South Africa's toughest and most hated white right-wingers, the notorious Dr Andries Treurnicht, leader of the Conservative Party. He and his party wanted a separate state for Afrikaners. He had been a Dutch Reformed minister and professed strong Christian faith. Testimonies from our pan-African colleagues clearly touched him, especially one from Kenya's John Gatu, a long-standing friend of AE. Gatu told how he had hated white people after going through the Mau Mau war, but after coming to Christ had learned to forgive. However, he spoke further of his residual hatred towards Afrikaners, and

> you, Dr Treurnicht, even more particularly . . . although I do not agree with your politics at all, or some of your interpretations of the Bible, the Spirit of God is convicting me of my attitude towards you and I want to ask

357

Team praying with Conservative Party leader, Andries Treurnicht

for your forgiveness . . . and give you the right hand of fellowship and greet you as my brother.[7]

The eyes of hard-hearted Treurnicht became wet with tears. 'Nothing like this has ever happened to me before,' he said. 'And certainly no black man has ever called me brother.'[8]

After urging him to rethink his views of the way forward for South Africa, we all laid hands on him and prayed.

Might he have changed his views? We will never know. A few weeks later he was dead from a heart attack.

President de Klerk

In September we met with President de Klerk in his office in the Union Buildings. Edward Muhima, our Ugandan Team Leader, spoke boldly: 'Mr President, we do thank God for the kind of man you are and for what you have achieved here in South Africa. Indeed we believe that you could be the Moses of South Africa.' It was one of those statements which takes one's breath away. 'But, Mr President, I would remind you that in order for Moses to lead the Children of Israel out of Egypt, he had to leave the courts of Pharaoh.'[9]

Team visit de Klerk

The price of liberation for the country's blacks would require a sacrificial handing over of power by the whites. Our extended time with de Klerk ended in prayer for him.

Could just praying for these leaders pay off? We believed it could.

ANC

Our next stop was Luthuli House, headquarters of the ANC, to meet with members of their executive. The ANC delegation of ten was led by Oliver Tambo, its president, who, on hearing that de Klerk had asked us to open in prayer, readily agreed for us to do the same!

An open time of sharing followed, during which we listened to their observations and then sought to minister spiritual encouragement, before gathering round Oliver Tambo to pray for his health, as he had suffered a stroke.

Afterwards, one member commented: 'Everyone who comes to Luthuli House talks politics or money to us, but you people ministered to our hearts.'

The barrel of a gun

In the street outside were several militant-looking youths wearing the T-shirts of Mkhonto weSizwe, the armed wing of the ANC. One of them asked who we were.

Team visit ANC at Luthuli House: Michael with Oliver Tambo

Edward Muhima answered, 'We're from other parts of Africa and we are here to encourage you all to negotiate and not try to solve problems through the barrel of a gun.'

'But,' replied one of them, 'certain people do not understand any language but the gun.'

Edward responded: 'You must iron out your differences and capitalize on the things which unite you. Otherwise you could end up going the way of Uganda where we lost 800,000 people because we began fighting.'[10]

The boys took that in.

When we spoke against violence in these different contexts, we often thought of Jacques Ellul's book *Violence*, where he speaks of its laws, two of them being the Law of Reciprocity (if you use violence on me I will use it on you), and the Law of Continuity, namely that once you get violence into the system and bloodstream of a country, it will continue to be very difficult to get it out.

PAC

Finally, we called on the Pan Africanist Congress leaders whose slogan was 'One settler, one bullet'. Benny Alexander, later calling himself Khoisan X, led the group.

Our discussion was deep. Little could we have realized then that two years later they would be asking us to help them change that slogan and call off their armed struggle.

Dialogue

With the election just 18 months away, we decided to concentrate our efforts on facilitating more of this kind of dialogue that had proved so transforming. We hit on the idea of organizing special weekends away at a game lodge called Kolobe near Pretoria. Over the course of a year from December 1992, we ran six weekends, involving nearly a hundred political leaders. These were among the most significant contributions we were to make at that politically important time.

Kolobe Lodge

361

Someone once asked me how we got the leaders to come. My PA Peter Kerton-Johnson and I promised them the weekend of a lifetime. I replied, 'And then we just harried and harried them till they agreed to come!'

Sadly, that great bull of a man, Eugène Terre'Blanche, head of the AWB, the Afrikaner Weerstandsbeweging (Afrikaner Resistance Movement), who was later to be murdered on his farm, declined to come. He was the only leader we contacted who just banged the phone down on me.

Kolobe offered fully private accommodation which was free of press intrusion. It lies deep in the bush and we went there by light aircraft, a heartwarming and relaxing adventure in itself, flying in to that little runway cut between the trees and shrubs.

Then we laid on good food. Kolobe Lodge is an upmarket facility, and the meals were out of the top drawer!

Next came plain fun together and encountering one another in our common humanity – a government leader plus a leader of a terrorist organization having coffee together, or leaders of opposition parties swimming together, or going on a game drive together, or having a picnic in the bush next to a four-wheel drive.

I recollect for myself the surreal experience of going jogging early one morning with a senior leader of the PAC, the guys who just the previous week had blown up a sports club in King William's Town, killing a number of whites. After our run we could talk about that. We also prayed together.

Beyond all this, the real key to Kolobe's power lay in our taking extended time as a group to share our personal stories.

Michael and Frank Mdlalose, later Premier of KwaZulu-Natal,
fly from Kolobe together in a small plane

Testimonies from Kolobe

So many life-changing stories came out of these weekends.

First there was Chris de Jager of the Afrikaner Volksunie (AVU), who told how his grandfather had been humiliated by British soldiers after the Boer War when he was made to walk round Pretoria with a sign round his neck that said: 'I am a donkey. I cannot speak English.' He said that after what the British had done to the Afrikaners, he and his people never again wanted to be subject to anyone. Least of all the blacks. That's why they wanted a separate Afrikaner state.

Then, there was John Nkadimeng of the Central Committee of the Communist Party, a close friend of Mandela and an ANC executive member. He told how he came out of a tribal background in northern Transvaal and how, as 'a kitchen boy', he was abused by a Christ-professing Afrikaans farmer. This drove him into the arms of the Communist Party, later landing him in prison for two years. After the Kolobe weekend, John asked for some books to help him look at Christianity afresh 'because for the first time at Kolobe I experienced real love and acceptance from Christians'.

I also recollect vividly Philip Mlambo's story. He was Deputy President of the PAC (Pan Africanist Congress) – the 'one settler, one bullet' people – and former commander-in-chief of the military wing of the PAC. He had spent 23 years of his life in prison on Robben Island. He told of assorted beatings and brutalizing from prison guards, plus one horrific experience of being made to dig a hole nearly two metres deep, after which he was told to get in it. The guards then filled it in with sand up to his neck and urinated on him.

With tears in his eyes one Afrikaner said: 'We deeply apologize to you, brother. Please forgive us. I never knew we did things like that.'

The mix

In these dialogues, first of all the enemy was humanized. Stereotypes were shattered.

Second, enemies became friends, not in the sense of all reaching identical postures, but in the sense of people finding and coming to like each other, even trust each other.

Third, people learned things in these encounters which they had never thought possible. Lekau Moyaha, a leader in Steve Biko's political party, the Azanian People's Organization (AZAPO), said: 'I learned more in my

One of the Kolobe Lodge gatherings, pre-game drive, mid-1993

first three hours at Kolobe than I could have learned in six years anywhere else.'

Fourth, many people found that their personal and even political ideas were much closer to those of others there than they could possibly have imagined. The only differences were how to achieve the desired ends.

Fifth, people were actually changed by the chemistry of encounter. When it came to the turn of politician Amichand Rajbansi's daughter, Vimleka, to share her story, she said with emotion: 'If I had had my turn yesterday, it would have been quite different from how I feel now. I have had several revolutionary encounters with some of these Afrikaners.'

In fact it was quite something for certain politicians to have to do 12 or 15 bits of listening before they could do their own bit of talking!

Addie van Rensburg, from the executive of the AVU, came to three Kolobes, each time bringing new colleagues from the extreme right wing. His great-grandfather had been President of the 'Zuid-Afrikaanse Republiek', and his mother came from the Strijdom family that produced former South African Nationalist prime minister, Hans Strijdom. Addie later wrote:

> Facing people who were on the wrong side of the apartheid fence made me realise with shame and sadness that apartheid had become a monster which dehumanised people and subjected them to the most degrading laws and regulations, and all in an attempt to preserve a *status quo* which could no longer be defended.

Addie became a changed man:

> So while I love my own people deeply and will always be an Afrikaner, I will never again be part of a system which denies other people the opportunities I have had. I found at Kolobe that the love of our Lord Jesus Christ lives in the hearts of many people, and in reaching out to our fellow people there are many willing hands to grasp one in reconciliation.[11]

Addie, like his boss Andries Beyer in the AVU, who joined de Klerk in unwinding apartheid, resigned from the party. He also took his reconciling message to his friend, General Constand Viljoen, who had some 400,000 Afrikaners ready to rise up and overthrow the process towards non-racial elections. Addie believed Viljoen was deeply affected by this.

Home Affairs Minister Danie Schutte added: 'I also believe Kolobe had a significant part in finally getting the right-wing Afrikaners into the elections.'[12]

Then there was the extraordinary post-Kolobe story of the PAC's Philip Mlambo from whom I got a phone call one day out of the blue. 'Michael,' he said, 'our leadership wants to meet with you. Will you come to Johannesburg?'

I agreed, of course. My personal assistant Peter Kerton-Johnson and I would go up. Once there, he and Benny Alexander (Khoisan X), told me they had decided to call off the armed struggle. And they wanted to know our thoughts and get our encouragement.

'Well, men,' I said, 'we obviously want to encourage this significant move. But one thing is for sure. You will have to receive with full force our insistence that you terminate your slogan "One settler, one bullet"!'

They agreed.

Five years later, when I was in the UK at a conference on reconciliation in Coventry, which happened the day after Princess Diana's tragic death in August 1997, who should be there but Philip Mlambo? He was sharing his testimony of what happened through the chemistry of the Holy Spirit's working in him at Kolobe.

In many ways our efforts at dialogue seemed small. But we felt led to press on with them by faith, even though we didn't know where they would lead.

29

Nation on a knife edge

More things are wrought by prayer than this world dreams of.[1]
(Alfred Lord Tennyson)

South Africa had become one of the most violent societies on earth. In France in the early 1990s the annual murder rate was 4 per 100,000 people. In the USA it was 10. In South Africa it was 98. In our province of Natal it was 213.[2] That translated to about 20 people dying daily, 60 or 70 at the weekends.

In March 1993 I was curiously the only Christian leader invited to be part of an inspecting delegation to go in military helicopters to the KwaZulu-Natal Table Mountain 'war zone' between ANC and IFP supporters near Pietermaritzburg. Needless to say, it was worse than horrific. On a spot where a massacre of schoolchildren had taken place, I asked if I could say a prayer for Natal, for South Africa, for our elections and for all of us as leaders. No one demurred. All bowed their heads as I prayed. Journalists too. After all, we were in theistic Africa.

The next day, astonishingly, a message came to me from Harry Gwala, the head of the Natal Communist Party who had also been at Table Mountain, inviting me to meet with Nelson Mandela the following day. This was a remarkable open door, for which I had in fact been praying. If nothing else, I had a signed leather-bound copy of Billy Graham's book *Peace with God* which the author had wanted me to give personally to Mandela. His prayers accompanied me too.

My conversation with the great man was warm and serious, and spiritually rather than politically focused.

When I gave Dr Mandela Billy Graham's book, he said: 'Do you know that he has preached many inspiring sermons? I was much touched by one of his sermons which I saw on television when I was in Pollsmoor Prison. In fact, you know, on Robben Island I never missed a church service or Bible study and I appreciated very much my regular visits from a Dutch Reformed minister. I wanted to send a gift from me to his wife, and all I

Michael with Nelson Mandela, 1993

had was a guava from my breakfast that morning. So that's what I gave. But when the wardens realized I was developing quite a friendship with this minister, they disallowed him from coming to see me any more. I thought that very sad.'

Mandela then added, 'I would like to keep going to church even now, but it is very difficult and complicated for me.'

Before we could close in prayer, some aides regrettably interrupted us to call an end to our time.

New issues out of the new constitution

Anyway, some surprising fruit came after Mandela had received a document on human rights which we at African Enterprise had prepared in a consultation at AE for political thinkers in the light of the deteriorating situation around us. We had been sceptical of anyone taking much notice of our document, but Mandela wanted us to take up our concerns with Albie Sachs of the ANC's Constitutional Committee and one of the main drafters of the new constitution for South Africa.

Our special concern was to see God recognized in our constitution.

Four of us met Sachs in Cape Town. Atheist communist though he was, Sachs was open: 'I don't see why not. After all, the great majority of our people are religious and God-fearing.'

There and then we suggested that the preamble to the Constitution should open with: 'In humble submission to Almighty God, we the people of South Africa . . .' And at the end, 'Nkosi sikelel' iAfrika' (God bless Africa).

367

Saying he would send our thoughts to the senior ANC leadership, Albie gave us a warm left-handed handshake as we left, his right arm having been blown off some years previously by a letter bomb sent to him by some in the South African security police. Another violent act by the dirty-tricks brigade!

In the final draft of the new 12 November 1993 version of the Interim Constitution was our preamble exactly as suggested, with God at the beginning and God at the end. How we rejoiced! The preamble was declaring that the state is not autonomous, but has a transcendent point of accountability to the divine.

But tragically, some academics who were influential in drafting the Constitution succeeded in getting this part of the preamble removed, 'because there are some 0.05 per cent of South Africans who are atheists, and the Constitution needs to be for them as well'!

My other bits of lobbying for the Constitution were on two fronts. The first concerned the wording of the clause on sexual orientation found in Chapter 2, section 9, which reads:

> Everyone is equal before the law and has right to equal protection and benefit of the law . . . [Prohibited grounds of discrimination include] race, gender, sex, pregnancy, marital status, ethnic or social origin, colour, sexual orientation, age, disability, religion, conscience, belief, culture, language and birth.[3]

It wasn't fully clear what exactly this clause was saying or would lead to, but as I saw it, it would be opening the way for same-sex marriage and for specially protected rights for homosexuals, instead of having such rights protected, with everyone else's, under general human rights.

It was not surprising, of course, that the issues of discrimination and rights were much to the fore in the Interim Constitution. The proposed Bill of Human Rights had an appropriate clause forbidding 'unfair discrimination' of any sort, including against homosexuals. So the issue in our view was whether *not* granting same-sex marriage to homosexual people was a denial of human rights or 'unfair discrimination'.

As we saw it, marriage had always had appropriate parameters around it, differentiating it as a particular relationship. Thus I cannot marry, nor do I have a right to marry, my sister, daughter or mother. A grown woman may not marry a boy of seven or claim her right to do so. One may not marry a person who is already married. Nor, up to that point, could one marry a person of the same gender. So, in a nutshell, it is a definitional issue and one relating to qualification for entry into a particular institution.

My involvement on this front eventually led me in 2004 to becoming the co-chairman, with my friend Moss Ntlha, of the Marriage Alliance of South Africa, in which our primary concern was that of contesting for marriage as heterosexual, monogamous and permanent. We were guided by what we believed were clear principles on marriage as laid out in the Bible, for example, in Matthew 19.4–6:

> He who made them from the beginning made them male and female, and said, 'For this reason a man shall leave his father and mother and be joined to his wife, and the two shall become one flesh' . . . So they are no longer two but one flesh. What therefore God has joined together, let [no one] put asunder.

But our Marriage Alliance efforts with constitution-makers over several years came to naught.

The other issue related to a clause which I knew would be used to relax abortion laws. This clause read as follows: 'Everyone has the right to bodily and psychological integrity, which includes the right – (a) to make decisions concerning reproduction; (b) to security in and control over their body'.[4]

Clearly this provision would grant women much greater freedom of personal choice about whether or not to have an abortion. My concerns were that the human rights of the mother were being taken into consideration, but not those of the unborn child. The reference in the Constitution looked obscure, but it was powerfully loaded. Again, we couldn't prevail with anyone.

Our worst fears on both accounts later proved justified. South Africa finally opted for something very close to abortion 'on demand' in 1997, and it was this clause which was used to justify this. Also, in due time in 2006, South Africa fully sanctioned same-sex marriage. And the term 'marriage' became same-sex inclusive.

Actually I always regretted that there weren't more Christian leaders willing to put their heads above the parapet on these issues while the Constitution was being drafted.

More violence

Meanwhile the violence, murder and mayhem continued, especially in Natal, but also in Johannesburg where there were thousands of IFP Zulus in the mines interfacing with ANC Zulus and others.

Many whites began to emigrate. This process was called PFP – not Progressive Federal Party, the name of our main opposition party, but

Packing For Perth! At one point several hundred people were taking this route every day.

People weren't safe even in churches. One person from a church in Ladysmith described to me the terrifying experience of ducking down below window level as a hail of bullets from an automatic rifle raked the church through the windows.

The man who helps us in our garden, David Sokela, told how he was in his church in Imbali during a night-long prayer vigil when, at midnight, bullets were randomly fired in by a cluster of gunmen, 32 penetrating his stomach, hands and thigh, and one going clean through his leg. Eleven people in the prayer meeting died. Scores were wounded. David – with others dead, dying or wounded – lay unattended on the floor through the night until 7.00 a.m. when an ambulance arrived. Quite miraculously he survived after 13 months in hospital. Many others lost family members and friends during those times.

In fact, as far away from Natal as Cape Town, St James Church in Kenilworth was attacked during a service by four gunmen from the Azanian People's Liberation Army (APLA), the military wing of the Pan Africanist Congress, peppering the church with bullets and lobbing hand-grenades. Eleven died horrifically, another 58 were wounded, and a number were maimed for life. The brave pastor, Frank Retief, called for forgiveness and soul searching.

In July 1993 I wrote to Mandela to wish him 'Happy Birthday' and to try humbly to suggest the notion of a Camp David-style private re-treat for just himself, Buthelezi and de Klerk. This was the formula used first by President Jimmy Carter in 1978 to get together Prime Minister Begin of Israel and President Anwar Sadat of Egypt, and then by President Bill Clinton to try to forge a peace agreement between then Israeli Prime Minister Ehud Barak and Palestinian Authority Chairman Yasser Arafat in 2000. Could not that sort of arrangement work wonders? Mandela, gra-cious to a fault, replied:

> I very much regret that I do not think your suggestion would be produc-tive at this time. Having separately met with both President de Klerk and Chief Minister Buthelezi recently, I do not feel that a further meeting will produce any additional results.
>
> Furthermore, I and my colleagues have always been of the view that as many parties as possible across the political spectrum in South Africa must be involved in discussion and negotiations, if we are to have the quali-tative and lasting peace we need. I do not think a meeting, involving only three parties to the peace process, is correct.

I fully appreciate and applaud your efforts towards the Camp David concept, but I feel that insofar as South Africa is concerned, at this time in our history, it would not be appropriate.[5]

Conservative Afrikaner concerns

By the end of 1993, despair hung like a funeral shroud over South Africa.

However, the fact was that the Natal Zulu issue was not the only centre of volcanic, nation-gutting rumblings. Elsewhere in South Africa, conservative and radical right-wing Afrikaners were flexing their muscles, refusing to come into the elections, and beginning to breathe fire and slaughter. At heart they wanted a separate white Afrikaner homeland (or Volkstaat). And they would fight for it.

Columnist Gerald Shaw wrote in the local newspaper, the *Natal Witness*: 'This is a dangerous moment in South African history. Clandestine forces on the right are poised to wreck the first democratic election if they can, and make the country ungovernable.'[6]

The homelands of Ciskei and Bophuthatswana were also calling for a federal form of decentralized government.

In northern Natal things were cooking among conservative Afrikaners who wanted to push the Zulus towards a break with a unitary state, and maybe even into going it alone. This would give added impetus to their own dream for independence.

Thus right-winger Leonard Veenendal, pressing for a free Volkstaat, made himself leader of the newly formed Natal Boere Kommando in northern Natal. Soon other areas in the province declared themselves part of the Volkstaat, and Veenendal believed that they could count on the support of almost three million whites to join them.

Veenendal admitted that the election date left him with a hollow feeling in his gut:

I hope it will be peaceful but if the election happens and if our land is taken from us, *'die skote sal begin klap'* [the shots will begin to be fired] . . . the boerevolk will not bend under the yoke of a NP [National Party], ANC or SACP [South African Communist Party] government.[7]

If the army were deployed, on whose side would it fight?

The *Daily News* reported a new kind of hazard, namely whether the South African Defence Force (SADF) could count on all its members to defend the government's election plans and processes. The newspaper stated:

> The SADF is planning its largest deployment of troops around the country in a major operation aimed at quelling election violence as the battle for the hearts of the security forces hots up.
>
> Senior defence sources confirmed that the massive call-up of troops for deployment in and around trouble-spots, to ensure an orderly run-up to the elections, had already begun in certain areas with a number of Citizen Force units already mobilised.[8]

Bear in mind that the South African Defence Force was made up mainly of conservative Afrikaners; one can readily see how they would feel massive conflicts of loyalty if called on to oppose fellow Afrikaners of a right-wing persuasion who were willing to fight for their own independence. So if the army were called in, on whose side would the soldiers fight?

The *Daily News* reported: 'Volksfront leader and former chief of the SADF, General Constand Viljoen, challenged a claim by President FW de Klerk that the security forces would be loyal to the Government.'[9]

Viljoen was still an incredibly influential man among the military leadership. Clearly he himself was torn between his loyalties to the South African Defence Force and his loyalties to his own Afrikaner *Volk*. Where finally would he throw his considerable weight?

It seemed that more and more gunpowder was daily being poured from different sides into the already explosive powder keg.

Natal Leaders' Forum

In the middle of all this, AE called a Natal Leaders' Forum for 24 February 1994, and over 250 leaders attended. The one thing everyone agreed on was that any breakaway of Natal or any other sectors from the rest of South Africa would be catastrophic.

We ended in powerful unanimity with three resolutions.

First, to give impetus to a meeting brokered by a Durban businessman for a face-to-face meeting between Mandela and Buthelezi.

Second, to urge all Christian leaders to embrace afresh and broker the backstage facilitation of encounters between alienated political leaders. The Church's role was emphasized as vital in helping the key players to find each other.

Third, to urge all Christians everywhere to embrace anew and with greater urgency the role of peacemaking.

*Colleen Smith holding things together behind the
scenes. She was Michael's secretary for many years*

The point once again was to try to get everyone doing his or her bit.

For our part, AE called for a 24/7 two-year prayer chain, which continued round the clock with deepened intensity and ever-increasing numbers. We were a nation on its knees. In this, I believe, in retrospect, lay the basis of our final breakthrough and miraculous national salvation.

The following week, Mandela and Buthelezi did in fact meet, in grim seriousness, and agreed to call for international mediation to try to help South Africa through to peaceful elections eight weeks later, especially finding a way for Buthelezi's IFP to enter the elections.

The big IFP reservation was that KwaZulu-Natal would lose its regional autonomy, land up with weakened political power, and have the King's jurisdiction over tribal trust lands removed.

Without some of these issues resolved, the IFP Zulus would not enter the elections. This would threaten to abort South Africa's first democratic elections, and, if that happened, it would prove calamitous.

Khosa Mgojo and Mmutlanyane Mogoba, Natal Leaders' Forum, 1994

Election registration deadline

Meanwhile in the Transvaal, after some heavy wrangling with extreme right-wingers, General Constand Viljoen resigned from the Afrikaner Volksfront and registered provisionally a new party, the Freedom Front (FF), with himself as its leader, to contest in the elections. The even more radical white right-wing group, the AWB (Afrikaner Weerstandsbeweging), declared Viljoen 'a political Judas-goat sent by the Broederbond/ANC/NP/Communist Party alliance to lead us to the slaughter'.[10]

The Freedom Front had registered in the nick of time, with minutes to spare before the registration deadline. What had changed Viljoen's mind was unclear. But Addie van Rensburg, one of General Viljoen's close friends and associates, a three-time attendee at the Kolobe Lodge weekends, later told me: 'Michael, you will never know the extent to which the Kolobe Lodge weekends contributed to Viljoen's army of right-wingers coming in to the election. You see, Viljoen had some 400,000 people willing to follow him into an all-out rebellion against the election, as well as 50,000 trained men. He just had to snap his fingers and they would all move. But after every Kolobe weekend I and others went back to him and said: "Constand, there is *another* way. We have seen it at Kolobe. We have met blacks with whom we can talk and negotiate. This is the way to go. The armed resistance way will never work. It will bring calamity."'

Jacob Zuma despairs, Roger Burrows reflects and Amichand Rajbansi wonders! Leaders' Forum, Durban, February 1994

While Viljoen was seeing another way, the defiant IFP had still not submitted its election candidate lists by the time of the election registration cut-off date (midnight, 9 March 1994).

Bophuthatswana homeland

There were further complications in the Bophuthatswana homeland. Two days before the registration deadline, President Lucas Mangope announced that Bophuthatswana would boycott the elections. For some in the homeland this was an extremely unpopular move and it led to a civil service strike as well as mutiny in the local armed forces. Three hundred police officers marched to the South African Embassy to demand reincorporation of Bophuthatswana into South Africa.

To add fuel to the fire, right-wing AWB radicals, who were hell-bent on keeping Bophuthatswana out of the elections, moved in, supposedly in support of Mangope and his government. Bophuthatswana police and military (all wanting to be part of the elections and part of South Africa) opened fire. In effect they carried out firing-squad executions of several white AWB members, who were photographed lying face down in pools of blood.

Dramatic photos of dead white Afrikaners, hovered over by armed black soldiers, greeted white readers of the *Sunday Times* on 13 March 1994. It was a spectacle never before seen, and it shocked the country.

Unrest lasted four days until eventually Mangope bowed to pressure

Jacob Zuma, Nkosazana Dlamini-Zuma, Cardinal Wilfrid Napier and Khosa Mgojo deep in discussion

Jacob Zuma and Michael, Durban, February 1994

and agreed that Bophuthatswana would participate in the elections. He then reversed his decision, and the SADF removed him from power and restored order.

With all these dramatic events unfolding, South Africa was nearly ready to vote, or was it? Or were we still a nation on a knife edge?

The answer would lie in KwaZulu-Natal.

30

Miracle

The ballot is stronger than the bullet.[1]
(Abraham Lincoln)

In reality everything was still extremely precarious. Beyond everything, there was still the vexed and seemingly intractable issue of KwaZulu-Natal. If it took a modest miracle to get right-wing Afrikaners almost ready to vote, it would take an even greater miracle to get the Inkatha Freedom Party (IFP) Zulus of Natal into the election. A miracle is what we needed, and a miracle is what we finally got.

But there were still many bridges to cross. One of these was the issue of international mediation which Mandela, Buthelezi and de Klerk had decided on in an attempt to break the ANC–Inkatha impasse. Could it possibly be made to work?

IFP Chairman Frank Mdlalose (who had been at Kolobe, remember?) now invited us in AE to submit a list of possible mediators for the international mediation process from Africa and around the world 'because our list is not complete'; after phone calls far and wide to linkages across the globe, we did as he asked.

Washington Okumu

One name we really pushed was Washington Okumu, a veteran Kenyan diplomat and economist whom we had met a couple of years previously during some very creative backstage conferences organized by Michael Schluter, the brilliant and energetic founder and director of the Newick Park Initiative in England. These gatherings drew together a wide spectrum of political thinkers and leaders from Europe, the UK, the USA and Africa, especially South Africa.

Schluter's agile brain and experience helped us to draw up many papers of relevance to the future of South Africa – which was our focus.

Anyway, when the list of mediators drawn up by the ANC and IFP appeared – to be led by Henry Kissinger and former UK foreign secretary, Lord Carrington – it was evident that none of our suggestions had made it, and unbelievably not even Washington Okumu, even though he knew Mandela and Buthelezi, and Henry Kissinger under whom he had studied at Harvard. Beyond that, no Africans at all were included, yet South Africa and its current convulsions constituted a profoundly African problem. This was bizarre.

Washington Okumu

We then asked Frank Mdlalose if he could get Buthelezi and Mandela to agree to Washington Okumu becoming the major advisor to the mediating group.

In hope that this could come to pass, we contacted Washington Okumu in Kenya, our message synchronizing with an urgent call to Okumu from

Lord Carrington and Washington Okumu

Michael Schluter, who also asked him to go to South Africa and try to contribute. Michael's mother graciously offered to cover the cost of the plane ticket.

Okumu demurred. Then, to his everlasting credit, he bravely agreed to come. He arrived on 27 March 1994, just four weeks before the now threatened elections.

We had lined up, again via Peter Kerton-Johnson's amazing and untiring efforts, an assortment of visits with key leaders in Natal, including Kolobe Lodge connections. One of the first politicians we had Okumu meet was Jacob Zuma, this happening on the same day Zuma had had his house burned down by IFP supporters.

I remember phoning Jacob that night and praying with him about his family's loss. In fact I did this sort of thing quite often with him, or his wife Nkosazana Zuma; or with Frank Mdlalose, the deputy leader of the IFP; or with Prince Mangosuthu Buthelezi himself. When leaders are between a rock and a hard place, and don't know which way to turn, to be prayed for and encouraged can mean the world. Likewise with Mandela and de Klerk we felt prompted to alert them to the fact that divine wisdom was their major need and that it was available. But the condition was to 'ask', and we gave them James 1.5–6: 'If any of you lacks wisdom, let him *ask* God . . . and it will be given him. But let him *ask* in faith' (my emphasis).

Our next port of call and visit of note for Okumu was with Buthelezi. We chartered a small two-engined plane and flew to Ulundi, where Buthelezi and Okumu warmly embraced like long-lost friends. At the end of our extended discussion Buthelezi said: 'I see the hand of the Lord in all this.' Even so, he insisted that the election needed to be delayed for eight weeks to allow some of the issues to be worked out. Okumu, Peter Kerton-Johnson and I felt Mandela would never agree to more than four weeks, if that.

Back in Pietermaritzburg that night, Okumu, now understanding the IFP position a bit better, felt, as did Peter and I, that we needed to get Danie Schutte, Minister of Home Affairs, a Kolobe graduate and the man in charge of the election, to come to my home that very night, regardless of the lateness of the hour. It was 10.00 p.m. and it was urgent. Time was not our friend.

'Thanks to what Kolobe had put in my heart,' said Schutte later, 'I decided to come.'

He shared with us his extreme fear that the election could not be pulled off in the four weeks remaining until its date on 27 April.

'The 900 electoral supervisors are nowhere near in place,' Schutte added, 'plus 50 per cent of our polling stations aren't in place either because they're in "no-go" conflict areas. Moreover, the wheels of the Independent Electoral Commission are perilously close to coming off.'

All very sobering for Okumu. But both he and Schutte agreed to stay in close touch, sharing information from both the government side and other leaders as Okumu met them.

We ended with fervent prayer together. We needed real faith to believe anything could come of all this. But from that moment, Danie became the vehicle conveying everything Okumu was finding out to President de Klerk. It was a critically important conduit of information. And it worked in reverse from de Klerk via Danie to Okumu, and from him to key black leaders. Okumu was beginning to get a real in-depth understanding of the dynamics.

Next day in Johannesburg Okumu met with members of the ANC leadership, got their perspective, and shared viewpoints from both the IFP and the government sides.

I remember I had a frighteningly vivid dream that night. Across a huge white screen came emblazoned the words: 'The last opportunity'.

For all of us, this added accelerated urgency as a word from the Lord.

Then came a more than welcome word. Okumu would be invited by both Mandela and Buthelezi to be the official African Advisor to the international mediating exercise.

That weekend, with Washington still in Johannesburg working his ANC linkages, an invitation came to me to go and see King Goodwill Zwelithini at his palace in Zululand. This was significant because a high percentage of Zulus gave huge loyalty to His Majesty. Also, Washington needed His Majesty's perspective, especially because the nub of the election problem was where the Zulus stood on issues of federal or centralized power, plus the King's authority over KwaZulu-Natal's tribal trust lands. Danie sent me the longest fax I have ever received, taking a whole roll of fax paper(!), presenting the government's view to share with the King.

Alfa Air, a private air charter company, flew me out. The promised car to pick us up never arrived, and palace officials said it was too dangerous to land at Nongoma where the King was. The airstrip was washed out or something. But the pilot, Dave Solomon, and I agreed to go for it. Negotiating grazing cattle, on a potholed strip more like a vegetable patch than a runway, Dave put the plane down with consummate skill.

Instead of going straight to the palace for our secret meeting, I was taken to an Easter Day church service where the King called me to stand with him while CNN filmed us. So much for the top-level secrecy of my visit, as promised! And so much for an Easter Day service with Carol and the family!

Thereafter came an extended palace meeting. The King gave his Zulu viewpoint graciously, but very firmly. I needed to convey this to Okumu and via him to Schutte and de Klerk. Again we ended with prayer. It never bothered me whether leaders were Christian, Muslim, atheists or communists; I always sought to end such encounters with prayer. And I was never blocked from doing so. Indeed, leaders always appreciated it. After all, they knew *they* didn't have all the answers.

On the way back to our mealie-patch airstrip, we passed gangs of youths, all carrying assault rifles or revolvers. Our driver too had such a rifle below his dashboard. All were ready to fight for the political integrity of the Zulu homeland. The driver said threateningly, 'Let de Klerk put one soldier in here, and we will declare war.'

Our province had become a tinderbox. How on earth could IFP and ANC Zulus, not to mention English and Afrikaners, vote shortly in a peaceful election? It was now 3 April. The election was set for the 27th, just three and a half weeks away.

Two days later Okumu was back, and I reported to him all the details and perspectives of the Zulu king as gleaned in my flying visit to his palace. After forty-eight hours of helter-skelter connections, Okumu was gone again.

In the meantime we in AE were also putting together a giant prayer meeting, the Jesus Peace Rally, which we had called for Sunday 17 April, in Kings Park rugby stadium, ten days before the election.

'Please call it the Interfaith Peace Rally,' urged one church leader to me.

'No, brother,' I responded firmly. 'There is no power in the word "interfaith". But there is power in the name of Jesus, the name above every name.'

He promptly ended the conversation.

In a terrifying semi civil-war situation, with people scared even to board buses for fear of being shot at, and scores dying every day, we wondered whether anyone would come to the stadium. A hundred? Three hundred? A thousand? The rugby stadium was big. We didn't want our faith to be small.

Mediation

The international mediation group was set to meet on 13 April. On Tuesday 12 April Okumu flew back in, amid the genocidal convulsions of

Rwanda getting under way further north. Eight hundred thousand were to die, including our own AE Rwanda Team Leader, Israel Havugimana, his family and some of our board. Would we suffer the same fate in South Africa?

Some incredible delays at the airport meant we were maddeningly late getting Okumu to the Carlton Hotel where the international mediators were meeting. Okumu was ushered in and put down next to Kissinger, who warmly hugged his former Harvard University pupil.

Then, abracadabra, Okumu was called on to conclude the evening, to the astonishment of the media and many others who didn't know who he was and how he got there. We of course knew. And gave thanks!

Next morning in the hotel lobby we met Kissinger. When I said, 'Sir, we will be praying for you to find solutions,' he looked at me a bit mystified and replied, 'Thank you. I hope we *will* find solutions.'

The mediators all set off, with Washington in tow, for a destination unknown and maybe for as long as a week. I headed back to Natal to an isolated farm for a few days to prepare for my message at the Jesus Peace Rally on the 17th. It was 14 April. Thirteen days to go to the election.

Just as I was leaving for the farm, a stricken Okumu rang.

The whole thing had fallen through. 'Everyone is going home,' said Washington, 'including me.' Kissinger's parting words were: 'Armageddon will be here in three weeks.' An unofficial word from the US State Department reached us via a well-placed American friend saying it anticipated a million dead in KwaZulu-Natal alone in the next few weeks.

The peace process had simply blown up in their faces, reported a disconsolate Okumu. Amid this darkness, resolution rose in my spirit and I replied to Washington: 'I see no way you can go. The Lord has not brought us this far only to let the whole thing fall apart now. Besides, you are in a very special way, I believe, God's man in this situation. Not that he has not used others. But you have a special role to play. Kissinger and Carrington may have to go, but not you. You need to soldier on alone. The Lord will help you and we will cover you constantly with prayer.'

'You think so?' said the big man reflectively.

'Yes, I think so.'

Okumu flies solo

In the hopes of meeting with Buthelezi, Okumu set off early next morning for Lanseria Airport on the outskirts of Johannesburg from where Buthelezi was to leave. But Buthelezi had already left the airport, on his way to report to the King. However, something happened, which I believe to be miraculous, to Buthelezi's plane. The compass began to gyrate violently which, though not life-threatening, required the pilot to turn back to Lanseria Airport. Okumu and Buthelezi accordingly had a critically important discussion, which breathed new life and hope into the mediation process. This enabled Buthelezi later in the day to bring a positive and encouraging word to the King, rather than a negative one.

In a rushed parting, with airport mechanics extraordinarily declaring there to be nothing wrong with the compass, the two men agreed to meet two days later at the Jesus Peace Rally at Kings Park Stadium. There they would decide whether a final agreement could be reached.

Okumu then connected to a mass of other key players, including advisors to the KwaZulu-Natal government, such as Dr Willem Olivier and Danie Joubert; business leaders such as Colin Coleman; and Judge Ziegler, head of the Independent Electoral Commission. Olivier and Joubert took details of their conversation with Okumu first to Danie Schutte, Minister of Home Affairs, and in charge of running the election. Then the three of them went to communicate the conclusions and suggestions to President de Klerk. Okumu and these men were coming up with a plan. Perhaps it could fly. Judge Ziegler agreed there was potential, and amazingly agreed to the possibility of a last-minute entry to the election of Buthelezi's Inkatha Freedom Party.

The issue

Let's backtrack now to reflect again on what was at issue here.

The IFP Zulus, then constituting the majority of the approximately seven million Zulus in Natal, and therefore the largest tribe in South Africa, feared losing their relative autonomy in a unitary state where an ANC government of Dr Nelson Mandela and Thabo Mbeki would be predominantly Xhosa-speaking.

This would require some adjustment to the new unitary state constitution already in place. IFP Zulus were unhappy with this and felt it should therefore be seen as interim, and renegotiated with the facilitation of post-election international mediation. The terms of reference for the post-election international mediation, wrote Okumu, would

> assume that the new Republic of South Africa will be a United Federal State with a single entity in international law and in which all its subjects have full and equal citizenship. Yet the constitution will also guarantee the devolution of certain specified powers to the regions.[2]

The IFP Zulus did not want to be politically overrun or dominated by another tribe. That was the nub of things. Okumu felt that these concerns needed to be recognized, faced and dealt with. They could scarcely be fully dealt with *before* the elections as time was so short, but could be addressed with the help of international mediation after the elections.

Also in the mix, of course, was the authority of Zulu King Goodwill Zwelithini over so-called tribal trust lands in parts of KwaZulu-Natal.

Would the parties, with the help of international mediation, negotiate their way into an adjusted federal and decentralized power model as the best for South Africa, even after the elections were over? If so, the Inkatha Freedom Party would in good faith enter the 27 April elections at the last minute. This was shortly thereafter agreed to by Buthelezi and Mandela, and they signed together.

I left my farm hideaway on the evening of Saturday 16 April, my sermon for the Jesus Peace Rally safely tucked under my arm, and my heart trusting for the peace of Christ to come from the rally. I felt the Lord say: 'There will be no disappointment.'

That evening, the King phoned our home and said he was praying. 'Only God can see us through,' he said, 'and God will not let us down. Above all, I am praying for the political parties to listen to each other, understand each other's problems and do some compromising so the nation can be saved.'

He added: 'Tolerance and restrained language are the important things. And I want all my people together, from all the parties. You must say that from me, please.'

He concluded the call by saying: 'Without our Lord Jesus Christ we cannot achieve anything or go anywhere. Say that too.'

I had planned to, for sure.

Jesus Peace Rally

The next day in Durban, Okumu, Buthelezi and I met to go together to the rally.

Just then we got a call from businessman Colin Coleman who had managed to secure an appointment for Okumu with Mandela in Cape Town, so that the great man could see Okumu's document. A private jet had been laid on. This seemed more than providential. Okumu must leave at once.

Giving Buthelezi a copy of his handwritten draft to share at the Peace

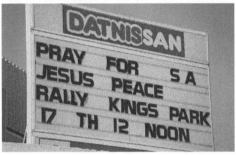

Jesus Peace Rally, Kings Park Stadium, Durban, April 1994

Rally with Danie Schutte and Jacob Zuma, Okumu headed to the airport to meet Coleman and a colleague to speed through to Cape Town.

As some 25,000 people entered that stadium for prayer, there was a palpable sense of occasion, of a *kairos* (Greek: divine opportunity) moment, a sense of history in the making. Media from South Africa and the world contributed also to the atmosphere. BBC reporters had been pulled away from Bosnia to get a ringside seat at the world's next major conflict.

Opening the rally, my great AE colleague Abiel Thipanyane first asked all who had lost loved ones in the Natal violence to stand so that we could pray for them. Hundreds stood, many weeping, as people around them rose to pray for them with hands laid on or arms enveloping them in hugs of comfort.

Moving worship, poignant Scripture readings, anguished prayers soared up to God as the desperate cries of a stricken nation reached heavenwards. Never ever had I seen South Africans, or anyone, pray with such intensity and emotion. Only God could save our country. People knew that.

Jesus Peace Rally: prayers call on the Lord to intervene

Meanwhile, up in the VIP lounge, the groaning prayers of a nation were beginning to be answered, all unbeknown to those in the stadium.

Buthelezi was showing Okumu's handwritten document to the two key players, Zuma and Schutte, representing Mandela and de Klerk respectively, both of whom had sent messages to the rally, as had the King.

Zuma said he thought it could work. So did Danie Schutte, who promptly phoned President de Klerk there and then. The President said: 'Get back here quickly.' Schutte's plane was alerted to fly. An exhilarated Buthelezi called an aide, instructing that the Central Committee of the Inkatha Freedom Party hold a meeting that very evening, for which Buthelezi would be flying back. By then, Okumu had flown into Cape Town to meet Mandela.

Something was happening. Something almost too good to be true.

In my own address I focused on the way Jesus offered forgiveness from the very agony of the cross to those inflicting that agony: 'Father, forgive . . .' (Luke 23.34). Such forgiveness was required now from us South Africans to one another.

I also in that address made a call for the IFP to do the seemingly impossible and enter the elections, even at this midnight hour.

That night in my study, I was played out and, O faithless Michael, really wondered if anything had been accomplished. Yet I sought to remind myself that the Lord was still sovereign and in charge. The conviction would have been mightily reinforced had I known what was going on in Cape Town with Mandela, Okumu, and Colin Coleman, head of the Consultation Business Movement (CBM) which had already made a significant contribution to the peace process; in Pretoria with President de Klerk and Danie Schutte; and in Ulundi with Chief Minister Buthelezi and his Central Committee.

But a strange thing happened at about 8.45 or 9.00 p.m. that night in my study. All of a sudden my deep oppression lifted and in my spirit I heard the words: 'The stronghold has been broken and has come down.' And of course my mind immediately turned to the apostle's famous words in 2 Corinthians 10.3–6 which speak of spiritual weapons, not part of any worldly war, destroying strongholds (areas of thought not in line with the Lord's) and 'taking every thought captive to Christ'.

Beginnings of breakthrough

In reality, as I later discovered, it was between 8.30 and 9.00 p.m. that evening that Mandela was giving a green light to proceeding to look at Okumu's document; likewise de Klerk and Schutte in Pretoria, and Buthelezi and his IFP Central Committee in Ulundi. As I saw it, the thoughts of the main players were becoming 'captive' to the divine will for that moment.

All groups in the three places agreed to meet the next day in the cabinet room in the Union Buildings in Pretoria under the chairmanship of de Klerk.

It was an intense day of debating details, dotting i's, and crossing t's. It spilled over to the morning of Tuesday 19 April.

The heart of the deal was that the very tricky matters of South Africa's final constitution – whether the nation would be a unitary, regional (confederal), or federal state, plus an appropriate recognition of the role and power of the Zulu king, especially his authority over the Zulu tribal trust lands – would be for the moment set aside until after the election, should the IFP come in, but after the election there would be a process of further international mediation, this time hopefully succeeding.

Buthelezi and the IFP agreed, on these conditions, to enter the election.

It was in fact on this issue that the first mediation efforts of Kissinger and Carrington had collapsed. Buthelezi later wrote of those first mediating efforts: 'When it became clear that Dr Kissinger and his team intended to redraft the Constitution as a [federal] form of state, backing the recognition of the Zulu Monarch and Kingdom, the ANC and NP [National Party] sent them packing.'[3]

All this would require recalling Parliament a day before the election, a happening without precedent. But it happened!

Eighty million ballot papers would need to be adjusted. Five hundred new polling stations and crews to man them would be needed in Natal alone – all of which happened.

At about 2.00 p.m. on Tuesday 19 April, de Klerk, Mandela and Buthelezi came on radio to announce they had found a way through for the elections to proceed on the planned dates of 26–27 April.

South Africa, its newsrooms, and indeed the world, went quiet. There was in the air a sense that a miracle had happened.

Celebrations at AE – Lois Stephenson leads staff in rejoicing, 19 April 1994

I wept.

Then at AE all our staff gathered and linked hands in a huge circle and poured out our hearts in praise and thanksgiving to our great God. Likewise, all believers across South Africa.

Editorial after editorial in South African newspapers used the word 'miracle'. So did *Time* magazine, the *Financial Times*, the *Wall Street Journal*, Natal's *Sunday Tribune*, *The Star* in Johannesburg, the *Natal Witness* in Pietermaritzburg, and so on. In the House of Commons, one member said: 'History has thrown up an authentic miracle.' The BBC announced: 'The Jesus Peace Rally tipped the scales.' President Kaunda of Zambia said: 'I would say without hesitation, it is a miracle.'

In the next few days Okumu did an amazing 136 radio and television interviews. Durban businessman Terry Rosenberg, who had worked miracles himself helping the 80 million adjusted ballot pages get printed and dispersed, said: 'I feel Washington Okumu's whole life and background had in some ways been a preparation for that particular week and for such a time as this.'[4]

Writing a tribute for Washington Okumu's family after the Professor's death in November 2016, Buthelezi stated:

> He played a significant role in assisting South Africa's transition to democracy . . . I will remember Professor Okumu for as long as I live, and I pray that history will remember him longer. He deserves a place not only in our hearts but in the collective memory of politics and Christianity.[5]

I have often felt that Okumu has not been adequately honoured in South Africa by most of our contemporary politicians and historical commentators. I don't deny that many of our own politicians were amazing. But enormous credit is owed to Washington Okumu.

Peter Kerton-Johnson and Michael thanking Washington Okumu

Election day at last

On 27 April, the main election day, a couple of big black limousines swept into our driveway at home. It was Danie Schutte, Minister of Home Affairs and in charge of the election, plus his bodyguards and entourage.

'Michael,' he said to me, 'I just felt I had to come to say on this historic day when we are having a peaceful election that this miracle for me began the night you called me late to come to your home and meet Washington Okumu. We political leaders on all sides had done everything political power, influence and money could achieve. And it all came to naught. Then God stepped in and honoured this little unlikely initiative from all of you, and especially Washington Okumu. From then, dialogue and communication could begin to flow from all the key players to one another. And the way through began to emerge.'

Early that morning Carol and I and our domestic helper Ntombi Ndlovu had gone to our community hall to vote peacefully like millions of other South Africans. I then came home and went back to bed where my doctor had consigned me because of chronic exhaustion. My minister, Ian Cowley, brought me communion in bed. But I didn't stay there long!

Election dramas

The 8.00 p.m. news showed Chief Buthelezi distressed that there were extensive breakdowns at many rural locations in KwaZulu-Natal; some places even had no polling stations, while in others ballot papers did not arrive, or else IFP stickers were not affixed to the ballot paper. Things were going so seriously wrong that the IFP might have to pull out of the election after all, even at this hour. The party was about to have a Central Committee meeting that very night to decide.

I was aghast. I phoned Danie Schutte at once and found him so dismayed that he felt he needed to fly out to Ulundi at dead of night. We decided to go together, along with advocate Dikgang Moseneke, Vice-Chair of the IEC (Independent Electoral Committee), and a very prominent figure in South Africa's landscape, who was also distraught.

When Carol heard I was going she said, 'You're not just sick; you're also insane.' But, being the amazing Carol that she is, she also said, 'Well, go. I'll call key intercessors to pray for you all.'

I met Danie and two associates in a darkened and deserted Pieter-maritzburg airport where a small military jet, flown down from Pretoria's

Election drama: Moseneke, Michael and Danie
Schutte and officials flying off in the dead of night

Waterkloof Airforce Base, landed with engines screaming. In it also was the advocate Moseneke.

Moments later we were in the air and then landing at Ulundi, where we joined an exhausted Buthelezi and some 12 other IFP leaders in a small conference room.

As I have written elsewhere:

> An extraordinary list of election irregularities, mishaps and organisational disasters was presented. It seemed to go on *ad infinitum*. There were situations where people turned up to find no polling station, or else there was a polling station but some of the equipment was missing, like the ultraviolet lamps or the invisible ink, or even the ballot boxes themselves. In a couple of cases the electoral officials themselves were missing!
>
> Sometimes people went through the electoral procedure, having their hands stamped with invisible ink, only thereafter to find there were no ballot papers at the end of the line, or that they could not vote for some other reason. One could well imagine the fury of such people, now marked as having voted, even though they had not voted! Nor would they be able to vote, for the fatal liquid stamp was upon them.
>
> Then there were cases where polling stations could only handle 3,000 people in the day but more than 10,000 turned up. Some then had to leave, often furious, having waited a whole day without voting.[6]

Schutte and Moseneke excelled themselves when faced with these desperate challenges. Planes were ordered to lift off from Pretoria with 60 extra personnel, ballot boxes, ballot papers, ink and ultraviolet lamps, all ready to be on the ground and on site in Natal by dawn.

In my remarks in those post-midnight hours with Buthelezi and his leaders, I urged realism in this first-ever democratic election for our country. Albeit convulsed, this was an undertaking which we dared not allow to fail, or else what? Whatever was needed to ensure success could be made to happen, maybe even securing an extra day for the electoral process. Buthelezi said an extra day would surely help.

Moseneke then said that he and the IEC would do whatever was necessary to pull it all off. I pleaded with the IFP leadership to accept the pledge from Schutte and Moseneke to set things right in the next few hours.

Some concord was reached. And in fact, in the event, an extra day was given.

I was touched to be asked by Chief Buthelezi to close off in prayer, reminding them all as I did so of 1 John 3.20, which says: 'God is greater ...'

We left Ulundi on a wing and a prayer at 2.00 a.m., and I collapsed into bed with amazing calm sometime after 4.00 a.m.

One final hitch

Was the drama all over?

Not quite.

We found that the Independent Electoral Commission (IEC) had been in crisis mode late the previous evening over multitudes of other crises and irregularities elsewhere in the country. In the Cape one person phoned a friend of mine and said, 'What do I do? I've just had 100,000 blank ballot papers thrown over my fence into my backyard!'

Transport to take ballot papers to polling stations also failed in many places, until the IEC had to use taxis to take bundles of ballot papers to this station or that. Also many more people were turning up to vote in some places than there were ballot papers. In one Orange Free State town an extra 200,000 people turned out to vote. No wonder ballot papers ran out.

My very dear entrepreneurial friend Terry Rosenberg was again contacted by frantic IEC commissioners at 6.00 p.m. on 27 April. Could he help by getting six million new ballot papers printed before dawn? Also, the IEC had run out of invisible ink. And of ultraviolet lamps – very necessary as Terry explained: 'Of course the forms are no use unless you have the ink. And the ink is no use without the ultraviolet lamps because you can't then check up if someone has voted.'[7]

First Terry mobilized a couple of local Durban printers at the dead of night. The first of six million extra ballot papers began rolling off the presses, getting tied up into thousands of bundles to be flown by helicopters and small planes from the South African Air Force to different venues around the country.

Then ink. Terry and some friends contacted a dining-out Barlows director. Could Barlows at dead of night come up with 4,000 one-litre containers for ink? And could they commandeer a plane to get them where needed? The Barlows director, rising to the occasion, answered both questions affirmatively.

But ultraviolet lamps? Terry put this matter to his operations team in Durban of about 60 volunteers. Amazingly a Jamaican lady said she recalled that Lesotho had used such lamps in its recent election. The appropriate government minister in Lesotho was then contacted in the small hours and connected them to Lesotho's electoral officer, whom they also woke up. He blearily agreed to supply the needed lamps. But the Maseru airport did not open until 7.00 a.m.

'No alternative,' said Terry. 'Our planes must fly and be hovering over the airport at 6.45 a.m. Then they can drop down at 7.00 a.m. and collect the hundreds of lamps.'[8]

And thus it was. The air force planes picked up 1,500 ultraviolet lamps before racing back to Durban where other aircraft picked them up to fly them to places throughout Natal.

'So now,' said Terry, 'we had forms going out in one set of planes, bottles coming in on another, and lamps being transported to different locations in yet another.'[9]

Terry told me later that scores of dedicated South Africans of all races, occupations and backgrounds laboured through that night. In Johannesburg, some church leaders worked on similar exploits through those days.

As people in KwaZulu-Natal and other places, all unaware of the night dramas, woke up to a new day, the first democratic elections of South Africa were back on track.

The final miracle

In the end the country voted during three of the most peaceful and crime-free days in the history of South Africa. A true miracle in and of itself. In our previously convulsed Pietermaritzburg area, police reported that over

Election day: Debbie, Martin and Carol Cassidy
queue to vote with domestic helper Ntombi Ndlovu

those three days there was not one single crime. Liberation and democracy had carried and won the day.

Mandela's ANC won, of course. President de Klerk's National Party lost. But conceding defeat, de Klerk memorably said: 'God has been very good to us.'

Buthelezi's IFP won Natal. A good outcome for that moment to stabilize the province.

General Constand Viljoen's Freedom Front had participated. It won nine seats in Parliament, one for General Viljoen himself, with 424,555 votes. And the FF is still there to this day with positive input to Parliament. Imagine if those 424,555 had decided to overthrow the electoral process by force.

It doesn't bear thinking about.

Queueing up to vote: jubilant voters

Danie Schutte visits Michael on election day

31

Genocide

> *We cannot trample upon the humanity of*
> *others without devaluing our own.*[1]
> *(Chinua Achebe)*

Just as South Africa in April 1994 was celebrating its liberation from catastrophe, Rwanda to our north plunged into its own abyss. Someone once said: 'All the devils that possessed South Africa, once exorcised, then fled to occupy Rwanda.'

Christians have been called to minister in areas of conflict down the centuries, and in the crucial years of 1994 and 1995, AE was called to engage in the conflict in Rwanda. For a long time we had had deep concerns about the country, and I made a point, in February 1994, of visiting to liaise with our team there. The Team Leader, Israel Havugimana, organized a gathering of church leaders which I addressed, drawing on our experience in South Africa. I urged a comprehensive ministry of reconciliation between political foes.

Israel Havugimana, a couple of weeks before the genocide
began, introducing Michael at church leaders' meeting

This is not the place to discuss what brought such extreme alienation between the Hutu and Tutsi. Suffice to say that it was rooted deeply in the histories, ancient and colonial, of these two people groups. As the situation deteriorated, it became more and more necessary for these political foes to be reconciled to one another.

The American ambassador, David Rawson, set up a meeting in his home for the heads of some 14 or 15 political parties, and asked me, along with my colleague Malcolm Graham, to tell the story of our Kolobe Lodge dialogue weekends in South Africa, with the hopes that something similar could happen in Rwanda.

Tragically, there was no time for this. On 6 April 1994, the deaths of the presidents of Burundi and Rwanda in a plane crash, caused by a rocket attack, set the country at war. And some eight weeks later many of the leaders we had met at that breakfast were dead. Hutu militants went on the rampage, and between 850,000 and 1,000,000 people, mostly Tutsi, died in one of the century's most brutal genocides. General Paul Kagame, leader of the rebel forces, took over the government and became *de facto* head of the country.

Our colleague Israel, a Hutu himself, who had prophetically challenged the Hutu government over its cruel suppression of Tutsis, was among the first to be lined up with his family and shot. Later some of our AE Rwanda Board suffered the same fate. It was a time of enormous pain.

Deep levels of alienation

In July of 1995, we sought to minister in this desperate situation by holding a mission in Kigali, the capital of Rwanda.

In our opening rally with about 7,000 in the local stadium, Antoine Rutayisire, our courageous new local AE Team Leader, asked people to stand if they had returned from exile. Hundreds stood, mostly Tutsi. Some had on their consciences that they had been forced at gunpoint to kill a husband, wife or children. How could such people be healed?

I chose to preach on how Jesus in Mark 4 calmed the storm on the Sea of Galilee, and how we needed his love, forgiveness, justice and power to calm the storm still raging in Rwanda. Several hundred responded to my appeal to take Christ into their hearts to help them forgive.

It may sound simplistic, but only forgiveness could even begin to bring healing to such a situation.

Among those who responded to the message was one man who was counselled by my colleague, Stephen Lungu, our Team Leader in Malawi at the time. The man said:

> All my relatives have been killed. I had been wounded myself and I survived by lying among dead bodies in the mass grave into which I had been thrown and also left for dead. Later I was able to move, but how can I forgive what those people did to me and to others?[2]

Stephen later prayed with him and he said at the end of the time: 'This man's face was shining with the love and forgiveness of God.'

A woman came forward for prayer after a hospital meeting led by David Peters from AE South Africa. She was crippled. But after giving her life to Christ and being prayed for, she was astonishingly healed and able to walk out of the hospital.

We met one man who, after killing a girl in Gisenyi in the south, had gone to ask the family for forgiveness. They then went to the authorities together and the mother said to the authorities that they should not put this fellow in prison or punish him because they had forgiven him. The authorities in Gisenyi then said: 'Well, if you have forgiven him, and God has forgiven him, then we forgive him as well!'[3]

One of our team was in a church where 10,000 people had been herded into the church compound and killed. After ministering in situations such as these, without precedent for them, the members of our team needed more than ever to come together, report back and listen to one another. We met every day, first thing in the morning.

Tears and a great weeping

I'll never forget one such team meeting. I called it the Team Meeting of Tears and a Great Weeping.

Ernie Smith, our great Pan African Missions Director, began to share how he had preached the night before and then called people for prayer. One woman came forward who had lost the use of her arm. Her fingers were clamped tightly shut with the hand unable to open. Her elbow was also jammed in a grotesque angle. When Ernie prayed for her, the fingers suddenly snapped open and the elbow came loose and there was huge rejoicing all round.

Ernie then told of two people who had come with similar prayer-needs. The first was a lady who had literally lost all her relatives and who was in great need of comfort and grace from the Lord. She especially wanted to be able to forgive so that she could fully live for Jesus.

A second woman had seen her husband and child butchered before her eyes and she herself had been beaten up and dumped in the bush. She said: 'I just want the power of Jesus so that I can go out and witness to him and tell others everywhere of the love of God.' This had profoundly moved Ernie, who said how slow we often are in our normal comfortable circumstances to witness to the love of God. But here were women who had experienced great trauma yet were eager for fresh power to testify to the love of God. That night, said Ernie, he cried before the Lord as he had never cried before, and was struggling to hold his emotions in check as he recounted what had happened.

My colleague, Leonard Mbilinyi, our Team Leader in Tanzania, was overcome as he began to tell of a soldier who had come forward in his meeting the previous night. He had seen all of his relatives killed and had been feeling dreadful bitterness. On top of that, he was experiencing hatred for his wife, something he longed to overcome and for which he needed prayer. The problem was that he, the soldier, was a Tutsi married to a Hutu woman, and some Hutu extremists had seized her and the children and then forced her to throw her own children into the river to be drowned. The hatred and bitterness he felt towards his wife was almost uncontrollable. He was longing for the power from the Lord to forgive her and live with her peacefully, and it was this for which he asked Leonard to pray.

As Leonard broke down, so too did Nathan Kamusliane of our Uganda team. So too did Singaporean AE team member Chye Ann. At this point a spirit of brokenness and weeping swept over the whole gathering, the tears of Jesus surely. Never in our ministry, before or since, have I seen anything comparable. One colleague said, 'The Lord has said to me: "Go and listen to them and weep with them!"'

The stories proliferated. Over lunch one day, one Tutsi returnee from Uganda who had spent 35 years in exile told me his neighbour had lost her whole family. She had been raped, but had then resolved to stay with the rapist and become his wife. He repented and agreed to become a responsible husband. So they were sticking to each other and looking to the Lord for help to become a true Christian couple.

Ntarama

While we were in Kigali, some of us went to the site of Ntarama, where some of the worst and most extensive killings took place. It was a horrific sight, with evidence of brutal torture and crude means of killing. I went there with Archbishop Desmond Tutu, who was participating in the

Ntarama massacre site, Rwanda. Michael prays for a broken Desmond Tutu

mission with us as an official guest of the government and whose celebrity meant that the press was ever with us. As we approached the church with its rotting remains, Desmond broke down and we thought he might faint. We rushed to hold him, and could only pray for him and for ourselves to cope with this overwhelming experience.

Following this visit, we were given some insight into the complexity of guilt in situations of genocide. This is what we were ministering to. We were told by a woman who was a field officer for the United Nations Commission for Human Rights that

> the killings were all done by ordinary people – neighbour against neighbour – with people being forced to kill one another and in many cases family members: husband killing wife, parents killing children and so on. Obviously in a situation like this deep trauma is also experienced by women who survive, because many of them were raped and violated, and may be having to cope with the children now being born.

In other words, without one-to-one ministry in helping people cope with the trauma and rebuilding of relationships at the lowest level where people are on a day-to-day basis, it is impossible to solve the problem. There is no shortcut. The question is 'How do we do it?' How can we help? Most unfortunately, because of the compromise of the Church and the involvement of many church leaders, especially in the institutional and mainline churches, who were lackeys of the previous regime and were involved directly in the genocide, it is said, and understandably so, that the people and the authorities now have no regard for the Church. This is of course a grave concern for us involved in the ministry of the Gospel. Unless the

Lord gives us favour and brings a deep spirit of repentance and revival to His people, and to this land, it would be almost impossible for us to contribute in any relevant, meaningful or effective ways.[4]

I hoped that the AE mission contributed to restoring the image of the Church. We were Christians from outside, and were linking with many in the local church whose hearts were in the right place. In this we were greatly helped by the new leader of our AE team, Antoine Rutayisire.

Stadium rally

Sunday 30 July was set for a rally in the local stadium. Ten thousand people were there, including the *de facto* leader Paul Kagame and his wife Janet – who herself had already been to the mission and been prayed for as well. Desmond Tutu kicked off and gave a brilliant talk on Daniel chapter 3 and the story of the young Hebrew men Shadrach, Meshach and Abednego, thrown by the Babylonian king into a fiery furnace. Desmond dramatized this account with genius. He acted out King Nebuchadnezzar counting one, two, three figures miraculously walking unharmed in the flames, then blinking his eyes as he saw a fourth, and then starting to count again in unbelief: one, two, three – surely not, but yes, my goodness – there are four! The Son of God was there. The Lord of heaven and earth had come to his children in their fiery ordeal and was with them. Desmond applied this to believers in Rwanda and it was powerful indeed.

I had been burdened about my message and had prepared it early that

Stadium rally: Michael and Desmond Tutu with political and church leaders, Kigali, July 1995

morning for two hours on my knees beside my bed. What came to me was the connection between the suffering of the Rwandan people and Christ's suffering and death on the cross. How wonderful that after Christ's death, there came his resurrection and the promise of forgiveness. No sin was too great for God to forgive. He bore every sin of humankind on the cross. And his gift of the Holy Spirit helps us to forgive others and to live full lives in obedience to him.

After my message Paul Kagame came to the platform, and I felt an impulse to ask if I could pray for him. He graciously agreed. I laid my hands on him and prayed publicly for him with a deep desire in my heart that the Lord should use and guide this brother in the leading of the nation.

Later, when our time in Rwanda was almost over, I was brought back to that moment with Kagame by one of my Rwandan colleagues, Paul Bahati.

He turned to me suddenly and said: 'You know what I think is the most historic thing that happened during this mission? It was in the closing rally when you prayed for Kagame and laid your hands on his head. Nothing like that has ever happened before in our country. The people say this was history and this was God coming to our country in a very special way.'

I guess on my part it was a case of the Lord's fools rushing in where angels fear to tread.

The prison

Desmond and I were particularly concerned to visit the prison in Kigali, and I had sought permission from the Minister of Justice. We were given the go-ahead.

I met Desmond at his hotel and once again we were off in a great cavalcade with the press thronging round the place, although they were not allowed into the prison.

Our first port of call was the women's section. They all began singing, shouting and cheering, especially when they saw Desmond, but of course we were all symbols of hope. We could scarcely move for the throng of forlorn young women. I could only reach out my hands and pray for them or for their child – and was glad of my fractured French.

Gershon Mwiti, our Kenya Team Leader, later told me he had met a woman who had heard of our experience in the women's prison and had broken down in tears and shared how 'those women in prison were the very people who killed some of our husbands and engineered the killing of other women's husbands'. Yet what we saw were people who were longing for rescue and hope in spite of their huge guilt or otherwise.

Michael amid prison throng, Kigali Prison, June 1995

We were then led to the men's section where the situation was even more horrifying. None of us in all of our days had seen such human congestion. As we came into each section and squeezed our way through the sardine-like crush of humanity, the men cheered, some even waving Bibles at us, others reaching out to touch us. If only we could have seen what lay behind each of the faces before us.

One man in one dark corridor was obviously blind, his empty marble-like eyes rolling upwards and his hand held out to me. He had a great semi-toothless grin, and I could only think of blind Bartimaeus and his healing encounter with Jesus.

At one point, when there was dancing going on, I rather impetuously seized a prison cap off one of the prisoners, put it on my head and began to dance as well, amid a tremendous cheer from those all around. But apart from that frivolity, one could only call out every two or three steps, 'We are praying for you . . . Jesus loves you . . . We want to see *amahoro* [peace] in Rwanda.'

The chapel

We were finally led through the throng of humanity to what they called 'the chapel'. In this, the largest room in the place, with a huge wall on one side and another smaller wall with wire netting going up to the roof on the other, Desmond was invited to address the group. He then called on me to say a prayer. I raised it to the Lord with, I must admit, much anguish of spirit.

Just as we were about to move out, a young man stepped forward and very boldly read a petition from the prisoners saying their situation was unacceptable and they were appealing to Desmond and to the international community for assistance in their plight. I think this initiative caught the prison authorities off guard, but once his public reading of the document had begun they were put in an awkward position of not knowing whether to stop it, which would have looked repressive, or allowing it to proceed, which could have very negative publicity consequences for them. Anyway, the petition was read in full and handed to Desmond.

Once outside the main prison building we were called for a press interview with masses of enormous cameras staring into our faces. We each sought to do our best and Desmond ended up making a quiet but powerful plea that this situation with its unacceptable overcrowding should be remedied.

Just before we left I saw the Minister of Justice and asked him whether he would make it possible for a few of us to come back and preach in the prison the next day. He answered in the affirmative. My heart leapt and I prayed something would come of it.

When I finally got back to our house I felt utterly overwhelmed and found the only response was to get into a very hot bath and wash myself frantically for about half an hour. I just felt a desperate need to get clean, as if the external washing could somehow reach into one's soul to cleanse one within from that environment of suffering, murder, crime, and injustice for the innocent, as well as guilt for the guilty and for man's whole inhumanity to man. Then, of course, it is hard to face one's human inadequacy in terms of any really appropriate response.

When I saw Antoine I told him, 'You won't have seen anything like what we saw in prison.'

Antoine then brought me down to size, saying quietly: 'Yes, I have seen something worse. Those are living bodies squashed in there in that prison. But I have seen dead bodies squashed and piled up, many of them friends, and people I know.'

I just hung my head in embarrassment.

Preaching in prison

We were delighted that the long-coveted opportunity to go back to the prison and preach was indeed given to us. Antoine had also secured a small van which was piled about four feet high with New Testament portions, tracts, and copies of the Psalms.

After some initial hassles with prison officials blocking us ('Where's your piece of paper?'), the doors swung open (remember Revelation 3.8), and we were in. Again we started in the women's prison.

I found a tiny space in the centre of one crammed corridor and, with Paul Bahati of our Rwandan team beside me, I began to share why we were there. It brought cheering, waving and even smiles to faces which one would have thought had long since lost the capacity to smile or laugh.

Calvary

I shared a little of God's word with the women, letting them know of the Lord's Calvary love and our concern for them, and that even Jesus knew what it was to be a prisoner. He had finally faced capital punishment and died on the cross to cover all our sins.

I then called on Steve Lungu to share his testimony, which he did as usual with great power, telling about his own background, semi-orphaned, living a life of despair and hopelessness, and finally getting into the world of robbery and violence until the Lord found him. It was riveting. When David Peters asked the women if those who would like to commit their lives to Jesus would raise their hands, it looked as if 100 per cent of the hands in the place went up.

There was such a longing that somehow the Lord might come and reach into their hell-hole and bring hope.

When David finished praying out loud for those wanting to give their lives to Christ, we gave them a few further words of encouragement and then began to hand out the New Testament portions. There was pandemonium as people tried frantically to lay hands on the material. We tried to assure them that there was enough available, and that if they did not get a piece of literature they could share one. We also suggested that at night in the cells they should pray and read God's word together, and worship. Although such exhortations seemed frail and feeble, there are good Old and New Testament evidences that God is the God of the prison cell, whether for Daniel in the furnace or the lions' den (Daniel chapters 3 and 6), or Paul and Silas in prison (Acts 16.23–24). And, of course, for multitudes of the condemned ever since.

Our hearts broke, leaving these stricken young women, but we were comforted in tiny measure that, amid all the tears and anguish, we had left behind a flood of written Scriptures which could surely bring some blessing and hope.

Then we moved into the men's prison and its main square, again jam-packed. I held up my Bible, waved, and called out *Amahoro à Rwanda* (Peace to Rwanda). This elicited a cheer and sustained clapping.

Picture the scene as my diary speaks:

> Again I had never seen such a press of humanity (even worse than last time) in what was the main quadrangle. I discovered that over in one place they had created a little space with a bench and a table. The thing to do seemed to be to squeeze through to that point and then stand on the table.[5]

Table-top preaching

My journal continues with its description of my unusual 'pulpit':

> Finally I was on the table with Paul Bahati who was translating for me. Picture then the rickety table in burning sunlight, the white preacher and black preacher; and directly in front of us an anguished sea of humanity giving way towards prison cells with one-square-metre windows from which eight to ten people might be peering out and straining to see or hear.
>
> Rigged up against the side of one wall appeared to be something like a few bunks with some cloth hung across them rather than bricks and mortar. So how would they cope if the weather got unpleasant? One would never know. Then on each of those precariously suspended bunks were several people peering out towards us. To my left was a sunken sector, perhaps two or three feet below the level on which our table was perched. It was maybe ten metres in width and 30 in length, but jammed with 300 or 400 people. There again were the familiar metre-square windows, obviously looking out from both sunken and elevated cells with once again eight or so faces peering from the dark rectangular cavity. Screwing up one's eyes to look past and beyond them, one saw yet more faces further back in the dark interior. Was this Dante's hellish *Inferno*? To our right was one solid black crush of humanity. Some had even clambered up onto dilapidated little rooftops covering other prison cells.
>
> As far as my eye could see down a dozen little side alleys, there must have been a thousand people there.[6]

How could any legal system cope with this catastrophe? In fact I recall a Rwandan government official saying to me: 'Our prisons were built for normal day-to-day civilian times when one has a handful of criminals locked up. They were not built to cope with the aftermath of genocide with nearly a million murders and maybe two million other people implicated.'

With an inadequate public address system and now a great hush, I preached for five or six minutes on the prisoner Barabbas and how he had been set free from his prison cell because Jesus died for his sins on Calvary's tree (see Luke 23.18–25). This was greeted with a mighty roar of approval and hope.

Sea of hands

After Steve and David added their contributions, there was once again an absolute sea of hands in response to the evangelistic call. It was not the automatic reflex of people wanting to please, although one never knows fully in these situations. But whatever allowances one would make for superficiality, or other extenuating factors, I for one did not diminish for one second what I believed God was doing in that prison in those mysterious moments.

Commitment

David led the men in a prayer of commitment which, after being translated sentence by sentence into Rwandese, they all echoed out loud, calling on the Lord. While David was praying I opened my eyes and looked around. I saw one prisoner on a roof, peering down towards me. He had his fingers up in a 'V for victory' sign. When I on impulse caught his eye and returned the sign, his face exploded with delight. He jabbed his neighbour and was obviously saying, 'Look, he saw me.' It was a funny kind of feeling. In fact again and again each of us sought with individuals to register them with meaningful and deep eye contact, rather than staring at the floor, or up into the heavens. As we looked each one in the eye, we tried to give the sense of the Zulu greeting '*Sawubona*', meaning 'I see you; you have registered on me as a human being; I know you are there. We have connected.'

I asked our Kenya Team Leader, Gershon Mwiti, who was once in the Kenya prison services, to close in prayer and to share some simple principles of discipleship, which he very meaningfully did.

Then a strong sense came to me from the Spirit that we needed to present a picture to convey the importance not just of vertical reconciliation with God, but also of horizontal reconciliation and forgiveness with one another. With Gershon and Antoine on the table preaching and translating respectively, Steve Lungu was standing with me while Paul Bahati was on the bench alongside the table. I rather unceremoniously seized David and asked him to stand between Steve and myself as I equally unceremoniously pulled Singaporean Soh Chye Ann to stand up on the bench next to Paul Bahati.

So here we all were, standing in a line on the bench with all eyes riveted upon us, a black Malawian, a brown South African Indian, an old whitey colonialist, a black Rwandese and a yellow Singaporean! We then all put our arms round one another to demonstrate our fraternal bonding in Christ. I then cried out to one and all (some 10,000 people in that prison with maybe 3,000 or 4,000 able to hear us) that here in Steve was a black man who had hated and wanted to kill whites, but now in Christ he had the capacity to forgive and love me as a representative white. Then there was David who likewise as an Indian had hated white people and had been caught up once in violent Indian politics. I added that in South Africa many blacks hated Indians even more than they hated white people. 'But here we are before you all, as brothers in Christ, and each of us is bonded here to a black Rwandese in Paul Bahati, and finally to the yellow man from the Far East. This is what the gospel is all about. So too here in Rwanda it requires the power of Jesus for Hutu to bond to Tutsi, and Tutsi to Hutu, and both of them to the Twa, and the Twa to both of them.'

The place was riveted. A mighty gospel truth of reconciliation in Christ came vividly, we believed, to them.

Our amazing Rwandan Team Leader Antoine, who had been through some of the worst fires of genocide, then led us in song. This exploded in deafening praises to Jesus Christ and up into the heavens unlike anything I had ever heard.

Before wrapping up I stood on the table again and conveyed that we were deeply concerned for them and what would come next. I said we had indicated to the Vice-President and Prime Minister that the overcrowded situation in the prisons was unacceptable.

Antoine, a true hero in Africa if ever there was one, then closed in prayer, with a sacred hush over the place that seemed to have heaven and earth and the whole wide universe holding their breath.

Stories to bring hope

Moving from the prison almost directly into a VIP dinner organized by Antoine and the AE team was like moving on to another planet.

But after our testimony and preaching it was amazing to see scores of people, cabinet ministers, parliamentarians, ambassadors, senior citizens, and numbers of VIPs all filling out cards indicating their spiritual response to Christ and desire for follow-up material.

At another level that day, Steve Lungu met two UN soldiers who had been at a loose end and had decided to come to our prayer rally. Both were terribly lost in their personal lives. Indefatigable Steve led them both into commitment to Christ.

Of course, in a place like Rwanda, and in that particular time, there were many extraordinary stories of the Lord's mysterious intervention.

One Anglican bishop I met, Alexis Bilindabagabo, told me of 7 April 1994, the day when the killings began. He had retreated with some 300 other people into a church hall, where they simply gave themselves to prayer. No one tried to bring in weapons for self-defence; they just saw prayer as their armour.

Then they saw hundreds of militia coming towards them with machetes, grenades and guns, but a couple of hundred metres from the church hall they all suddenly stopped. Alexis then walked out across the open space to the attackers and met three of them, who told him that everyone in the hall was going to be attacked. Alexis replied that even as Elijah saw the armies and angels of the living God, so they in that hall would be protected: 'If the angels allow you to come and attack us, you will be able to; otherwise you will not be able.'

The attackers then advanced to within 100 metres of the hall, but at that point suddenly and inexplicably scattered. Other waves of attackers came towards them, and each time at the very same spot, about 100 metres from the hall, they all scattered and dispersed.

'It was at the same spot each time,' said Alexis. 'I believe we experienced the miracle of angelic protection.'

Overcrowding taken seriously?

We had been made very warmly welcome by the new Rwandan government, even being invited to meet with the Transitional National Assembly together with the Embassy Corps and the wider leadership of Kigali. In one of our last meetings with the three main leaders, Desmond Tutu again made the point that the overcrowding in the prison was quite unacceptable. He was clear on the importance of justice, but that it should be tempered with mercy.

Obviously 200,000 or more people could not be put on trial, but distinguishing between the different levels of crimes was almost as difficult. Perhaps some kind of international tribunal could help.

We later heard from the Red Cross that if all the accused in Rwanda were processed by English law it would take 40 years, and by US law, 140 to 200 years. Imagine several hundred thousand O. J. Simpsons!

Desmond and I sought to interact with the struggles of these Rwandan brethren, and make a number of suggestions. We ended with a good word of prayer for them.

This was not the last word on the subject of overcrowding. We mentioned it to many others in positions of influence, not least the German Ambassador, as I recall.

Subsequently, upon our return to South Africa, we saw a newspaper article reporting that prisoners were being moved from overcrowded prisons to warehouses. So someone somewhere had registered something. We had to accept that even a little change was better than nothing.

Tears at last

On the flight home I reflected in perplexity on my own dominant emotion throughout our time in Rwanda. Desmond had wept. Our team had wept. People counselled had wept. Prisoners had wept. Pastors had wept.

Everyone had wept. But I had not – which is unlike me. I had just gone ice-cold and frozen inside by the horrific enormity of it all.

Until I got into my home church the following Sunday back in Hilton, South Africa. The minister said: 'Michael is just back from Rwanda. I'm sure if you ask him some questions over tea, he'll tell you a bit about Rwanda.'

That's when I wept. And wept.

I wept for Rwanda. Oh yes!

But I also wept for my home church.

32

Project Ukuthula

We politicians can't fix this thing.[1]
(Nelson Mandela)

Back in South Africa, despite our miracle 1994 elections, all was not resolved, especially in KwaZulu-Natal. Provincial elections were set for the middle of 1996, but the situation in Natal was so volatile that its participation was in doubt. If the elections were to go ahead, and peaceably, some more miracles were needed!

Buthelezi's Inkatha Freedom Party was nursing a grievance that promises made before the 1994 elections had not been honoured. Only recently, in 2017, I sat down with Buthelezi at a private lunch and he told me that Mandela's failure to engage his government in international mediation was 'in my view the one blemish on Mandela's otherwise stellar career'.

On 19 April 1994, a week before the elections, Buthelezi, Mandela and de Klerk, with Washington Okumu as witness, had pledged themselves to the principle of international mediation. I have in my possession the text of that document. Clause 4 states that 'Any outstanding issues in respect of the King and the 1993 Interim Constitution as amended will be addressed by way of international mediation which will commence immediately after the said elections.'[2]

With pressures from the ANC on Mandela, and the IFP's increasing disillusion, the violence once again had mounted. As early as February 1996, with the provincial elections some six months away, Natal's situation was said to be 'calamitous'.

It was at this point that we were drawn in, and African Enterprise became part of something remarkable in KwaZulu-Natal – a movement for peace.

KWACLA

In the first place, we decided to call a KwaZulu-Natal Christian Leadership Assembly (KWACLA) which was coordinated by AE's Singaporean team member Soh Chye Ann – an organizational eager-beaver if ever there was one. As he said, 'Things usually start to go wrong at the leadership level.'[3]

Hence our resolve to gather 600 to 1,000 Christian leaders from the churches, businesses, the professions and the government. As it was reported in the *Natal Witness*: 'Fears that the ongoing violence in KwaZulu-Natal could erupt into full-scale civil war or even genocide have led to a major gathering of Christian leaders being called in Pietermaritzburg.'[4]

In the event, some 600 leaders came and agonized together over our province for three powerful days.

There was at least one light moment.

As I got to the lectern to deliver the opening address, one of our media team, Alex Theophilus, came to adjust the microphone. Poker-faced, he passed me a piece of paper with a message on it. I thought it would say something like: 'The Lord guide you, Michael, and mightily anoint you with the Holy Spirit.'

But, no! It was the score in the World Cup cricket match between South Africa and the West Indies! And we were doing well.

So tickled was I that it almost put me off my stroke – I had to tell the assembly that cricket came a close second to the things of the kingdom of God. I think South Africa lost in spite of the prayerful support of 600 Natal Christian leaders!

Despite our KWACLA endeavours, the provincial elections in KwaZulu-Natal continued to be under threat. The local ANC leaders cited the lack of free political activity and rampant violence as reasons for postponing Natal's participation. Mandela was against this, but ANC Natal leader Jacob Zuma said: 'No one is going to force the ANC to go into this election when we know it's not free and fair. It's like walking into a group of armed men bare-handed.'[5]

Things came to a head when the royal household of Zulu King Goodwill Zwelithini was attacked on 26 April and six princesses, plus one of his wives, Queen Buhle Zulu, were seriously injured. A few days later another princess, Nonhlanhla Zulu, was hacked to death, and her funeral almost turned into a violent free-for-all. My colleague, Jamie Morrison, and I went to see Queen Buhle in hospital and pray with her. A real Christian, and indeed an intercessor, she was much touched by this visit. I believe she was already in this polygamous relationship with the King when she came to Christ.

In the attack mentioned, some IFP supporters had supposedly come to believe that the King had 'swopped political allegiances' and become 'a firm ANC supporter'.[6]

Needless to say, Mandela was worried because he thought it would be very embarrassing for South Africa if its first provincial elections after the famous 1994 general election were to turn into a disaster. The world would ask: 'Is this really a democracy after all?'

In the middle of all this, Anglican Bishop Matthew Makhaye of Ladysmith found himself at a gathering where Mandela was present. Did Mandela feel that some Natal church leaders could help in KwaZulu-Natal?

The President leapt at the notion, and said: 'Yes, and draw in African Enterprise.'

Makhaye phoned me about this, as well as Bishop Mmutlanyane Mogoba, Presiding Bishop of the Methodist Church and based in Durban. 'And Mandela wants to meet the three of us at his presidential home in Durban in a few days' time.'

This put me in a dilemma because I was due in a matter of days to go to Australia on a five-week ministry tour. All the meetings and speaking engagements were set up. Yet here was a big problem in my own back yard and the President was asking us in AE to help.

My mentor, Dr Calvin Cook, and the Father of AE's work in South Africa, said: 'Nothing should take you away right now.'

Carol and I prayed about it and she felt strongly I should stay.

That was it. Mike Woodall, our AE Australia Director, and as able and nimble-footed a colleague and administrator as AE ever had, worked wonders to negotiate the way for my Singaporean colleague Soh Chye Ann to take my place. Thus was I able to stay.

Mandela meeting

Early on the morning of 2 May, we were ready for the trip to Durban. Carol sent me off saying, 'May the Lord give you today great wisdom and a Christian independent spirit so that you are not fooled by power.'[7]

But just as we were leaving, we learned that there had been a multiple-lorry pile-up with oil spills on the motorway to Durban, and that route would now be closed for hours. What now? We felt we couldn't miss our appointment with Mandela.

The ever-resourceful Jamie Morrison immediately phoned our local airport and said we wanted to hire a small aircraft plus a car at Durban airport. If the Lord doesn't take you through the deep waters, or the fiery flames, he can certainly fly you over them!

Within half an hour we were in the air, flying over the massive traffic jam at the scene of the accident. Minutes later we were in Durban, and then on the way to Madiba's provincial residence, which we reached at the stipulated time. Madiba, incidentally, is Mandela's clan name and is used to signify respect and affection.

As was Madiba's way, he received us with characteristic warmth and graciousness, and then guided Makhaye, Mogoba and myself into lunch. Jamie, poor guy, had to content himself with lunching with Jacob Zuma and a few other ANC heavyweights!

Madiba kicked off our two-hour luncheon with some fascinating reminiscences which made me wish I could have recorded them! Then, finally getting to the horrific KwaZulu-Natal election violence, he launched in: 'You know, we politicians can't fix this thing. That's why we need you people and the Church to come to our aid and see what you can do. It would be more than tragic if our first provincial elections post '94 should fail. And what would the world think?'

We listened intently, shared and exchanged ideas, and said we would seek to activate the whole Church of Christ in KwaZulu-Natal and everyone we could into the ministries of reconciliation. Though it was 2 May and there were only nine weeks to go, we all agreed it was worth pulling all the stops out with the Lord's help. The elections were set for 26 June. Just nine weeks to bring the death rate down from 20 a day to zero, so that peaceful and fair elections could be held.

After a few photographs, we headed to the airport and flew back to 'Maritzburg, marvelling at Mandela, and the spirit and humility of the man.

Meeting at Presidential House, Durban: Mmutlanyane Mogobo,
Matthew Makhaye, Nelson Mandela and Michael, 1996

The ministry of reconciliation

Makhaye, Mogoba and I agreed, along with our AE South Africa team, that we needed to try to activate all Christians in the province for the ministry of reconciliation. If everyone 'did their bit' something could change. In fact, if churches would really combine, the simple principles we put together for these ministries of reconciliation could be repeated anywhere.

We would call the venture 'Project Ukuthula' (Zulu for peace).

My role was to sit with political leaders to try to understand the intricacies of the province's conflicts. One such leader was Johan Marais, a Natal Nationalist Party MP, who had been at one of the Kolobe Lodge weekends. He stressed that we needed to try to get people to focus on something that would be bigger and better for everyone in the province, and do it positively without looking back at the negatives of the past. A simple message, but potentially very powerful if embraced.

On the same day I met Marais, I met with Archie Gumede, the former president of the United Democratic Front. This had been a cluster of groups opposed to the Nationalist government, a sort of ANC 'inside the country' while the ANC leaders were still in exile before de Klerk's 1990 unbanning of the liberation movements.

Archie, a courageous Christian man, said that Mandela, Zuma, and the ANC leadership who had either been in prison or in exile, needed to understand the grass-roots dynamics of those who had *not* been imprisoned or exiled. Archie said that if he and Jacob could get together, and have a meeting of minds, it could save a lot of lives.

He added that 'no war could be settled by lieutenants and infantry on their own without the generals'.[8] We needed to work with all three – the generals, the lieutenants and the infantry.

Two days later we were with a dejected Frank Mdlalose, the Premier of KwaZulu-Natal, who lamented how 'elusive' peace was. The political leaders couldn't 'contain their followers'. He couldn't see Buthelezi and Mandela getting together and was finding it very hard to connect to Jacob Zuma. We urged him to keep trying. In fact he succeeded three days later. It was a beginning.

On 7 May there was a Project Ukuthula meeting in the Anglican cathedral in 'Maritzburg. Bishops Nuttall and Fennell, and church and lay leaders were there. Everyone resolved to spread the reconciliation challenge.

At a press conference, we asked editors and journalists to change their rhetoric from hostility and enmity to reconciliation and forgiveness. We did this in Durban too. 'Report some good stories,' we told them, 'not all bad. Stop polarizing.'

Papers and radio stations began in earnest to do just that.

The churches also launched a Democracy Campaign to teach afresh the concepts of political tolerance. Churches sent significant leaders to all areas of the province to meet with pastors, lay leaders and congregations.

Visits were made to police headquarters and stations to challenge police officers to carry out their work with impeccable impartiality.

The Mothers' Union held marches. Medical people took the peace message to patients in their hospitals. Christian laypeople went to the different IFP and ANC hostels in the different cities.

With the South African communication services, we began formulating other plans. TV and radio would be activated. There would be some concerts for the peace process, and music festivals. The security forces, police and army would be drawn in to make their contribution. They promised to drop thousands of leaflets from helicopters over rural areas.

One word that we received from God was: 'Don't form committees to do the work of reconciliation, forgiveness and peace. You do it.' Someone once said: 'If Moses had formed a committee the children of Israel would still be in Egypt!'

A great Zulu brother, Daniel Ngubane, joined us full-time to go from

Project Ukuthula discussion group

end to end in the province, especially speaking to the traditional chiefs, or *amakhosi*. Sipho Sokela from the South African Council of Churches undertook to go everywhere, speaking to youth. Coordinating the whole project was a very able brother, Derek Batte, who came on board full-time over these months.

Breakfasts for business and professional people proliferated across the province, and the peace message was conveyed, plus our appeal for Ukuthula funding. The financial response was stunning. Believers in every sector were doing their part.

Another interesting development was that two notorious 'warlords' – Sifiso Nkabinde (ANC), whom Dave Peters and I had the privilege of leading into commitment to Christ before he was assassinated, and David Ntombela (IFP) – now declared themselves 'peace-lords', and even said they would hold 'joint rallies'. We were getting somewhere.

Other good news was that the daily death rate began dropping.

Making progress

On 18 May, the South African Parliament finally ratified a new constitution for the country. Although some federal concessions had been made, they were not enough for the IFP, whose representatives walked out of Parliament as Buthelezi said he would still challenge the Constitution in the Constitutional Court. He and the IFP felt that provincial powers had, if anything, been reduced.

This left KwaZulu-Natal still sizzling. To try to address this, a letter was drawn up and signed by all major church leaders. The heart of the letter was a call to cease violence and promote a climate of peace for the elections:

> It is clear that the future of our region cannot be built on the ashes of our homes, soaked in the blood of our brothers and sisters . . .
>
> We ask all ministers of the Gospel to preach on the theme of forgiveness, reconciliation and peace in these coming weeks. We call all political parties to refrain from utterances which could foment violence among followers. We implore all political parties to renew the Peace Accord agreement and openly support all peace initiatives to encourage free political activities in all areas. We urge the media to report in a responsible manner, avoiding sensational reporting. We urge the police to make their work of protecting communities felt on the ground and hasten the development of community policing forums. We urge all to support the families of victims of violence.[9]

We particularly emphasized the Electoral Code of Conduct drawn up in February 1996, and urged people to have the integrity to honour it. Among other things was this commitment:

> Parties, candidates and representatives acknowledge and undertake not to contravene the right of any party, candidate, representative, voter or participant in the election to express divergent political and other opinions, to canvass freely and safely for membership and support from voters and to have free and safe access to any area.[10]

This letter went far and wide to every conceivable type of constituency, including to 5,000 school heads to give to their kids to give to their parents. The Lord had opened the way via the Department of Education for this to happen. Thousands of families were thus reached.

I sought to report back to Dr Mandela every few days with news of progress or setbacks!

Meanwhile on 11 June, Buthelezi made a call for peace in KwaZulu-Natal, saying he would 'join hands with anyone of any party who wishes to take action for peace'.[11] He also testified that this provincial peace initiative was different, as the talks were not just on a diplomatic level, but involved members of the ANC and IFP talking deeply to one another. Buthelezi said: 'We will join in action with church and business leaders to establish a culture of tolerance.'[12]

The politicians clearly felt that in the Ukuthula climate they were making progress. There was hope. Hundreds of Christians once again participated in 24/7 chains of prayer. That was a critically important component.

What I just loved was the way everyone got in on the act. Thus the *Mercury* newspaper and Spar supermarket declared that their annually sponsored 10 km Ladies' Challenge race would be 'a Race for Peace'. *The Mercury* carried a photograph of Bishop Mogoba and Mrs Eunice Mdlalose, wife of the Premier of Natal, and First Lady of the Province, meeting to encourage the race organizers. In the event 5,000 women ran!

Also encouraging was the South African Broadcasting Corporation for Natal throwing a huge function, with the Durban Mayor and assorted lords and ladies all there to announce their commitment to involvement in Project Ukuthula.

And you know what? All these endeavours from business people, editors, politicians, church leaders and ordinary Christian men and women began to make a difference.

God was doing something

The numbers of deaths per day continued to decline. Over the weekend of 8–9 June seven people died from violence when only weeks previously the death toll had been approximately 60 per weekend.

Premier Frank Mdlalose, a deep Christian and great friend of our ministry, tabled in Parliament on 12 June a comprehensive programme of action to take the peace message to all people in KwaZulu-Natal.

I honestly believe that when Christian people are deeply praying for politicians, a climate of change begins to prevail.

One major initiative now remained for Project Ukuthula leaders, and that was conducting a Peace Summit which we had initiated in Durban for some 300 leaders just 13 days before the provincial elections. Leaders from across the political spectrum were represented, including from the Church; the business, education, media and communication sectors; the police and army; and other parts of the diplomatic corps.

Even Queen Buhle and Princess Sibusile, who had been seriously injured in the palace attacks, were there. It was encouraging too to hear the King urge 'all citizens in the province to support the peace initiatives',[13] in spite of the fact that his family had been among the victims of violence.

Jacob Zuma said he was confident the initiative would succeed because all parties supported the church leaders' Ukuthula initiative.[14]

The Mercury's editorial on 14 June said:

A genuine peace initiative seems to have evolved. Led by churches and backed by political rivals, the peace summit in Durban can be seen as the first step towards a lasting solution to the reign of terror.

How joyous it would be if, in future years, the month of June, 1996, might be remembered in SA, not only for the tragedy of Soweto Day, but as the time when the people of KwaZulu-Natal finally came to their senses.[15]

Provincial parliament

The Mercury also reported:

Last week saw perhaps some of the most extraordinary happenings in the provincial legislature to date. The KwaZulu-Natal parliament has always been a place of political conflict and heated debate, and for the past two years not a single session of the house has passed without at least one massive outbreak of the political divides and tensions between the IFP and ANC.

419

So, to come to a week where opposing politicians were being extremely polite and nice to each other, and where the debate actually focussed on the real issues surrounding the 1996/97 provincial budget, proved to be an eye-opener to the most hardened of political observers.[16]

Perhaps, then, with this kind of spirit prevailing, it was not surprising that Bishop Makhaye and I were invited not long before the election to address the KwaZulu-Natal Parliament. We were received with appreciation and saw the politicians really working together.

The Natal papers made a bit of a fuss about the contribution the churches had made to bringing peace in the province, and commended them for it. This was gratifying. It's not often that the press hands the Church a bouquet!

The daily and weekend death rates came down to zero.

The 'God' factor

Anyway, the elections were held on 26 June in total peace. Apart from a couple of very minor incidents reported to police, there was no violence to mar the electoral process.

I had learned that in the most conflicted of situations, earnest peace-making initiatives can change the socio-political environment, provided there is deep, fervent and ongoing prayer to the Lord of peace who says: 'Nothing is too hard for [me]' (Jeremiah 32.17 NIV).

Yes, in Project Ukuthula, day-and-night prayer was the underlying key. And God had made a way.

33

Threads of prayer and writing

━━━●◆●━━━

*Prayer ushers in order out of chaos, pulls peace out of confusion
and destruction, and brings joy in the midst of sorrow. It
takes what Satan meant for evil and brings us good.*[1]
(Cindy Jacobs)

The people of South Africa had shifted their gaze away from the giants
they faced, to Christ, who is the real agent of change in our lives. The God-
given passion in me for the gospel to be worked out in every aspect of life
is what has inspired my whole ministry.

Throughout the years of my life, amid everything else, the closely en-
twined threads of prayer and writing have charted my footsteps in what
God called me to do, and thus it was through my next 25 years of ministry.

Prayer

The apostle Paul wrote: 'Don't be weary in prayer; keep at it; watch for
God's answers, and remember to be thankful when they come' (Colossians 4.2 TLB).

We need to hang in there with our prayers, even as Jesus commended
the importunate man who kept waking his neighbour and calling on him
in the night for help (Luke 11.5–13). This story speaks of persisting in
prayer from the depths of the soul until God finally answers.

It's a case of 'PUSH', which stands for: Pray Until Something Happens!

Of course for all of us, personal prayer will be the key prayer dimension
of our lives. I will always be thankful that within weeks of my Christian
commitment back in October 1955, I was taught to make prayer a daily
part of life. My daily devotional time, or 'quiet time', as some call it, has
been without doubt the single greatest habit in my life. Together with my
Bible reading at that time, I was encouraged to make a prayer diary and I
have used one ever since.

I have found it helpful in a small notebook to divide my praying into three cycles – a daily one, a weekly one and a monthly one, because one can't pray for everyone and everything all in one day. I use photographs stuck into my notebook of my family members, friends or missionaries as a visual reminder as I pray for them.

In the daily section I follow the well-known acrostic 'ACTS'. A stands for Adoration (worship), C for Confession, T for Thanksgiving, and S for Supplication (asking).

Likewise with the weekly cycle. I mark the pages Monday to Saturday and list people, needy situations, aspects of our work, and needs of society, including leaders.

In the monthly cycle I note people who may not be very central to my life but whom I don't want to lose contact with and want to lift to the Lord from time to time.

The blessings of this prayer habit are far too extensive to enumerate, but if I were to shut down this aspect of my life it would be like switching off my oxygen supply. So too would it be if the Church, in groups large or small, ceased to pray to the Lord of heaven and earth for his blessings, which we so desperately need in our world.

Prayer in the evenings before bed is also important to me. I don't take a long time on this because of tiredness, but 10 or 12 minutes is wonderful, and, using a devotional book rather than big chunks of the Bible, I find I can go to sleep with a scriptural or devotional thought as the last thing on my mind for that day. It also helps to have godly thoughts going into our subconscious as our day ends.

Without this personal dimension to our praying, I believe we would not be able to pray effectively in a church or corporate setting.

One of the great rewards of prayer is seeing the Lord answer. Of course, this isn't always the case in a visible way, and we have to be open to his will, timing and choosing.

Prayers have gone up from both Carol and me individually and to-gether for our extended family to come to know the Lord. If I think of my own parents, though my dad had truly sought to follow the Lord for years, it meant much to me that literally on his deathbed he prayed, like the thief on the cross, 'Lord Jesus, remember me.' As to my Doubting Thomas mum, she attempted prayers of commitment several times, but it again meant the world to me when the last word she uttered as she breathed her last was: 'Jesus'. Thank you, Lord.

Then there was Carol's dad, John. He too struggled with faith. He actually was a pretty tough guy. Very self-sufficient and independent. I was always terrified to try to talk to him about the things of the Lord. But

Carol's parents: Noenkie and John Bam

prayer went up for him for decades. Anyway, several rough things happened to him in his late eighties. He lost his beloved wife of over 60 years, Noenkie, and had a heart attack, a car accident, and a few other problems.

One day I was on the phone to him and suddenly felt emboldened to say, 'Dad, I think after all these things happening in your life the Lord is trying to say something to you. Don't you feel it's time now to yield your life to Christ and take him as your Saviour, Lord and Friend? I can pray right now over the phone a prayer of commitment you can echo in your heart.'

'Yes, Mike, I'd like to do that.' Grandpa at 89 was saying an unequivocal yes to Jesus Christ. And it was a deep thing for him. He endlessly wanted to talk about heaven, and even asked me what I thought Granny would be wearing when he got up there! I'm afraid four years of theological training hadn't equipped me to answer that!

Prayer mysteries

Sometimes there are deep mysteries attached to our prayer lives, especially with seemingly unanswered prayers or delayed answers.

Actually I believe there are no unanswered prayers which are sincerely lifted to our Lord. The Lord can say either 'Yes', 'No' or 'Wait'. An example of the latter is when I prayed so earnestly throughout my twenties for the Lord's choice for my wife, and then desperately as I entered my thirties! My prayer was answered, in the Lord's sovereign timing, when Carol so miraculously entered my life, but I had had to wait quite a while.

In the case of my poor eyes and, in later life, my deteriorating hearing, the Lord seemed to say a single 'No'! And that was that.

There have been times when I have prayed out in a forest, or during a prayer walk, or on a hilltop in tearful pleading for African Enterprise – when something was going wrong and I didn't see how it could be fixed without a mighty intervention from the Lord. Sometimes things only righted themselves slowly. On occasion it was sudden and immediate. The Lord has his way and timing.

But what about those gutting and heart-rending mysteries when the Lord seems to leave us or our loved ones or friends in the darkness of devastation or tragedy?

For example, our young nephew, Richard Evans, aged 11, son of Carol's sister Lynn and her husband Trevor, died of leukaemia, even though we had prayed mightily for him. What about that?

Or what of our friends John and Beth Fyvie, three of whose four children died over several years of a fearsome affliction called Batten disease? Never will I forget my jangled emotions while speaking at three separate funerals over those little coffins, one of whom carried a godchild of mine.

After all that prayer! Where was God? And how does faith in God survive such tragedy?

Well, first of all we daren't throw all our faith away, nor suddenly doubt in the darkness what God has shown in the light. Second, one has to enter the category of mystery and grasp that it is better to live with mystery than with bad answers. After all, one day we will no longer see through a glass darkly, but will 'understand fully, even as [we] have been fully understood' (1 Corinthians 13.12). So we just don't know what is going on. And we need to admit it. Nor will we know until we meet the Lord face to face.

This is why John the apostle says that faith is 'the victory that overcomes the world' (1 John 5.4), meaning all that the world throws at us. It is faith alone which knows there is an answer and which enables us to wait for the answer.

When we come with lament and deep questionings, we need to put everything back in God's hands, and remember that even Jesus, in his wounded but real humanity, cried out 'Why?' on the cross: 'My God, my God, why have you forsaken me?' (Matthew 27.46 NIV). Of course, that was the climactic moment of atonement when, bearing the sins of the world, he experienced the 'cut-off-ness' from God which we sinners deserved. Even so, at that moment, he gathered up all the 'whys' which ever tumbled from the human breast, and bore them on the cross, even as he bore our 'griefs and . . . sorrows' (Isaiah 53.4) and our 'transgressions [and] iniquities' (Isaiah 53.5).

Our challenge when it comes to perplexities and mysteries is to relinquish them to the Lord, allowing him to carry our 'whys'.

Mark Stibbe put it well: 'We declare, Lord, that You can. We believe that You will. We know You might not. We'll trust You if You don't.'[2]

Carol's weekly prayer group

Carol has a deep, faithful and persistent prayer-life which is an inspiration to me. Not only does she lift family needs or friends' needs to the Lord in her private devotions, but she also has a group of women meeting without fail every Friday morning for an hour to pray for South Africa – not personal things this time but for the country!

On the occasions when I can join them, it is a deep and instructive experience to hear these women calling on the Lord for our government institutions, for change in our country, for the end of corruption, and much else besides. They have no doubt been joining hundreds of other small groups around the country praying similar things, and we have indeed seen all sorts of corruptions come to light for public scrutiny and protest.

One also never knows what seriously negative things might have been held at bay by the prayers of God's people coming together to call on their heavenly Father for his intervention.

What we do know is that our Jehovah God and his Son Jesus Christ do call on us constantly to pray and to ask him for what we want or need. He wants us to bring everything to him in prayer, because this keeps us connected to him, keeps it all relational, and keeps us dependent on him for his blessings.

As an example, this is why I have been so committed to national prayer movements such as Angus Buchan's Mighty Men's gatherings (a couple of them numbering over a million), and the Global Day of Prayer, which began in South Africa and then finally embraced over 200 nations. This was envisioned and led by Cape Town businessman Graham Power who had been launched on his Christian faith journey through an AE leadership mission in Cape Town. I was much privileged to be asked to be patron of this movement.

Writing

Ever since I started writing in diaries and in letters home through my young years, putting pen to paper has been almost second nature. It has also been an integral part of my ministry. Quite apart from thousands of letters, essays, talks, sermons and addresses, I have written tracts and leaflets for our missions, and several books, some of which grew out of shorter written pieces or talks.

My first public writing was a newspaper column in our daily local newspaper, the *Natal Witness*. This resulted from a word coming into my spirit back in 1967, a whisper from the Lord, after a five-month youth outreach in the southern suburbs of Cape Town: 'My son, take up your pen. You will reach more people by writing than you will ever reach by talking.'

As well as my column, I did a 12-week newspaper series for seekers or doubters who wanted to explore the Christian faith and understand how to respond to Christ. The series was well received so I said to my then secretary, Dorothy White, 'Why don't you get them together in a nice format and send them off to the American student publishers, Inter-Varsity Christian Fellowship? Let's make the title *Christianity for the Open-Minded: An Invitation to Doubters.*' Doing this was relatively straightforward – less so for subsequent publishing projects: I have always written everything out in longhand, which then creates incredible problems for my secretaries such as Colleen Smith and Brenda Harrison to type up, because they tell me I write in tongues!

To my delight, InterVarsity Christian Fellowship accepted this volume at once and continued to reprint it, even up to this year. The book has sold well over 100,000 copies, has been reprinted 16 times, and has been widely used on American campuses and in AE missions.[3]

My next effort arose out of a series of talks I gave in 1968 in a high school mission. It seemed worthwhile to write them up into a little book called *Decade of Decisions*, which I proudly took to the publisher Hodder & Stoughton of London, offering it to the religious editor, Edward England, who would one day become my literary agent.

He took my typescript, cast his eye over it for a few moments, and then said, 'No, Michael, I think not.'

I must have looked disconsolate.

'Anyway,' he went on, 'don't look too disappointed. Perhaps you should know I also turned down *The Cross and the Switchblade* by David Wilkerson which went on to sell six million copies!'[4]

Edward gave me a gift volume of sermons by James Stewart of

Edinburgh and a cup of tea, before I stepped out feebly into a foggy day in London town. It was my first lesson in learning that the path to any sort of writing success at all is paved with rejection slips.

In due course I took the manuscript to Marshall, Morgan & Scott, another London publisher, whose editor rescued my rather battered ego by accepting it. And the book did quite well. In the USA, Regal Books in California took it, changed the title to *Where Are You Taking the World Anyway?* and sold some 130,000 copies.[5] That restored a little bit of confidence.

Alan Paton, whom I often visited in his home to talk about South Africa, once said to me, 'Michael, with any book you write, you must read it 13 times before sending it to the publisher!'

I hope I had taken this advice seriously when I later went back very nervously to my straight-talking publishing friend, Edward England at Hodder & Stoughton in London, with my new script, *Bursting the Wineskins*, on the person and work of the Holy Spirit.

'Tell me about it . . .' Edward said over a cuppa.

'We'll take it,' he pronounced a few minutes later, without even looking at the script.

'Come on, Edward,' I remonstrated, 'you can't do that. You don't even know if it's a good book.'

'I *smell* one,' he said with a sort of Sherlock Holmes intuition.

The Lord used *Bursting the Wineskins* in special ways, and I know of one person whose life was changed completely as a result: Tim Holmes, son of Jack and Ruth Holmes, whom you may remember I had met with his family on board ship going out from Southampton to Cape Town in early 1959.

Tim was a lonely bachelor hydrologist working out in the remote Namib Desert region in Namibia. In the midst of mightily coveting and praying about finding a wife, he found himself reading a copy of *Bursting the Wineskins*, sent to him I guess by his family because he sort of knew the author!

In the book, he read how the Lord had most miraculously brought Carol and me together. Tim registered that he had a month's annual home leave coming up and he was going back to England. He said to the Lord: 'If you could do that for Michael, could you not do something similar for me?'

So the day after Tim arrived home in Worcester, he startled his family by saying firmly that he urgently needed to go back to Sevenoaks, Kent, where he had been born and grew up (taking seriously the instruction to Isaac when looking for a wife that he needed to go back to the country of his birth). And with no explanations given, Tim did just that and went to stay with an old childhood friend, now working for Mission Aviation Fellowship (MAF).

Next day his friend said, 'Tim, I'd like to take you down to our MAF offices and have you meet some of our staff.'

And off they went. Arriving at the office, he introduced Tim to the receptionist. 'This is Tim Holmes.'

Then from behind an office screen came a lady's voice: 'Tim Holmes! I once knew a Tim Holmes.' And out came a young woman called Ros.

'My word, it's you, Tim. I remember you from when we were in primary school as kids.'

Big chit-chat and a happy reunion followed. Then Tim said, 'You know, I once sent you a Valentine's card.'

'Oh, my,' said Ros, 'was that from you? I remember it!'

More chit-chat. Then Ros said: 'Why not come round to my place for lunch tomorrow, if you're free?'

And there it was. Overnight Tim's heart was pounding. He believed this was the girl for him.

He astonished himself at lunch the next day by asking, 'Ros, will you marry me?'

She was easily as thunderstruck as Carol had been on 18 August 1969 when I popped my question.

'Well, let me go out into the garden and pray!'

A few moments later she returned and exulted, 'Yes, Tim, *yes!*'

'Well, Ros, I'm only in England for just over three weeks. So we've got just three weeks to plan a wedding.'

Jack and Ruth were bowled over as they got the blockbuster story. And planning began with a frenzy.

When it came to going back to Namibia, Tim's airline said his flight was already over-full. No place even for one more person. Tim and Ros prayed hard. A few days later an airline representative phoned. There had been several cancellations. Ros was taken off the waiting list and now firmly booked on the plane.

Tim and Ros's fairy-tale story took them back to Namibia and later into full-time missionary work, along with a happy little brood of children!

Chasing the Wind

The bug had now well and truly bitten and I found myself itching to write a fuller book on defending and explaining the Christian faith and introducing people to Jesus. The jump-off point was Solomon's story in the book of Ecclesiastes, where he tells of his quest for meaning. He tries everything: wine, women, song, wealth, social and political exploits – you name it. But his conclusion? 'I have seen all the things that are done under the sun; all of them are meaningless, a chasing after the wind' (Ecclesiastes 1.14 NIV). *Chasing the Wind* was my title.[6]

One story coming out of *Chasing the Wind* that really touched my heart was told to me personally by a lady called Margaret Dickerson from Cape Town. She was grief-stricken after losing her husband of many, many years. Viewing herself as an atheist she was void of all comfort. But one day she surprised herself by going into a church, where she felt a numinous presence. Once outside again, she made a request: 'God, if you really exist, and I don't think you do, but if you do, you know I'm a reader. So I am going to go to the Cape Town City Library and go to the religious section. Lead me to a book which will help me find you.'

'Michael, it was extraordinary,' she told me when we actually met. 'My hand somehow reached out and laid hold of a copy of *Chasing the Wind*. And that was that. I read it twice in the next 48 hours and came into a glorious conversion and found Christ as my Lord, Saviour and Friend.'

Some years later in Cape Town I came across Margaret running a book table at a church. Promoting and selling Christian books had become her ministry!

Yes, writing – it's something I've loved ever since I was a boy. And with prayer meaningfully in the mix, the Lord can sometimes do something significant when pen is put to paper.

Michael at his writing desk

That's why it has been both fun and rewarding to keep these two threads of prayer and writing going in my life – until finally, this memoir notion came forth.

It started as a quiet request to the Lord that he would enable me to do it. Then it was Carol who encouraged me to make a start: 'I think you should do it,' she told me, 'while you've still got a memoir!'

34

New priorities

I know, Lord, that's all I am
At Best,
Thy Passing Guest,
Here Today,
Gone tomorrow.
Brief Meal with Thee, my Host,
Joy now, then Sorrow.
Tastes bitter now, then sweet,
Heart skips a beat.
All shared with those loved most,
Until the Journey's done,
And hopefully the Crown is won.
And I see, not just a Guest,
But, Oh, so blessed,
A son.[1]

Everyone in Christian ministry will be familiar with the temptation to keep going until the job is done – against the odds at times, and asking a lot of our nearest and dearest. That was the story of my life: taking on too much. 'You can never say no, Michael,' was my executive assistant David Rees's constant rebuke to me. I couldn't argue with that. Somehow holding on to obvious priorities was always problematic for me. You know, getting first things second was one of my habits. I deeply regret this.

But at the end of 2009 I was brought up short.

Near miss

The year had been brimful. Too full. As well as the usual AE activities, I had a major research trip to India, and was also significantly involved in planning for the third Lausanne Congress on World Evangelization set for Cape Town in October 2010, as I had been deeply committed to the Lausanne movement since its inception in 1974. But I ended the year exhausted.

As we prepared for our annual leave in the middle of December, I had one last engagement to fulfil. It was to preach at my nephew Charlie Bester's wedding, my sister Judy's son. I was up at 4.30 a.m. to prepare my address, and by the time we had packed and got away, the sun was high and it was baking hot.

We were cruising along KwaZulu-Natal's main motorway up to Johannesburg. The road was shimmering in the glare of the sun. Carol went to sleep. You know, when wives do something seemingly sensible, you just have to follow their example. So dutifully I fell asleep too!

We woke with the sound of a thunderclap as we hit who knows what. We were heading off the road down an angled grass bank and still travelling at well over 100 kilometres per hour (60 mph)!

In that split second, I knew I had to try to get the vehicle back on to the road. The sliding front wheel touched the tarmac, and with the sound of screaming rubber our car turned nearly 360 degrees and landed up stalled, and straddling the highway sideways on. It was the time of the Christmas rush and holiday traffic, but at that moment no vehicle was anywhere in sight! I restarted the engine and pulled quickly off the road.

Carol burst into tears.

In due course an Indian couple pulled up to ask if we were all right. Thankfully we were. And we drove on until we came to a garage with a little café. 'Some strong coffee, please!'

We realized that probably nowhere else along that stretch of motorway could we have gone off the road at speed and not plunged down a much steeper bank and turned over, or hit a culvert, or a tree or a telephone pole. We had been truly spared from becoming yet another tragic Christmas traffic statistic.

Our son, Martin, advised us to make an unscheduled stop to sleep at a guesthouse that night and try to recover before heading off again early the next day. In the small hours of the morning I had a vivid dream. I saw the back view of our familiar green car bumping violently along the angled bank with sticks, stones, dust and grass flying in all directions.

Then into the picture and right across it in huge black capital letters appeared the word 'GOD'! Larger than life.

'Well, Lord,' I said, 'you've sure got my attention now. What do you want to say?'

And the words seemed to flow immediately into my soul.

'My son – yes – I was there. I saw it. I allowed it. I spared you. And I want you to hear from me. I want you to change your priorities, cut back on administration and fundraising, and focus on encouraging younger leaders, and writing and preaching.'

I have always believed that God speaks on occasion through dreams. Not often. But sometimes. I dream every night and normally cannot recall anything. But a compelling dream deserves prayerful attention, and has often given me guidance I could never otherwise have got. And of course dreams are in the Bible from cover to cover.

So the near miss on the motorway, and this dream, really made me pause. It was time to take stock.

The practicalities of untangling myself from my many commitments presented quite a challenge, and took more time probably than it should have done. It was hard to extract myself. I made a list of priorities; resigned from some committees; and talked to people about what I thought the Lord was calling me to do at this stage of my life.

The first thing that became clear was my mentoring role.

Barnabas Groups and Facilities

Of course informally I had always tried to support those around me whom the Lord put on my heart to encourage. I had also adopted a more specific mentoring role on some occasions. But this was different.

'I believe you need really to get into "relational mentoring" of younger and rising leaders,' a friend told me before I had got very far in think-ing about it. Then, shortly afterwards, I found myself among hundreds of thousands of younger men at the Mighty Men's Conference (MMC) organized by my extraordinary farmer-evangelist friend Angus Buchan. What a man! Tents stretched as far as the eye could see at his farm, Shalom, out near Greytown. My attendance was a last-minute opportunity which in retrospect seemed like another example of the Lord's timing.

My accommodation was not a tent but a nearby house lent for the occa-sion, together with seven co-lodgers, mostly from George in the Western Cape. As I was introduced to them, one of them said, 'Hey, wow! This is something. We have been praying during this weekend somehow to have a "spiritual father experience" with an older leader. We think you are an answer to our prayers.'

Well, this was nothing if not humbling. I told my group that, curiously enough, the Lord had been pressing me into a discipling and mentoring role with younger leaders.

'Why don't you start with us?' they said.

Thus out of dear Angus's ministry was born my own Barnabas ministry, with the George lads becoming my first Barnabas Group.

Strangely, a number of other younger leaders in other places had out of the blue begun writing to me. Would I in some way seek to mentor them? These included both women and men.

So almost overnight eight other groups, in eight other cities, were born – Johannesburg, Cape Town, Pretoria, Bloemfontein, Port Elizabeth, East London, Durban and Pietermaritzburg.

By Dave Rees's astonishing administrative and organizational efforts, he and I were personally able to visit each of these groups three times a year, over the next few years, and in one particular year four times. It was challenging, but exhilaratingly worthwhile. We looked at themes like developing one's devotional life, how to lead someone to Christ, how to read and interpret the Bible, discipling someone, making the most of our time, relating to the Church, basic apologetics and defending the faith, and so on.

I just became so very deeply fond of all these 'Barnabees'. They give me so much hope for our beloved South Africa. And this same hope is what I felt recently while watching my son Martin cross the finish line of the 90-kilometre 2018 Comrades Ultra-Marathon from Pietermaritzburg to Durban. What a picture of the rainbow nation working: crowds and runners alike cheering one another along, regardless of race or background. South Africa truly is the world's most wonderful country. And AE's amazing Foxfire Youth Teams show the young are open and ready to roll.

The Barnabas Groups continue, even if over the last while I have needed, for health and other reasons, to cut back while other colleagues have done the running for me.

Health challenges

Of course, as Scottish poet Robbie Burns reflected, 'The best laid schemes o' mice an' men/Gang aft agley',[2] usually paraphrased as 'The best-laid plans of mice and men go oft awry'.

And for me the 'going awry' was due to my health. I was well under way with my reordered priorities when I was diagnosed with not one but two illnesses with the potential to take me out altogether – leukaemia and lupus. This slowed me down, make no mistake. Carol and I, ever closer, were thrown into a round of wondering and waiting, and great dependence on our Lord, especially when the extra rascal myasthenia gravis descended upon me:

> To you, O LORD, I lift up my soul,
> O my God, in you I trust . . .
> O guard my life, and deliver me;
> do not let me be put to shame,
> for I take refuge in you.
>
> (Psalm 25.1, 20 NRSV)

My editorial assistant Megan Whatley who, together with my ultra-efficient secretary Brenda, was helping me with putting together the autobiography I had at last prioritized, gave me a Scripture which, from that poignant day of diagnosis to this, has anchored me in the sovereignty of God over both my life and my death. 'In [your] book', says the psalmist, 'were written, every one of them, the days that were formed for me, when as yet there was none of them' (Psalm 139.16). My life from conception to the time of my departure is marked out for me by my supernatural Lord and Creator.

Oh, the peace-giving blessing of knowing that!

Whenever I felt stronger, I got back to work.

It's an instructive thought that often when severe testings come upon us, life's temporary allures of comfort, money, belongings, career success, or whatever, become relatively unimportant as we live intentionally and of necessity in deep closeness to the Lord. And we grasp that while many blessings come our way, they are never to be mistaken for Home.

But then the trial lifts and we go back to our former ways, losing sight of what we learned.

Teamlet: Dave, Brenda, Megan and Michael

C. S. Lewis in his classic book *The Problem of Pain* comments along these lines about severe human tribulations:

> At first I am overwhelmed, and all my little happinesses look like broken toys. Then, slowly and reluctantly, bit by bit, I try to bring myself into the frame of mind that I should be in at all times. I remind myself that all these toys were never intended to possess my heart, that my true good is another world and my only real treasure is Christ. And perhaps by God's grace, I succeed, and for a day or two become a creature consciously dependent on God and drawing its strength from the right sources. But the moment the threat is withdrawn, my whole nature leaps back to the toys. I am even anxious, God forgive me, to banish from my mind the only thing that supported me under the threat because it is now associated with the misery of those few days. Thus the terrible necessity of tribulation is only too clear.[3]

I was a slow learner.

During times of solitude, when I was deep in conversation with my Lord, I penned what I called 'MC Musings'. These often took the form of poetic prayers, and a couple of them have sneaked into this chapter! Thus, in Hyrax Cabin by the Kariega River, I penned the following:

> **What if . . . ?**
> I woke this morning, dozed, prayed, and thought –
> What if . . .? Am I being taught?
> What if I only have another year?
> What if then I face the tear
> That tears me from this Earth's clutches
> Pressing on me Heaven's Embrace,
> And Angel touches,
> In Another Place . . .
> Even just a year from now?
> And I began to wonder how
> To live it
> And to what to give it.
> Thoughts crowded in.
> Just live it. Life is for living.
> And for giving.
> Yes, Your best shot.[4]

Respite

During this time, there was a moment when God seemed to lift the curtain over his sovereign plans and give me a glimpse into the future that still awaited me on his beautiful earth.

View from Hyrax Cabin of Kariega River: solitude retreat

I was recovering from double pneumonia and facing a potentially serious operation when my good friend, Robin Stephenson, a man full of faith, came to pray with me and lay hands on me.

'Michael,' he said, 'I believe the Lord has shown me that all is going to be well tomorrow.'

I woke the next day with huge peace, in spite of the prospect of who knows what. My physician, on an early visit, ordered one last scan, and the cardiovascular surgeon checked it before ushering me into the prepared theatre.

I believed I knew what he would find and, sure enough, he returned with good news.

'It's all dramatically improved,' he said. 'Almost gone, completely clear. The tumour has virtually vanished and there is no necessity even for a bronchoscopy or biopsy. You can go home!'

'Do you mind if I say, "Thank you, Lord?"' I asked him with the deepest relief possible.

'Fine, but not to me,' he replied with a twinkle.

'No,' I said, 'I am thanking *him*. It's an answer to prayer.'

The year 2018, with seven hospital visits and four in ICU, was a long weakening journey, with the Lord deepening my dependence on him, rescuing me, and putting me on another trajectory into my future and my home straight. Arthur Scott, my son-in-law Jonathan's dad, sent me this lovely stanza by an anonymous author to which he added his own final line:

> Lord, I am willing to receive what you give;
> To lack what you withhold;
> To relinquish what you take;

To suffer what you inflict;
To be what you require;
And to do what you send me to do.

Home straight

It's difficult to know when a home straight begins. In a 200-metre race, the home straight would be the last 50 metres. In a 1,500-metre race it would be the last 300 metres. In the Comrades Ultra-Marathon it would be the last 6 or 7 kilometres. When can any of us know we are in the home straight? I *think* mine began in our near-death experience on the motorway to Johannesburg in December 2009.

I thereafter dipped in and out of Psalm 90, which calls for us to 'number our days' (verse 12). The psalm reminds us: 'The years of our life are threescore and ten, or even by means of strength fourscore' (verse 10).

And I was very close to that fourscore. Recognizing this made me thankful for so much. The old gospel song says:

Count your blessings, name them one by one,
And it will amaze you what the Lord has done.

How fortunate I am to have been alive at all! My destiny was not just to be a being, but a *human being*. We are made in the image of God, to know something of what God is like. I have rationality, a moral sense, aesthetic appreciation, an ability to love, a capacity for laughter and also for tears. I know all these characteristics are in my heavenly Father and I can relate to him.

I also recognized the supreme blessing of being deeply loved by my parents. I remember at Fuller Seminary we were obliged to fill out 'The Minneapolis Multiphasal Personality Inventory' (MMPI), a clever psychological tool (with a ghastly name!) to assess all sorts of capacities in the students. I asked my psychology professor for the findings on me.

'Well, Mike,' he said, 'you have suffered some deep hurts, but you have one of the deepest senses of personal security I have ever seen. This I believe comes from having been deeply and unconditionally loved by your parents, giving you a great capacity for rebound. You may get knocked down. But you'll never be knocked out. You will bounce back.'

And I think that has been true. I have had many insecurities but also a basic sense of self-worth, a confidence in who I am, and a consequent capacity to ride out quite a few storms of life and hang in there.

Many other things have helped me. I give thanks for the rest and the fun afforded by regular holidays, which have perhaps been among my greatest privileges. Breaks are important for everyone, whatever shape they take.

Seeking solitude has also been vital for me, time to pause and seek the Lord and his guidance. Such solitude times, if we will only treat ourselves to them, stand out as high-water marks of blessing in any given year. But I also believe they are a necessity if we want to last out, and not conk out.

Once when on sabbatical in Vancouver, Canada, I spoke to the psychology counsellor at Regent College, and asked her what her one word of counsel would be to me as I returned to all the stresses of ministry.

Without hesitating she said: 'Michael, get solitude.'

Then, I owe so much to Carol, family, friends and colleagues for running the race with me, and for so often going the extra mile. I couldn't have done it without them.

I won't say teamwork is easy. It is challenging, like being married to a couple of dozen people! But there is a special depth to friendships when you have a shared interest and commitment, a task you passionately want to do together. And what a blessing to be able to share things, even failures or sins, and know that what has been shared will be held safely in total confidentiality, prayer and care. Sometimes we find it difficult to share deep needs or areas of failure, maybe due to our pride getting in the way, but doing so can bring peace, rescue and healing.

I would add here that when AE has been truly synergistic, at its best and producing exceptionally high levels of performance, it was because our friendship and relational levels were really good, our goals focused and our mutual cooperation deep. And when our performances were poor, it was because our relationships were tatty and our goals unclear.

There is also great value, especially for any in ministry or Christian leadership, to have older friends who become mentors to us and guide us through the assorted challenges of the Lord's work. I have been blessed with several, most notably Calvin Cook, Bruce Bare and Stephen Neill.

Thankfully I am at peace about AE, its international leadership by Stephen Mbogo of Kenya, and its South African leadership by Theuns Pauw, in South Africa where I reside, both highly capable leaders, like our other nine national team leaders, with a strong vision for evangelism.

Alongside my gratitude for so much, I do have regrets, such as not spending more time with my precious Carol and the family, both immediate and extended. I probably sought to be too messianic, rushing here and there to try to save situations! However, the key is to know when to jump in oneself, and when to leave it to others. If I had life over again, I would be a lot lazier! And a lot more caring.

Of course, if one short-changes one's family, it is equally likely that we will short-change the Lord. My prayer life and times of devotion have not been a patch on those of my heroes, or so it seems to me.

I would have loved to have gone deeper with the Holy Spirit too. The apostle Paul urges us to 'walk in the Spirit' (Galatians 5.16–18 KJV), which surely means having a moment-by-moment connection to the Spirit throughout any given day, and I regret not having entered more into that, especially in the area of healing.

Take the analogy of the smartphone. One may master phone calls, text messages, the internet, and still not understand all the variety of options available through the device. It is a bit like that with the Holy Spirit. Reading 1 Corinthians 12 and 14, I realize how far I have yet to go.

What I know more than ever is that Christ is my all in all. Nothing else is certain. And every day is a gift. Carol, family, extended family, friends and colleagues are even more precious to me. And I have surrendered AE more fully into the Lord's hands.

Life is for living

As 2017 got under way, my creative work was flourishing, thanks to great help from the members of my closest team. In fact it is thanks to them that I have been able to do anything at all in these later years, really.

I was also enjoying relaxed time with Carol, my beloved and gem of all gems, as well as opportunities to be with my precious wider family.

One such occasion happened recently when the whole family, including Cathy who had come over to South Africa from the USA, but sadly without her husband Jonathan and the two boys, got together for Easter at Namirembe, our home in Hilton. The gathering gave me a sudden sense of overwhelming happiness and family delight, and it all seemed too rich for words.

Again there came to me an extraordinary sense of Christian salvation and Christian family as God's two supreme gifts to human beings.

What gave the extra sense of tonic was the constant symphony of sounds where somehow children's peals of laughter fitted together with strumming on the piano, the nicks and knocks of carpet bowls, shrieks of irritation as a naughty brother provoked his little sister, and from outside the house the thump of a rugby ball kicked around. Rising from the braai,

Family time over Easter: Carol, Cathy, Martin and Debbie with Michael, 2017

our South African-style barbecue, were the smoky scents and sounds of Gary and Martin's chops and steaks sizzling on the fire.

The only thing missing that weekend was our granddaughter Josie Kirsten's little outgrown dress which stated: 'If you think I'm cute, wait till you see my granny!'

One discussion over those days particularly centres itself into my retrospective consciousness. It began over dinner and continued for a while afterwards, and related to the obsessive use, by all of us, but probably particularly by the kids, of cell phones and other electronic devices, this leading into a vigorous discussion of all the horrific stuff that can now be accessed at the push of a button.

What impressed me was that at no point did the discussion get heated or out of control, but rather there was a distinct sense of godly wisdom and rationality descending from the adults of the family as a deposit down into the lives of the younger ones. It was the older generations passing on to the younger generation something memorable and important. It gave me a very good feeling to hear and witness this.

And of course, as it was Easter, the whole occasion was impregnated with the sense of Christ's Calvary love and resurrection power.

My prayer for you

For any believer reading my story, my prayer for you is that you find your life's calling, and that you finish well.

Sometimes I think back and wonder what on earth would have happened to me had I not responded to the gospel when I first understood it back in 1955. I might have become a lost soul indeed – maybe lost my way morally; got into unsatisfying or soul-destroying work; missed my life partner or botched up my marriage.

But, no. I responded to the gospel. In some ways it is hard for me to think it might ever have been otherwise. Does this throw me into the debate of predestination and free will? Maybe. Somehow I feel both are true. It's as if one comes up to a door which says: 'Choose'. So you choose and go through it. Then when you look back, you see on the inside of the door: 'Chosen'. Thus I believe in October 1955 I made a full, free, non-robotic, non-pre-programmed and genuine choice to follow Christ, exercising my powers of both free choice and contrary choice. Then, from within the world of knowing him, I feel I was indeed somehow chosen. With the apostle I feel that 'he chose us in him before the foundation of the world . . . He destined us in love to be his [children] through Jesus Christ, according to the purpose of his will' (Ephesians 1.4–5).

Throughout my life and work subsequently, I think what has delighted me most has been to try to live *sub specie aeternitatis* (under the aspect of eternity), as the medieval theologians used to urge. So, on the cover of my diary I have a quote from Martin Luther which I love: 'There are only Two Days in my Diary. Today and That Day.'

My old friend and mentor, Ted Engstrom, used to say to me, 'Mike, you must pray: "Lord, may I finish better than I started."' This has been my

Michael and Carol, Pater Noster, August 2015

442

prayer for every footprint I have made in the African sand. And my testimony now is of God's faithfulness to me every step of the way.

Others now, like those below, must carry the work forward.

Leaders of the 10 national AE teams who will carry on making footprints in the African sand. From left to right: Dr Melisachew Mesfin (Ethiopia), Guide Makore (Zimbabwe), Leonard Kiswangi (DRC), Dr Stephen Mbogo (International Team Leader), Enoch Phiri (Malawi), Michael Macha (Tanzania), John Kalenzi (Rwanda), Benson Omondi (Kenya), Paul Ssembiro (Uganda), Bernard Sachie (Ghana), Theuns Pauw (South Africa)

Do please consider supporting and praying for these leaders. Our international website is: <https://international.africanenterprise.com>.

Sadly, space has not allowed the telling of ministry footprints graciously granted in other places around the world, such as Israel, Ireland, Belgium, Central and South America, the USA, Canada, Australia, New Zealand, the UK, the Far East and so on. All very humbling, undeserved and amazing to me.

But my primary calling has been Africa and it is those footprints accordingly on which this memoir has focused.

What I do know is that everywhere, whether in Africa or beyond these shores, it has all been about mercy. The apostle says that we have 'this ministry by the mercy of God' (2 Corinthians 4.1).

Oh yes, indeed.

Thank you, Lord! And all for your glory.

Deo gratias.

Epilogue

C. S. Lewis once said, 'Aim at Heaven and you will get earth "thrown in"; aim at earth and you will get neither.'[1]

Sadly, during his time on earth I missed getting to meet the great man at Cambridge. And I was always sorry about this. He was just a five-minute bicycle ride from my college, but I was unaware at the time of his legendary presence and never availed myself of the opportunity to go round to his rooms at Magdalen and say, 'Mr Lewis, could I have tea with you?' I am sure he would have replied: 'Come on in, boy. Do you like it with milk and sugar? And how about a crumpet?'

But I surely look forward to sitting down with him in heaven one day!

Yes, and isn't heaven just the most glorious prospect imaginable? I don't, of course, fancy the process of dying. But, even in that, I know that 'surely goodness and mercy shall follow me all the days of my life; and I shall dwell in the house of the LORD for ever' (Psalm 23.6).

As the apostle Paul declares: 'Eye has not seen, nor ear heard, neither has there entered the heart of man the things God has prepared for them that love him' (see 1 Corinthians 2.9).

Life here on earth is all prelude, and ahead lies a new heaven and a new earth:

> Then I saw a new heaven and a new earth; for the first heaven and the first earth had passed away, and the sea was no more. And I saw the holy city, new Jerusalem, coming down out of heaven from God, prepared as a bride adorned for her husband; and I heard a loud voice from the throne saying, 'Behold, the dwelling of God is with men. He will dwell with them, and they shall be his people, and God himself will be with them; he will wipe away every tear from their eyes, and death shall be no more, neither shall there be mourning nor crying nor pain any more, for the former things have passed away.' And he who sat upon the throne said, 'Behold, I make all things new.' Also he said, 'Write this, for these words are trustworthy and true.' And he said to me, 'It is done! I am the Alpha and the Omega, the beginning and the end.' (Revelation 21.1–6a)

I sign off with the principles of life I was requested to write down for inclusion in an anthology on leadership. They have served me pretty well. This is what I wrote: 'My creed is simple: Jesus Christ is God, Lord, Saviour of humankind, and coming King; from that flows my code of conduct and the path to significance.'

1 Hand everything over to Him, stay His friend, and be true to Him.

2 Stand firm on the Bible as God's authoritative guide for life and living.

3 Aim to correlate behaviour to profession but rejoice in God's forgiveness for failure.

4 Be always willing to tell others about the One whom to know is life eternal.

5 Keep all life's primary relationships strong and intact, for this is the heart of things.

6 Discern God's place and calling for life and stay at the centre of His will.

7 Give everything your best shot.

8 Make forgiveness a way of life and do not retaliate for wrongs inflicted, because vindication of His own is God's business.

9 Be strong and very courageous, as God told Joshua, because life is tough, but it yields to courage.

10 Aim to finish better than you started, remembering too that when this Day is done the best is yet to be, because Heaven is our Final Home.[2]

It comes down to this: 'Seek first his kingdom and his righteousness, and all these things shall be yours as well' (Matthew 6.33).

Thank you, Lord!

Notes

Foreword

1 F. W. Boreham, 'The Candle and the Bird', *Boulevards of Paradise*, London, Epworth Press, pp. 103–13.

2 Roots

1 *Burke's Landed Gentry*, 4 vols, ed. Peter Beauclerk Dewar and Charles Mosley, 19th edn, Burke's Peerage and Gentry LLC, 2001–6; originally published 1883–5.
2 D. Reitz, letter to Edward Reading, 11 April 1934.
3 Charles Cassidy, letter to Dee Cassidy, 21 January 1936.
4 D. Cassidy, letter to parents, 17 October 1936.

3 Shadows of war

1 Winston Churchill, *Never Give In! The Best of Winston Churchill's Speeches*, Pimlico, London, 2006, p. 198.
2 D. Cassidy, letter to Edward and Molly Reading, 10 May 1940.
3 D. Cassidy, letter to Edward and Molly Reading, 21 May 1941.
4 D. Cassidy, letter to Edward and Molly Reading, undated, 1941.
5 D. Cassidy, letter to Edward and Molly Reading, 21 April 1941.
6 Favell Lee Mortimer, *Peep of Day*, Free Presbyterian Publications, Glasgow, 1997, pp. 5–6.
7 D. Cassidy, letter to Edward and Molly Reading, 21 April 1941.
8 D. Cassidy, letter to Edward and Molly Reading, 1 March 1942.
9 D. Cassidy, letter to Edward and Molly Reading, 11 March 1942.
10 D. Cassidy, letter to Edward and Molly Reading, 12 March 1941.
11 D. Cassidy, letter to Edward and Molly Reading, 12 February 1942.
12 D. Cassidy, letter to Edward and Molly Reading, 11 March 1942.
13 D. Cassidy, letter to Edward and Molly Reading, 14 June 1942.
14 D. Cassidy, letter to Edward and Molly Reading, 20 August 1942.
15 D. Cassidy, letter to Edward and Molly Reading, March 1943.

4 When I was a child

1 Edith Eger, *The Choice*, Rider Books/Penguin Random House, London, 2017, p. 14.

2 D. Cassidy, letter to Edward and Molly Reading, 14 July 1943.
3 D. Cassidy, letter to Edward and Molly Reading, 8 March 1943.
4 D. Cassidy, letter to Edward and Molly Reading, 8 August 1944.
5 D. Cassidy, letter to Edward and Molly Reading, undated 1946.
6 C. M. A. Cassidy, letter to Charles Cassidy, undated, 1945.
7 D. Cassidy, letter to Edward and Molly Reading, 14 December 1941.
8 D. Cassidy, letter to Edward and Molly Reading, 22 February 1942.
9 D. Cassidy, letter to Edward and Molly Reading, 29 March 1942.
10 D. Cassidy, letter to Edward and Molly Reading, 1 March 1942.
11 D. Cassidy, letter to Edward and Molly Reading, 17 July 1944.
12 D. Cassidy, letter to Edward and Molly Reading, 3 August 1942.
13 D. Cassidy, letter to Edward and Molly Reading, June 1943.
14 Author's scrapbook.
15 D. Cassidy, letter to Edward and Molly Reading, 21 May 1945.

5 Boarding school

1 C. S. Lewis, quoted in *The Hodder Book of Christian Quotations*, ed. T. Castle, Hodder & Stoughton, London, 1982, p. 69.
2 D. Cassidy, letter to Edward and Molly Reading, 13 January 1946.
3 D. Cassidy, letter to Edward and Molly Reading, 28 January 1946.
4 C. S. Cassidy, letter to Michael Cassidy, 29 January 1946.
5 C. M. A. Cassidy, letter to Dee Cassidy, 12 September 1946.
6 C. M. A. Cassidy, letter to Charles and Dee Cassidy, 25 July 1946.
7 C. M. A. Cassidy, letter to Charles and Dee Cassidy, 24 September 1946.
8 C. M. A. Cassidy, letter to Charles and Dee Cassidy, 19 June 1949.
9 C. M. A. Cassidy, journal, 24 September 1947.
10 D. Cassidy, letter to Edward and Molly Reading, 28 August 1946.
11 D. Cassidy, letter to Edward and Molly Reading, 15 May 1946.
12 C. M. A. Cassidy, journal, 8 December 1949.
13 C. M. A. Cassidy, journal, 9 December 1949.

6 Patrick Duncan – childhood hero

1 D. Cassidy, letter to Edward and Molly Reading, 25 May 1948.
2 C. J. Driver, *Patrick Duncan: South African and Pan-African*, David Philip Publishers, Cape Town, 2000, p. 50.
3 Driver, *Patrick Duncan*, p. 50.
4 Driver, *Patrick Duncan*, p. xiii.
5 Driver, *Patrick Duncan*, p. 82.
6 Deborah Lavin, ed., *Friendship and Union: The South African Letters of Patrick Duncan and Maud Selborne, 1907–1943*, Van Riebeeck Society, Cape Town, 2010, p. xvi.
7 Lady Duncan's reminiscences written in the days after Sir Patrick's death, quoted in Lavin, ed., *Friendship and Union*, p. xvi.

8 Sir Patrick Duncan to Pat Duncan, 9 July 1937, quoted in Lavin, ed., *Friendship and Union*, p. xxiv.
9 Lavin, ed., *Friendship and Union*, p. xxv.
10 Lavin, ed., *Friendship and Union*, p. xxvi.
11 D. Cassidy, letter to Edward and Molly Reading, undated, 1943.
12 D. Cassidy, letter to Edward and Molly Reading, 21 March 1943.
13 D. Cassidy, letter to Edward and Molly Reading, 1 August 1943.
14 Driver, *Patrick Duncan*, pp. 106–7.
15 D. Cassidy, letter to Edward and Molly Reading, 13 December 1943.
16 D. Cassidy, letter to Edward and Molly Reading, undated, 1943.
17 Driver, *Patrick Duncan*, p. 279.
18 Driver, *Patrick Duncan*, p. 282.

7 Michaelhouse

1 James Cameron Todd, quoted in *Michaelhouse, 1896–1968*, ed. A. M. Barrett, Michaelhouse Old Boys Club, Pietermaritzburg, 1969, p. 13.
2 C. M. A. Cassidy, letter to Charles and Dee Cassidy, 11 February 1950.
3 C. Cassidy, letter to Michael Cassidy, 6 May 1951.
4 D. Cassidy, letter to Michael Cassidy, 9 May 1951.
5 M. Reading, letter to Michael Cassidy, 9 May 1951.
6 E. V. Lean, letter to Michael Cassidy and Paul Chapman, 9 May 1951.
7 C. M. A. Cassidy, letter to Charles and Dee Cassidy, 28 August 1951.
8 Hendrik Verwoerd, quoted in *Apartheid: A History*, ed. B. Lapping, Grafton Books, London, 1986, p. 109.
9 C. M. A. Cassidy, letter to Charles and Dee Cassidy, 5 May 1952.
10 C. M. A. Cassidy, letter to Charles and Dee Cassidy, 5 May 1952.
11 C. M. A. Cassidy, letter to Charles and Dee Cassidy, undated, 1952.
12 C. Cassidy, letter to Michael Cassidy, 21 September 1952.
13 C. M. A. Cassidy, letter to Charles and Dee Cassidy, 10 March 1953.
14 C. M. A. Cassidy, letter to Charles and Dee Cassidy, 25 October 1953.
15 F. Snell, letter to Michael Cassidy, 21 January 1954.
16 C. M. A. Cassidy, letter to Charles and Dee Cassidy, 24 August 1954.
17 C. Morgan, testimonial for Michael Cassidy, October 1954.
18 J. B. Chutter, letter to Charles Cassidy, 29 October 1954.

8 Cambridge and conversion

1 P. and C. Duncan, letter to Michael Cassidy, 24 February 1955.
2 Form III, PTS (Parktown School), letter to Michael Cassidy, undated, 1955.
3 C. M. A. Cassidy, letter to Charles and Dee Cassidy, 1 September 1955.
4 C. M. A. Cassidy, letter to Charles and Dee Cassidy, 19 September 1955.
5 I have been unable to locate a written source of this quote, but it is authentic. Temple Gairdner may have preached it in a sermon.

9 Theological perplexities and politics

1 Kahlil Gibran, *Wings of Thought*, Open Road Media, New York, 2011, p. 165.
2 C. Cassidy, letter to Michael Cassidy, 6 November 1955.
3 C. M. A. Cassidy, letter to Charles and Dee Cassidy, 13 November 1955.
4 C. M. A. Cassidy, letter to Charles and Dee Cassidy, 27 November 1955.
5 D. Cassidy, letter to Michael Cassidy, 19 February 1956.
6 D. Cassidy, letter to Michael Cassidy, 19 February 1956.
7 D. Cassidy, letter to Michael Cassidy, 19 February 1956.
8 C. Cassidy, letter to Michael Cassidy, 19 February 1956.
9 C. M. A. Cassidy, letter to Charles and Dee Cassidy, 27 February 1955.
10 J. I. Packer, *'Fundamentalism' and the Word of God: Some Evangelical Principles*, Inter-Varsity Fellowship, Leicester, 1958, p. 49.
11 M. Nuttall, A. Macaulay, C. M. A. Cassidy, letter to *The Times* (London), South African Affairs, 9 May 1956.
12 P. Duncan, letter to Michael Cassidy, 24 May 1956.

10 An academic mountain to climb

1 Enid Blyton, *Mr Galliano's Circus Story Collection*, Hodder & Stoughton, London, 2016.
2 CICCU Bible study leaders had a sort of infallibility attached to them, though we students didn't always understand clearly what they were saying, as in this instance.
3 C. M. A. Cassidy, letter to Charles and Dee Cassidy, 27 May 1956.
4 'Robin Hood and the Widow's Three Sons', ballad, quoted in *The Oxford Dictionary of Quotations*, 2nd edn, Oxford University Press, London, 1953, p. 31.
5 C. M. A. Cassidy, letter to Charles and Dee Cassidy, 21 October 1956.
6 C. M. A. Cassidy, letter to Charles and Dee Cassidy, 25 November 1956.

11 A 'great work'

1 Speaker, quoting from an unacknowledged source, High Leigh Conference, Hoddesdon, June 1956.
2 C. M. A. Cassidy, letter to Charles and Dee Cassidy, 7 July 1956.
3 Duke of Windsor (Edward VIII), quoted in *America in Quotations*, ed. B. Dehgan, McFarland and Co., Jefferson, NC, 2003, p. 74.
4 John Updike, in Dehgan, ed., *America in Quotations*, p. 59.
5 Carl Gustav Boberg (1859–1940), 'How Great Thou Art', quoted in *Singing the Faith*, ed. The Methodist Church, Canterbury Press, Norwich, 2013, p. 82.
6 M. S. Cassidy, letter to Charles and Dee Cassidy, 12 August 1957.
7 G. Cassidy, letter to Charles and Dee Cassidy, 16 August 1957.
8 D. Cassidy, letter to Michael Cassidy, 11 August 1957.

9 Martin Luther King, quoted in *Eyes on the Prize: America's Civil Rights Years*, ed. Clayborne Carson, David J. Garrow, Vincent Harding, Darlene Clark Hine, Penguin Books, New York, 1987, p. 44.

10 King, quoted in Carson et al., eds, *Eyes on the Prize*, p. 45.

12 Facing brokenness

1 C. M. A. Cassidy, journal, 19 October 1958.
2 C. M. A. Cassidy, journal, 31 October 1958.
3 C. M. A. Cassidy, journal, 31 October 1958.
4 Edith Schaeffer, *L'Abri*, The Norfolk Press and Henry E. Walter Ltd, Worthing, 1969, p. 173.
5 C. M. A. Cassidy, letter to Charles and Dee Cassidy, 23 March 1958.
6 C. M. A. Cassidy, journal, 3 February 1959.
7 C. M. A. Cassidy, journal, 8 February 1959.
8 C. M. A. Cassidy, journal, 6 February 1959.
9 C. M. A. Cassidy, journal, 15 February 1959.
10 Editorial, *Evening Standard,* Salisbury, 26 February 1959, page unknown.
11 C. M. A. Cassidy, journal, 4 February 1959.
12 C. M. A. Cassidy, journal, 28 March 1959.
13 C. M. A. Cassidy, journal, 5 April 1959.
14 C. M. A. Cassidy, journal, 6 April 1959.
15 C. M. A. Cassidy, journal, 7 April 1959.
16 C. M. A. Cassidy, journal, 24 August 1959.
17 C. M. A. Cassidy, journal, 26 August 1959.

13 Fuller Theological Seminary

1 George Marsden, *Reforming Fundamentalism: Fuller Seminary and the New Evangelicalism*, Eerdmans, Grand Rapids, MI, 1987, p. 67.
2 C. M. A. Cassidy, letter to Charles and Dee Cassidy, 13 October 1959.
3 J. Bester, letter to Michael Cassidy, 22 May 1960.
4 D. Cassidy, letter to Michael Cassidy, 8 April 1960.
5 C. M. A. Cassidy, journal, 4 March 1960.
6 C. M. A. Cassidy, journal, 5 March 1960.
7 C. M. A. Cassidy, journal, 9 May 1960.
8 C. M. A. Cassidy, journal, 13 May 1960. See Romans 11.33.
9 Helmut Thielicke, *Encounter with Spurgeon*, trans. John W. Doberstein, Fortress Press, Philadelphia, 1963, pp. 6–7.
10 Thielicke, *Encounter with Spurgeon*, p. 7.
11 African Enterprise mission statement: 'Evangelising the cities of Africa in word and deed, in partnership with the Church'.
12 Marsden, *Reforming Fundamentalism*, p. 67.
13 John Stott, quoted in Michael Cassidy, *The Church Jesus Prayed For: A Personal Journey into John 17*, Monarch Books, Oxford, 2012, ch. 7, pp. 141–2.

14 Summers trying our wings

1 C. M. A. Cassidy, journal, 2 August 1960.
2 B. Burnett, letter to Michael Cassidy, 10 August 1960.
3 C. M. A. Cassidy, journal, 16 November 1960.
4 C. M. A. Cassidy, journal, 16 November 1960.
5 C. M. A. Cassidy, journal, 14 December 1960.
6 C. M. A. Cassidy, journal, 31 December 1960.
7 John Stott, *The Preacher's Portrait*, Eerdmans, Grand Rapids, MI, 1961, p. 42.
8 Robert H. Mounce, *The Essential Nature of New Testament Preaching*, Eerdmans, Grand Rapids, MI, 1960, p. 110.
9 C. M. A. Cassidy, journal, 15 June 1961.
10 C. M. A. Cassidy, journal, 17 July 1962.

15 Early lessons in evangelism

1 Oswald Chambers, *My Utmost for His Highest*, ed. J. Reimann, Christian Art Publishers, Nashville, TN, 2010, January 14.
2 C. M. A. Cassidy, letter to Charles and Dee Cassidy, 1 January 1963.
3 C. M. A. Cassidy, letter to Charles and Dee Cassidy, 4 February 1963.
4 C. M. A. Cassidy, letter to Charles and Dee Cassidy, 6 November 1963.
5 C. M. A. Cassidy, journal, 17 July 1964.
6 C. M. A. Cassidy, journal, 19 July 1964.
7 C. M. A. Cassidy, journal, 11 September 1964.
8 C. M. A. Cassidy, journal, 26 September 1964.
9 C. M. A. Cassidy, journal, 9 October 1964.
10 C. M. A. Cassidy, journal, 10 October 1964.
11 C. M. A. Cassidy, journal, 12 October 1964.
12 C. M. A. Cassidy, journal, 13 October 1964.
13 C. M. A. Cassidy, journal, 15 October 1964.

16 Taking a stand against racism

1 Martin Luther King, quoted in *The Words of Martin Luther King, Jr.*, ed. C. S. King, Collins Fount, 1985, p. 42.
2 Policy conclusions, Volkskongress (People's Congress), Bloemfontein, 1944.
3 Michael Cassidy, 'The Ethics of Political Nationalism', in *One Race, One Gospel, One Task: World Congress on Evangelism, Official Reference Volumes, Papers and Reports*, vol. 2, ed. C. F. H. Henry and W. S. Mooneyham, World Wide Publications, Minneapolis, 1967, pp. 313–14.
4 Cassidy, 'Ethics of Political Nationalism', pp. 315–16.
5 Cassidy, 'Ethics of Political Nationalism', p. 316.
6 Carel F. A. Borchardt, 'Die Afrikaner Kerke en die Rebellie', in *Teologie en Vernuwing*, ed. I. Eybers, A. Konig and C. Borchardt, University of South Africa, Pretoria, 1975, p. 113.

7 David Bosch, 'Church, State and Power', an unpublished paper read at the Rhodesian Christian Leaders' Consultation, Salisbury, 23 November 1977, p. 4.
8 Bosch, 'Church, State and Power', p. 5.
9 Francis A. Schaeffer, *A Christian Manifesto*, Crossway Books, Westchester, IL, 1981, pp. 90–1, 130; italics are Schaeffer's.
10 Martin Luther King, quoted in King, ed., *Words of Martin Luther King Jr.*, p. 42.

17 In the days of our youth

1 Michael Cassidy, *Let the Earth Hear His Voice: International Congress on World Evangelisation, Lausanne, Switzerland*, ed. J. D. Douglas, World Wide Books, Minneapolis, 1975, pp. 749–59.
2 J. V. Tooke, letter to Michael Cassidy, 10 July 2015.
3 R. T. S. Norwood, conversation with Michael Cassidy, date unknown, 1969.
4 R. T. S. Norwood, 'Rector's Address on Speech Day', *S. Michael's Chronicle*, October 1968, vol. 20, p. 15.
5 D. Hotchkiss, email to Michael Cassidy, 27 June 2015.
6 G. Sklar-Chick, email to Michael Cassidy, 1 July 2015.
7 A. Smedley, email to Michael Cassidy, 1 September 2015.

18 Romance

1 C. M. A. Cassidy, letter to Carol Bam, 8 October 1969.
2 C. M. A. Cassidy, letter to Carol Bam, 9 October 1969.
3 Michael Cassidy, *Bursting the Wineskins*, Hodder & Stoughton, London, 1983, pp. 69–71.
4 Cassidy, *Wineskins*, pp. 52–61.

19 Marriage and ministry

1 Michael Cassidy, *Prisoners of Hope*, African Enterprise, Maseru, 1974, p. 23.
2 Michael Cassidy, 'The Sign of the Cross', *The Star*, Johannesburg, 18 April 1970.

20 Prisoners of hope

1 Michael Cassidy, *Prisoners of Hope*, African Enterprise, Maseru, 1974, p. 33.
2 B. J. Vorster, letter to Michael Cassidy, 22 November 1972.
3 Connie Mulder, quoted in Cassidy, *Prisoners of Hope*, p. 40.

21 Heaven is opening

1 Editorial, *Natal Mercury*, 14 March 1973.
2 Edward Perronet (1726–92), 'All Hail the Power of Jesus' Name'.
3 Michael Cassidy, *Prisoners of Hope: The Story of South African Christians at a Crossroads*, African Enterprise, Maseru, 1974, p. 49.

4 Alphaeus Zulu, quoted in Cassidy, *Prisoners of Hope*, p. 51.
5 Michael Green, quoted in Cassidy, *Prisoners of Hope*, p. 48.
6 David Bosch, quoted in Cassidy, *Prisoners of Hope*, p. 80.
7 Douglas Webster, quoted in Cassidy, *Prisoners of Hope*, p. 60.
8 Billy Graham, quoted in Cassidy, *Prisoners of Hope*, p. 103.
9 Manas Buthelezi, quoted in *I Will Heal Their Land: Papers of the South African Congress on Mission and Evangelism*, ed. C. M. A. Cassidy, African Enterprise, Maseru, 1974, pp. 269–70.
10 Beyers Naude, quoted in Cassidy, *Prisoners of Hope*, p. 123.
11 David Jenkins, 'Conveying the Christian Message to South Africa', *Cape Times*, 10 March 1973.
12 '700 Map Out New Church Line', *Drum*, 8 May 1973, p. 21.
13 'Commendable', *Natal Witness*, 26 March 1973.
14 John de Gruchy, quoted in Cassidy, *Prisoners of Hope*, pp. 160–1.

22 Family

1 Story quoted in Tim Elmore, *Nurturing the Leader within Your Child: What Every Parent Needs to Know*, Thomas Nelson, Nashville, TN, 2001, p. 203.
2 Deborah Kirsten, *Chai Tea and Ginger Beer: My Unexpected Journey . . . Cricket, Family and Beyond*, Struik Christian Media, Cape Town, 2015, pp. 4–5.
3 C. M. A. Cassidy, journal, 30 June 2015.
4 Ruth Bell Graham, quoted in Billy Graham, *The Journey: How to Live by Faith in an Uncertain World*, Thomas Nelson, Nashville, TN, 2006, p. 265.

23 Leadership as the possession of difficulties

1 C. M. A. Cassidy and G. Osei-Mensah, eds, *Together in One Place: The Story of PACLA*, Evangel Publishing House, Nairobi, 1978, p. 32.
2 Simone Ibrahim, quoted in Cassidy and Osei-Mensah, eds, *Together*, p. 46.
3 Janani Luwum, quoted in Cassidy and Osei-Mensah, eds, *Together*, p. 216.
4 Luwum, in Cassidy and Osei-Mensah, eds, *Together*, p. 290.
5 Festo Kivengere, *I Love Idi Amin: The Story of Triumph under Fire in the Midst of Suffering and Persecution in Uganda*, Fleming H. Revell, Old Tappan, NJ, 1977.

24 Reaching for the rainbow

1 Archbishop Desmond Tutu, a phrase repeatedly uttered publicly after the 1994 first South African democratic elections.
2 John Bunyan, *The Pilgrim's Progress from This World, to That Which Is to Come*, 1678.
3 C. M. A. Cassidy, journal, 2 February 1977.
4 Anonymous ancient proverb.
5 C. M. A. Cassidy, letter, 28 August 1977.

6 Michael Cassidy, *Bursting the Wineskins*, Hodder & Stoughton, London, 1983, pp. 119–20.
7 Thomas Chisholm (1866–1960), 'Great Is Thy Faithfulness'. Words: Thomas O. Chisholm. Copyright © 1923, Ren. 1951 Hope Publishing Company, Carol Stream, IL 60188. All rights reserved. Used by permission.
8 M. Ntlha, letter to Michael Cassidy, 9 May 2016.
9 D. Richardson, letter to Michael Cassidy, 11 April 2016.

25 Open doors to Africa

1 Stephen Lungu, *Out of the Black Shadows: The Amazing Transformation of Stephen Lungu*, Monarch Books/African Enterprise, Oxford, 2001.
2 Abiel Thipanyane, quoted in *African Harvest: The Captivating Story of Michael Cassidy and African Enterprise*, ed. A. Coomes, Monarch Books, London, 2002, pp. 262–73.
3 D. Richardson, letter to Mike Woodall, May 2013.
4 Victoria Wilson, quoted in Coomes, ed. *African Harvest*, p. 292.
5 Quintus Septimius Florens Tertullianus, *Apologeticus* (AD 197), ed. J. E. B. Mayor, trans. Alex Souter, Cambridge University Press, Cambridge, 1917, ch. 50.

26 Reconciliation

1 Desmond Tutu, quoted in *African Harvest: The Captivating Story of Michael Cassidy and African Enterprise,* ed. A. Coomes, Monarch Books, London, 2002, pp. 451–2.
2 Michael Cassidy, *The Passing Summer: A South African Pilgrimage in the Politics of Love*, Hodder & Stoughton, London, 1989, p. 34.
3 *Natal Witness*, 13 June 1987.
4 Allan Peckham, quoted in Cassidy, *Passing Summer*, p. 36.
5 Jack Garratt, quoted in Cassidy, *Passing Summer*, p. 36.
6 Klaus Nurnberger, paper for NIR National Strategy and Theology Group, 1985.
7 Nurnberger, paper for NIR National Strategy and Theology Group.
8 Carl Ellis, *Beyond Liberation: The Gospel in the Black American Experience*, InterVarsity Press, Downers Grove, IL, 1983, p. 29.

27 The Mandela moment

1 Charles Bester, quoted in Michael Cassidy, 'Conscience, Challenges and Christian State', in *Conflict and the Quest for Justice*, ed. Klaus Nurnberger, John Tooke, Bill Domeris, Encounter Publications, Pietermaritzburg, 1989, pp. 389–90.
2 <https://en.wikipedia.org/wiki/Nkosi_Sikelel%27_iAfrika>.
3 J. Bester, letter to Michael Cassidy, 17 November 2017.

4 Michael Cassidy, *The Politics of Love: Choosing the Christian Way in a Changing South Africa*, Hodder & Stoughton, London, 1991, p. 20.
5 F. W. de Klerk, quoted in Cassidy, *Politics of Love*, p. 21.
6 F. W. de Klerk, quoted in Cassidy, *Politics of Love*, p. 22.
7 F. W. de Klerk, quoted in Cassidy, *Politics of Love*, pp. 22–3.

28 Life at full stretch

1 D. E. Hoste, quoted in *A Prince with God*, ed. Phyllis Thompson, China Inland Mission, London, 1947, pp. 130–1.
2 Willie Jonker, quoted in *The Road to Rustenberg: The Church Looking Forward to a New South Africa*, ed. L. Alberts and F. Chikane, Struik Christian Books, Cape Town, 1991, p. 92.
3 Desmond Tutu, quoted in C. M. A. Cassidy, *A Witness for Ever: The Dawning of Democracy in South Africa*, Hodder & Stoughton, London, 1995, pp. 98–9.
4 John Hall, quoted in Cassidy, *Witness*, p. 101.
5 Antonie Geldenhuys, quoted in Cassidy, *Witness*, p. 101.
6 John Hall, quoted in Cassidy, *Witness*, p. 103.
7 John Gatu, quoted in Cassidy, *Witness*, pp. 36–7.
8 Andries Treurnicht, quoted in Cassidy, *Witness*, p. 37.
9 Edward Muhima, quoted in Cassidy, *Witness*, pp. 37–8.
10 Edward Muhima, quoted in Cassidy, *Witness*, pp. 39–40.
11 Addie van Rensburg, quoted in Cassidy, *Witness*, pp. 83–4.
12 Danie Schutte, quoted in Cassidy, *Witness*, p. 84.

29 Nation on a knife edge

1 Alfred Lord Tennyson, quoted in *The Oxford Dictionary of Quotations*, 2nd edn, Oxford University Press, London, 1953, p. 531.
2 Carole Cooper et al., *Race Relations Survey*, South African Institute of Race Relations (SAIRR), Johannesburg, 1994, pp. 297–8.
3 South African Constitution, Chapter 2, Bill of Rights, section 9.
4 South African Constitution, Chapter 2, Bill of Rights, section 12.2.
5 N. Mandela, letter to author, 6 August 1993.
6 Gerald Shaw, 'Total Strategy Conspirators', *Natal Witness*, 28 February 1994.
7 Shaw, 'Total Strategy Conspirators'.
8 M. Grenelli, 'Mass Call-up Begins', *Daily News*, 2 March 1994.
9 Grenelli, 'Mass Call-up Begins'.
10 Dirk van Eeden, 'Front Split Looms as Viljoen Quits', *Sunday Times*, Salisbury, 13 March 1994.

30 Miracle

1 Abraham Lincoln, *Speeches and Letters of Abraham Lincoln (1832–1865)*, ReadHowYouWant, United States, 2008, p. 77.

2 Washington Okumu, 'Suggested Terms of Reference for International Mediation to Be Considered by Inkatha Freedom Party, the African National Congress and the National Party', 5 May 1995 (presented to author by Mangosuthu Buthelezi, December 2016).

3 Tribute by Prince Mangosuthu Buthelezi sent to Okumu family – to be read at the Professor's funeral, 19 November 2016.

4 Terry Rosenberg, quoted in C. M. A. Cassidy, *A Witness for Ever: The Dawning of Democracy in South Africa*, Hodder & Stoughton, London, 1995, p. 193.

5 Tribute by Prince Mangosuthu Buthelezi sent to Okumu family.

6 Cassidy, *Witness*, p. 205.

7 Terry Rosenberg, quoted in Cassidy, *Witness*, p. 204.

8 Rosenberg, quoted in Cassidy, *Witness*, p. 207.

9 Rosenberg, quoted in Cassidy, *Witness*, p. 207.

31 Genocide

1 Chinua Achebe, quoted in S. Mthethwa-Sommers, *Narratives of Social Justice Educators: Standing Firm*, Springer, New York, 2014, p. 79.

2 Michael Cassidy, *Ruination and Resurrection in Rwanda: A Diary of the AE Rwanda Mission, July–August 1995*, African Enterprise, Maseru, 1995, p. 15.

3 Cassidy, *Ruination and Resurrection*, p. 38.

4 Cassidy, *Ruination and Resurrection*, p. 57.

5 Cassidy, *Ruination and Resurrection*, p. 82.

6 Cassidy, *Ruination and Resurrection*, p. 83.

32 Project Ukuthula

1 N. Mandela, conversation with Michael Cassidy, 2 May 1996.

2 Typed text of ANC, IFP, NP Joint Statement, 19 April 1994, as handed to the author by Mangosuthu Buthelezi at a private lunch, 31 January 2017, Durban.

3 Soh Chye Ann, 'Christian Leaders Tackle Violence', *Natal Witness*, 7 February 1996.

4 Keith Ross, 'Fears of Civil War Expressed', *Natal Witness*, 22 February 1996.

5 Jacob Zuma, quoted in Nicola Jones, 'Elections on A Knife Edge', *Natal Witness*, 20 April 1996.

6 Nicola Jones, 'A Family Under Fire', *Natal Witness*, 3 May 1996.

7 C. M. A. Cassidy, journal, 2 May 1996.

8 C. M. A. Cassidy, journal, 4 May 1996.

9 Church leaders, Project Ukuthula Peace Letter to people of KwaZulu-Natal, 29 May 1996.

10 Church leaders, Project Ukuthula Peace Letter.

11 Nicola Jones, 'Buthelezi's Call for Peace', *Natal Witness*, 11 June 1996.

12 Jones, 'Buthelezi's Call for Peace'.

13 Nicola Jones, 'Peace for the Province', *Natal Witness*, 14 June 1996.
14 Jones, 'Peace for the Province'.
15 David Wightman and Leon Marshall, 'Steps to Peace', *The Mercury*, 14 June 1996.
16 Yvonne Grimbeek, 'Peace Must Now Prove Itself', *The Mercury*, 4 June 1996.

33 Threads of prayer and writing

1 Cindy Jacobs, *The Power of Persistent Prayer: Praying With Greater Purpose and Passion*, Baker, Grand Rapids, MI, 2010, p. 17.
2 Mark Stibbe, quoted in *A Year's Journey with God*, ed. Jennifer Rees, Hodder & Stoughton, London, 2010, p. 211.
3 Michael Cassidy, *Christianity for the Open-Minded: An Invitation to Doubters*, InterVarsity Press, Downers Grove, IL, 2010; originally published Inter-Varsity Christian Fellowship, 1976.
4 David Wilkerson, *The Cross and the Switchblade*, Zondervan, Grand Rapids, 2002; originally published Pyramid, New York, 1962.
5 Michael Cassidy, *Where Are You Taking the World Anyway? The Ten Most Important Years of Your Life and How to Make the Most of Them*, Regal Books, Glendale, CA, 1973; originally published under the title *Decade of Decisions*, Marshall, Morgan & Scott, London, 1970.
6 Michael Cassidy, *Chasing the Wind: Man's Search for Life's Answers*, Hodder & Stoughton, London, 1985.

34 New priorities

1 C. M. A. Cassidy, journal, 2 February 2015.
2 Robbie Burns, 'To a Mouse (on Turning Her Up in Her Nest with the Plough)', 1785.
3 C. S. Lewis, *The Problem of Pain*, Macmillan, New York, 1962, p. 106.
4 C. M. A. Cassidy, journal, 20 January 2015.

Epilogue

1 C. S. Lewis, in *Mere Christianity*, quoted in *A Year with C. S. Lewis*, ed. P. S. Klein, William Collins, London, 2013, p. 358.
2 Michael Cassidy, quoted in *A Gathering of Eagles*, ed. J. D. Coy, Evergreen Press, Mobile, AL, 1999, p. 173.

Copyright acknowledgements

African Enterprise

———————

African Enterprise, founded in 1961 by Michael Cassidy, is a global partnership that empowers Africans to transform the continent through urban evangelism, discipleship, leadership development, trauma healing and reconciliation, and empowerment of women and youth.

In light of its mission to 'Evangelize the Cities of Africa through Word and Deed in Partnership with the Church', AE employs its model of stratified evangelism to unite church leaders in a given city to engage in evangelistic outreach. In this outreach, both AE and local evangelists 'fish where the fish are' by sharing the gospel in hundreds of gatherings in offices, factories, hospitals, universities, schools and marketplaces. New believers are integrated into local churches to be discipled and grow in their effectiveness as witnesses to Christ. And through a multi-year process of training local church pastors and lay leaders in evangelism, counselling and discipleship, the capacity of churches in a city to continue to reach their local area is greatly enhanced.

AE has over the last generation been a catalyst in gathering the Church around Africa to face into the challenges of making the gospel relevant across a continent struggling with poverty, disease, corruption, poor leadership and often intractable violence. These gatherings have included the 1973 South African Congress on Mission and Evangelism in Durban, South Africa; the Pan African Christian Leadership Assembly in Nairobi, Kenya, in 1976 and 1994; the South African Christian Leadership Assembly in Pretoria in 1979 and 2003; and the National Initiative for Reconciliation in South Africa in 1985.

Addressing the dire need for gospel training of emerging young leaders, AE spearheaded the Foxfire Youth Empowerment programme in 1980 in Zimbabwe, which has now expanded into South Africa, Malawi and Kenya, with plans to extend further into Congo-DRC, Ethiopia, Ghana, Rwanda, South Sudan, Tanzania and Uganda. Young people aged 18 to 25 give a year of their lives to being trained in evangelism, discipleship, counselling and the teaching of life skills to their peers. They also learn professionally choreographed dance moves, which they use to attract audiences in schools, youth groups and on stratified evangelistic missions. Thousands of young Africans each year come to faith through the Foxfires and learn biblical principles of navigating life successfully, especially with regard to issues of sexuality, drugs, alcohol and recovering from abusive childhoods.

With so much violence around Africa, AE has for decades been involved in ministering trauma healing and reconciliation to bring inner healing to those who have suffered from war, violence and sexual abuse. This often involves 'training of trainers' sessions in which this vital ministry can be multiplied out through populations where tens and hundreds of thousands need such healing.

AE currently has ministry teams in ten countries in Africa – Congo-DRC, Ethiopia, Ghana, Kenya, Malawi, Rwanda, South Africa, Tanzania, Uganda and Zimbabwe – with ongoing ministry in South Sudan and into North Africa.

Please contact our offices by visiting: www.africanenterprise.com

Australia
+61 (02) 9889 1799
ae@aeint.org
www.africanenterprise.com.au

Belgium/Europe
europe@aeint.org
Belgium.africanenterprise.com

Canada
(604) 744-0930
admin@africanenterprise.ca
www.africanenterprise.ca

Ireland
ireland@aeint.org
ireland.africanenterprise.com

New Zealand
ae@aeint.org
www.africanenterprise.co.nz

South Africa
aesa@ae.org.za
southafrica.africanenterprise.com

United Kingdom
+44 1707 663314
info@africanenterprise.co.uk
http://africanenterprise.co.uk

United States
(800) 672-3742
info@aeusa.org
www.africanenterprise.org

Index

Schutte, Danie 365, 379–81, 383, 385–7, 390–2, 395, 456
Scott, Andrew 268
Scott Arthur 268, 437
Scott, Cameron 268
Scott, Catherine (Cathy), née Cassidy 229–30, 254–5, 257, 259, 261, 264, 267–9, 301–3, 339, 440–1
Scott, Jonathan 267–8, 437, 440
Scott, Joyce 206
Serwanga, Dan 276
Sewell, Chris 310
Shaumba, Pierre 161
Shaw, Gerald 371, 456
Shea, George Beverley 115
Sibusile, Princess 419
Sikakane, Ebenezer 195, 197, 224, 225, 235, 244, 253
Sikakane, Emily 225
Silk, Dr Mary-Jean 222
Silverthorn, General Merwin 158–9
Sisulu, Walter 346
Sklar-Chik, Gavin 204
Slater, Charlotte 205
Slater, Raymond 204–5
Smart, Karefa 159
Smedley, Alan 205, 453
Smith, Barbara 172, 181
Smith, Chris 140, 163–4, 172, 181, 197, 206–7, 211–12, 216
Smith, Colleen 426
Smith, Ellen 327
Smith, Ernie 398–9
Smith, Mary-Jane 154
Smith, Dr Nico 327
Smith, Professor Wilbur 154
Smuts, Jan 24, 47–8, 50, 162, 168
Snell, Fred 54, 56, 63, 449
Snelling, John 131
Snelling, Olave, née Cassidy 6, 15–16, 21–3, 25, 27, 44, 122–3, 126, 129, 131, 163–4, 171, 209, 215, 267, 340
Sobhuza II 349
Soh Chye Ann 399, 407, 412–13, 457
Sokela, David 370
Sokela, Sipho 417
Solomon, Dave 380

South African Christian Leadership Assembly (SACLA) 287–9, 292–3, 295–301
South African Communist Party (SACP) 343, 371
South African Congress on Mission and Evangelism 201, 224, 229, 231–2, 235, 241, 251, 454
South African Council of Churches (SACC) 223–4, 353, 417
South African Defence Force (SADF) 338, 341, 371–2, 376
South African Liberal Party 52, 182
Spurgeon, Charles 144, 451
Staggers, John 297
Stephenson, Lois 191
Stephenson, Dr Robin 437
Stevens, Richard 126
Stewart, James 426
Stibbe, Mark 425, 458
Stott, Dr John iii, 126, 147, 157–8, 162, 189, 280, 283, 451–2
Strijdom, Hans 364
Sudan Interior Mission Home 176
Sutherland, Kathleen 246

Tambo, Oliver 359–60
Taylor, Jane 131
Taylor, Maurice 131
Tennant, Ralph 24
Terre'Blanche, Eugène 362
Terren 99, 101–2
Tertullian, Quintus 317, 455
Theodoric 123–4, 126–7
Theophilus, Alex 412
Thielicke, Helmut 144, 451
Thipanyane, Abiel 195–8, 224, 313, 385, 455
Thipanyane, Jemina 196, 225
Thomas, Bob 148–9
Thomas, Timothy 314
Todd, James Cameron 54, 449
Todd, Richard 342, 449
Tooke, John 195, 197–8, 200, 232, 237, 240, 293, 343, 453, 455
Tooke, Rona 195, 200, 343
Tracey, Gill 242